# This

... is an authorized facsimile made from the master
copy of the original book. Further unauthorized
copying is prohibited.

❧

Books on Demand is a publishing service of UMI.
The program offers xerographic reprints of more
than 130,000 books that are no longer in print.

❧

The primary focus of Books on Demand is academic
and professional resource materials originally published by university presses, academic societies, and
trade book publishers worldwide.

## U·M·I
### BOOKS ON DEMAND

University Microfilms International
A Bell & Howell Company
300 North Zeeb Road
P.O. Box 1346
Ann Arbor, Michigan 48106-1346
1-800-521-0600   313-761-4700

Printed in 1994 by xerographic process on acid-free paper

# The Thinking Organization

## Dynamics of Organizational Social Cognition

*Henry P. Sims, Jr.*
*Dennis A. Gioia*
*and Associates*

# The Thinking Organization

 Jossey-Bass Publishers

San Francisco • London • 1986

THE THINKING ORGANIZATION
*Dynamics of Organizational Social Cognition*
by Henry P. Sims, Jr., Dennis A. Gioia, and Associates

Copyright © 1986 by: Jossey-Bass Inc., Publishers
433 California Street
San Francisco, California 94104
&
Jossey-Bass Limited
28 Banner Street
London EC1Y 8QE

Library of Congress Cataloging-in-Publication Data

Sims, Henry P. (date)
   The thinking organization.

   (A Joint publication in the Jossey-Bass management
series and the Jossey-Bass social and behavioral
science series)
   Includes bibliographies and indexes.
   1. Organizational behavior. 2. Cognition. 3. Social
perception. I. Gioia, Dennis A. (date)
II. Title. III. Series: Jossey-Bass management series.
IV. Series: Jossey-Bass social and behavioral science
series.
HD58.7.S584 1986      302.3'5      85-45913
ISBN 0-87589-690-1

Manufactured in the United States of America

The paper in this book meets the guidelines for
permanence and durability of the Committee on
Production Guidelines for Book Longevity of the
Council on Library Resources.

JACKET DESIGN BY WILLI BAUM

FIRST EDITION

*Code 8619*

*A joint publication in*
The Jossey-Bass Management Series
*and*
The Jossey-Bass
Social and Behavioral Science Series

Consulting Editors
Organizations and Management

Warren Bennis
*University of Southern California*

Richard O. Mason
*Southern Methodist University*

Ian I. Mitroff
*University of Southern California*

*To*
*Laura Smail Sims*
*and Judith Albrecht*

# Preface

This is a book about thinking and thought in modern organizations—an emerging area of interest known as organizational social cognition. Social cognition refers to the ways we think about people in social situations in general. This book is concerned specifically with social cognition in organizations. It is based on the fundamental assumption that thinking and thought are the lifeblood of organizations, that social cognition lies at the heart of decision making, communication, strategic action, interpersonal behavior, organization design, and virtually every other important organizational process. Consequently, our main goal in writing this book is to offer in-depth treatments of key topics in organizational thinking that will be useful both to management practitioners and scholars.

Indeed, the issues covered in this volume will be of lasting interest to anyone concerned with the way modern organizations work. Why should this be so? Why should a reader be tempted to proceed further into a book that adopts the view that insight into cognitive processes gives us an advantage in understanding how organizations work? One answer is effectiveness—understanding ourselves, understanding others, and understanding the organizational social setting are all critical to effective management and organizational achievement.

Typical issues and problems that executive readers might encounter are explored in this book. Examples are

- the manager who has a vision of an innovative strategic direction, but must instill a new way of thinking to implement that vision

- the executive who must think through possible new organizational structures to meet a changing environment
- the vice-president of human resources who must consider designing a strategy to alter ineffective modes of interpersonal interaction in an organization
- the CEO who must deliberately select or create highly visible symbols as keynotes for changing an entrenched culture
- the manager who finds herself in conflict with another manager, but who must find ways to establish a "meeting of minds" in order to cope
- the manager who must write a performance appraisal for a high-performing subordinate whom he personally dislikes
- the executive who needs to understand how patterns of speech and talk can enhance or diminish organizational objectives

These are the kinds of issues this book examines through the lens known as "social cognition." A fundamental purpose of this book is to help improve executives' effectiveness in dealing with other people and with the socially-influenced situations in their organizations. We believe that insight into our own cognitive processes helps us make our own thoughts and actions more effective. Moreover, understanding how other people think enables us to answer "why" questions about their behavior and can provide insight that will improve our ability to manage.

Philosophers and scientists have long recognized that cognition is an essential defining characteristic of humanity. The word *cognition*, after all, derives from the Greek word *cognos*, meaning "to think." What might be less obvious is that organizations also are an essential characteristic of our human experience, especially in contemporary society. We are now well described, not only as societies of individuals but also as societies of organizations. And organizations are most usefully viewed as fundamentally social enterprises. Given this recognition, it might be somewhat surprising that works on social cognition in organizations are not prevalent on the scholarly or practitioner bookshelf. This book is intended to fill that void.

Thought about thinking in organizations has been sporadic, disconnected, or even superficial in the past, perhaps because the conceptual and empirical tools for understanding cognition in organizations have been underdeveloped. Within the past decade, however, that pattern has begun to change. We now have the tools. The study of how executives and employees think is being revitalized. As academic researchers and writers about management and organizational processes, we see ourselves as part of that movement and we want to facilitate its progress and development. This book is the manifestation of that desire.

In our initial planning, we considered putting together a volume of previously published work about cognitive theory in organizations. We reviewed the literature carefully and identified about two dozen articles that we would have included in such a book. Upon further consideration, however, we realized that we needed more up-to-the-minute information. To do justice to this fast-developing field that has captured the attention and interest of many of the best thinkers in the study of organizations, we decided that a book of original contributions was essential.

We sent our brief prospectus and invitations to participate in the book to over a dozen scholars whom we knew to be active in the field, including the authors from our working list of reprint candidates. We were gratified when about 90 percent of our invitees indicated their willingness and their enthusiasm about the project. Their responses validated our perception of the worthiness and timeliness of the proposed book.

Among the authors of chapters in this volume are some of the most innovative and well-known contributors to theory, research, and applications of social cognition in organizations. The works they have produced for this book integrate previous research with the newest ideas about the role of cognition in organizations. In many ways, the chapters are mixtures of established and vanguard notions.

We encouraged our contributors to express innovative ideas that might be somewhat speculative in nature—and not to be bound by more conservative or traditional conventions. In many cases the speculative stance contributes to exciting explorations into the nature and functioning of modern organizations.

Because we subscribe to the notion that *action* is a domi-

nant characteristic of organizations, we are less interested in
"cognition for cognition's sake," and more interested in *cognition-action* linkages. Consequently, we asked our contributors
to de-emphasize pure theory and to address managerial and organizational implications in their conceptualizations. As a result, each chapter, by design, includes a section addressing
applications and implications. Thus, despite its nature as a compendium of leading-edge work, this book contains a much greater emphasis on pragmatics than do other volumes of this type.

Nevertheless, we emphasize that this book is primarily a
vehicle for conceptual development on important organizational
topics. Therefore, we expect that a major audience will be organizational scholars and students. The book will also be useful
to management practitioners and consultants who are interested
in learning about sophisticated advancements in theories of organizations. Although this is not a basic book, written at a simple level, readers of *Harvard Business Review, Organizational
Dynamics, Business Horizons,* and other high-level executive
journals will find the ideas in this book accessible.

*The Thinking Organization* is comprised of three main
sections consisting of four chapters each, preceded by an introduction and followed by a concluding chapter. The introductory chapter sounds out major themes and provides a brief overview of the book. The three main parts of the book are entitled
"Foundation Concepts for Organizations," "Transition from
Concept to Practice," and "Applications of Social Cognition to
Organizations." Their sequence depicts the natural flow of the
book from discussions of fundamental organizational cognitive
processes to more applied concerns, processes, and techniques.
The concluding chapter provides a state-of-the-art synthesis of
the book's main themes.

The section on foundations covers the use of knowledge
structures by organization members, focusing specifically on
schemas, scripts, causal reasoning, cognitive maps, symbols, and
sensemaking. The concept-to-practice section draws on these
and other fundamental notions to discuss issues of increasing
relevance to the understanding of organizations. Topics include
the role of language and communication, implicit theories, im-

pression management and self-justification processes, and affect and emotion. Finally, the applications section treats topics that are currently most directly applicable to modern management, including issues of managerial understanding, learning, decision making, and strategic management.

We believe that scholars will be interested in all sections of the book, and that practitioners and consultants will be interested primarily in the introduction, the concept-to-practice and applications sections, and the conclusion. We also believe that the works comprising this volume are seminal and will become standards of reference in the years to come.

In summary, this book is the manifestation of our belief that the study and management of organizations will benefit substantially from a carefully structured and integrated work that presents in one place a substantial body of the advanced thinking on how cognitive theory can be applied to organizations. We hope that it will stimulate thought about thinking in organizations and that that thinking will be related to action.

We are indebted to colleagues Alfredo Jaccoud, Clinton Longenecker, Daniel Brass, Charles Manz, and Richard Mason for reviews, encouragement, and ideas. We especially appreciate the continuing support of Laura Frye, Shirley Rider, and Diane Snyder. We also thank our contributors for their extremely professional responses to exigencies of time and consistency. While the editing process is never entirely painless, we have been pleased that it has proceeded smoothly.

*University Park, Pennsylvania*                    Henry P. Sims, Jr.
*March 1986*                                        Dennis A. Gioia

# Contents

# Contents

# The Authors

*Henry P. Sims, Jr.,* is professor of organizational behavior in the College of Business Administration at Pennsylvania State University. He received his B.S. degree (1961) in engineering from Purdue University, his M.B.A. degree (1967) in industrial relations from the University of Detroit, and his Ph.D. degree (1971) in management from Michigan State University.

Sims's research on leadership and managerial/employee psychology has been published in over 65 journal articles and over 100 presentations and proceedings. He is coauthor, with Charles Manz, of *SuperLeadership: Discovering How to Lead Others to Lead Themselves to Excellence* (1986). He is former president of the Eastern Academy of Management, and in 1981, his research was prominently summarized in a feature interview in *U.S. News & World Report.*

*Dennis A. Gioia* is assistant professor of organizational behavior in the College of Business Administration at Pennsylvania State University. He received his B.S. degree (1970) in engineering science, his M.B.A. degree (1972), and his doctorate degree (1979) in management from Florida State University.

His current research and writing focus on the nature and use of complex cognitive processes by organization members and the way those processes combine with sensemaking, communication, and influence processes to facilitate organizational change. He is a contributor to the *Academy of Management Review, Business Horizons, Journal of Management, Journal of Applied Social Psychology,* and *Organizational Behavior and Human Decision Processes,* among other professional publications.

*Lee Roy Beach* is professor and associate chair of psychology at the University of Washington. He received his B.A. degree (1957) in psychology from Indiana University and his M.A. (1959) and Ph.D. (1961) degrees from the University of Colorado. He also did postdoctoral work at the University of Michigan.

Beach's research work is mainly in judgment and decision making, in which he has published numerous articles and given presentations at national and international meetings. He is a fellow of the American Psychological Association and a member of the Society for Organizational Behavior and the Judgment and Decision Making Society.

*Nancy E. Bell* is a doctoral candidate in organizational behavior and industrial relations at the University of California at Berkeley. She received her B.A. degree (1974) in philosophy from the State University of New York at Binghamton and her M.B.A. degree (1983) from the University of New Mexico. Her current research involves the relationship of attitudes and intentions to behavior and the relationship of personality to job attitudes and job behaviors.

*Michel G. Bougon* is assistant professor of organizational behavior at Pennsylvania State University. He received his M.S. degree (1958) in general engineering from the Advanced National School of Arts et Metiers (Paris, France), his M.B.A. degree (1973) in finance and organizational behavior from the University of Illinois in Champaign, his M.A. degree (1977) in organizational behavior and his Ph.D. degree (1980) in organization theory, both from Cornell University.

Bougon's research is directed at the cognitive basis of organizations as well as the cognitive difference between novice and master executives. His work has been published in *Administrative Science Quarterly, Organizational Behavior and Human Performance, The Journal of Management,* and the *Journal of Behavior Research Methods and Instrumentation.* A chapter presenting his cognitive organization theory and the "Self-Q" interview technique that he developed to research his theory appears in *Beyond Method,* edited by Gareth Morgan. This chapter is now being expanded into a book.

*Arthur P. Brief* is professor of management and organizational behavior at New York University's Graduate School of Business Administration. His research on various facets of organizational behavior has been published in over five dozen journal articles and in five books of which he is coauthor or editor. With Walter Nord, he is now writing a book on the meaning of work.

Brief is a fellow of the American Psychological Association, past president of the Midwest Academy of Management, and a member of the American Sociological Association. He has served on the editorial boards of the *Academy of Management Journal, Academy of Management Review,* and the *Journal of Management.* In addition, with Benjamin Schneider, he is consulting co-editor to Garland Publishing on a series of ancestral books in administrative science. He is also consulting editor to Lexington Books on a new series of books on under-attended issues in management and organization.

*Jennifer A. Chatman* is a doctoral candidate in organizational behavior and industrial relations at the University of California at Berkeley. She received her B.A. degree (1981) in psychology from the University of California at Berkeley. Her research interests include examining organizations at several levels from the individual to the total environment of an industry. In particular, she is concerned with the bases of organizational commitment, impression management, and the justification of individual and organizational performance. Her current writings involve decision making and communication and the impact of source credibility on information system use.

*Anne Donnellon* joined the faculty of the Graduate School of Business, Harvard University in 1986. She was formerly visiting assistant professor in the College of Business, University of Colorado at Boulder. She received her B.A. degree in English from the University of Cincinnati, her M.A. degree in applied linguistics from Teacher's College Columbia University, and is a candidate for the Ph.D. degree in business administration from Pennsylvania State University. Her research interests are the cognitive and communicational aspects of organizing and managing. Areas of current work include power, leadership, symbolism, and qualitative research methods. She is coauthor of articles that have appeared in the *Journal of Management* and *Education Administration Quarterly*.

*H. Kirk Downey* is professor of management at Texas Christian University. He received his B.A. degree (1965) in economics from Kansas Wesleyan University, his M.B.A. degree (1967) from Wichita State University, and his Ph.D. degree (1974) in organizational behavior from Pennsylvania State University.

Downey's research and writings have been published in *Administrative Science Quarterly, Academy of Management Journal, Academy of Management Review, Journal of Management, Human Relations,* and *Organizational Behavior and Human Performance.* He is a past editor of the *Journal of Management.*

*Jack M. Feldman* is professor and chairman of the Department of Management at the University of Texas at Arlington. He received his B.A. (1966), M.A. (1968), and Ph.D. (1972) degrees from the University of Illinois at Urbana, specializing in social and industrial/organizational psychology.

Feldman has published research in a variety of theoretical and applied areas, including stereotyping, minority group relations, cross-cultural differences in work values and behaviors, and social cognition applied to performance appraisal. His current interests include the relationships between person categorization processes, appraised performance, interpersonal behavior, and independently measured abilities and job performance. He was named a fellow of the American Psychological Association in 1983.

*Michael Finney* is an organizational consultant specializing in long-term strategic change efforts. He received his B.S. degree in psychology from the University of Central Arkansas, his M.A. degree in organizational communications from the University of Arkansas at Little Rock, and is currently completing his Ph.D. degree in business administration at the University of Southern California. Finney's recent works include *Models of Management Consultancy* (with Craig Lundberg) and *The Current MBA: Why Are We Failing?* (with Caren Siehl).

*Roseanne J. Foti* is an assistant professor of psychology at Virginia Polytechnical Institute and State University. She received her B.A. degree in psychology from Millersville State College and her M.A. (1982) and Ph.D. (1984) degrees in psychology from the University of Akron.

Foti's current research work is in cognitive processes in social perceptions, perception of political leaders, and stress at work. She has published in *Organizational Behavior and Human Performance* and the *Journal of Applied Psychology*.

*Daniel J. Isenberg* is assistant professor of business administration at the Harvard Graduate School of Business Administration. He received his B.A. degree (honors, 1974) in psychology from the University of Oregon and his M.A. (1980) and Ph.D. (1981) degrees in social psychology from Harvard University. From 1974 to 1976 he was a consultant at the Israel Institute of Work Productivity.

Isenberg's research has been in the areas of managerial thinking, interpersonal relations, small group behavior, and the management of change. His research has appeared in the *Harvard Business Review, Journal of Personality and Social Psychology, Organizational Behavior and Human Performance, Journal of Applied Social Psychology, American Statistician, Contemporary Psychology*, and he has contributed to several books, including *Leadership: Beyond Establishment Views* (Hunt and others, eds.), *Leadership on the Future Battlefield* (Hunt and Blair, eds.), and *Thinking* (Bishop and others, eds.). He is currently completing a book on his studies of how senior managers think, to be entitled *Managerial Thinking: Towards Strategic Opportunism*.

*Robert G. Lord* is professor of industrial and organizational psychology at the University of Akron. He received his B.A. degree (1968) in economics from the University of Michigan, and his M.S. (1972) and Ph.D. (1975) degrees in psychology from Carnegie-Mellon University.

Lord's research focuses on leadership, small group behavior, and motivation. Central to each of these areas is the application of information processing models and cognitive theories to explain organizational behavior. Lord's recent work has appeared in *Organizational Behavior and Human Performance, Journal of Applied Psychology, Academy of Management Review,* and *Research in Organizational Behavior.*

*Terence R. Mitchell* is the Edward E. Carlson Distinguished Professor of Business Administration at the University of Washington. He received his B.A. degree (1964) in psychology from Duke University, his Advanced Diploma in Public Administration (1965) from the University of Exeter, and his M.A. (1967) and Ph.D. (1969) degrees in psychology from the University of Illinois.

His research interests are leadership, motivation, and decision making. He has published three books and over 80 journal articles and has made numerous presentations at national meetings. He is coauthor, with W. Scott and P. Birnbaum, of *Organizational Theory: A Structural and Behavioral Analysis* (4th edition due in 1987) and coauthor, with James Larson, of *People in Organizations* (3rd edition due in 1987). He is a fellow of the American Psychological Association and a member of the Society for Organizational Behavior.

*Ian I. Mitroff* is the Harold Quinton Distinguished Professor of Business Policy in the Department of Management and Organization, University of Southern California. He received his B.S. degree (1961) in engineering physics, his M.S. degree (1963) in structural mechanics, and his Ph.D. degree (1967) in engineering science with a strong minor in the philosophy of social science, all from the University of California at Berkeley.

Mitroff is a member of the American Association for the Advancement of Science, Academy of Management, American

Psychological Association, American Sociological Association, Philosophy of Science Association, and the Institute for Management Science. He has published over 140 papers and seven books in the areas of business policy, corporate culture, managerial psychology and psychiatry, strategic planning, and the philosophy and sociology of science. His most recent book is *Corporate Tragedies: Product Tampering, Sabotage, and Other Catastrophies*, with R. Kilmann.

*Stephan J. Motowidlo* is associate professor of organizational behavior at Pennsylvania State University. He received his Ph.D. degree in industrial and organizational psychology from the University of Minnesota. Prior to joining Pennsylvania State University, Motowidlo was a research psychologist with Personnel Decisions Research Institute in Minneapolis. He has also served as a member of the faculty at the University of Toronto and the State University of New York at Binghamton. His research interests include motivation, job satisfaction, occupational stress, the selection interview, performance appraisal, job choice, turnover, and prosocial behavior. His works have appeared in the *Journal of Applied Psychology, Journal of Personality and Social Psychology, Educational and Psychological Measurement, Motivation and Emotion,* and *Academy of Management Journal.*

*Oh Soo Park* is associate professor of organizational behavior in the College of Business and Economics at Inha University (Incheon, Korea), where he has also served as assistant dean for academic and student affairs. He received his B.A. degree (1975) in business administration and his M.B.A. degree (1977) from Seoul National University, Seoul, Korea, and will soon receive his Ph.D. degree in business administration from Pennsylvania State University.

Park's current research and writing focus on affect and cognition in leadership, performance appraisal, and culture in organizations.

*Joseph F. Porac* is an associate professor of business administration at the University of Illinois at Urbana-Champaign. He received his B.A. degree (1975) from the University of Pittsburgh, and his Ph.D. degree (1979) in psychology from the University of Rochester. Porac's recent work is concerned with the causative and affective substrates of human action.

*Kenneth J. Rediker* is a Ph.D. candidate at the Graduate School of Business Administration, University of Washington. He received his B.A. degree (1974) in English literature from Westmont College and his M.B.A. degree (1976) in accounting and quantitative methods from the University of Oregon.

Rediker's research involves strategic decision processes as a source of organizational adaptation, forms and implications of organizational diagnostic processes, and causal modeling of organizational-environmental relationships.

*Gerald R. Salancik* is IBE Professor of Organization at the University of Illinois at Urbana-Champaign and associate editor of *Administrative Science Quarterly*. He received his B.A. and M.A. degrees in journalism from Northwestern University and his Ph.D. degree in psychology from Yale University.

Salancik's recent work concerns attitudes, organizational power, and forms and evolution of organizing.

*Barry M. Staw* is a professor in the School of Business Administration and currently chairs the Organizational Behavior and Industrial Relations Group at the University of California at Berkeley. He has taught previously at Northwestern University, the University of Illinois, and the University of Iowa. Staw is co-editor of *Research in Organizational Behavior* and serves on the editorial boards of *Administrative Science Quarterly, Organizational Behavior and Human Decision Processes*, and the *Journal of Applied Psychology*. His research has focused on organizational commitment, decision making, and job attitudes. He is currently completing research on a dispositional theory of job attitudes and is beginning a program of research on creativity in organizations.

*Karl E. Weick* holds the Harkins and Company Centennial Chair of Business Administration at the University of Texas, Austin.

He received his Ph.D. degree (1962) in psychology from Ohio State University.

Before moving to Texas, Weick held positions at Purdue, University of Minnesota, and Cornell. Weick served as editor of *Administrative Science Quarterly* from 1977 to 1985, and is currently on the editorial boards of *Contemporary Psychology; Accounting, Organizations, and Society; Journal for the Theory of Social Behaviour;* and *International Journal of Small Group Research.*

# The Thinking Organization

*Dynamics
of Organizational
Social Cognition*

# Introduction:
# Social Cognition in Organizations

Dennis A. Gioia
Henry P. Sims, Jr.

People in organizations are not simply "actors." They are unique in that they do not just *do,* they also *think.* More accurately, perhaps, they often take action as a result of their thinking. In a related vein, organizations themselves do not "behave" independently of the people who construct and manage them. At their essence organizations are products of the thought and action of their members. Yet organizations also seem to take on a life of their own. An apparent paradox is thus created. For some, organizations are entities guided by thinking individuals who shape the actions of the organization. For others, the distinction between organizations and their members is blurred enough that treating the two as independent entities is problematic.

We have chosen our title, *The Thinking Organization,* to reflect the paradoxical nature of organizations. In one sense the title is merely an expressive metaphor intended to reflect the notion that thinking organization members make the decisions that influence the actions of themselves, others, and their organizations. In this view, everybody "knows" organizations do not think; it is people in organizations who think. Thus, the distinction between an organization and the people in it is taken for granted.

In another sense, however, "the thinking organization" is a rich metaphor chosen to recognize the view that there is no

1

essential difference between organizations and their members. According to this position, people *are* the organization; their cognitions, visions, and consequent actions define the essence of "being organized." Thus, when people in organizations think, organizations think. In this interpretation the metaphorical title therefore applies more literally.

In yet another view of the paradoxical nature of organizations, people can be seen as so immersed in the organizational context and its influence on their perception and thought that individual thinking cannot be usefully distinguished from organizational thinking. This position is conceptually similar to the one taken by March and Shapira (1982), who explored the difficulty of distinguishing between individual and organizational decision making.

It so happens that the editors as well as their associates are conceptually divided over the issue of how best to characterize the nature of organizations. Consequently, it seems only appropriate to produce a volume on the dynamics of organizational social cognition with a paradoxical title that encompasses and represents all these views and yet simultaneously captures the essence of the book as a whole, which emphasizes the profound role of human cognition relating to organizations. The fundamental purpose of this book is to explore how people in organizations think about their experiences and how they act in conjunction with their thoughts. A useful by-product of this exploration is an in-depth, multiple-perspective probing into the basic nature of organizations themselves.

Successful members of organizations are typically proficient processors of information and creative architects of meaningful experience. They engage in active attempts to make sense of the myriad of information cues that surround them. They forge understanding out of some very limited and ambiguous cues, and on the basis of that understanding, they act. As organizational scholars, we frequently focus on the limitations and problems of people in organizations. Yet by and large, these people are very successful at dealing with information, constructing a workable world, and taking effective action.

In many ways, this portrait of people in organizations

might seem self-evident. We all know that people think, that they expend time and mental energy trying to understand "what's happening" around them, and then, consciously or not, deciding what to do about it. Paradoxically, however, this portrait does not seem to fit very well with many of our scholarly historical views about the nature of organizational life. With the notable exceptions of expectancy theory (Vroom, 1964), goal-setting theory (Locke, Shaw, Saari, and Latham, 1981), and more recently, attribution theory (Mitchell, Green, and Wood, 1981), much of what has been written about organizations has focused mainly on behaviors and outcomes, without an in-depth understanding of the cognitive processes that influence those behaviors and outcomes.

Until recently, our formal understanding of these processes has been rather limited. To manage organizations more effectively, we must understand their internal workings in greater depth. Therefore, we should attempt to comprehend and articulate the reasons behind action in organizations. In particular, we must develop substantially more insight into the individual cognitive antecedents of *concerted action*—that is, action that individuals undertake together because of a common purpose. Concerted action, of course, is the essence of organizing.

The complexities of human cognition, such as those involved in concerted action, are in fact not easy to understand or measure. In general, we have not known very much about how organization members think, and at times, organizational theorists, in their role within the field of management study, seem to have reached a paralyzing conclusion that they can "satisfice" (Simon, 1957) without understanding organizational cognition in any serious depth. After all, this philosophy suggests, organizations seem to work well enough without our having to worry about what might be going on inside some executive's head. The notion that the cognitive aspects of organizations do not require exploration serves only, however, to severely limit our vision of the wonderfully complicated world of organizations. We have arrived at a point where the picture of organizational action must be extended. To do so requires a deeper probing into the nature of organizational cognition.

One obvious conclusion about organizations is that, fundamentally, they are social entities. Activities within organizations do not take place in a vacuum or in an impersonal environment. Instead, those activities are embedded firmly in an interpersonal milieu that strongly influences virtually everything that occurs. And no phenomenon is more strongly influenced by the social milieu than cognitive processing (and vice versa). For that reason, studying cognition for its own sake can be a somewhat sterile approach to the richness found in modern organizations. Rather, the essential thrust of this book is toward "social cognition in organizations"—that is, the study of cognitive processes within the social context of organizations.

This is a book about the way people think, especially managers and executives. More specifically, organizational social cognition is the study of human information processing (both conscious and unconscious) as it influences, and is influenced by, the complex social and structural phenomena within the modern organization. Notice that this definition emphasizes that social cognition and organization mutually influence each other. We might view social cognition as "how people think about people, situations, and people in situations."

While this overly simple definition specifies the domain of this book, it does not quite convey the scope of the territory covered by our contributors. In effect, virtually any form of cognitive processing that occurs in organizations falls within our purview. Our examination of the topic includes, for example, wide-ranging perspectives on strategy, language, and interpersonal affect.

## Sounding Our Overarching Themes

In order to preview some of the themes addressed in the following pages, we here identify some of the major issues and characteristics of our social cognitive view of organizations.

*Why Social Cognition?* We believe that the study of organizations is in truth embryonic. There are so many processes about which we have very little understanding. Most people working in organizations have a seat-of-the-pants knowledge about "what will work," but they do not know why. As organizational beings, we have learned to influence other people, other departments, and even other organizations without having a comprehensive grasp of the underlying processes.

One should naturally expect that an enlightened discipline would proceed sequentially from the process of understanding a given phenomenon to the processes of trying to predict, influence, and control that phenomenon. However, the field of study known as *management* does not always seem to have done it that way. Rather, we seem to have concentrated predominantly on obtaining results, before gaining a comprehension of the underlying processes that bear on the reason for those results. Does the discipline of management really understand the complex internal and social influences that affect and drive organizational behavior? A major theme and really the raison d'être of this book is the articulation and elaboration of the social cognitive basis for organizational behavior.

*The Connections Between Action and Cognition.* Within this social cognitive context, a related theme that we wish to reiterate is that of understanding the links between cognition and action. The chapters contributed to this book do not focus myopically and exclusively on social cognition at the expense of a concern with behavior, action, and outcomes. Instead, we hope to demonstrate that a more complete picture emerges, and a more effective management derives, only when the interactive aspects of the relationship between cognition and action are considered within the context of the human organizational experience.

Overall, the issue of the links between cognition and action has received surprisingly little attention in the organizational literature (exceptions are Pondy, 1983, and Weick, 1979 and 1983). Given the issue's obvious importance, the lack of attention it has received is probably related to the complexity of the problem. Although the study of organizational behavior is still youthful, we believe that the field has clearly moved beyond the point of predicting, influencing, and controlling behavior by focusing exclusively on so-called objective behavioral and environmental factors. Through this book, we propose a fundamental focus on how people think—how they think as both individuals and as organized groups—and then as a consequence, on how they act, and especially on how they act in an organized fashion. We will also devote attention to the interaction of thought and action—that is, to the issue of how action influences thought and thought influences action.

*Eclecticism and Beyond.* Traditionally, the fields of management and organizational behavior have been very eclectic, borrowing substantially from other, more fundamental disciplines. Organizational theorists and practitioners have been ready recipients of the most useful ideas and research from such diversified disciplines as psychology, linguistics, anthropology, economics, and sociology. This volume continues that venerable tradition by working to extend and integrate some of the most recent notions in these fields as a means of understanding the nature of organizations.

There is a difference, however, between the approach this book takes and the traditional eclecticism of the field of organizational science. In effect, we have made every effort to reduce the lengthy lag between discoveries in the fundamental disciplines and their translation to management and organizational scholarship. The work represented in this volume is intended to be state-of-the-art and to accelerate this process of translation.

The chapters in this book represent a trend that we also wish to emphasize. Despite the relative youth of the study of organizations, the field is nonetheless a relentlessly maturing one. One of the hallmarks of a maturing discipline is the tendency toward creation of its own knowledge, thus implying a reduced dependency on the borrowing of ideas from other disciplines. Certainly, we believe the characteristic of originality is very evident in the chapters contributed here. Our contributors go significantly beyond mere borrowing from the fundamental disciplines. The study of organizations is now truly coming into its own. Not only is the work presented here advanced eclecticism, but it also signals a step beyond eclecticism toward very original organizational scholarship in its own right.

*Individuals and Organizations.* One of the most omnipresent entities of modern society is now the organization. In stark terms, we live in a world of organizations. They are pervasive in both our personal and professional lives. They are instruments for goal accomplishment; they are theaters for acting out roles; they are cultural systems with often idiosyncratic values and world views; they are political arenas where people exert influence and are targets of influence; and they are self-sustaining organisms that can be treated as living systems (see Morgan, in press, for an elaborated treatment of the multiple views of organization). Finally, organizations are simply places to be, where many of us spend the majority of our waking lives. For these reasons, among many others, organizations require study. Our contribution to that study consists of conceptualization and reconceptualization about the nature and role of cognition in organizations.

Concluding that we now inhabit a world of organizations, however, does not dismiss the importance of the individual; it merely makes the distinction between what derives from the individual and what derives from the organization problematic. Given the nature of organizations as socially constructed entities, and the nature of individuals as socially immersed and influenced, the lines defining what is an individual phenomenon and what is an organizational phenomenon are very blurred indeed. Organizations are social entities created by individuals, where individuals engage in the social functions of concerted action, collaboration, conflict, and so on, but they are also entities that manage to take on a life of their own. This complex interaction between organizations and the individual makes the organization one of the richest of all possible contexts and a most difficult arena for study, but one that demands an approach that can adequately capture people's cognitive capacity for creating the organizational structures and processes that affect them.

*Cognitive Consensuality.* Because this book emphasizes the interactive and integrative nature of organizational social cognition, it will also explore how cognitions might evolve from an individual's idiosyncratic thought process into some form of shared aggregate that is useful for concerted purposeful action. How do individuals, each with their own individualistic thought patterns, find shared meaning in an organizational environment, so that a reasonable degree of understanding and action is possible?

Many of the contributors to this volume have used the word *consensual* to indicate commonly shared cognitive processes. That is, after a time individuals within a group or an organization tend to think, at least to some degree, alike. Some would call this shared meaning *organizational culture.* Consensuality does not necessarily imply perfect agreement, nor that individuals have conducted a formalistic process of "reaching consensus." It merely implies that, whatever the process—conscious or unconscious, deliberate or not—individuals have achieved a certain similarity in the way they process and evaluate information.

Cognitive consensuality is extremely important for organizational systems, because concerted action frequently depends on cooperation and a certain degree of shared values and understanding of "how things are done." Thus, cognitive consensuality facilitates organizational action. But cognitive consensuality can also retard organizations and is perhaps the most reasonable explanation why organizations can be slow to change. Because change implies new ways of thinking and doing, new patterns of cognitive processing are frequently necessary. Sometimes cognitive consensuality must be destroyed and rebuilt in order to bring about organizational change.

Clearly, cognitive consensuality is an important element to consider when organizational social cognition is the topic of focus. Organization is impossible without some reasonable degree of cognitive consensuality. What are the processes by which the cognitions of groups of individuals become coaligned and thus facilitate focused social action within organizations? This is an important question that lies at the heart of many of the contributions to this book.

*A Focus on Pragmatic Implications.* Another recurring theme in this book is our concern with the practical implications of the concepts, theories, and research. By design, this book is devoted to an exploration of rather esoteric, state-of-the-art topics. Typically, such a book is aimed at a very high level of abstraction, and often makes little or no attempt to make the leap from abstract scholarship to practical implication. We have made a conscious and overt attempt to rectify this typical shortcoming in works of this kind. Each contributor has been asked to devote a part of his or her chapter to an exposition of the implications and applications of the points made in the chapter. We hope to avoid the usual tendency to give short shrift to the usefulness of the concepts to the practitioner.

Indeed, our intent was to create a volume that is accessible to executives and managers interested in advancing their profession. Although the contributions in the book are of the "cutting edge" variety, the authors of each chapter have tried to strike a balance between purely academic and popular styles of writing, without compromising the intended message of each chapter. We think that aim has been accomplished in a way that should engage members of both the professional management community and the academic community.

*Toward a Cognitive View of Organizations.* The world of organizational cognition is populated with many interesting and provocative concepts. Perhaps a capsule preview of some of them will be worthwhile here. Among the most important notions is that of a *schema,* which is a mental structure that serves to organize knowledge in some systematic fashion, often operating unconsciously. Although a schema is an abstract mental construct, it can be thought of as a sort of coherent network of thought about something that might be important to a manager. One basic type of schema is a *category,* which is said to be represented by a *prototype,* another mental abstraction that captures the defining characteristics of people and situations (see Rosch, 1978). For instance, when a manager considers one of her employees a low performer, that simple act of labeling the employee brings forth her low-performer schema, a host of traits and behaviors that are typically characteristic of low-performing people (not necessarily those associated with any given individual). The existence of the schema in the manager's mind leads to an assumption of attributes the employee might not have and causes missing information to be filled in with typical, but not necessarily accurate, information. The use of schemas saves a lot of cognitive work—that is, it is efficient—but it also can result in inaccurate performance appraisals (Feldman, 1981).

Schemas and prototypes might sound like abstract notions with questionable relevance to the manager's everyday job. There is strong and rapidly accumulating evidence, however, that everybody categorizes and that everybody uses prototypes. More succinctly, everybody uses schemas to some significant degree to cognitively organize his or her experience (see Cantor and Mischel, 1979). For that reason, the issue is not just a matter of learning about some new concepts that probably apply to organizations. It is a matter of understanding concepts that influence the way people in organizations work.

There are some obvious ramifications that stem from the example of the schema for a low-performing subordinate. Categorizing people as low performers not only causes managers to assign them negative traits they might not have (the phenomenon of *halo*), but also causes managers to treat them in a fashion consistent with the expectations provided by the schema (the *self-fulfilling prophecy* phenomenon). As an anonymous sage once said, "If you don't know how it works, how are you gonna fix it?" By understanding the fundamental cognitive processes involved, we can gain a deeper understanding of some of the most persistent problems in organizational behavior, along with some renewed faith in our ability to do something about them.

Other potentially new concepts include other forms of schemas, such as *implicit theories,* which are naive, personal collections of assumptions about how things are related and the way the organizational world works. For example, one's implicit theory about whether organization life is competitive or collaborative can govern whether one's actions are political or altruistic.

Yet another concept prevalent in the book is that of the *script,* which is a schema devoted to understanding and enacting dynamic patterns of behavior. A script supplies knowledge about expected sequences of events and then guides one's behavior so that it is appropriate to the given situation. For instance, when a manager conducts a strategy meeting, neither the stages in the meeting nor the steps in the strategic decision-making process need be carefully thought out beforehand. The sequence and patterning of events is already known and stored in memory in the form of scripted understanding.

Symbols also play a strong role in organizational life (Pondy, Frost, Morgan, and Dandridge, 1983). *Symbols* are simply meaningful representations that convey understanding. They can range from the visual (the corporate logo), to the verbal (advertising slogans), to the material (medals for service), to the abstract (information gathering as evidence of rational activity devoted to decision making—see Feldman and March, 1981). All have significance for cognition and action.

Indeed, we believe that all these potentially unfamiliar concepts and ideas provide required perspectives on the study of organizations as manifestations of cognition and action. All these notions, and many others that will appear in this book, can help us understand the workings of the modern organization and the people within. With such improved understanding, we can hope to improve the effectiveness of the management of organizations and our understanding about theories of organizational behavior. We believe that especially in recent years substantial progress in understanding cognitive processes in organizational settings has taken place. We are beginning to build a base of knowledge that transcends our previous inability to satisfactorily address the role of social cognition in organizations. Perhaps more importantly, we have now begun to understand the connections between cognition and action. Once understood and articulated, these developments suggest, in a way not previously possible, real implications for the transference of esoteric knowledge to the world of pragmatic management.

### An Overview of the Book

This book is divided into five sections: an introduction, a concluding chapter on the state of the art, and three major groups of contributor chapters. The fundamentals of organizational cognition are covered in Part I, which is entitled "Foundation Concepts for Organizations." These and other concepts are further developed in the "Transitions from Concept to Practice" section that forms Part II, with an eye toward bridging the transition from fundamentals to pragmatics. Finally, the relevance for organizations is demonstrated in Part III, "Applications of Social Cognition to Organizations."

We lead off with perhaps the most basic notions in modern social cognition, a treatment of schemas in human information processing by Robert G. Lord and Roseanne J. Foti entitled "Schema Theories, Information Processing, and Organizational Behavior." This article applies schema theory to understanding the problem of information processing and behavior in organizational settings. Four principal types of schema—self-schema, prototype schema, script schema, and person-in-situation schema—are compared in terms of their structural similarity and their effects on memory for information. The topics of schema growth and change and schema choice are then discussed. The implications of schema theory for understanding organizational behavior and processes are then analyzed by focusing on the consequences of using or not using schema and on ways that schema use can be effectively managed.

Next up is a chapter called "Symbols, Scripts, and Sensemaking," by Dennis A. Gioia. It explores the social cognitive processes used by organization members to make sense of their experience. It focuses on the means by which people in organizations construct definitions of organizational reality that serve as vehicles for understanding and action. The thesis of the chapter is that symbols and schemas, especially script schemas, are the primary organizational sensemaking devices. Understanding is accomplished and communicated mainly by means of symbolic processes (employing overt symbols, metaphors, analogies, and stories) that are then retained in schematic form via scripts. The scripts, which are dynamic webs of structured knowledge oriented around event sequences, then serve as a basis for action that further facilitates meaning construction and sensemaking processes. The chapter concludes by discussing the implications for understanding how organizations work and how an awareness of these fundamental processes might facilitate more effective management.

Next, Gerald R. Salancik and Joseph F. Porac expound on "Distilled Ideologies: Values Derived from Causal Reasoning in Complex Environments." The chapter focuses on the use of a simplification heuristic as part of the art of causal reasoning by practicing managers. Salancik and Porac argue that ideologies are beliefs derived from processes used in reasoning about causes in complex environments. They also reason that managers process such complexity in a simplified manner by attending to the interdependencies that exist among the factors in the environment in order to arrive at an understanding of the relative importance of each factor for a decision or outcome of concern. The authors conclude by discussing how recent research can be used to show the ways that usable ideologies can be distilled from interdependence, and they illustrate the problem with a review of the reasoning processes that went into some rather major decisions.

Concluding Part I's discussion of fundamentals is a piece related to Salancik and Porac's chapter. Karl E. Weick, Jr., and Michel G. Bougon explore the metaphor of "Organizations as Cognitive Maps." In their view, organizations are often depicted as consciously coordinated tools to accomplish ends. Cognitive representation of coordinated means-ends relations takes the form of causality assertions, which connect concepts abstracted from experience. The resulting *cause maps* provide cognitive structures that are imposed on events to create meaning, which means that cause maps often *are*, in fact, the organization. The chapter reviews the background for the idea of cause maps and then goes on to compare methods for data collection. A selective review of research findings is followed by a concluding section in which implications for research and practice are discussed.

The first chapter in the section "Transitions from Concept to Practice" is Anne Donnellon's in-depth exploration of the role of "Language and Communication in Organizations." Donnellon has two main theses: (1) that there is a need to develop a better understanding of human cognitive processes and (2) that much of what is done in organizations, both substantively and symbolically, is accomplished through language and other systems of communication. Drawing on perspectives from psycholinguistics and sociolinguistics, she discusses the processes by which individuals in organizations develop, modify, and display their cognitions through their communication. The influence of communication on organizational action is also considered. Finally, the research on and practical implications of language use in organizations are discussed. Donnellon argues that research on the role of communication in person perception, socialization, learning, and influence will yield significant benefits for organizational practices like selection, training, decision making, and change.

H. Kirk Downey and Arthur P. Brief next engage in a bit of informed speculation about implicit theories of organizing, dealing with the issue of "How Cognitive Structures Affect Organizational Design." In their view, the cognitive structures of an organization's members are not only essential to organizational functioning but also might, in some large measure be responsible for the structure that organizations develop. A substantial portion of this chapter is devoted to an exploration of the reasons why it is important to understand the ways in which cognitive structures, especially on the part of governing executives, might exert influence on many facets of organizational performance, including organizational design.

Next, Jennifer A. Chatman, Nancy E. Bell, and Barry M. Staw provide an exposition of "The Managed Thought: The Role of Self-Justification and Impression Management in Organizational Settings." Their chapter argues that cognition in organizations is influenced both by individual motivation and by social context. An understanding of cognition in organizations must therefore reach beyond a mechanical or dispassionate information-processing view. Investigators of social cognition must recognize that cognitions can be "managed" in the sense of being subject to motivational and contextual forces. Their chapter examines two "motivational" cognitive theories, self-justification and impression management, which bring individuals into models of social cognition because they emphasize bias and the adjustment of beliefs to fit behavior. These theories also bring the social context to bear on social cognition since they help identify interpersonal influences in information processing and the transmission of data. The two theories are first reviewed and contrasted, and then an attempt is made to expand the current literature on self-justification and impression management by explicitly applying the theories in organizational settings.

"Affect in Organizations: How Feelings and Emotions Influence Managerial Judgment," by Oh Soo Park, Henry P. Sims, Jr., and Stephan J. Motowidlo, considers the influence of feelings and their relationship to cognition. Recently the role of affect in cognition, the role of cognitive processes in understanding affect, and other affect-related phenomena have become compelling issues in the field of organizational behavior as well as in cognitive social psychology. Previous research has been concerned with affect-like variables, such as satisfaction, valence, and preferences. Nevertheless, little organizational research has focused on the role of affect within the social information-processing realm, especially in organizational behavior contexts such as motivation, leadership, performance appraisal, and decision making. This chapter focuses specifically on the performance appraisal situation. Recent research on performance appraisal has emphasized and attempted to understand its processes in terms of social information processing. For this line of research, affect and affect-related variables can provide a more comprehensive understanding of performance appraisal processes.

In Part III's focus on applied organizational cognition, Daniel J. Isenberg first tackles "The Structure and Process of Understanding." His own field research on managerial thinking has identified the practical importance of how managers come to understand the situations that confront them in their work. Isenberg identifies three concepts that have direct implications for how managers plan and implement action. First, plausible reasoning functions to increase the manager's confidence to the threshold of feasible action. Second, schematic information processing helps to explain a number of observed phenomena, including the prevalence of intuitive decision processes. And finally, probabilistic thinking captures the manager's attitude toward the uncertain nature of his or her organizational and business environment. Examples from the field research illustrate these three concepts and their usefulness in understanding managerial thinking processes.

Jack Feldman's contribution, "On the Difficulty of Learning from Experience," considers the criteria by which the adequacy of learning is assessed as well as some general ideas of how learning takes place and how learning is influenced by task characteristics and environmental factors, rendering feedback more or less meaningful. He then considers some phenomena studied by social cognition researchers (for example, hindsight bias, salience effects, social explanation, Pygmalion effects) that act to make learning more difficult as well as factors allowing substantial accuracy (for example, the robustness of linear models in prediction). Finally, he provides some recommendations for improving the efficiency and accuracy of experience-based learning.

The chapter "Image Theory and Organizational Decision Making," by Terence R. Mitchell, Kenneth J. Rediker, and Lee Roy Beach presents the central ideas of a new theory of decision making and extends some of these ideas to organizational decisions. It begins with the considerations that gave rise to image theory, its background, its descriptive rather than prescriptive nature, and how it differs from both the "normative" and the "heuristics and biases" views. This theory suggests that people have images about themselves, their pasts, and their futures. These images are composed of policies, goals, strategies, and tactics in a descending order of behavioral specificity. The theory argues that most decisions are made based on a simple process of seeing whether an alternative "fits" with the image and that only under special circumstances do people resort to a cost/benefit or expected-value type of thinking. The authors then extend the theory from individual decisions to organizational decisions by drawing theoretical parallels between the two and elaborating upon these parallels in terms of organizational culture.

Our final entry in the applications section is "Strategic Plan Failures," where Michael Finney and Ian I. Mitroff characterize "The Organization as Its Own Worst Enemy." They argue that social cognitive processes at varying levels of complexity (organizational, functional unit, group, and individual) play a critical role in the success or failure of an organization's strategic plan. These processes exist as sometimes visible and more frequently invisible facilitators or barriers. An organization concentrating on the external environment as the major source of threat and uncertainty does so at great risk. Its internal environment may create and unwittingly nourish a more formidable foe: itself. Finney and Mitroff present organizational self-reflection as a method for exploring the cognitive processes operating in an organization. The method can provide information for the design or correction of an organization's strategy. Having a fairly accurate self-reflection makes it possible to design a better-informed future strategy. Existing barriers and their associated meanings can be brought to the surface and changed so that future strategies have a better chance of success.

Finally, in the concluding chapter Dennis A. Gioia comments on "The State of the Art in Organizational Cognition." This chapter is devoted to the identification and synthesis of the common themes that emerge from the preceding comprehensive discussion of organizational cognition. The chapter and the book then conclude by turning the lens of organizational cognition on the issue of organizational change and by asking how what we now know about cognitive processes in organizations might facilitate the improvement of efforts to generate change.

These works comprise the current thinking on cognitive processes in organizations, rendered by scholars who have contributed much to that body of thought. Taken together, they represent our state of progress to date. In many ways, this volume shows how much organizational theorists have done. In many other ways, it also shows how much the field has left to do.

## References

Abelson, R. P. "Script Processing in Attitude Formation and Decision Making." In J. S. Carroll and J. W. Payne (eds.),

*Cognition and Social Behavior.* Hillsdale, N.J.: Erlbaum, 1976.

Cantor, N., and Mischel, W. "Prototypes in Person Perception." In L. Berkowitz (ed.), *Advances in Experimental Social Psychology.* Vol. 12. Orlando, Fla.: Academic Press, 1979.

Feldman, J. M. "Beyond Attribution Theory: Cognitive Process in Performance Appraisal." *Journal of Applied Psychology,* 1981, *66,* 127–148.

Feldman, M. S., and March, J. G. "Information in Organizations as Signal and Symbol." *Administrative Science Quarterly,* 1981, *26,* 171–186.

Locke, E. A., Shaw, K. N., Saari, L. M., and Latham, G. P. "Goal Setting and Task Performance: 1969–1980." *Psychological Bulletin,* 1981, *90,* 125–152.

March, J. G., and Shapira, Z. "Behavioral Decision Theory and Organizational Decision Theory." In G. Ungson and D. Braunstein (eds.), *Decision Making: An Interdisciplinary Inquiry.* Boston: Kent, 1982.

Mitchell, T. R., Green, S. G. and Wood, R. E. "An Attributional Model of Leadership and the Poor-Performing Subordinate: Development and Validation." In B. Staw and L. Cummings (eds.), *Research in Organizational Behavior.* Vol. 3. Greenwich, Conn.: JAI Press, 1981.

Morgan, G. *Images of Organization.* Beverly Hills, Calif.: Sage, in press.

Pondy, L. R. "Union of Rationality and Intuition in Management Action." In S. Srivastva and Associates, *The Executive Mind: New Insights on Managerial Thought and Action.* San Francisco: Jossey-Bass, 1983.

Pondy, L. R., Frost, P. J., Morgan, G., and Dandridge, T. D. (eds.). *Organizational Symbolism.* Greenwich, Conn.: JAI Press, 1983.

Rosch, E. "Principles of Categorization." In E. Rosch and B. B. Lloyd (eds.), *Cognition and Categorization.* Hillsdale, N.J.: Erlbaum, 1978.

Simon, H. A. *Models of Man: Social and Rational.* New York: Wiley, 1957.

Vroom, V. H. *Work and Motivation.* New York: Wiley, 1964.

Weick, K. E. *The Social Psychology of Organizing.* (2nd ed.) Reading, Mass.: Addison-Wesley, 1979.

Weick, K. E. "Managerial Thought in the Context of Action." In S. Srivastva and Associates, *The Executive Mind: New Insights on Managerial Thought and Action.* San Francisco: Jossey-Bass, 1983.

# 1

# Schema Theories, Information Processing, and Organizational Behavior

### Robert G. Lord
### Roseanne J. Foti

*I have so much to do and so many things to keep track of that I use this notebook as a second memory.*

*There are so many new tasks that I keep lists of everything I have to do.*

—Comments from two
newly hired assistant
professors

Like these two new employees, most people experience some degree of information overload when adjusting to new jobs. This is because they have not yet developed the cognitive schemas that allow more experienced employees to do many tasks automatically. The nature of cognitive schemas and how they help organizational members efficiently process information is the focus of this chapter.

Most organizations provide complex and noisy informational environments in which organizational participants gather information about other individuals and relevant work tasks, which they must then integrate with their own thoughts, feelings, and work behaviors. To manage these multiple information-processing demands, people accomplish many cognitive activities without conscious awareness, attention, or much forethought. In other words, people rely on highly structured, preexisting knowledge systems to interpret their organizational world and generate appropriate behaviors. Such a knowledge system, which is often called a *schema,* is the major focus of this chapter. (Note that although the plural of *schema* from the Greek is *schemata,* we will use the anglicized plural, *schemas.*) In this chapter, we will describe the various types of schemas that are commonly used, noting their parallels and unique properties. We will then discuss their relation to information processing and to the generation of organizational behavior. We will conclude by discussing the practical implications (both positive and negative) of schema use and the ways in which schema use can be managed.

To fully appreciate the role of cognitive schemas, it is necessary to first distinguish between two forms, or modes, of information processing: automatic and controlled processing. *Controlled processing* places heavy demands on our limited capacity to pay attention, focuses on one activity at a time, is easily altered or reversed by subjects, and is very sensitive to cognitive load (Shiffrin and Schneider, 1977). Controlled processes are activated when we are thinking about a task we are doing and explicitly planning how it should be done, as is often the case with new work tasks. *Automatic processes,* however, demand less attention; can be applied to several activities simultaneously; are difficult to alter, suppress, or ignore once learned; and are virtually unaffected by cognitive load. In familiar situations and for familiar work tasks, they allow us to operate with little thought or cognitive strain, enabling us to simultaneously manage several cognitive tasks.

To illustrate, in a group meeting complex organizational problems such as developing a corporate strategy can be solved with controlled processes because other related issues are handled using automatic processes. That is, perceptions of others and oneself, the expected flow of events in the group meeting, and the relation of a corporate strategy to other areas such as production or marketing can all be understood using automatic processes. Moreover, these later tasks can be handled automatically because we have ready-made and appropriate schemas for forming social and self-perceptions, for understanding how familiar events like meetings are sequenced, and for understanding how abstract principles, such as corporate strategies, can be interrelated with more concrete factors, such as the needs of production departments in accomplishing organizational goals. Using the more precise cognitive terms that we will explain in the next section, we can say that the traits of others are assessed automatically by matching their characteristics or behaviors with *person schemas*; richly developed *self-schemas* are used to form self-perceptions; meeting events are anticipated using *weak scripts*; and the set of activities related to accomplishing goals are organized and sequenced using *strong scripts*. How such automatic processes operate can be understood by more carefully describing cognitive schemas and their interrelation with fundamental cognitive processes, such as memory, perception, and decision making.

Bartlett (1932) first introduced the term *schema* as a description of a hypothetical mental structure controlling attention and the subsequent reconstruction of memory. For our purposes, a schema is a cognitive structure that represents organized knowledge about a given stimulus—that is, a person or situation—as well as rules that direct information processing. In essence, a schema provides observers with a knowledge base that serves as a guide for the interpretation of information, actions, and expectations (Graesser, Woll, Kowalski, and Smith, 1980; Taylor and Crocker, 1981). Schemas help people simplify and effectively manage the information in the complex task and social environments characteristic of applied settings.

The schema concept specifically maintains that social information is stored in an abstract form, not simply as a collection of all the original encounters with a specific "type" of person or situation. For example, a good-supervisor schema is stored in memory and a general case abstracted from specific good supervisors that have been known. The schema would contain information common to these supervisors, such as knowledge that a good supervisor is well organized, delegates responsibility, makes sound decisions, develops employees' capabilities, and clearly communicates attainable tasks.

## Types of Schemas

Social schemas essentially fall into four groups (Taylor and Crocker, 1981). The first type is a *self-schema* (Markus, 1977), which contains information about one's own personality, appearance, and behavior. A *person schema* focuses on trait and behavior information common to certain groups or types of people. Examples of person schemas include introvert and extrovert (Cantor and Mischel, 1979), leaders (Foti, Fraser, and Lord, 1982; Lord, Foti, and Phillips, 1982; Lord, Foti, and De Vader, 1984), and good workers versus bad workers. *Script or event schemas* include knowledge about the typical sequence of events in a given situation. Typical scripts include eating lunch with co-workers and going to a job interview (Gioia and Manz, 1985; Gioia and Poole, 1984; Schank and Abelson, 1977). The final type of schema is a *person-in-situation schema*. This type of schema contains information about people and behavior typically found in specific social situations. Examples of this type of schema include a job applicant at an interview and a practical joker at a party (Cantor, Mischel, and Schwartz, 1982).

The research on social schemas—whether focused on self, person, script, or person-in-situation—shows that they all have similar effects on information processing. Specifically, each type of schema affects the perception of incoming information, the retrieval of stored information, and inferences based on that information. Nevertheless, for the sake of clarity, each type of schema will be discussed separately, with the greatest emphasis placed on person and script schemas.

*Self-Schemas.* This type of schema consists of cognitive generalizations about the self that are derived from past experience. Most people have clear conceptions of themselves in relation to some attributes and less clear self-conceptions in relation to others. People have a self-schema for dimensions that are important to them, for dimensions for which they think of themselves as extreme, or for dimensions on which they are sure the opposite does not hold (Markus, 1977). Thus, if independence is important to you, and if you think of yourself as extremely independent and not at all dependent, this implies that you have accumulated considerable knowledge (that is, a self-schema) about yourself on that dimension. In short, self-schemas represent the way the self has been differentiated and articulated in memory.

Having a self-schema for a particular dimension allows a person to quickly filter incoming information about that dimension in social situations. Going back to the example of independence, individuals who have a self-schema for independence consistently and quickly recognize traits related to independence as descriptive of themselves; they do not show this pattern with respect to dependence traits. Therefore, having a self-schema for a particular dimension means that an individual is a rapid judge of himself or herself on that trait or behavior in a variety of circumstances. In addition, people with a self-schema for a given attribute also note it in other people (Fong and Markus, 1982).

Markus and Smith (1981) have elaborated on the impact of self-schemas in judgments and evaluations of other people. They have found that individuals with a certain self-schema will process information about others that is relevant to their schema differently from an individual without this schema. Their key finding was that an individual possessing a certain self-schema will elaborate another person's behavior relevant to that schema with information from his or her own schema, resulting in a more extreme evaluation of that person's behavior. Thus, a schema-relevant target person is seen as either more independent or more dependent by an individual with an independence self-schema than by someone without this self-schema.

In terms of memory and inference, self-schemas help people to remember relevant information. Thus, people with an independence schema can remember many examples of independent behavior; they also expect to behave independently in the future and resist people telling them they are not independent (Markus, Crane, Bernstein, and Siladi, 1982). It is important to point out, however, that knowledge about oneself and others differs in several ways. First, knowledge about oneself is more accessible in memory than knowledge about others, and the self-judgment is far more memorable (Rogers, 1981). However, the relative memorability of self-judgments decreases as the other person being judged becomes more familiar (Bower and Gilligan, 1979). Finally, knowledge about the self is more affect-laden than is knowledge about others, especially unfamiliar others. Several researchers have suggested that the advantage of self-relevant information in perception and memory is due in large part to its emotional importance (Bargh, 1982; Rogers, 1981).

*Person Schemas.* This second type of schema has most often been related to a categorization process. Individuals sort other human beings into groups, types, or other categories according to similarities in their essential features. One characteristic of person categories is that these categories are not clearly bounded sets. Rather, they are more like "fuzzy sets" in which members of one category have overlapping features in common with members of other categories. Thus, the boundaries distinguishing membership in one category from membership in another closely related category are neither sharp nor reliable (Cantor and Mischel, 1979; Lord, Foti, and Phillips, 1982). For the sake of distinctiveness, categories are represented cognitively by *prototypes,* an abstract set of features commonly associated with the members of a category (Cantor and Mischel, 1979; Lord, Foti, and Phillips, 1982). Once a prototype of a category has been formed, membership in the category is assessed in terms of *prototypicality* or perceived similarity of the stimulus to the prototype. In other words, categorization of a person is based on the extent to which the features of that stimulus person match those features contained in the prototype. In addition, knowledge about any given category is structured around and represented in long-term memory as a prototype (Cantor, Mischel, and Schwartz, 1982). The example we gave earlier of the good supervisor is an illustration of a person schema.

A main issue related to the categorization process is the structure of person categories and the level at which categorization occurs. Specifically, it has been found that categories for people are hierarchically organized and that there is one level of organization that is most basic or functional in relation to information processing (Brewer, Dull, and Lui, 1981; Cantor and Mischel, 1979; Lord, Foti, and De Vader, 1984). An example of this hierarchical structure for the category of leaders is as follows: leader is the superordinate or most global level in the hierarchy; below this level come the basic categories that include different types of leader—for example, political, business, and sports leaders; finally, at the lowest level in the hierarchy are the subordinate categories that further differentiate each basic-level category (that is, democratic or republican political leaders). It is the basic-level categories that are significantly richer in detail and more differentiated from contrasting categories— for example, from nonleaders—and that are therefore most useful in processing social information.

In terms of retrieving information from memory, once an observer places a person into a particular category, the observer is likely to misremember the presence of consistent but never seen attributes. In two very similar studies, Phillips and Lord (1982) and Phillips (1984) investigated the effects of leadership categories on descriptions and recognition of leader behaviors. Participants in the study viewed a videotaped interaction of a four-person problem-solving group, received bogus (good or poor) performance information, and then completed a recognition memory measure. The results showed that memory for behavioral information was highly dependent on the labels consistent with the bogus performance feedback. Specifically, good performance information led to recognition of leader prototypical behaviors and poor performance information led to recognition of antiprototypical leader behavior. Even more interesting, they found that behaviors that were consistent with the schemas but that had not in fact occurred were given recognition ratings that were not significantly different from ratings of behaviors actually seen.

The importance of labels and cognitive categories in retrieving information is also illustrated by a study of perceptions of real political figures (Foti, Fraser, and Lord, 1982). Using Gallup poll data from several surveys of perceptions of United States presidents and presidential candidates, they found marked changes over time and across candidates in the percentage of respondents who believed strong leadership qualities were possessed by the person being rated. They posited that as these leadership perceptions changed, so would perceptions of other characteristics that were strongly associated with leadership. Consistent with this expectation, correlational results clearly showed a pattern of greater change for more prototypical items when leadership ratings changed either for the same person over time (former President Carter at several time periods) or between politicians (President Carter versus Senator Kennedy).

Another particularly interesting effect of person schemas on memory is the *point-of-view effect,* in which the point of view taken during recall affects the information recalled. For example, Anderson and Pichert (1978) manipulated the perspective at retrieval by asking participants in the study to imagine they were either prospective home buyers or burglars; they found significant effects on the recalled details from a previously read story. This suggests that memory involves a working backward (search) from a current perspective through relevant schema structures to the desired information. Information irrelevant to that perspective often cannot be accessed, although it may be retrievable at some other time when another point of view is taken. This type of bias may help explain why subjects given good performance feedback recall different processes than subjects given poor performance feedback (Binning and Lord, 1980). Namely, different information may be retrieved from these alternative performance-related points of view. It also suggests that supervisors would "remember" different behaviors for the same employee after learning of good as compared to poor employee performance.

Turning to the impact of person schemas on inferences and judgments, we note that the structure of these schemas may affect the ease of retrieval and therefore the judgments that are made. In particular, two types of judgments, frequency ratings and causal assessments, may be highly dependent on the way information is retrieved. Tversky and Kahneman (1974) maintain that frequency judgments are most often made by using heuristics such as availability. Specifically, more available behaviors are judged to have been exhibited more frequently. Availability, in turn, may depend on the schematic structure underlying memory that occurred weeks or months before. Interestingly, more prototypical information is more available in memory. For example, while investigating leadership categories, Lord, Foti, and De Vader (1984) had subjects make prototypicality ratings for various leadership behaviors and found that the time taken to make these ratings decreased as the item prototypicality increased. These results are consistent with the operation of an availability heuristic. Furthermore, Murphy, Martin, and Garcia (1982) have concluded that as time between observing behavior and making frequency judgments increases, reliance on person schemas will also increase. However, further research is required to determine whether frequency ratings are more likely to reflect the internal structure of the person schema into which a particular individual has been categorized rather than the actual behavior of that individual.

Availability heuristics may be important in memory-based causal or responsibility attributions as well. More available information may be more salient and may therefore be given increased causal importance (Taylor and Fiske, 1978). Also, as noted by Lord and Smith (1983), observers making attributions may only search memory until they find a plausible cause for an event. Such a limited search for cause implies that schema organization would substantially impact on the causal explanations. Thus, as Lord, Foti, and De Vader (1984) found, stimulus persons classified as leaders were seen as being more responsible for their organization's performance and as having more causal impact on performance than stimulus persons not classified as leaders.

To sum up, then, person schemas include prototypic representations of attributes and behaviors, such as leadership, and shape the processes of perception, memory, and inference to conform to our general assumptions about different types of people. Using these schemas does not necessarily produce accuracy in identifying individual attributes and behaviors. Person schemas are used by observers to manage complex social information economically, but not always accurately.

*Script Schemas.* In addition to self and person schemas, the third type of schema is a script or event schema. Simply stated, a script schema is a cognitive structure that describes the appropriate sequence of events in a given situation (Abelson, 1981; Schank and Abelson, 1977). Scripts serve a dual purpose for people. First, scripts enable the understanding of situations and play an important role in comprehension and inference making (Gioia and Manz, 1985). Second, scripts provide a guide to behavior that is appropriate to those situations. For experienced workers, one would expect scripts to be a potent determinant of behavior. Unlike self- and person schemas, scripts possess a temporal ordering, and the associations among events in a script have a certain causal relationship. Lichtenstein and Brewer (1980) have postulated that actions within a script are organized into a series of goal-subgoal relationships; that is, early events in the script produce, or at least enable, the occurrence of later events (Nisbett and Ross, 1980). For example, a selection interview asking questions about an applicant's education and work experience contains a subgoal for assessing his or her qualifications. Putting the applicant at ease is in turn a subgoal aimed at allowing the applicant to provide more complete information, which in turn enables a more accurate assessment.

Abelson (1981) has proposed that scripts possess a hierarchical structure similar to person schemas. The script itself is the basic level in the hierarchical structure—that is, the level most functional in processing information about everyday situations. Analogous to superordinate categories are what Abelson calls *metascripts*—that is, scripts that are more abstract and that lack detail. *Script tracks* are analogous to subordinate-level categories. A particular script track contains many additional contextual details not shared by other tracks. Thus, a manager could hold a generalized meeting with a metascript and retain specific events and behaviors appropriate to different types of meetings in different tracks. This process allows a repertoire of related contextual scripts to be retained: one for conducting a planning meeting, one for conducting a similar but distinctive planning meeting, another for a brainstorming meeting, and so on (Gioia and Poole, 1984).

Abelson (1981) also distinguishes between two categories of scripts people hold in memory. *Weak scripts* resemble other forms of cognitive structures such as person schemas (extrovert or good supervisor) and serve to organize expectations about the behavior of people in certain situations, but they do not specify the exact sequence of these behaviors. For example, independent events that usually occur together are organized by weak scripts. The distinctive feature of *strong scripts* is, in contrast, the expectation of an exact sequence of events due to the enabling relationship (goal-subgoal) between script events.

Scripts impact on perception, memory, and judgment processes in much the same way as person schemas in that observers match external stimuli to pre-existing scripts. This process leads to two types of errors: distortion of present but slightly inconsistent information to fit the script, and inferring additional events or behaviors implied by the script but not actually observed. Such errors are indicated by the finding that unobserved script-consistent actions are as recognizable to observers as script-consistent actions that were actually seen (Graesser, Gordon, and Sawyer, 1979; Graesser, Woll, Kowalski, and Smith, 1980). This gap-filling process appears to be exaggerated by repeated encounters with the script (Bower, Black, and Turner, 1979). Larger inconsistencies between the external stimulus and the script may be explicitly noticed, triggering additional processing to distinguish the action in memory. Thus, observers may "tag" a particular script to indicate a noticed inconsistency (Graesser, Gordon, and Sawyer, 1979; Graesser, Woll, Kowalski, and Smith, 1980). Initially, these inconsistencies are remembered more easily than script-consistent actions, but they may also be forgotten more quickly over time.

To summarize, scripts describe appropriate sequences of activity in particular situations. Like other schemas, scripts guide the perception of ambiguous information, often shape memory toward script-consistent information, and fill in gaps where stimulus information is missing. In contrast to person schemas, the sequential and enabling aspects of a script may make inconsistencies or interruptions harder to ignore.

*Person-in-Situation Schemas.* The fourth and final type of schema to be discussed combines characteristics of both the person and event schemas. Cantor, Mischel, and Schwartz (1982) have posited that observers' knowledge systems may not be organized around such discrete entities as persons and events. Rather, the richest, most lifelike, and most useful cognitive structures may be compound in nature. These structures are essentially generalizations about people-in-situations or scripts for behavior in situations, such as an applicant at a job interview.

Most of the research conducted on person-in-situation schemas has been concerned with the content and structure of this type of schema in relation to person and event schemas. Cantor, Mischel, and Schwartz (1982) compared the number of features subjects could agree on in person-in-situation schemas to the number of features in the corresponding but separate person and event schemas. They found in most cases the compound schemas contained more features than the separate schemas. Additionally, the authors found a hierarchical structure for the compound schemas with categories at the basic level being described in more concrete and vivid terms due to greater numbers of characteristics related to behavior and physical appearance. Finally, the authors also found that subjects could form images of different person-in-situations faster than simple person images alone.

In summary, each type of schema discussed has similar effects on information processing by guiding our attention, biasing our memory in terms of schema-consistent behaviors or events, and filling in gaps where stimulus information is missing. In addition, person schemas, scripts, and person-in-situation schemas share a similar hierarchical structure. Yet each type of schema has some unique characteristics. Self-schemas contain more affect than the other types of schemas, which explains why self-knowledge is more accessible and more memorable than knowledge about other people. Script schemas often contain a temporal ordering because actions within a script are organized by a series of goal-subgoal relationships. Finally, person-in-situation schemas may be richer, more accessible, and therefore more widely used than either person or script schemas.

## Schema Growth and Change

Given the pervasive effects of schemas on perception, memory, and inference processes, an important issue becomes the "state" of the schema itself. Specifically, two topics need to be addressed: How easily do schemas change, and how do they develop?

*The Perseverance Effect.* Schemas facilitate information processing by allowing the general case to fill in for the specific example. A fellow employee may not fit your "co-worker" schema perfectly, but he may fit well enough to permit a generic co-worker schema to be used to predict and understand his behavior. Small discrepancies between the generic co-worker schema and the employee's behavior would be overlooked, forgotten with time, or explained by situational factors. This sort of reliance on schemas simplifies processing, but it also makes generic schema resistant to change. Known as the *perseverance effect*, this resistance represents a major feature of schemas: they often persist stubbornly even in the face of contrary evidence (Fiske and Taylor, 1984).

Schemas can be so robust that they persist even when people are informed that the evidence in support of them is false. In an interesting study designed to demonstrate this point, people were told that a new personality test showed them to be socially sensitive. Presumably, these people then activated or began to build a self-schema for social sensitivity and to think of all the reasons they were socially sensitive. When informed that the test was not genuine, participants in the study still continued to believe they were socially sensitive (Ross, Lepper, and Hubbard, 1975). Thus, once convinced of their social sensitivity, people remained convinced even when the initial reason was disqualified.

What can be done to make people more responsive to

contradictory evidence? Telling people that the evidence to support their schemas is mixed and that they should try to be unbiased does not minimize the perseverance effect. However, telling people to think carefully about how they are evaluating the evidence and to watch for biases as they interpret the data (Lord, Lepper, and Thompson, 1980), as well as having people argue against their schemas (Anderson, 1982), has been shown to moderate this effect.

*Schema Development.* Since schemas are so robust, it is important to know how they develop in the first place. Although schema development has not been explored extensively, some principles are clear. Schemas are built from experience with relevant instances, and they become more abstract, more complex, and more organized with experience (Fiske and Taylor, 1984). This occurs because people generalize schemas from experiences with instances of the category in question, and it occurs for many types of schema, such as learning about an organization (Martin, 1982). Several properties of schemas are likely to change with increasing experience. The schemas of experts contain more characteristics than do the schemas of novices, and mature schemas also become more organized. Specifically, expert schemas contain more information (Lurigio and Carroll, 1985), more links among the elements and characteristics, and possibly a more efficient hierarchy (McKeithen, Reitman, Reuter, and Hirtle, 1981).

While most accounts of schema development assume that schemas are built from experience with relevant examples, much less attention has focused on examining the process of schema development. In a recent paper, Fiske and Dyer (1985) presented a learning approach to schema development. Specifically, they suggested that a schema begins as a collection of individual components or features, and through experience, associations among related components are strengthened until the entire schema can be activated in an all-or-none fashion. Thus, schema development progresses along a knowledge continuum from novice to expert level, with experience strengthening the links among related components.

Viewing schema development as a kind of knowledge

continuum led Fiske and Dyer (1985) to make some intriguing predictions about the effects of schema development on the transfer of learning. Specifically, the authors wanted to know whether knowledge of one schema facilitated or inhibited learning a second somewhat similar schema that was composed of some elements in the old schema and some new elements. They found that if the schema was in a novice state of development and existed as many isolated, barely familiar components, then the prior schema facilitated learning the new schema because it increased the familiarity of part of the new schema content. However, if the schema was in an intermediate stage of development and existed as many loosely linked components, then the prior schema interfered with learning the new schema. Finally, if the schema existed as a unified whole (an expert schema), the prior schema did not affect learning a new schema.

To summarize, schemas develop out of repeated exposure to relevant instances, and they become more abstract, complex, and organized over time. Depending on the level of schema development, knowledge of one schema may either facilitate, inhibit, or have no effect on learning a second, related schema.

## Choice of Schema

Given the variety of schemas available for an observer to use, choice of schemas becomes an important issue that can affect perceptions, memory, or behavior. The way subordinates are perceived may be affected substantially by the schema used by their superiors in organizations. Choice of schema is a joint function of the target (either the person or the situation) and the perceiver. It is affected by the perceiver's goals, recently used information, salient aspects of the target, and differences among perceivers.

*Observational Goals.* The purpose for which an observer plans to use the information gathered has been shown to affect the processing of that information in many different ways. Perceivers with different observational goals will chunk a sequence of behavior differently (Cohen and Ebbesen, 1979), store the information differently in memory (Cohen and Ebbesen, 1979;

Hamilton, Katz, and Leirer, 1979), and retrieve different information from memory (Hoffman, Mischel, and Mazze, 1981).

In a study designed to test the effects of these four observational goals, Hoffman, Mischel, and Mazze (1981) constructed a series of written behavioral episodes that could be alternatively categorized in terms of the goals or traits of the stimulus person. Subjects categorized the episodes using either a memory, empathy, impression formation, or behavior prediction purpose. The results indicated that people with either the memory or the empathy purpose organized the episodes according to the stimulus person's goals, whereas the impression formation and behavior prediction purposes leads to participants organizing the episodes in terms of traits. Additionally, only the goal organizational strategy enabled a second group of participants to remember the behavioral episode.

Since goal relationships are an integral part of script or event schemas, it seems quite likely that qualitatively different types of information will be noticed when script as compared to person schemas are guiding perception. Script schemas will focus attention on actions or situational features that facilitate or prevent goal attainment, whereas person schemas will direct attention to behaviors or attributes that define these categories. Thus, the same objective social situation may be "seen" quite differently by a perceiver relying on these alternative schemas to guide perception. For example, managers implementing MBO programs will "see" things differently than managers concerned with performance appraisal, the former using scripts and the latter emphasizing person schemas.

In one of the few studies comparing the effects of alternative perceptual schemas on person perceptions, Foti and Lord (1985) showed subjects a videotape of a board meeting that could be encoded using widely held scripts about how board meetings operate. It could also be encoded in terms of person schemas emphasizing leadership, since the situation was depicted as a formal organizational meeting and hierarchical differences in authority were quite evident. They induced subjects to use a leadership schema by asking subjects to form an impression of the chairman of the group while watching the videotape.

To induce a script schema, Foti and Lord used two manipulations. First, they asked subjects to remember as much information as possible from the videotaped stimulus. Second, they also informed some subjects about the goals of group members. This information should produce script-related processing since scripts are widely recognized, goal-related sequences of events. Foti and Lord found that subjects in script-relevant conditions remembered more script-relevant information on a free-recall task than did subjects in the person schema conditions. These latter subjects, however, remembered more leader-relevant information than did subjects in the script-relevant conditions. Clustering analysis based on recall order also indicated that subjects used a script-relevant organization in the script-relevant conditions and a leader-relevant organization in the person schema conditions. Recognition accuracy depended on how consistent the items were with appropriate memory schemas.

*Priming.* In addition to observational goals, recently used information will impact on the interpretation and retrieval of information. Specifically, priming has to do with the issue of whether previous exposure to a particular schema will affect subsequent descriptions and evaluations of persons or situations. Research has shown that exposing people to positive or negative trait terms—for example, "adventurous" versus "reckless"— causes people at a later time to rate and recall behaviors that can be interpreted in many ways—for example, shooting rapids —as correspondingly positive or negative (Higgins, Rholes, and Jones, 1977).

Priming can have long-term as well as short-term consequences, affecting ratings as much as two weeks later, and there is evidence to suggest that priming effects increase over time (Higgins and King, 1981). This is an important point. It suggests that a transitory and perhaps arbitrary context can affect the way a person is permanently categorized in memory.

*Salience.* A person can be salient relative to the perceiver's context and thus become the focus of attention in a number of ways (Fiske and Taylor, 1984). Novelty, being the only person of a certain race, sex, or hair color in a group, causes that person to be the center of attention. Physical features of the stimulus (size, brightness, loudness, movement, uniqueness) may make the stimulus stand out from the immediate context and thus attract attention. A person can become salient if he or she behaves in ways that do not fit the perceiver's prior knowledge about that *individual,* his or her *social category,* or *people in general.* All these types of salience are based on expectations. A somewhat different principle of salience is that salience can be created by a person deliberately dominating the visual field in social settings. For example, salience can depend on seating position in a group; a person who wants to have the maximum impact on the leadership of a meeting should sit at the head or foot of a long table (Taylor and Fiske, 1978).

Regardless of the way salience is created, its effects are robust and wide ranging. The most dominant consequence of salience is exaggerated perceptions of causality. Salient behavior is also seen as less under the control of the situation and more indicative of the person's underlying tendencies. Salience does not reliably enhance the quantity of recalled information, but it does increase the organization and consistency of memory in several ways. The more attention an observer pays to another person, the more typical of a certain category the person becomes. Attention will structure impressions, emphasizing features that fit, and adjusting those that do not. Thus, salience affects causally relevant memory, which in turn leads to exaggerated attributions.

The impact of salience on leadership perceptions has been illustrated in an empirical study by Phillips and Lord (1981). They had observer-subjects view one of two fifteen-minute videotapes of the same four-person problem-solving group. The videotapes were filmed concurrently and differed only in that the camera angle of one tape made the person being rated more salient than in the other tape. Along with explicit instructions to attend to the entire group or to concentrate on the target individual, this difference between tapes formed the researchers' manipulation of the salience of the target. Leadership ratings were substantially higher under the salient than the nonsalient conditions, illustrating that manipulating attention affected recognition of leadership. It appears that subjects in the high-salience condition saw the target as fitting better with their pre-existing leadership schema and thus having more causal impact than did subjects in the low-salience condition. Thus, as previously discussed, salience affected causally relevant memory, which in turn led to higher leadership ratings.

## Implications of Schema Use for Organizations

*Consequences of Schema Use.* The consequences of relying on social schemas and automatic processes are both good and bad. The benefits are that cognitive capacity is conserved so that it can be allocated to other tasks, that one's social world seems more predictable than it may actually be, and that social interactions produce less mental strain and anxiety. The costs are that we view others in overly stereotypical ways, that we may be less accurate in rating others' behaviors or performance, and that we may be unknowingly biased by salient personal characteristics (race, age, or gender) that are automatically used to classify others. In this section, we will discuss these consequences in more detail and also explain how schemas can be used to integrate one's social and task activities.

Schemas help reduce the information-processing demands associated with social activities by providing a ready-made knowledge system for interpreting and storing information about others. They also provide a set of rules or operations that guide the automatic processing of social information. For example, Lord (1985b) has explained how schemas can automatically guide selective attention/comprehension, encoding, storage, retrieval, and judgment steps in perceiving and evaluating others. In addition to controlling cognitive processes, the general content of social schemas fulfills an important function since it provides a ready-made system for storing information. Returning to the business meeting example offered at the beginning of the chapter, one may perceive the CEO as a leader on the basis of his or her position, dress, and behavioral style—that is, on the basis of the fit with the content of leadership prototypes. Once this classification is made, we do not need to preserve all the specific details about our CEO in memory; instead, we merely have to store the label—leader—and any particularly salient exceptions we notice. We can then rely on generic leadership information to fill in information (usually but not always accurately) that is not specifically stored in memory. Such simplifications are especially useful since storage of information into permanent memory is slow compared with the speed of other cognitive operations; thus, a potential bottleneck is avoided. Unfortunately, accuracy in perceiving and evaluating others may also be reduced and biases may be introduced.

By providing a generic way of perceiving and storing information about others, the use of social schemas can reduce the accuracy of social information processing. Although others may be classified or labeled fairly accurately, descriptions of specific behaviors or activities may be based as much on the content of generic schemas as on the actual behaviors of the person being described (Lord, 1985a). Two weeks after our corporate meeting, we would describe the behavior of our CEO in stereotypical terms rather than recalling each specific behavior. Such simplifications produce measurement problems for researchers interested in accurate descriptions of leader behavior (see Lord, 1985b, for more detail) or for practitioners interested in accurate performance appraisals. However, from the viewpoint of the organizational participant, these measurement problems are of little importance. What is crucial is that cognitive tasks are simplified and the use of generic schemas allows one to easily form expectations about future behaviors of our CEO. We know how future meetings would be conducted, what type of influence or control tactics he or she would use, how specific problems would be handled, and how effective our CEO would be by virtue of having classified our CEO as a leader.

Although the role of social schemas in guiding perceptions, memory, and evaluations of others has received extensive attention, their impact on the production of social or task behaviors has been underemphasized. Here the impact of self-schemas and scripts becomes particularly important. Since self-schemas contain both information about how we perceive ourselves and how we are perceived by others, they can be used to generate behaviors that are appropriate both to the self and to social situations. They provide a general answer to the question "How should I act?" Given familiarity with a situation, a self-schema may become a particularly important type of person-in-situation schema: me-in-situation. Since self-schemas are highly elaborate and person-in-situation schemas are the most detailed and useful form of social schemas (Cantor, Mischel, and Schwartz, 1982), it seems reasonable that a me-in-situation schema would be both highly elaborate and very useful. Part of this elaboration would involve linkages to well learned and previously enacted scripts, and part would involve linkages to associated affective information. Thus, our CEO conducts the corporate meeting, in part, by enacting scripts that the CEO and others view as being appropriate. This allows him or her to use controlled cognitive processes to focus on the problems being discussed at the meeting. Our executive also knows what his or her affective reactions will be during the meeting and how they can be managed. He or she knows in advance whether conducting a meeting will make him or her nervous and, if so, how to manage this anxiety.

Script schemas are also a potent means to guide task-relevant behavior, particularly for repetitive tasks. Scripts contain information on goal-subgoal relations or means-ends chains that, when coupled with feedback, can efficiently guide behavior and attention. Control theorists (Carver and Scheier, 1981) argue that we automatically monitor the consistency between feedback and goals, directing attention to sufficiently large differences or obstacles that prevent goal attainment. Moreover, the organization in scripts (sequencing of subgoals) provides organization to our task activities.

Problem-solving behavior for unfamiliar tasks can be conceptualized as merely constructing script schema where none previously existed. Thus, if our hypothetical corporate meeting was called to increase profits, much of the problem-solving activity would involve developing strategies, tactics, and activities to accomplish this objective and organize them into a coherent plan. When completed, this plan would probably have a hierarchical organization of goals and explicit sequencing information. Efficient execution of this plan would also require feedback relevant to each goal level.

In other words, our business executives would be using their controlled cognitive capacity to develop the type of script-based control system that automatically guides behaviors in familiar situations. Interestingly, the goal-oriented nature of this corporate meeting would also affect the social perceptions of our executives. Knowing the goals of the CEO (to increase profits) would elicit script rather than person-based perceptual schemas from others (Foti and Lord, 1985). This common schema would guide expectations and communication during the meeting, suggest appropriate behaviors or activities, affect impressions of others, and influence the information that was stored in memory.

Our hypothetical business meeting can be used to illustrate what would happen if no cognitive schema existed. First, our CEO would have no ready-made agenda for the meeting and no set of subroutines for handling familiar meeting activities. Affective components would be unclear and difficult to manage, and his or her problem-solving activities would be unorganized. Other executives would have no clear expectations concerning the CEO or task activities. They might focus their attention on sizing up the CEO rather than solving the problem at hand. Even if they were problem-oriented, they might be uncertain how they could contribute to task activities. Communication would be much more elaborate and difficult, and misunderstanding and misperception would be much more common. Given sufficient time, motivation, and intelligence, our business executives could, of course, work through these difficulties. However, the meeting would be much more cognitively and emotionally demanding than it would be when person, self, and script types of schemas efficiently guide cognitive activities.

*Control of Schema Use.* The previous example as well as the theory developed in this chapter imply that organizations may benefit when members of the organization use social and task-related schemas appropriately. Two questions are relevant to this issue. It is important to determine, first of all, whether controlled information processing is preferable to schema-guided automatic processing, and second, which schemas are in fact guiding automatic processing.

Some organizational functions would probably benefit

from the use of controlled processing (defined at the beginning
of this chapter). For example, selection processes and performance appraisals could be improved, the accuracy of behavioral
measures could be increased, and biases in perceiving others
could be reduced. However, if organizational participants used
controlled processes for such activities, cognitive resources
would be drained from other tasks and social activities would
be more fatiguing (see Lord, 1985a, for a more thorough discussion of this issue). Thus, we doubt whether we should try to
avoid using social schemas; the costs of this alternative are too
great.

Which schemas should be used is a more practical question. In most situations, a mix of self-schemas, person schemas,
and script schemas will be used, but the relative predominance
of these schemas could be changed. Increasing the evaluative or
personal nature of activities should increase the use of self-
schemas; emphasizing the formation of impressions or expectations should increase the use of person schemas; emphasizing
accurate memory for events or the goals of activities should
elicit the use of script schemas. Changes in the use of such schemas will affect the perceptions formed, the information remembered, and the evaluations made.

Although no general recommendations can be made, two
possibilities can be offered to illustrate the potential of effectively managing schema use. Consider, for example, the performance appraisal process. The timing of performance appraisal is
generally directed by the calendar; appraisals occur every six
months or every year. Appraisals cover multiple tasks performed by employees over the period, and person schemas are
probably the most convenient means to organize these activities
in forming an overall evaluation and set of expectations. However, performance appraisals are characterized by global halo
and inaccuracies in rating specific events. Shifting to script-
guided performance appraisals could be produced by emphasizing the goals of subordinates and by performing appraisals
when major projects are completed rather than when dictated
by the calendar. Such a shift might be very effective in reducing
halo and in producing a more accurate rating of events.

A second possibility concerns the use of various types of

person schemas. Since gender, race, and age are highly salient, they will often be used to automatically process social information. Admonitions to avoid bias in social perceptions would probably have little impact on such automatic processes. However, priming other schemas could be more effective. For example, organizational norms that emphasized professionalism could provide an effective prime for less biased schemas. Further, training perceivers to develop more appropriate work-related schemas could be a desirable method of reducing bias. Learning categories for good, average, or poor employees or co-workers could be made part of organizational training programs. Teaching techniques to develop more balanced, data-based schemas might also be appropriate. In this respect, training people to think carefully about how they are evaluating evidence and to watch for bias as they interpret data might be helpful (Lord, Lepper, and Thompson, 1980), just as having people argue against their schema seems to be (Anderson, 1982).

*Broader Applications.* We have described four types of cognitive schemas, arguing that they all affect information processing (albeit somewhat differently) and can serve as a basis for generating appropriate organizational behaviors as well. Our focus has been on the micro and cognitive aspects of schemas, but schemas are also relevant to more macro and affective aspects of organizations. Commonly held schemas provide a basis for informal organizations, and they facilitate interpersonal communication. They may also help us assess causality, guiding our affective reactions to our own behavior or to the actions of others. Schemas also facilitate learning from tasks or social experiences (Gioia and Manz, 1985). Such aspects of organizational life all involve the integration of new information within existing cognitive structures of organizational members. Hence, the identification of different types of schemas and their impact on information processing is a fundamental step in understanding many important organizational processes.

## References

Abelson, R. P. "Script Processing in Attitude Formation and Decision Making." In J. S. Carroll and J. W. Payne (eds.),

*Cognition and Social Behavior.* Hillsdale, N.J.: Erlbaum, 1976.

Abelson, R. P. "Psychological Status of the Script Concept." *American Psychologist,* 1981, *36,* 715–729.

Anderson, J. R. *The Architecture of Cognition.* Cambridge, Mass.: Harvard University Press, 1982.

Anderson, R. C., and Pichert, J. W. "Recall of Previously Unrecallable Information Following a Shift in Perspective." *Journal of Verbal Learning and Verbal Behavior,* 1978, *17,* 1–12.

Bargh, J. A. "Attention and Automaticity in the Processing of Self-Relevant Information." *Journal of Personality and Social Psychology,* 1982, *43,* 425–436.

Bartlett, F. C. *Remembering: A Study in Experimental and Social Psychology.* Cambridge: Cambridge University Press, 1932.

Binning, J. F., and Lord, R. G. "Boundary Conditions for Performance Cue Effects on Group Process Ratings: Familiarity Versus Type of Feedback." *Organizational Behavior and Human Performance,* 1980, *26,* 115–130.

Bower, G. H., Black, J. B., and Turner, T. J. "Scripts in Memory for Text." *Cognitive Psychology,* 1979, *11,* 177–220.

Bower, G. H., and Gilligan, S. G. "Remembering Information Related to One's Self." *Journal of Research in Personality,* 1979, *13,* 404–419.

Brewer, M. B., Dull, V., and Lui, L. "Perceptions of the Elderly: Stereotypes as Prototypes." *Journal of Personality and Social Psychology,* 1981, *41,* 655–670.

Cantor, N., and Mischel, W. "Prototypes in Person Perception." In L. Berkowitz (ed.), *Advances in Experimental Social Psychology.* Vol. 12. Orlando, Fla.: Academic Press, 1979.

Cantor, N., Mischel, W., and Schwartz, J. "Social Knowledge: Structure, Content, Use, and Abuse." In A. Hastorf and A. Isen (eds.), *Cognitive Social Psychology.* Hillsdale, N.J.: Erlbaum, 1982.

Carver, C. S., and Scheier, M. F. *Attention and Self-Regulation.* New York: Springer-Verlag, 1981.

Cohen, C. E., and Ebbesen, E. B. "Observational Goals and

Schema Activation: A Theoretical Framework for Behavior Perception." *Journal of Experimental Social Psychology,* 1979, *15,* 305-329.

Ebbesen, E. B., Cohen, C. E., and Allen, R. B. "Cognitive Processes in Person Perception: Behavior Scanning and Semantic Memory." In N. Cantor and J. F. Kihlstrom (eds.), *Personality, Cognition, and Social Interaction.* Hillsdale, N.J.: Erlbaum, 1982.

Fiske, S. T., and Dyer, L. M. "Structure and Development of Social Schemata: Evidence from Positive and Negative Transfer Effects." *Journal of Personality and Social Psychology,* 1985, *48,* 839-852.

Fiske, S. T., and Taylor, S. E. *Social Cognition.* Reading, Mass.: Addison-Wesley, 1984.

Fong, G. T., and Markus, H. "Self-Schema and Judgments About Others." *Social Cognition,* 1982, *1,* 191-205.

Foti, R. J., Fraser, S. L., and Lord, R. G. "Effects of Leadership Labels and Prototypes on Perceptions of Political Leaders." *Journal of Applied Psychology,* 1982, *67,* 326-333.

Foti, R. J., and Lord, R. G. "Prototypes and Scripts: The Effects of Alternative Methods of Processing Information on Rating Accuracy." Unpublished manuscript, 1985.

Gioia, D. A., and Manz, C. C. "Linking Cognition and Behavior: A Script Processing Interpretation of Vicarious Learning." *Academy of Management Review,* 1985, *10,* 527-539.

Gioia, D. A., and Poole, P. P. "Scripts in Organizational Behavior." *Academy of Management Review,* 1984, *9,* 449-459.

Graesser, A. C., Gordon, S. E., and Sawyer, J. D. "Recognition Memory for Typical and Atypical Actions in Scripted Activities: Tests of a Script Pointer and Tag Hypothesis." *Journal of Verbal Learning and Verbal Behavior,* 1979, *18,* 319-332.

Graesser, A. C., Woll, S. B., Kowalski, D. J., and Smith, D. A. "Memory for Typical and Atypical Actions in Scripted Activities." *Journal of Experimental Psychology: Human Learning and Memory,* 1980, *6,* 503-515.

Hamilton, D. L., Katz, L. B., and Leirer, V. O. "Cognitive Representation of Personality Impressions: Organizational Processes in First Impression Formation." *Journal of Personality and Social Psychology*, 1979, *39*, 1050–1063.

Higgins, E. T., and King, G. A. "Accessibility of Social Constructs: Information-Processing Consequences of Individual and Contextual Variability." In N. Cantor and J. F. Kihlstrom (eds.), *Personality, Cognition, and Social Interactions.* Hillsdale, N.J.: Erlbaum, 1981.

Higgins, E. T., Rholes, W. J., and Jones, C. R. "Category Accessibility and Impression Formation." *Journal of Experimental Social Psychology*, 1977, *13*, 141–154.

Hoffman, C., Mischel, W., and Mazze, K. "The Role of Purpose in the Organization and Information About Behavior: Trait-Based Versus Goal-Based Categories in Person Perception." *Journal of Personality and Social Psychology*, 1981, *40*, 211–225.

Jeffrey, K. M., and Mischel, W. "Effects of Purpose on the Organization and Recall of Information in Person Perception." *Journal of Personality*, 1979, *47*, 397–419.

Lichtenstein, E. H., and Brewer, W. F. "Memory for Goal-Directed Events." *Cognition Psychology*, 1980, *12*, 412–445.

Lord, C. G., Lepper, M. R., and Thompson, W. C. "Inhibiting Biased Assimilation in the Consideration of New Evidence on Social Policy." Paper presented at the meeting of the American Psychological Association, Montreal, Sept. 1980.

Lord, R. G. "Accuracy in Behavioral Measurement: An Alternative Definition Based on Rater's Cognitive Schema and Signal Detection Theory." *Journal of Applied Psychology*, 1985a, *70*, 66–71.

Lord, R. G. "An Information Processing Approach to Social Perceptions, Leadership, and Behavioral Measurement in Organizations." In L. L. Cummings and B. M. Staw (eds.), *Research in Organizational Behavior.* Vol. 7. Greenwich, Conn.: JAI Press, 1985b.

Lord, R. G., Foti, R. J., and De Vader, C. L. "A Test of Leadership Categorization Theory: Internal Structure, Information Processing and Leadership Perceptions." *Organizational Behavior and Human Performance*, 1984, *34*, 343–378.

Lord, R. G., Foti, R. J., and Phillips, J. S. "A Theory of Leadership Categorization." In J. G. Hunt, V. Sekaran, and C. Schriesheim (eds.), *Leadership: Beyond Establishment Views.* Carbondale: Southern Illinois University Press, 1982.

Lord, R. G., and Smith, J. S. "Theoretical, Information Processing, and Situational Factors Affecting Attribution Theory Models of Organizational Behavior." *Academy of Management Review,* 1983, *8,* 50–60.

Lurigio, A. J., and Carroll, J. S. "Probation Officers' Schemata of Offenders: Content, Development, and Impact on Treatment Decisions." *Journal of Personality and Social Psychology,* 1985, *48,* 1112–1126.

McKeithen, K. B., Reitman, J. S., Rueter, H. H., and Hirtle, S. C. "Knowledge Organization and Skill Differences in Computer Programmers." *Cognitive Psychology,* 1981, *13,* 307–325.

Markus, H. "Self-Schemata and Processing Information About the Self." *Journal of Personality and Social Psychology,* 1977, *35,* 63–78.

Markus, H., Crane, M., Bernstein, S., and Siladi, M. "Self-Schemes and Gender." *Journal of Personality and Social Psychology,* 1982, *42,* 38–50.

Markus, H., and Smith, J. "The Influence of Self-Schema on the Perceptions of Others." In N. Cantor and J. Kihlstrom (eds.), *Personality, Cognition and Social Interaction.* Hillsdale, N.J.: Erlbaum, 1981.

Martin, J. "Stories and Scripts in Organizational Settings." In A. Hastorf and A. Isen (eds.), *Cognitive Social Psychology.* New York: Elsevier North-Holland, 1982.

Murphy, K. R., Martin, D., and Garcia, M. "Do Behavioral Observation Scales Measure Observation?" *Journal of Applied Psychology,* 1982, *67,* 562–567.

Nisbett, R. E., and Ross, L. *Human Inference: Strategies and Shortcomings of Social Judgment.* Englewood Cliffs, N.J.: Prentice-Hall, 1980.

Phillips, J. S. "The Accuracy of Leadership Ratings: A Cognitive Categorization Perspective." *Organizational Behavior and Human Performance,* 1984, *33,* 125–138.

Phillips, J. S., and Lord, R. G. "Causal Attributions and Perceptions of Leadership." *Organizational Behavior and Human Performance*, 1981, *28*, 143–163.

Phillips, J. S., and Lord, R. G. "Schematic Information Processing and Perceptions of Leadership in Problem-Solving Groups." *Journal of Applied Psychology*, 1982, *67*, 486–492.

Rogers, T. B. "A Model of the Self as an Aspect of Human Information Processing." In N. Cantor and J. Kihlstrom (eds.), *Personality, Cognition, and Social Interaction.* Hillsdale, N.J.: Erlbaum, 1981.

Rosch, E., and Mervis, C. "Family Resemblances: Studies in the Internal Structure of Categories." *Cognitive Psychology*, 1975, *7*, 573–605.

Ross, L., Lepper, M. R., and Hubbard, M. "Perseverance in Self-Perceptions and Social Perception: Biased Attribution Processes in the Debriefing Paradigm." *Journal of Personality and Social Psychology*, 1975, *32*, 880–892.

Schank, R. C., and Abelson, R. P. *Scripts, Plans, Goals, and Understanding.* Hillsdale, N.J.: Erlbaum, 1977.

Shiffrin, R. M., and Schneider, W. "Controlled and Automatic Human Information Processing: II. Perceptual Learning, Automatic Attending, and a General Theory." *Psychological Review*, 1977, *84*, 127–190.

Taylor, S. E., and Crocker, J. "Schematic Bases of Social Information Processing." In E. T. Higgins, C. P. Herman, and M. P. Zanna (eds.), *Social Cognition: The Ontario Symposium.* Vol. 1. Hillsdale, N.J.: Erlbaum, 1981.

Taylor, S. E., and Fiske, S. T. "Salience, Attention, and Attribution: Top of the Head Phenomena." In L. Berkowitz (ed.), *Advances in Experimental Social Psychology.* Vol. 2. Orlando, Fla.: Academic Press, 1978.

Tversky, A., and Kahneman, D. "Judgments Under Uncertainty: Heuristics and Biases." *Science,* 1974, *185*, 1124–1131.

# 2

Symbols, Scripts,
and Sensemaking

*Creating Meaning
in the Organizational Experience*

Dennis A. Gioia

*An idea, in the highest sense of that word, cannot
be conveyed but by a symbol.*

——Coleridge

*For the most part we do not see first and then de-
fine. We define first and then see.*

——Lippmann

*What's happening here and how do I deal with it?*

——Tacit generic question
asked by all new organ-
ization members and
most old hands

How do people in organizations understand what is going on
around them? How do they come to know the ropes, to learn

*Note:* I would like to thank Daniel Brass and Henry P. Sims, Jr.,
for helpful reviews of an earlier version of this chapter.

49

the system, to discern the culture? How do they know what values to hold and what actions to take? How do they create a meaningful day-to-day world out of the many complex events taking place in a modern organization? In short, how do they make sense of their organizational experience?

Many of the attempts to delve into this question have approached it from a socialization perspective (Louis, 1980; Van Maanen, 1976) and have generated very rich descriptions of such processes. This chapter is intended to address the question on a more elemental level. It focuses on the means by which people in organizations construct definitions of organizational reality that serve as vehicles for understanding and action.

The main thesis is that symbols and scripts act as primary organizational sensemaking devices. *Symbols* are signs or representations that signify some wider concept or meaning; *scripts* are dynamic event-sequence-oriented webs of structured knowledge held in memory. I argue that understanding is accomplished and communicated mainly by means of symbols (most notably in the form of metaphorical language) that are then retained in a structured or schematic form via scripts. The scripts subsequently serve as a basis for action that further facilitates the meaning construction and sensemaking processes.

## Ground Assumptions

A fundamental assumption of this chapter is that people in organizations are engaged in ongoing attempts to understand what is happening around them; they are presumed to be involved in a search for meaning, in much the same way that people in their personal lives are. This assumption does not mean, however, that they are rational, active, or even conscious processors of information, but it does mean that they engage in a process of ascribing meaning to, or imposing meaning upon, experience (including their own actions), and use the imposed meaning as a basis for subsequent understanding and action. In this process, behaviors, acts, and events in and of themselves are not important. It is the meaning associated with the behaviors or acts or events that matters (Blumer, 1969; Weber, [1947] 1968). A key issue for understanding organizational behavior thus becomes one of understanding how meaning is derived. Put more simply, the issue becomes one of first understanding how people in organizations understand and then exploring how that understanding is associated with action.

A second fundamental assumption is that sensemaking is a process involving the social construction of reality. People who are organizing can do so only on the basis of some sense of collective understanding. The understanding arrived at is dependent on the interpretations given to the shared experience; and because those interpretations can be markedly different within varying contexts and with different organization members, the reality constructed is relative to the actors and their immediate context. Thus, the reality with which people must deal is of their own making. Organization members, therefore, do not engage in a process of *discovering* some existing reality but of *creating* it and/or learning it from others who are mutually involved in its construction.

Thus, to both recapitulate and prefigure the argument of this chapter, the main purpose is to explore processes used by organization members to accomplish the potentially intimidating task of making sense of their experience. Meaning created is seen as influencing action taken. Similarly, action taken is seen as influencing meaning created (Weick, 1969, 1979). Both processes are viewed as inextricably reciprocal. What is intended, then, is an exploration of the origins of understanding and action. The main thesis is that the construction of meaning is accomplished mainly through, first, the use of symbols and, second, the reliance on cognitive scripts. Symbols are a primary means whereby meaning is communicated and understood; scripts are the cognitive vehicles for structuring experiential knowledge and for guiding appropriate action. The chapter offers brief overviews of the topics of organizational symbols, scripts, and sensemaking as well as an elaboration of the main thesis and a discussion of the implications of these concepts for organizations. To begin, we will discuss symbolism as a source of organizational knowledge and understanding.

## Organizational Symbolism

One of the ways that organization members engage in the fundamental process of sensemaking is by using symbols to convey meaning and understanding. A symbol is some representative sign that stands for some other object, entity, or concept. It is a means of communicating that expresses the concept in relation to some other one, often employing figurative imagery to establish meaning and importance (for example, "Business competition is war"). A sign becomes symbolic when it is interpreted in a way that suggests meaning in terms that have organizational significance (Morgan, Frost, and Pondy, 1983). Symbols transcend the literal to represent some wider domain of meaning. The assertion that competition in an industry is a war is not literally true, but the symbolism conveyed by the characterization casts organizational life as a survival enterprise, which imputes seriousness, gravity, and a "must win" value to the situation.

Geertz (1973) said that a symbol is *any* object, act, or event that serves as a means for conception. Cassirer (1944) contended that *all* human understanding is essentially symbolic in nature. Both these positions suggest the pervasiveness of symbols in defining the texture of understanding. Yet despite the essential accuracy of these observations, such statements are so encompassing that they tend to preclude a definition of what is *not* a symbol, thus limiting the usefulness of the concept for organizational analysis. While recognizing that virtually anything can be a symbol, this chapter will take a symbol to be a sign (for example, a concept, event, or action) that serves as a meaningful representation of some significant element of the organizational experience.

There are many possible symbols in organizational life, including *logos* (the Presidential seal, the Chrysler pentagon, or Mickey Mouse's ears); *slogans* ("Quality of work life" and "Service is our business"); *stories* (the ubiquitous variations on the theme of an underling standing up to the boss and living to tell about it—see, for example, Martin, Feldman, Hatch, and Sitkin, 1983); *actions* (the CEO's public declarations of support for some new program); *nonactions* (a CEO's studied neglect of the VP's pet project or, in the political arena, the "pocket veto"); *visual images* (organization charts that ostensibly display the way things work or graphic depictions of wished-for work procedures); and *metaphors* (verbal representations that treat something as if it were something else). All these are organizational symbols because they convey relationships to concepts already understood and thus facilitate the construction of meaning by the person or group experiencing them.

In this list of kinds of symbols, the use of metaphor as a special case of organizational symbolism is of particular importance. Metaphorical communication defines one thing in terms of another: for example, "Organizations are theaters where everyone plays out a role." Lakoff and Johnson (1980) assign a special significance to the role of metaphor and have developed a compelling argument that metaphorical communication is essential to understanding. Indeed, their position holds that metaphors not only facilitate communication but also (and more important) shape thought. By implication, metaphors also shape understanding and action.

Consider again the often used war metaphor as it applies to organizations. People within organizations are said to be "engaged in power struggles" and "political battles." They "attack the positions" of others and try to "sabotage others' plans." The boss is labeled the "general," and the other employees are called "soldiers." At a more global level, organizations "defend a market position" and are very careful about their strategy lest they "fail to capture our share of the market." These terms and concepts are more than simply colorful phrases. They are ways of seeing and means for defining a consensual reality; they are also the stuff of organizational culture.

People make sense of their situations with subjectively constructed and intersubjectively agreed upon symbols that promote understanding. Thereafter, they can treat those symbols as if they were objectively real (Morgan, Frost, and Pondy, 1983) and act accordingly. To perceive the role of symbols in understanding and action, it is important to recognize both their pervasiveness in organizational life as well as their subjective nature, which imbues many (perhaps most) organizational phenomena with symbolic possibility. As Morgan, Frost, and Pondy (1983, p. 13) point out, "Symbols are socially constructed as symbols." In other words, although a lion, for instance, has no intrinsic symbolic significance, the lion has been fashioned into a symbol of courage—or of Metro-Goldwyn-Mayer, Inc. Many things can serve as symbols, and the same thing can serve as a symbol of many different things, depending on the context and, of course, the subjective meaning associated with it.

*Symbols in Understanding and Action.* As noted previously, actions often are symbolic. The understanding of the meaning of an action is negotiated collectively by those perceiving it; that understanding then facilitates the actions of the perceivers. Actions that are symbolic thus give meaningful form to experience. Probably the most fundamental action in organizations is decision making. The gathering of information to make decisions can itself be a symbolic activity—one that both signals and symbolizes an ostensibly rational, intelligent, and legitimate decision (Feldman and March, 1981). Symbolic actions also influence beliefs and values, and thus can either sustain a given construction of reality or stimulate the fabrication of a new one (Feldman and March, 1981).

Problems and problematic situations are perceived symbolically, often metaphorically. When a problem situation is described, for instance, as a "political football," the metaphorical imagery is understood to mean a sensitive, delicate issue that requires tact, finesse, and maybe even coalition, collaboration, and favor trading to arrive at a solution. The important point here is that at the fundamental level of the comprehension process, seeing something as "like" something else seen before is at its essence a symbolic process. The study of symbols can provide insight into processes that are both expressive and instrumental in organizations (Gioia and Chittipeddi, 1985; Pfeffer, 1981). A focus on symbols gives us a way of recognizing the extreme complexity and depth of the human organizational experience, and a way of learning how organization members go about the confusing task of figuring out what the many actions and events that occur in organizations might mean. They also provide a way of learning how consensual understanding leads to coordinated, collective activity (Dandridge, Mitroff, and Joyce, 1980; Gray, Bougon, and Donnellon, 1985).

Given the symbolic nature of understanding, social cognition itself can be viewed as essentially a symbolic process. In a fundamental sense, cognitive structure *is* symbolic structure. Mental representations of experience and knowledge are what are retained in memory (Rumelhart and Ortony, 1977), and these representations are symbolic in nature (Ortony, 1979). When an organizational event or action with symbolic possibility is experienced, it is related to existing knowledge to generate meaning. That is, as a current symbol becomes associated with symbolic networks, understanding occurs. In a sense, there is a resonance between symbols experienced and symbols retained. In a more general sense, understanding can only occur if new information can in some way be related to what is already known. A question of interest then becomes, In what fashion is the "already known" retained in memory? For an answer to that question, we turn to a brief examination of schemas, especially script schemas.

## Organizational Scripts

People are not pure information processors; that is, they do not rationally deal with all available information in an information-rich environment, and they do not reprocess information anew every time it is presented. To do so would bring about information-processing paralysis. Instead, people develop ways to engage in cognitive economy to lessen the task of handling the myriad of potentially meaningful cues available in an organizational setting. The first key to this kind of cognitive efficiency is to be able to interrelate the information according to some criterion of similarity. Once accomplished, the next critical requirement is to retain the information in memory in a way that preserves the interrelationships among pieces of information. That function is performed by cognitive frameworks called *schemas*.

A schema is a cognitive structure composed of a network

of expectations learned from experience and stored in memory (see Taylor and Crocker, 1981). It is a built-up repertoire of tacit knowledge that is used to impose structure upon, and impart meaning to, otherwise ambiguous social and situational information to facilitate understanding (Gioia and Poole, 1984). A schema thus provides a basis for the interpretation of information, events, and actions (Graesser, Woll, Kowalski, and Smith, 1980). The interrelated, ordered nature of schemas enables shortcuts to be taken during cognitive work. In effect, a contextual cue that suggests that a present situation is similar to an existing schema for related situations means that fresh processing is not required. The processing has already been done before and has been stored in some representational form—that is, not according to exact memory, but according to some transformation that has made the information meaningful in relation to something already known. It is this same structured character that also allows what has been termed "automatic" (Feldman, 1981) or "mindless" (Langer, 1978) information processing. That is, well-established schemas enable one to process information essentially unconsciously if a good match between current context and existing schema is obtained, thus freeing cognitive capacity to handle other more pressing or more novel demands.

Understanding thus occurs most readily when we can relate current experience to something already understood. The "something already understood" is retained in human memory in schematic form. Nothing is processed completely *tabula rasa*. Even for discrepant or novel information, the means for making sense of it is to relate it to some sort of existing knowledge. Information that cannot be so related remains meaningless unless it can somehow be forged into a new pattern of internally consistent meaning. Of course, meaning construction is not only a process of recalling existing schemas. If that were true, no new learning could occur (see Eoyang, 1983). Instead, meaning construction and understanding involves association of experience with existing knowledge, alteration of existing schemas by incorporating new knowledge, and occasionally a dramatic restructuring or creation of knowledge by intuition or revelation. Palermo (1986) has identified two means of schema-related adjustment: first, assimilation involves the alteration of a perception to fit an existing schema; and second, accommodation involves alteration of a schema to fit current experience.

*A Specialized Schema for Action.* Many types of schemas have been identified and confirmed, ranging from self-schemas (Markus, 1977) to generalized interpretive schemes (Bartunek, 1984; Ranson, Hinings, and Greenwood, 1980; Schutz, 1967). Most of the schemas currently acknowledged are treated essentially as frameworks for comprehension but are not typically seen as guides to action. A notable exception is the notion of a script schema, which is a cognitive structure devoted specifically to the retention of context-specific knowledge about events and event sequences and to the guidance of action on the basis of that knowledge (Abelson, 1976, 1981). Thus, a script might be viewed as the schema that is tied most directly to behavior and that therefore serves as an instructive vehicle for exploring the connection between cognition and action (Gioia and Manz, 1985).

The fundamental proposition of the script concept, then, is that people possess categories of structured knowledge about common or conventional events, behaviors, and actions that can be brought forth by situational cues to facilitate understanding and action. These categories are represented by *protoscripts* (Gioia and Poole, 1984), which are generic or prototypical scripts composed of sets of features that are common to a class of contexts (for example, problem-solving meetings). The experiencing of a new situation (a problem-solving meeting with a new department head) triggers a comparison-with-prototype process that either affirms the use of the protoscript to handle the new situation or suggests the modification necessary to enact the behaviors appropriate to the similar-but-different situation (Donnellon, Gioia, and Sims, 1985; Longenecker, Gioia, and Sims, 1983).

Typically, scripts have been treated as cognitive structures that are appropriate solely to well-learned and well-understood situations and are therefore automatically and unconsciously executed. This view does not seem to bear close scrutiny, however (refer to Gioia and Poole, 1984). Rather, scripts seem to be called into play, if only in outline form, whenever sense must be made of many facets of organizational experience.

Scripts are constructed from component parts that become successively more elaborated. These components range from the most elemental features called *vignettes* to strings of vignettes called *scenes* to a collection of scenes that ultimately is termed the *script*. This structure of scripts suggests that any given feature can be modified for adaptability to many different contexts. It also suggests that people are capable of using both automatic (unconscious) and controlled (intentional) processing, as the situation demands: automatic processing is used if a specific vignette or scene will do; controlled processing is used if the nature of the situation makes appropriate behavior problematic.

Pondy (1983) contends, for instance, that managers think in both rational and intuitive modes within a stream of action over time. One likely explanation for the way that progressive process is accomplished, I would argue, is by means of a subtle switching between controlled and automatic attention to the experiencing of action and outcomes. When a person is experiencing situations that are problematic, processes that are more rational and analytical typically are brought into play initially. As elements of the situation are recognized as stereotypical or can be associated with patterns of previous experience, processes that are more holistic and intuitive are then more likely to be used. (In one sense the essence of creativity and creative problem solving often involves a subversion of these typical modes to allow intuition to bear on the initial perception of a problem.) In either case, my general position is that most sense-making is accomplished, to some degree, by the use of schematized (especially scripted) knowledge. People rely on their structured knowledge of related experience, whether unconsciously or consciously engaged, to manage cognitive processing and subsequent action.

The implications of the use of scripts in organizations, however, involve both costs and benefits. Script processing provides for efficient, but not necessarily effective, cognitive processing. In particular, recall of specific information is inhibited by the existence of scripts, because information that has been incorporated into a script has necessarily been transformed to fit the script. Recall is therefore based on the script, not necessarily on events actually experienced. The script also serves to fill in the gaps of missing information, so long as the information is consistent with the existing script, thus resulting in remembrance of events that did not actually take place. Clearly, there is a price paid for the wonderful cognitive economy available from script processing: a trade-off is made that paves the way for an insidious sort of inaccuracy in remembering events, in which the perceiver may not know that he does not know what actually happened. This characteristic of schemas in general and scripts in particular is without question the most dangerous aspect of their nature. It is important but sobering to recognize that given the pervasiveness of scripts in human cognitive functioning, much of what is remembered amounts to revisionist history. In Loftus's words, what is rendered is a "current picture of the past" (1980, p. 50). Or as Mead (1929) long ago noted, the past is continually recreated in the present as it structures the understanding of what is currently happening.

*Relating Symbols and Scripts.* Because the stream of experience has a perceived sequential character (Schutz, 1967; Weick, 1969), scripts would seem to be the primary cognitive structure used to apprehend and enact experiential activity. A fundamental issue then concerns the elemental nature of the scripted knowledge. What is scripted? Given that understanding is rooted in symbols, I would contend that what has become structured into a script is symbolic knowledge of events, actions, and concepts. Knowledge is stored semantically, that is, according to meaning. That knowledge could be in the form of episodes (Schank and Abelson, 1977), visual images (Pylyshyn, 1973), or verbal codes describing sequences (Paivio, 1971). For example, when an executive "understands" how to act during top-echelon strategy meetings, that understanding does not occur according to step-by-step recall of events that should take place. It is composed instead of symbolic (often metaphorical) understanding. One executive has described such meetings as "think-tank sessions" and another as "the place where battle lines are drawn"; other executives have described these meetings as "a time for a strong will" and as "head-butting contests." To reiterate, these symbolic characterizations do more than simply lend richness to descriptions of organizational life; they specify ways of seeing and understanding, and thus structure behavior and action because of their symbolic nature. It is for this reason that I maintain that structured, symbolic knowledge comprises a script.

There is also another side to the relationship between symbols and scripts. One role of organizational symbols is to cue scripted action. One of the great values of repeating an acknowledged organizational story or myth is to elicit expected or desired actions from employees. Thus, symbols serve not only to express the values and culture of an organization (Pfeffer, 1981) but also to trigger action (Gioia and Chittipeddi, 1985). A symbol acts as a label or tag that accesses a specific script to be enacted (another instance of the resonance between current experience, cognitive structure, and subsequent action). For example, a new competitor characterized as a "threat" is often handled by heightening the perception that "we are a team that must stand and fight" in the grand tradition of the organization, thus cueing a group cohesion script.

In any case, the interrelationships stored in a script are meaningful symbolic representations of personal or vicarious experience. These webs of structured, symbolically based, action-oriented knowledge are the foundation on which sensemaking is built. Organizational sensemaking might therefore be seen as essentially a symbolic process, as, in effect, a social construction process conducted through the manipulation of symbolic information stored in symbolic structures.

## Organizational Sensemaking

*Sensemaking* is perhaps one of the few terms in the social and organizational sciences that means literally what it says: sensemaking refers to the concern with making sense of events and experience. A grasp of the human process of sensemaking, however, is not quite so straightforward because of the complex cognitive processes involved. Sensemaking *is* meaning construction. It is the process whereby people attempt to construct meaningful explanations for situations and their experiences within those situations. Sensemaking thus entails intricate (and often unconscious) processes of attending, comparing, attributing, relating, reflecting, retaining, and so on.

The layperson's view that sensemaking involves ongoing, rational processing of current informational cues to arrive at some cognitive conclusion has been challenged and generally discredited by philosophers and organization theorists. The most widely accepted view of sensemaking is known as retrospective sensemaking (Schutz, 1967; Weick, 1969, 1979). This position argues that one cannot make sense of events and actions until they have been completed and one then glances backward in time to construct the meaning of the events. That is, one "brackets" a segment of one's stream of experience and then analyzes it, as an outside observer would, in order to decide what the meaning of this portion of experience is (Weick, 1969).

A moment's self-reflection about how we come to understand events and actions can demonstrate the validity of this view. Unless we can examine the outcomes of our actions, it is not easy to discern their meaning. Such observations led Weick to conclude that "all knowing and meaning arise from reflection" (1969, p. 64). This is an important observation for the understanding of comprehension and action in organizations. It means that the notion that people fashion understanding through ongoing cognitive processing is essentially a fallacy. The view that sensemaking is a retrospective construction of meaning is typically seen as unusual by those first exposed to it and is often experienced as a revelation when accepted as valid later on. It is clearly the case, however, that to make sense of events, one typically steps outside one's lived experience and analyzes it retrospectively.

As we noted earlier, understanding and action are reciprocal, but it is useful to assume the primacy of action in the process of "normal" sensemaking. As Weick has put it: "How can I know what I think until I see what I say?" (1979, p. 133). Action drives "new" or revised sensemaking. It is the perception of action that becomes structured into a script. That is, organization members learn a script by retrospectively thinking about their own (and others') actions in a given setting, and deciding upon their appropriateness. Once specified, structured, and retained, the script then supplies the knowledge necessary to act in subsequent similar settings. Thus, action creates (scripted) understanding, and that understanding creates action.

The dependence of sensemaking on action and the orientation of scripts toward the structuring of knowledge about action is indicative of the close relationship between scripts and sensemaking. Sense made and action to be taken reside in scripts.

Weick (1979) argues that it is not only behaviors that become structured in organizations but also information and shared meaning—meaning that has been socially constructed, negotiated, and consensually validated. Again, because symbols are a primary vehicle for understanding, they can be construed as the unifying force that facilitates the construction of consensual scripts for action. Through the development and structuring of shared meaning and understanding, cycles of interlocked behavior become sensible. The storehouse of knowledge about "cycles of interlocked behavior" are the individual and consensual scripts held by organization members. They *are* the symbolic, meaning-oriented cognitive frameworks that are used in the enactment process described by Weick (1969) to make sense of experience.

There are profound consequences of reflective meaning construction derived from schematized (scripted) knowledge. As Walter Lippmann remarked in one of the quotations introducing this chapter, "We do not see first and then define. We define first and then see." Or as Weick (1979, p. 135) has put it, "Believing is seeing." Scripts and symbols supply the means for defining, and thus the mode of seeing. Sense is made of any current experience by imposing an existing framework on the current observation. People do not see or respond to a world of meaning that is objectively there; they create it from the interpretive schemes they have (Ranson, Hinings, and Greenwood, 1980; Schutz, 1967).

*Prospective Sensemaking.* So powerful is the reflective property of sensemaking that Schutz (1967) and Weick (1969, 1979) have invoked its role even during the consideration of future-oriented planning of intended action. The essence of this argument is that even when people are contemplating future action, they must think about it as if it had already occurred to be able to make sense of the intended outcomes. Thus, thought is said to occur not in the past tense typically associated with retrospection ("This happened") or in the presumed future tense ("This will happen") but in the future perfect tense ("This will have happened"). This intriguing proposition apparently unifies all sensemaking, even the difficult-to-grasp notion of future-oriented thinking, and casts it as fundamentally retrospective in nature. It is an explanation that has a nonobvious and revealing elegance—one that deserves a closer look.

Although I agree with the essential correctness of the observation that the origin of all sensemaking is in retrospection, this encompassing definition of the process tends to obscure some of the nuances involved in the execution of sensible action, particularly with processes concerning the affirmation of meaning (that is, those engaged when previously constructed meaning is assumed to be appropriate). Thus, to conclude that all facets of sensemaking are purely retrospective seems a bit too strict with the phenomenology of occurrences.

When events occur in predictable sequences and patterns, they trigger the use of scripts as guides to sensemaking. Scripts permit an artificial short-circuiting of the necessity to retrospectively bracket a discrete phase of experience to make sense of it. They do so in two mutually supportive ways: first, scripts specify the expectation of meaningful occurrences in advance of their happening; second, they create a self-fulfilling process (because one expects something to happen, one either makes it happen as expected or interprets the event as consistent with the expectation). Use of a script thus has a strong prospective element to it. For that reason, script-based sensemaking and action might be usefully distinguished as *prospective sensemaking.* The prospective element here is greatly dependent on prior experience that has evolved into a scripted structure of expectations. Meaning, therefore, is not something to be determined; it has been determined in advance because of reliance on the script. Thus, we can say that meaning is "prospectively affirmed."

Such a distinction between retrospective sensemaking and its special case, scripted prospective sensemaking, preserves the recognition that although retrospective sensemaking enables the formation of a script, the script facilitates future-oriented sensemaking. For instance, when an executive who is trying to decide what new product might fill a market niche uses a known heuristic procedure (that is, a decision-making script) to project the possible outcomes of various decisions, he or she can be described as engaging in a prospective sensemaking procedure. This is true even though the heuristic procedure was itself evolved through retrospection.

*Introspective Sensemaking.* Another possible subset of sensemaking might be characterized as "introspective," although the existence of this form is admittedly more difficult to pinpoint. Most sensemaking is construed as an "overt" process of social construction. We interact with others; we compare our perceptions with theirs; we test reality; we negotiate meaning and reality. All of these processes focus on the social nature of sensemaking. Yet to consider only these processes limits the definition of organizational understanding. How, for instance, can we account for intuition, imagination, vision, revelatory flashes of insight, apparent prescience in making critical decisions, and creative problem solving?

Introspective sensemaking may be a way of accounting for such esoteric processes. It may be a starting point for the study of self-based processes such as intuitive knowing ("I don't know how or why I know, I just know"). To date, these issues have been a bit too slippery for serious consideration within the discipline of organizational science. Yet these processes are attributed to our most creative and effective leaders, decision makers, and problem solvers. A reasonable conclusion is that such knowledge is retained in schemas, and that intuition is essentially an unconscious rendering of previously unseen relationships among concepts. Perhaps. But that still does not provide us with a satisfying explanation of significant sensemaking events, such as Einstein's revelations, which he himself could

not explain, or Kekulé's "dreaming" about the correct structure of the benzene ring, or many less famous instances of trans-
cendent organizational creativity. Our dependence on existing
conceptions of sensemaking may, in fact, be limiting our ability
to understand visionary processes that are important to organizations. At the least, we should be more open-minded about
considering the role of the introspective and unconscious processes used by people in organizations.

## Implications for Organizations

It is difficult to envision an organizational life that is not
infused with symbolism. Symbols and metaphors are the stuff
of communication. They are the way we create, understand,
and share meaning. Astute leaders of organizations implicitly
recognize the important roles of symbols and have learned to
manage them, because symbols can be one of the most effective
means not only for influencing culture but also for bringing
about substantive action.

*Managing with Symbolism.* Perhaps part of the romance
and attractiveness of managing through symbols is that the effect of doing so is often subtle and therefore less likely to engender resistance or countervailing measures. Political leaders
certainly understand this point, if mainly in a tacit sense (Edelman, 1964), as do business leaders who have "organizational
savvy." Attempts to lead, motivate, and exercise influence that
do not make use of the symbolic aspects of a situation miss an
important and facilitating feature of modern management technique.

When leaders use symbols effectively, they must first
identify the ideas and interpretations that are important to
members of the organization and then create symbols that address those issues (see Eoyang, 1983; Peters and Waterman,
1982; Pfeffer, 1981; Smircich and Morgan, 1982). When leaders
successfully use symbolism, they themselves become part of the
symbolic milieu because they represent the important values
held by their constituencies (see Burns, 1978; Eoyang, 1983).
What is more, the status acquired by such leaders works to gar-

ner further support for the legitimacy of their leadership. Such leaders create and then manage symbolic interactions in a way that supports the values and meets the needs of those led (Burns, 1978).

Symbolism also can have its dark side, however, and can be used as an instrument of dominance and control. By their nature, symbols are tenuous representations of concepts whose meaning can be manipulated in Machiavellian ways. The ambiguity of symbols implies that those in power can more easily impose their own desired meaning, often to the detriment of other people. However, the control fostered by the use of symbols can be used in a positive way, as a subtle and effective form of influence.

As Wilkins (1983) points out, control of this type has the hallmarks of Perrow's (1979) "second-order" and "third-order" controls. First-order control has to do with direct managerial control of action, and thus requires substantial energy and attention by executives. Second-order control is the control derived from programs, policies, and standardized procedures. Given that such understanding and meaning is often retained schematically in a script (a kind of mental program), direct managerial control is not required; when effectively constructed through teaching and training, the script supplies the requisite control. Third-order control, however, is even more removed; it derives from the understandings of, or meanings ascribed to, a context or setting by an organization member. Control resides within the interpretation system of the employee and is dependent upon his or her social constructions, although those constructions are capable of being influenced and managed by the leadership of the organization. Once the leaders of the organization decide on the "correct" symbols, third-order control follows as a matter of individual, albeit consensual, interpretation by lower-level members of the organization. Symbolic management can, therefore, serve as an effective way of encouraging self-management—that is, of having employees learn to lead themselves.

The main implication of the sensemaking perspective on organizations is that organization members both create and sustain their own particular reality. As esoteric as this perspective on organizations might seem, it offers an important and pragmatically relevant view for enlightened managers and scholars to consider. The essence of the position is that people respond only to things that have meaning for them. Understanding and action are directed on the basis of some internal and socially influenced interpretation given to occurrences. Thus, organizing and organization are a product of some workable, consensual vision of meaningful purpose. The practical relevance of this view is that it suggests a heightened role for proactiveness. If one creates one's own reality, then better to do so on the basis of one's own image of the nature of desired reality rather than reacting to a reality imposed from the outside. Accordingly, skill in defining a reality that can gain a consensual following constitutes the essence of leadership (Smircich and Morgan, 1982).

*Symbolism and Organizational Change.* Perhaps in no facet of organizational life is the role of symbols, scripts, and sensemaking more evident and important than during a period of change. Change typically involves some alteration in the organization's culture, which is both expressed and learned through symbolic processes (Dandridge, Mitroff, and Joyce, 1980; Louis, 1983; Smircich, 1983). Symbols serve to create the culture, sustain that culture, and increasingly to facilitate the transformation of the culture to meet new conditions.

The language used by an organization "defines" its reality and thus influences its culture (see Evered, 1983). Symbolic management, therefore, is first and foremost the management of the language used to describe the organizational values and aspirations. The task of management thus becomes the task of managing the symbols that provide labels, explanations, and meanings to the members of the organization (Pondy and Mitroff, 1979; Pfeffer, 1981; Weick, 1979). For this reason, a good deal of managerial activity involves political, theatrical, and linguistic skills (Pfeffer, 1981). Even more important for modern management is the recognition that the accomplishment of organizational change requires a change in the definitional symbols (Gioia and Chittipeddi, 1985) and the language used to shape reality (Evered, 1983, and Chapter Five of this volume). Ultimately, the symbolic redefinitions must be fashioned into consensual scripts that specify the actions involved in the "new way of doing things." Attempts to foster change, however, must take explicit recognition of the socially constructed nature of symbols, inasmuch as the overt symbols used to communicate the character of desired change should not have different meanings for different individuals and groups. It is important to develop symbols for change that have consensual bases to them: ones that are likely to engender common (and desired) meanings, and ones that are not specific only to the dominant coalition's view of the organizational world.

The role of symbols is exemplified in the case of a university that recently hired a new president who was charged with the task of "seeing the university through the eighties and beyond." He had some innovative ideas that he felt would equip the university to deal with the environmental uncertainty expected in the coming years. Yet he faced an entrenched culture that seemed rather ineffective even in the current climate. The new president's task was, in short, one of bringing about a significant change in a large, complex, inertia-laden organization. How best to steer such an organization in a new direction? Decreeing change by fiat was considered, then discarded. The approach had failed repeatedly in the past. Instead, the president concluded that change had to come from a collective understanding of the need for change.

The president chose to pursue change and to express his new vision of the university's role by the more subtle method of symbolism. The overarching metaphor chosen to characterize the change was that the university was to become "a top-ten public university." This metaphor was adopted and soon became consensual; who would not want to be in the "top ten"? Yet the notion was effective because it simultaneously implied that the university was not now in that elite group and thus galvanized effort toward a change in that direction. The operational metaphor chosen was that the university now was to engage in "strategic planning." As Cohen and March (1974) have pointed out, plans themselves are symbolic; they signify goals and aspirations. The notion of "strategic planning" was doubly significant because it indicated a "new" way to doing something that had of course been done in the past but that now was to be qualitatively different because it would be aimed specifically at capitalizing on "market opportunities for the university." A special University Strategic Planning Committee was nominated to lend legitimacy and importance to the task of strategic planning.

Other symbols also accompanied the effort to change. The university decided on a new, modern-looking logo that was widely accepted as a symbol of the "new" university. Some restructuring of the reporting relationships at the higher echelons was also accomplished, which was not only a substantive change but also symbolized that the old guard had been eased out to reduce resistance to the progressive vision of the university. Finally, a new college was created out of existing departments, and along with three other colleges, these colleges were dubbed "centers of excellence" to connote their symbolic status as the leading edge of the new wave.

All these steps had an impact on the way the university's members viewed the university's role. The various metaphors not only expressed a revitalized vision of the university but also set the stage for accomplishing the change. The stage setting amounted to a new pattern of perceiving and doing (a new set of scripts) that was consistent with the accepted vision of the university's altered role. Once the new scripts were consolidated, some of the symbolic devices (the Strategic Planning Committee, for instance) became instrumental in actually carrying out the proposed changes. At the time of this writing, some substantive alterations in the university's structure and mission have taken place, and further changes in line with the previously expressed vision are underway. Through attention to the symbolic aspects of management, progress toward strategic objectives has been made where previous attempts using other approaches have not succeeded.

It is important to make several observations about the evident symbolism in this mini-case. First, the symbols used were eminently sensible. They were similar to concepts that the many constituencies of the university already understood, yet they conveyed in clear and meaningful terms that a significant, but not radical change was underway. Secondly, the symbols used were not merely colorful, expressive devices; they defined a mode of sensemaking and were both influential and instrumental in facilitating change. The use of symbols and metaphors eased the intimidating task of transition. Finally, although not enough time has passed to draw a conclusive judgment about the effectiveness of the effort to bring about change, it is fair to say that some substantial shift in the culture of the university has already occurred.

## Conclusion

If we are to gain an understanding of organizing and organizations, we must develop conceptualizations that reflect their nature and complexity. As Pondy and Mitroff (1979) have noted, those conceptualizations must have features that account for the nuances of language and the processes involved in meaning construction. Such conceptualizations should recognize the higher capacities of organized human beings (Daft, 1983) and should thus engage in the kind of study that characterizes the human organizational experience. That experience begins with symbolic processes and is affirmed and maintained by scripted understanding and action. This chapter has explored the ways that organization members use symbols and scripts to facilitate the process of sensemaking so that understanding and meaningful action can be accomplished.

## References

Abelson, R. P. "Script Processing in Attitude Formation and Decision Making." In J. S. Carroll and J. W. Payne (eds.), *Cognition and Social Behavior*. Hillsdale, N.J.: Erlbaum, 1976.

Abelson, R. P. "Psychological Status of the Script Concept." *American Psychologist*, 1981, *36*, 715–729.

Bartunek, J. M. "Changing Interpretive Schemes and Organizational Restructuring: An Example of a Religious Order." *Administrative Science Quarterly*, 1984, *29*, 355-372.

Blumer, H. *Symbolic Interactionism: Perspective and Method.* Englewood Cliffs, N.J.: Prentice-Hall, 1969.

Burns, J. M. *Leadership.* New York: Harper & Row, 1978.

Cassirer, E. *An Essay on Man.* New Haven, Conn.: Yale University Press, 1944.

Cohen, M. D., and March, J. G. *Leadership and Ambiguity: The American College President.* New York: McGraw-Hill, 1974.

Daft, R. L. "Symbols in Organizations: A Dual Content Framework of Analysis." In L. R. Pondy, P. J. Frost, G. Morgan, and T. C. Dandridge (eds.), *Organizational Symbolism.* Greenwich, Conn.: JAI Press, 1983.

Dandridge, T. C., Mitroff, I. I., and Joyce, W. F. "Organizational Symbolism: A Topic to Expand Organizational Analysis." *Academy of Management Review*, 1980, *5*, 77-82.

Donnellon, A., Gioia, D. A., and Sims, H. P., Jr. "Speech Act Analysis and Script Inference: An Exploration of Cognition and Communication in Organizations." Unpublished manuscript, Division of Organizational Behavior, Pennsylvania State University, 1985.

Edelman, M. *The Symbolic Uses of Politics.* Urbana: University of Illinois Press, 1964.

Eoyang, C. "Symbolic Transformation of Belief Systems." In L. R. Pondy, P. J. Frost, G. Morgan, and T. C. Dandridge (eds.), *Organizational Symbolism.* Greenwich, Conn.: JAI Press, 1983.

Evered, R. "The Language of Organizations: The Case of the Navy." In L. R. Pondy, P. J. Frost, G. Morgan, and T. C. Dandridge (eds.), *Organizational Symbolism.* Greenwich, Conn.: JAI Press, 1983.

Feldman, J. M. "Beyond Attribution Theory: Cognitive Processes in Performance Evaluation." *Journal of Applied Psychology*, 1981, *66*, 127-148.

Feldman, M. S., and March, J. G. "Information in Organizations as Signal and Symbol." *Administrative Science Quarterly*, 1981, *26*, 171-186.

Geertz, C. *The Interpretation of Cultures.* New York: Basic Books, 1973.

Gioia, D. A., and Chittipeddi, K. "Symbolism and Strategic Change in Academia: A Study of Sensemaking and Influence in a University." Unpublished manuscript, Pennsylvania State University, 1985.

Gioia, D. A., and Manz, C. C. "Linking Cognition and Behavior: A Script Processing Interpretation of Vicarious Learning." *Academy of Management Review,* 1985, *10,* 527-539.

Gioia, D. A., and Poole, P. P. "Scripts in Organizational Behavior." *Academy of Management Review,* 1984, *9,* 449-459.

Graesser, A. C., Woll, S. B., Kowalski, D. J., and Smith, D. A. "Memory for Typical and Atypical Actions in Scripted Activities." *Journal of Experimental Psychology,* 1980, *6,* 503-515.

Gray, B., Bougon, M. G., and Donnellon, A. "Organizations as Constructions and Destructions of Meaning." *Journal of Management,* 1985, *11,* 83-98.

Lakoff, G., and Johnson, M. *Metaphors We Live By.* Chicago: University of Chicago Press, 1980.

Langer, E. J. "Rethinking the Role of Thought in Social Interaction." In J. H. Harvey, W. J. Ickes, and R. F. Kidd (eds.), *New Directions in Attribution Research.* Vol. 2. Hillsdale, N.J.: Erlbaum, 1978.

Loftus, E. *Memory.* Reading, Mass.: Addison-Wesley, 1980.

Longenecker, C. O., Gioia, D. A., and Sims, H. P., Jr. "Consensual Cognitive Scripts for Performance Appraisal." Paper presented at meeting of the National Academy of Management, Dallas, Aug. 1983.

Louis, M. R. "Surprise and Sensemaking: What Newcomers Experience in Entering Unfamiliar Organizational Settings." *Administrative Science Quarterly,* 1980, *25,* 225-251.

Louis, M. R. "Organizations as Culture-Bearing Milieux." In L. R. Pondy, P. J. Frost, G. Morgan, and T. C. Dandridge (eds.), *Organizational Symbolism.* Greenwich, Conn.: JAI Press, 1983.

Markus, H. "Self-Schemata and Processing Information About the Self." *Journal of Personality and Social Psychology,* 1977, *35,* 63-78.

Martin, J., Feldman, M. S., Hatch, M. J., and Sitkin, S. S. "The Uniqueness Paradox in Organizational Stories." *Administrative Science Quarterly*, 1983, *28*, 438–453.

Mead, G. H. "The Nature of the Past." In J. Cross (ed.), *Essays in Honor of John Dewey*. New York: Holt, Rinehart and Winston, 1929.

Morgan, G., Frost, P. J., and Pondy, L. R. "Organizational Symbolism." In L. R. Pondy, P. J. Frost, G. Morgan, and T. C. Dandridge (eds.), *Organizational Symbolism*. Greenwich, Conn.: JAI Press, 1983.

Ortony, A. "Metaphor: A Multi-Dimensional Problem." In A. Ortony (ed.), *Metaphor and Thought*. Cambridge, England: Cambridge University Press, 1979.

Paivio, A. *Imagery and Verbal Process*. New York: Holt, Rinehart and Winston, 1971.

Palermo, D. S. "From the Marble Mass of Language, A View of the Developing Mind." *Metaphor and Symbolic Activity*, 1986, *1*, 5–23.

Perrow, C. *Complex Organizations: A Critical Essay*. Glenview, Ill.: Scott, Foresman, 1979.

Peters, T. J., and Waterman, R. H., Jr. *In Search of Excellence*. New York: Harper & Row, 1982.

Pfeffer, J. "Management as Symbolic Action: The Creation and Maintenance of Organizational Paradigms." In L. L. Cummings and B. H. Staw (eds.), *Research in Organizational Behavior*. Vol. 3. Greenwich, Conn.: JAI Press, 1981.

Pondy, L. R. "Union of Rationality and Intuition in Management Action." In S. Srivastva and Associates, *The Executive Mind: New Insights on Managerial Thought and Action*. San Francisco: Jossey-Bass, 1983.

Pondy, L. R., and Mitroff, I. I. "Beyond Open Systems Models of Organization." In B. M. Staw (ed.), *Research in Organizational Behavior*. Vol. 1. Greenwich, Conn.: JAI Press, 1979.

Pylyshyn, Z. "What the Mind's Eye Tells the Mind's Brain: A Critique of Mental Imagery." *Psychological Bulletin*, 1973, *80*, 1–24.

Ranson, S., Hinings, B., and Greenwood, R. "The Structuring of

Organizational Structures." *Administrative Science Quarter-ly*, 1980, *25*, 1–17.

Rumelhart, D. E., and Ortony, A. "The Representation of Knowledge in Memory." In R. C. Anderson, R. J. Spiro, and W. E. Montague (eds.), *Schooling and the Acquisition of Knowledge*. Hillsdale, N.J.: Erlbaum, 1977.

Schank, R. C., and Abelson, R. P. *Scripts, Plans, Goals, and Understanding*. Hillsdale, N.J.: Erlbaum, 1977.

Schutz, A. *The Phenomenology of the Social World*. Evanston, Ill.: Northwestern University Press, 1967.

Smircich, L. "Organizations as Shared Meanings." In L. R. Pondy, P. J. Frost, G. Morgan, and T. C. Dandridge (eds.), *Organizational Symbolism*. Greenwich, Conn.: JAI Press, 1983.

Smircich, L., and Morgan, G. "Leadership: The Management of Meaning." *Journal of Applied Behavioral Science*, 1982, *18*, 257–273.

Taylor, S. E., and Crocker, J. "Schematic Bases of Social Information Processing." In E. T. Higgins, C. P. Herman, and M. P. Zanna (eds.), *Social Cognition*. Vol. 1. Hillsdale, N.J.: Erlbaum, 1981.

Van Maanen, J. "Breaking In: Socialization to Work." In R. Dubin (ed.), *Handbook of Work, Organization, and Society*. Skokie, Ill.: Rand McNally, 1976.

Weber, M. "The Interpretive Understanding of Social Action." From *The Theory of Social and Economic Organization*. Reprinted in M. Brodbeck (ed.), *Readings in the Philosophy of the Social Sciences*. New York: Macmillan, 1968. (Originally published 1947.)

Weick, K. E. *The Social Psychology of Organizing*. Reading, Mass.: Addison-Wesley, 1969.

Weick, K. E. *The Social Psychology of Organizing*. (2nd ed.) Reading, Mass.: Addison-Wesley, 1979.

Wilkins, A. L. "Organizational Stories as Symbols Which Control the Organization." In L. R. Pondy, P. J. Frost, G. Morgan, and T. C. Dandridge (eds.), *Organizational Symbolism*. Greenwich, Conn.: JAI Press, 1983.

# 3

# Distilled Ideologies

## Values Derived from Causal Reasoning in Complex Environments

### Gerald R. Salancik
### Joseph F. Porac

*If there weren't God, the foreman'd probably blame the blizzard on us too.*

> —Mother of one of the
> authors to a co-worker,
> 1958

*You tellin' me . . . s__t, when the bosses ain't around, the place runs like clockwork.*

> —Father of one of the
> authors in a bar after
> work, 1960

The more complex an environment is, perhaps ironically, the more simplified its representation is in causal reasoning. It is this simplification that we will address in this chapter. We will pursue one question: How are the important aspects of a causal structure distilled from the web of interdependencies creating it? That is, how do we know what is important for causing effects? We propose that a psychological process of association reveals the relative importance of causal elements in snapshots reflecting the contingencies we experience.

The worlds we live in are complex environments. They comprise many events melded from other events. When displayed as graphs, these environments appear as tangles. Yet people tear through the mire most of the time and get to the heart of what is important with surprising élan. We believe that people understand complex causal structures well because they distill meaning holistically rather than as a mass of bivariate associations. Moreover, we believe that the operation of such a process is ecologically sensible, for it directs attention to the elements in an interconnected system that are important for determining the system's effects.

As an example of simplicity in a complex causal structure, consider a recent "Heard on the Street" column by Doron Levin in the *Wall Street Journal* (Levin, 1985). The column outlines the investment potential for Upjohn's stock. As with most "Heard on the Street" material, Levin interviewed several Wall Street analysts to construct a model of effects on the stock. The specific issue prompting the column was that Upjohn had been telling security analysts its patented hypertension drug, Minoxidil, seems to grow hair on men who are going bald. The stock zoomed as the news spread in an otherwise dull summer and Levin analyzed its future value. With bravura that might startle many social scientists, the analysts weaved thirteen causal factors into six interlocking causal models to generate seven specific predictions. All this in an article of 650 words!

We graphed this implied model in Figure 1 to illustrate its basic characteristics. To summarize briefly what the figure shows, Levin believes that the prospects for Upjohn are great if Minoxidil is sold as a cure for baldness, since there is a ready market of the balding wealthy. This will require FDA approval, which is uncertain, but even if approval is not given or is delayed, the market for Minoxidil is still good, since pharmacists can convert the hypertension pills into a lotion. The market could be slowed if the FDA decides to delay approval, which is thought likely. Even then, the stock may be a good bet because of promising markets for other Upjohn products. One glitch for

Figure 1. Causal Model from "Heard on the Street" (Levin, 1985).

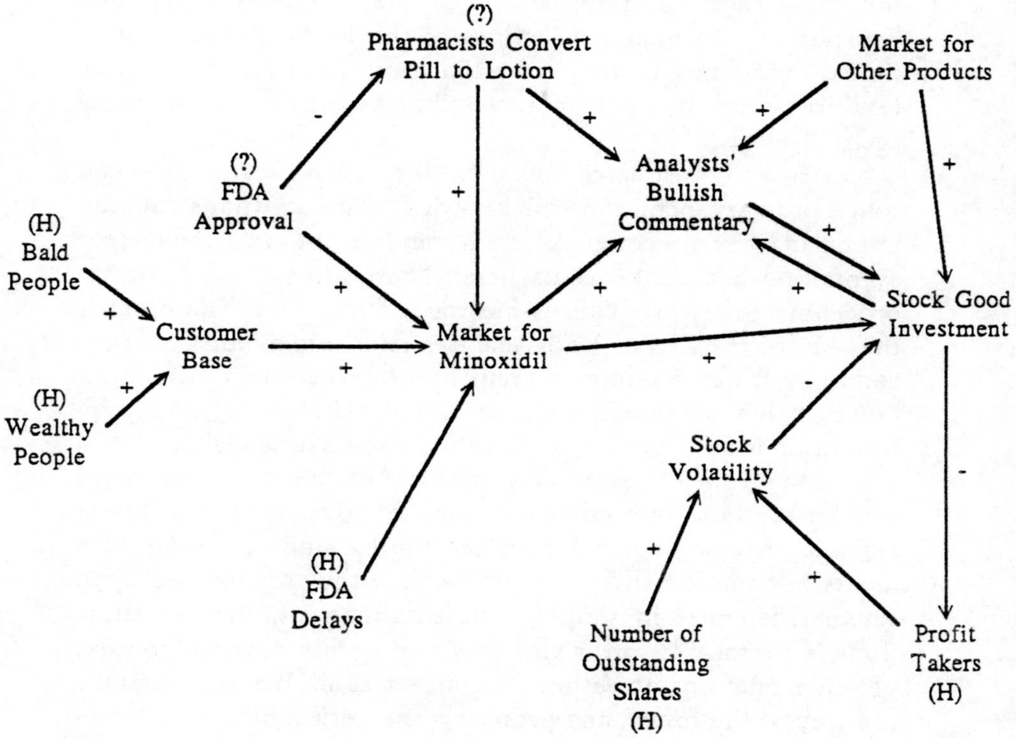

Key: (H) means the causal factor is considered likely
(?) means the status of the causal factor is uncertain
+ or - next to a connection is the direction of the effect predicted for the causal factor

the stock's value is that Upjohn's small number of outstanding shares leaves it vulnerable to risk from stock speculators taking their profit when the price rises as Upjohn's promise becomes known through bullish investment advisers. Profit taking will lessen the stock's investment value, slowing the profit takers and the bullish tendencies of analysts.

Despite the causal feedback loops and appearance of complexity, the model is an elegant simplification that pin-points the most relevant and immediate factors the analysts believe will determine Upjohn's and its investors' fortunes. Indeed, the entire model can be reduced to one statement: everything depends on the unknown actions of the FDA. These are mentioned by Levin's sources more than any other factors, and the text notes that the smart money will be keyed to this one causal agent.

How sophisticated analysts like Levin's colleagues and other ordinary people distill knowledge about what's causally important from complex environments of interdependent events is what concerns us here. There are two ways of approaching this issue. One is the way of the trees. The other is the way of the forest. Both analyses rely on perceptions of covariation in determining an event's causal role. Their difference, however, has to do with assumptions about how covariation information is used by people when making a causal claim.

We begin by examining the way of the trees. Our point will be to show that current models of covariation assessment and causal reasoning are of limited use for understanding judgments in complex environments because they are focused upon causal inferences in simple, isolated situations. In such situations, a causal relation is viewed either within a partial context of other relations or within no context at all. We then examine the way of the forest, and propose a theoretical model of "ideological distillation" to account for causal reasoning in complex environments. Along the way, we will present original evidence from a few of our own empirical studies that demonstrate the psychological validity of the distillation process.

### The Trees: Bivariate Causal Reasoning and the Limitations of Contemporary Theory

For the moment, consider Figure 1 from the vantage point of the Upjohn CEO. If Levin's analysis of the situation is correct, the company must base at least part of its long-term corporate strategy on whether Minoxidil is effective in growing hair. The CEO must also be concerned with whether Wall Street analysts will influence stock prices in a favorable way. But how does he make these determinations with sufficient confidence to convince skeptical shareholders that the drug will be good for the company in the future? More important, perhaps, would he recommend Minoxidil and Upjohn stock to a balding friend?

Since J. S. Mill introduced his "eliminative methods" in *A System of Logic* ([1843] 1941), scholars have argued that answers to questions such as these are to be found in people's assessments of simple covariations in the environment (Mackie, 1980). The use of covariation information in causal judgments is evident when a person explains an event by attributing it to another event with which it is associated over time. Kelley (1967, 1971), following Heider (1958), formalized covariation analysis as a basic psychological principle by showing how observers clarify simple causal textures by untangling bivariate associations. In doing so, Kelley argued, a person behaves much as a scientist might, conducting thought experiments, processing a few contingent associations, and unravelling what affects what. It is probably historically more accurate to suggest that scientists behave much as other people, since epistemological principles are simply refinements of the clever ways ordinary people decipher relations in their environments.

Most of the published literature on causal reasoning has followed this line of analysis. Thus, research and theory have been focused on understanding people's intuitive thought experiments involving a few isolated causal events. To illustrate the gist of this concern, consider the Upjohn CEO once again. One of his tasks is to know whether bullish analyses would lead to long-run stock appreciation or depreciation. By retrieving from memory past instances of bullish commentary and of company stock prices, the executive could attempt to complete the contingency table shown in Figure 2. In this way, the manager would flesh out a description of the co-occurrences over time of favorable or unfavorable analyst opinions and gains or losses in company stock prices. By making use of all four cells in his contingency analysis, the pharmaceutical chief would generate an intuitive equivalent to a formal chi-square test of association. High degrees of association over time would lead him to infer some degree of causal connection between analyst commentary and Upjohn stock value.

Contemporary research and theory have raised two im-

Figure 2. Hypothetical Contingency Table for Analyzing the Association
Between Stock Analyst Opinion and Changes in Stock Prices.

Analyst Opinions

|  | Favorable | Unfavorable |
|---|---|---|
| Gains |  |  |
| Losses |  |  |

Stock
Price
Changes

portant questions regarding this contingency table view of causal inference. The first concerns human information-processing skills: Given a set of co-occurrences over time between one event (say, analyst commentary) and another (say, change in company stock prices), are human observers able to process the complete set of bivariate events when asked or forced to make a causal claim? The second question concerns the supposed link between covariation assessments and causal judgments: To what extent is it justified to infer a causal connection between two events that have been shown to covary? Let us address each of these questions in turn.

*Accuracy in Covariation Assessment: Local Cues and Global Knowledge.* To inquire about accuracy in the assessment of environmental covariations might strike some as a bit silly, since our daily lives attest to our abilities to integrate covariation cues. A car rarely accelerates without the driver's pressing a foot to a pedal; lights rarely turn on without benefit of a hand clicking one of an odd variety of switches (more often they turn off!). A person would have to be dense, dead, or terribly in the dark not to notice these everyday co-occurrences.

However, data from psychological experiments tell a very different tale. In reviewing the large number of studies that have been conducted to assess people's ability to use covariation information, Crocker (1981) noted that biases have been found to enter into the judgment process in several significant ways: first, observers tend to skew their selection of evidence toward instances confirming an association instead of using both confirming and disconfirming instances; second, small samples of co-occurrences are sometimes considered overly representative of the entire population of co-occurrences; and third, judgments tend to ignore the statistical principle of regression to the mean. Crocker (1981) concluded her review by suggesting that "evidence has accumulated indicating that intuitive covariation judgments are subject to several sources of bias. In all likelihood our conceptions of our social world, which are based on these judgments, are simply incorrect much of the time. Indeed, one of the functions of social science research is to revise our often erroneous judgments about the relationships between events" (p. 288).

As it stands, this conclusion is rather disheartening since it suggests that predicting the future is a crapshoot, where success and failure are functions of random chance rather than deep-seated knowledge about events. Will Minoxidil be good for Upjohn's growth? Hire a cadre of enlightened social scientists to provide an accurate and objective assessment of the important contingencies. Otherwise, roll the dice and hope for the best.

But things are not so simple. Nor are they so bleak. In a recent paper, Alloy and Tabachnik (1984) argue persuasively that a person's accumulated world knowledge plays an important role in assessments of covariation. Noting that everyday life provides many examples of people negotiating their environments successfully, these authors distinguish between local *situational* data that can be used as evidence for or against covariation and global *expectations* that a covariation is present between the events in question. They suggest that when current situational information is present but prior expectations are nil, people will rely on the situational cues; when the opposite conditions exist, they argue that people will rely on prior expectations. The most interesting case is when both prior expectations and situational information about covariation are present, for then the current information may either concur in its implications with the prior expectations or conflict. The first situation —that is, when expectations and current information concur— is unproblematic, and Alloy and Tabachnik expect people to make correspondent inferences with extreme confidence. The second leads to a cognitive dilemma that people frequently resolve in favor of their prior expectations, except when a "substantial amount of belief-contradictory evidence or particularly salient contradictory evidence confronts them" (Alloy and Tabachnik, 1984, p. 116).

In suggesting that people's background knowledge helps to guide them in their judgments, Alloy and Tabachnik take a more moderate position regarding the accuracy of covariation assessments. When a local inference of association departs from the pattern of data present in the situation, it could indeed suggest an inability to process the information without bias. The CEO of Upjohn could be hopelessly constrained by his own information-processing limitations. On the other hand, such a departure could mean that incomplete and ambiguous data presented in a partial context is being filled in with a host of assumptions about the situation and other environmental associations that are in fact pertinent to the judgment at hand. Thus, the simple query "Will bullish analyst commentary influence stock prices?" might be answered by retrieving information not just about the covariation between analyst reports and stock values but also about market research data, the number of outstanding shares of stock, the docket of other new products being developed by the company, and so on. Only if we knew this additional multivariate information and how it is used could we determine whether the CEO is "accurate" in his assessment of the bivariate situation. Unfortunately, although much evidence has accumulated to suggest that human judgments often diverge from bivariate data, very little research has been conducted to explore the extent to which background multivariate knowledge about the entire associational structure motivates the "biases" that are often found. In a later section of this paper, we will examine the nature and influence of such knowledge more thoroughly.

*Covariations and Causal Inferences.* Regardless of people's ability to use covariation data, there is still the question whether such data say anything about a causal connection between the covarying events. Would an Upjohn manager be justified in inferring that analyst commentary *causes* movement in stock prices if, on the completion of all four cells in Figure 2, the evidence suggested a strong covariation? Behind this question is an issue familiar to most first-year students in a research methods course: correlation does not imply causation. How would the manager know whether the causal agent for stock price movements was analyst commentary and not the investors' *own* assessments of the market for Minoxidil? How would the manager know that an influx of profit takers did not occur on Wall Street at about the time Minoxidil was discussed in the business press? How, indeed, would the manager be able to rule out all possible counterexplanations for the supposed covariation?

Theorists have attempted to address this issue in two ways. Some have argued that covariation data is only one of several cues that people process when inferring causality (for example, Mackie, 1980; Nisbett and Ross, 1980). The claim is made that although covariation assessments are important, other information such as contiguity in time and space, similarity in magnitude between cause and effect, and temporal succession are important as well. By employing multiple cues, it is suggested, people winnow out irrelevancies in the environment and capture those associations that are most likely to be causal links. Thus, for example, it would be unlikely, assuming no hidden connections, that bullish analyst commentary causes price movements in Upjohn stock if the commentary always follows rather than precedes the price changes. By using a temporal succession cue, accidental or irrelevant covariations of this nature could be filtered from any causal inference.

In a relatively simple environment, a multiple-cue approach to causal reasoning would clarify the texture of bivariate associations a great deal. When the number of potential causal events is small, testing for continuity in space and time, temporal succession, and similarity of magnitude would narrow the focus sufficiently to allow one to select a likely causal candidate. However, not all environments are simple. In a recent study, for example, Salancik and Meindl (1984) identified a total of fifty-five causal factors named by top executives in accounting for the performance of their firms. In such complex structures, a causal judgment using multiple cues would still result in a large number of eligible causal events. Even in our restricted Upjohn environment, the use of multiple cues would probably fail to isolate a single causal agent responsible for the price of Upjohn stock. Thus, the concern for ruling out possible counterexplanations for a supposed causal covariation would still exist, with accurate assessments of covariation possibly remaining inaccurate assessments of causality.

Some of the more prominent accounts of causal reasoning in the published literature (for example, Kelley, 1967, 1971) approach the covariation-causation issue in a second, slightly different way. Rather than assuming that observers use multiple cues about a single covariation to determine a causal effect, this approach assumes that observers rely mainly on covariation data, but covariation data across several events simultaneously. If an individual processes information about multiple covariations, an "intuitive partial regression" could be performed in which the unique contribution of each causal candidate is ascertained. Thus, for example, one could suggest that an Upjohn executive would be able to keep in mind both analyst commentary and the market for Minoxidil as possible factors causing a change in stock value. When such a change occurs, the covariation cues relevant to these three factors could then be assessed, rival explanations considered, and a reasoned causal statement made about why the price change occurred. The presence of a plausible rival causal factor could be used to "discount" (Kelley, 1971) the causal force of the other, and corporate strategy could be written accordingly.

There is little doubt that humans are wonderful information-crunching machines. At the same time, however, there is good reason to question the generality of this second account of causal inferencing. What is known about short-term information-processing capacities leads to the conclusion that any environment containing more than a few potential causal candidates will overload even the most conscientious observer (for example, Kahneman, 1973; March and Simon, 1958). The ability to examine simultaneously large numbers of causal candidates in an effort to reveal unique causal contributions requires massive parallel processing capabilities. Because short-term information capacity is limited, however, complex environments must be assessed in serial snapshots, each of limited scope. One large-scale "mental path analysis" incorporating all unique bivariate causal relations is simply not possible when the number of such relations gets large. Thus, it is again the case that an existing model of causal reasoning falls short in describing how people assess complex environments, leaving open the question of how serial snapshots of causal effects are integrated into a general statement of what affects what.

Traveling the Way of the Trees and Getting Lost. A few years ago, the authors succumbed to an urge to return to nature and went backpacking in southern Indiana. The area chosen was one of dense hardwood forests compacted across rolling terrain. Precautions, such as the purchase of detailed topographical maps of the area, were taken beforehand to ensure that all would go smoothly. To make the story a short one, we got lost, right in the middle of the forest that we had so carefully reviewed on our maps. The problem was not with the maps; they were completely accurate. Our problem was missing the forest because of the trees. The hardwood was so densely packed together over miles and miles of land that we could reckon distance and terrain for only a few hundred yards at a time. Our maps were useless because everything seemed the same to us—just trees, one after another. Indeed, when we tried to use the configural information contained in the maps, we traveled in frustrating circles. Although we eventually found our way through trial and error, we vowed never to return to southern Indiana again.

In general terms, we were lost in Indiana because we could use only local situational cues to determine where we stood at any moment. In a simple and differentiated environment, this would have been no problem at all. But with thousands of tall trees for miles around, all looking very much the same, local cues provided little information to help us find our way. We chose our route of travel every two hundred yards or so, coursing through the woods in a random search for an outlet. We lacked configural information about the lay of the land. Our maps had this information, but unfortunately we could not match their configurations to the real world.

Inferring causality in complex environments by using local bivariate information is much the same as traveling in southern Indiana during a hot summer—one will often miss the forest for the trees and get lost. By isolating a few of the relationships from the many, one separates them from their configural context. In itself, this is not wrong; it is just incomplete. Unless local snapshots of covariations are woven into a more global configural pattern, the causal texture of the environment as a whole will never be apparent. Moreover, the need for such a summary increases with the complexity of the environment, since it is in highly interconnected structures that local situational snapshots are least informative.

The problem with existing research on causal reasoning is that scholars have been studying people's perceptions of small stands of timber and have ignored their understanding of the forest as a whole. To some degree, this has led to misconceptions about observer accuracy and information-processing ability. If Alloy and Tabachnik (1984) are correct, global configural information is used as often as situational cues in assessing environmental covariations. Is this being inaccurate? After all, we had an accurate map of the land, and we still could not find our way. More importantly, the past emphasis upon bivariate situational cues in causal inference has tended to promote the view that a complete theory of causal inference can be developed by researching local inference processes only. We hope to show in the next section that this is not the case.

## The Forest: Causal Reasoning from
## Configurations of Interdependencies

Without discounting what is known about reasoning in simple environments, we suggest that a strategy other than bivariate analysis may be used to extract inferences about the causal importance of events in complex environments. We propose that individuals derive much of their knowledge of causal importance by abstracting from snapshots of the associational structure existing in the environment as a whole. A photographer friend once explained the value of such a process most succinctly. He noted that the difference between a professional and an amateur photographer was that the amateur struggled hard to take the perfect shot—lining people into their poses, angling the camera in relation to the sun—but the professional just clicked the shutter again and again, taking dozens of photos. The key to this difference shows up when they sort among their prints later. The amateur, with only one picture to view, has to hope that this was one of those rare occasions when his actions perfectly correlated with the rich reality he remembered. The professional, floundering among his few dozen shots from different angles, glimpses, and lens, instead becomes immersed in the associations between the pictures taken until one photo emerges that seems to connect the slew of images into a whole more successfully than any of the other photos.

Causal reasoning, we propose, is also a matter of distilling sense from snapshot associations. On any particular occasion, an assortment of snapshots is primed from memory by information in the ongoing local environment, by the nature of the problem presenting itself, by odd recollections, by the fix of attention in small corners of the moment, or by the questions of colleagues. We retrieve parts of the complex causal structure we retain in memory—not as solid full-blown theories or reasoned arguments, but as bits and pieces of associated knowledge about contingencies, frequencies, typicality—to be refined or modified by local informational conditions and constructed into schemes for presentation or action. We further propose that from these snapshots of associations, an individual distills an impression of the causal importance of specific elements for global use, an impression that we will call a *distilled ideology*.

The credibility of this proposal rests on several issues, two of which we will address in the remainder of this chapter. One is whether it is possible, in theory, to obtain a description of a rich environment that captures global causal configurations. We will show that such a description is possible by examining one common organizational environment. A second issue is whether a configural description of an environment has psychological validity. We will argue that it does and provide empirical evidence to support our conjectures.

*Environmental Interdependence: Another Example.* The causal model determining the value of Upjohn stock presented earlier is a good example of an *interdependent environment:* that is, an environment in which the value of each element determines partially or completely the values of other elements. We have exhausted our journalistic liberties, however, and have abused Upjohn and its executives enough. We prefer to move to another causal environment, one much closer to our own academic occupations.

For a few years in the early 1980s, one of the authors ventured into the role of an academic administrator, making decisions about such things as teaching loads, TA's, budget allocations, and so on. In this role, strategic decisions usually revolved around such themes as preserving the quality of instruction while maintaining a high level of research productivity. Of course, this sort of goal can only be met if the administrator understands the causal context influencing teaching quality and faculty research. Otherwise, it would be impossible to choose the strategic levers necessary to attain the desired end. Thus, we return once again to the problem of causal reasoning in a complex environment.

To understand how people *do* describe an interdependent environment, it is necessary to consider how the environment *can* be described. In Figure 3 we have plotted a hypothetically valid causal structure for an imaginary academic department. The structure contains six elements: the total department budget, faculty teaching load, grant income brought into the department, the number of enrolled graduate students, the number of teaching assistants, and the scholarly productivity of the faculty. As in the Upjohn case, the arrows indicate the presence and direction of causal effects and the signs indicate whether the effects are positive or negative. Thus, for example, increases in faculty teaching loads would be associated with decreases in faculty research productivity. Such decreases would themselves

Figure 3. Hypothetical Causal Structure for an Academic Department.

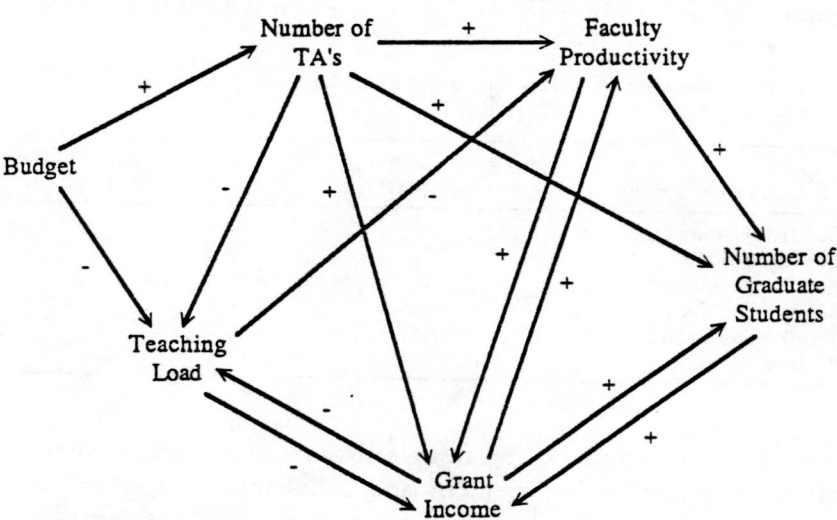

be associated with decreases in grant income, and grant reductions would further diminish research productivity.

Observing the links in this structure, one is tempted to just grant its complexity and move on to simpler fare. It is a messy tangle of lines and circles. But is it possible to make the structure more orderly, more understandable? Could we develop a way to address questions concerning the importance of grant income in the total structure, or how much would change if teaching loads were altered? In short, what do we do with a structure like that depicted in Figure 3?

A number of scholars have grappled with this problem, each developing rigorous methods for unravelling interdependence such as that in Figure 3 (for example, Bougon, Weick, and Binkhorst, 1977; Porac and Salancik, 1982; Salancik, 1984; Weick, 1979). Although there are differences in complexity among these methods, all share a basic similarity in that they use the number of interconnections between system elements as an indication of causal impact. The simplest way of enumerating such interconnections is to determine the number of direct connections between one element and the others in the structure.

In our hypothetical example, the breakdown shown in Table 1 is such a summary of Figure 3. From the table, it can be

**Table 1. Number of Direct Links Between Each Element and Others (from Figure 3).**

| Causal Element | No. of Elements It Affects | No. of Elements That Affect It | Total Links |
|---|---|---|---|
| Grant Income | 3 | 4 | 7 |
| Teaching Load | 2 | 3 | 5 |
| Faculty Productivity | 2 | 3 | 5 |
| Number of TA's | 4 | 1 | 5 |
| Number of Grad Students | 1 | 3 | 4 |
| Budget | 2 | 0 | 2 |

seen that the number of teaching assistants in the department is affected by one other element and influences four other elements. For faculty productivity, comparable links number three and two, respectively. By tallying up the two figures for each element, one obtains an index of the direct links between one element and the remaining causal structure. This index is shown in the third column of the table. It can be seen that grant income is the most interdependent causal element, while departmental budget is the least. From the third column in the table, one can infer that grant income will most likely be an important source of variation in the hypothetical operation of the department.

There are clearly more complex and complete methods for summarizing interdependence than that shown in Table 1. One might, for example, consider indirect as well as direct causal links between elements or inquire about nuances of structure such as whether an element has more causal inputs than causal outputs. One could weight each causal element according to its supposed links with factors not included in our more limited graph. However, our point is not to develop a method for a complete description of an interdependent system (as useful as such a method would be). Rather, it is to provide a conceptual foundation for an analysis of causal reasoning within an interdependent environment. Our previous commentary should suggest that there is good reason to question the psychological validity of any complex method for summarizing environmental causal relations—people simplify their inferences too much to entertain such procedures. Indeed, it is entirely possible that a very restricted description like that shown in Table 1 is close to the summary inferences an individual might make if forced to judge, for example, the importance of grant income to the operation of the department as a whole. We will explore this possibility in more detail next.

*Distillation of a Configural Causal Ideology from Local Bivariate Associations.* Our concern is with an interdependent environment from the point of view of an individual acting within it. How, for instance, would an administrator of our hypothetical academic department make sense out of the causal pattern illustrated in Figure 3? We have noted that most research to date on causal reasoning would lead one to suggest that a department head would process local situational information and then assess the degree of association between two (perhaps three) causal elements via a mental contingency analysis. We have also suggested that a bivariate analysis is incomplete in complex environments because it misses the richness of the interdependence. In our example, a complete bivariate assessment of the connections among the six environmental elements would require, at minimum, $(6^2 - 6)/2$, or fifteen, covariation assessments. These could be conducted only serially across time, implying that at any single moment the department head was reasoning from limited local information. There is clearly a need for cognitive simplification—the administrator must distill from the local data a configural representation of the environment as a whole.

We propose that a central component in the distillation of configural causal information is the retention in memory of only the conclusions reached via local assessment and not the raw situational evidence itself. During the reasoning that occurs in processing bivariate covariations, observers presumably choose to allocate their mental resources to the selection and interpretation of very detailed situational evidence. They retrieve instances of co-occurrences and determine the merits of

the data. However, once a conclusion is reached with a reasonable degree of certainty, the situational evidence is no longer of
great importance in the reasoning process. It can thus be discarded from short-term processing. What is retained, however, is
a simplified statement of perceived contingency, which is a
proposition about the likelihood of a causal connection between the local events. By retaining only the *conclusions* of the
bivariate search, observers minimize the necessity for expending
additional cognitive resources examining the same situational
evidence in the future. The retained causal proposition contains
the essence of the linkage between two events distilled from the
background clutter of attention-demanding local data. By serially processing local snapshots of bivariate data and retaining a
summary conclusion from the evidence, an observer builds a
repository of stored causal propositions about an environmental
domain. This knowledge can then be used when he or she wishes
to infer an element's configural importance in the environment
as a whole. It is this repository of retained causal information
about a given environment that we are calling a *distilled ideology.*

   Possessing a causal ideology permits an individual to sample generously information provided by large segments of the
environmental structure without investigating the covariational
minutia of each local situation. The forest can be ascertained
without being overwhelmed by the tangle of trees composing it.
In the case of our imagined academic administrator, questions
concerning the general importance of grant income or the likely changes that would come from a change in teaching loads can
be asked and answered. In doing so, causal propositions would
be retrieved from memory and integrated into configural statements such as "Grant income is crucial to our success as a department." Organizational strategies could then be formulated
with these global considerations in mind.

   This analysis thus implies that three levels of information
are used in understanding complex causal environments: first,
raw data about environmental covariations is presented in local
situational snapshots; second, causal conclusions from the situational evidence are retained in memory (as a distilled ideology);
and third, configural statements are used to summarize the envi-

ronment holistically. These three levels of information are
generated by two types of causal inferences: an inference that
abstracts from a sample of local data to a causal conclusion, and
an inference summarizing a sample of causal beliefs with a configural judgment. Although the inferential process involved in
the former has been studied extensively in the past, very little is
known about the latter. An observer can use a variety of strategies to sample from the retained store of causal beliefs in order
to infer the configural properties of the environment. Are some
strategies more reasonable than others? We will examine this
issue empirically next.

*Use of Causal Beliefs in Configural Judgments:*
*Evidence for Simple Strategies*

An observer attempting to ascertain the global configura-
tion of a causal environment is faced with the same problem we
encountered in constructing a summary of Figure 3. How many
connections (causal propositions) does one select from the total
store of retained beliefs? Should such beliefs be combined in
complex ways to ascertain indirect causal influences, or should
only simple direct links be summarized? Because of information-
processing limitations, a trade-off exists between the complexity of the integration rule and the number of causal propositions that can be sampled from the ideological store. Complex
integrations of retained beliefs are accomplished only by limiting the range of propositions sampled. Thus, only partial summaries of the interdependence in the environment are possible.
However, more holistic descriptions can be achieved when
many propositions are integrated with simple rules. Although
this trade-off is likely to be resolved differently in different situations, depending on the task at hand and the questions asked,
it is likely that observers favor simple strategies and large numbers of retained beliefs when attempting configural summaries
of the environment as a whole.

As evidence to support this claim, we offer the results of
two studies we have conducted at the University of Illinois. The
logic of both studies was essentially the same. From our organi-

zational respondents we obtained a set of causal propositions regarding a sample of elements from an important environmental domain. We then requested that they construct configural judgments about these same environmental elements. In this way, we were able to estimate the relationship between simple summary indices of the stated causal propositions and the global judgments.

*Study One (Porac, Salancik, and Ferris, 1983).* The thirty-seven men and forty-five women employees in this study were thirty-five to forty years of age, had been with the University of Illinois for about nine years, worked as cooks, maintenance staff, or office clerks, and earned about $12,000. They were asked to indicate the relationships among nine work outcomes by answering seventy-two questions ($72 = 9^2 - 9$) of the general form "If I had more *respect and fair treatment* from my boss, I would have _____ *freedom* to do my job the way I think it should be done," where the blank line was provided for the employee to indicate whether the first outcome would lead to more or less of the second outcome or have no effect. Employees also rated how *pleased* they were with the present levels of each outcome and how much they *wanted* each as an outcome from their work. We expected that their responses to the "want" questions would reveal how important, in a configural sense, each outcome was to them.

Several points about the data were noteworthy. First, the employees did not appear to have any difficulty in answering whether one outcome would lead to more or less of another or not affect it at all. Most people made their seventy-two judgments in twenty minutes. Their judgments also appear to be systematic and not a haphazard scatter of "more," "less," or "no effect" answers. Responses to all seventy-two pairs of outcomes were significantly nonrandomly distributed across the three categories. The employees did reflect, however, a common bias observed in experiments on causal reasoning—shying away from negative relationships, when one outcome decreases another. Only 1.8 percent of the 5,900 reported relationships were negative, and 51 percent were positive. Finally, the causal maps are fairly complex and interconnected. On the average, an outcome was seen to lead to two and a half to three others and to be affected by a similar number.

Partly because of the numerous connections, a simplified graph is difficult to present, so we will summarize the main linkages that held for most employees. *Promotion* was the outcome that was believed to lead to the most other outcomes—in fact, to all but *security. Respect* and *variety* were the two other most central outcomes in the set, each interlocked reciprocally with *promotion* while also affecting other outcomes in their own spheres of influence. *Respect* from bosses was believed to lead to *recognition* and *freedom* and *variety* to *challenge*. Nothing stood out as affecting *security,* although it was considered important for bringing about *freedom* to work in one's own style. *Friendship, pay,* and *recognition* were given minor roles in generating other outcomes.

We expected that the employees would use a very simple summary rule, much like the one we used in generating Table 1, for integrating these seventy-two beliefs into configural judgments about how much they wanted more of each outcome. To test this hypothesis, we derived an "importance index" for each outcome by simply tallying up all direct connections with the others in the set. The mean ratings for how much each outcome was wanted and the importance indices are presented in Table 2. Also presented are the correlations between the want ratings

Table 2. Key Results from Study One.

| Outcome | Want from Work | Derived Importance | Correlation of Want with Interdependence |
|---|---|---|---|
| Challenge | 5.38 (3) | 3.80 (4) | .42* |
| Freedom | 4.95 (9) | 3.08 (8) | .41* |
| Friendship | 5.09 (6) | 3.40 (6) | .41* |
| Pay | 6.35 (1) | 3.06 (9) | .25* |
| Promotion | 5.52 (2) | 5.34 (1) | .29* |
| Recognition | 5.02 (8) | 3.25 (7) | .34* |
| Respect | 5.15 (5) | 4.20 (2) | .51* |
| Security | 5.05 (2) | 3.52 (5) | .47* |
| Variety | 5.21 (4) | 4.15 (3) | .41* |

*$p < .01$.

and the importance indices for the nine outcomes separately. As can be seen, the causal importance of outcomes derived from respondents' seventy-two causal beliefs corresponded well with their own reports of what they consider important outcomes from work. For six outcomes, the reported and derived importance was only one rank apart (challenge, freedom, friendship, promotion, recognition, and variety). In addition, the correlations across employees between an outcome's importance for an employee and the interdependence that was summarized in the derived indices were significantly greater than zero for all nine outcomes. It should be mentioned that the values of these correlations did not change when satisfaction with current levels of each outcome was held constant. Also, more complex summary indices that considered first- and second-order indirect effects between the nine outcomes were not correlated as strongly to want ratings, indicating support for the notion that a simple direct summation rule was being used at the time of the configural judgments.

One whopping inconsistency was found for *pay*, which employees reported as being on the top of their lists of what they wanted from work but which they also reported as playing a very minor role in affecting other outcomes in the set. Although *pay* was believed to be affected by *promotion* and *respect* from bosses, it was not thought to lead to any other outcomes included in the study.

Of course, these nine outcomes hardly include all the outcomes employees might desire. The set was restricted arbitrarily to outcomes generally transacted within a work setting. Outcomes that are transacted outside of work, such as food for the table, house payments, movies, or respect from neighbors, were excluded. These are also the kinds of outcomes we get from our wages. Thus, the poor predictability of the *pay* outcome is not so much evidence that value is not derived from an outcome's role in a causal network as it is recognition of our inadequate sampling of the outcomes relevant to pay.

*Study Two (Porac and Salancik, 1982).* In this study, we studied thirty-six academic department heads from the University of Illinois. Collectively, our sample was responsible for two-thirds of the university's teaching and research. They had been in their jobs an average of four years and represented the natural, social, and behavioral sciences, engineering, agriculture, the humanities, the arts, and the military. Again, our purpose in studying them was to assess the relationship between their causal ideologies and the configural judgments we requested that they make about the importance of various elements in their environments.

As our sample of environmental elements, we selected twelve operating variables that are commonly associated with academic departments and which pilot analysis showed varied among departments. The variables were: grant income, instructional units taught, average teaching loads of faculty, receipts of endowment, numbers of graduate students, teaching assistants, course offerings, state budget appropriations, average teaching evaluations, internal research grant awards, and key committee assignments of faculty in the department.

Our respondents were interviewed in their offices and asked to state their beliefs about all possible bivariate causal connections among the twelve operating variables. They were also asked to make a series of configural judgments regarding the importance of each operating variable for their own department's success. Since academic departments typically view themselves as having two missions, we asked for ratings in each domain—teaching and research. The educational question asked the department head to rate the extent to which the variable had a "determining influence" on the level of the department's success in meeting the educational goals of the department's students. The research question asked about the variables' determining influences on the "scholarly productivity" of the department's faculty.

Our analysis was straightforward. For each of the thirty-six departments, we generated summary indices of interdependence for each of the twelve operating variables. The index was simply the total number of direct links to other variables in the sample. Thus, each department's data consisted of twelve summary indices, twelve educational importance ratings, and twelve scholarly importance ratings. Our test of the expectation

that interdependence would predict configural importance judgments was simply computing, for each department, two correlations: one between the summary indices and educational ratings,
and one between the indices and scholarly ratings. The results
were in line with our expectations. Across departments, the
average correlation between the interdependence indices and
educational importance was .75; for scholarly importance the
correlation was .54. As in Study One, more complex indices did
not correlate as well with configural importance.

To summarize, in both Studies One and Two, we obtained separate measures of a respondent's causal ideology
about an organizational domain and his or her configural judgments about the importance of elements in the domain. In both
studies, it was observed that a simple additive index of direct
causal connections predicted importance ratings. In both, more
complex indices did not predict as well. Such results support
our contention that configural judgments integrate samples of
retained causal propositions in very simple ways.

### Implications: Sawing Trees to See the Forest

We opened our discussion with a question concerning
people's ability to untangle causal effects in complex and interdependent environments. Along the way, we have suggested an
answer by arguing that causal reasoning takes place at two levels
of information processing. On the one hand, observers sift
through the data provided by local situational cues and build an
understanding of the relationship existing between a causal element and its effect. This is the way of the trees. On the other
hand, observers make broad-brush assessments of configural
relationships among many elements in the environment. This is
the way of the forest. We have placed emphasis upon what we
have labeled a *distilled ideology* as an intermediate level of generalization: a retained store of causal propositions that summarizes the evidence obtained through multiple snapshots over
time and that can be integrated succinctly into global causal
inferences. It should be clear from what we have said that it is a
causal ideology of this sort that acts to bridge the ways of tree

and forest. In effect, by employing distilled causal representations, an observer saws enough covariational trees to allow him or her to perceive the broad structure of the causal forest as a whole.

Our account of the dual nature of causal reasoning clarifies the place of previous research and theory on human causal judgment. By emphasizing the way of the trees, previous research has provided useful information about how people assess local covariational data. But such research is limited. A complete theory of causal inference will be constructed only when an equally large body of data is collected examining the way of the forest. Our arguments and those of others (for example, Bougon, Weick, and Binkhorst, 1977; Weick, 1979) provide useful beginnings for such an inquiry.

Throughout this paper, we have illustrated our points by drawing from various examples of administrative decision making—both real and imagined. The managerial mind seems a particularly rich source of information about how configural representations are gleaned from complex interdependent systems. Administrators act within an interdependent operating environment in which strategic action demands knowing the causal texture that will produce success or failure. Without configural information abstracted from retained causal beliefs, administrators would be condemned to a prison of local covariational evidence. Like the authors during their backpacking trip in Indiana, they would make important decisions considering a few variables at a time, hoping to reach strategic objectives, but most likely getting lost in the trees. In contrast, a causal ideology and the configural judgments based on it permit them to see the strategic lay of the land.

## References

Alloy, L. B., and Tabachnik, N. "Assessment of Covariation in Humans and Animals: The Joint Influence of Prior Expectations and Current Situational Information." *Psychological Review*, 1984, *91*, 112-249.

Bougon, M., Weick, K., and Binkhorst, D. "Cognition in Or-

ganizations." *Administrative Science Quarterly*, 1977, *22*, 609–632.

Crocker, J. "Judgment of Covariation by Social Perceivers." *Psychological Bulletin*, 1981, *90*, 272–292.

Heider, F. *The Psychology of Interpersonal Relations.* New York: Wiley, 1958.

Kahneman, D. *Attention and Effort.* Englewood Cliffs, N.J.: Prentice-Hall, 1973.

Kelley, H. H. "Attribution Theory in Social Psychology." In D. Levine (ed.), *Nebraska Symposium on Motivation.* Vol. 15. Lincoln: University of Nebraska Press, 1967.

Kelley, H. H. "Causal Schemata and the Attribution Process." In E. E. Jones and others (eds.), *Attribution: Perceiving the Causes of Behavior.* Morristown, N.J.: General Learning Press, 1971.

Levin, D. "Heard on the Street." *Wall Street Journal,* May 31, 1985.

Mackie, J. L. *Cement of the Universe: A Study of Causation.* Oxford, England: Oxford University Press, 1980.

March, J. G., and Simon, H. A. *Organizations.* New York: Wiley, 1958.

Mill, J. S. *A System of Logic and Ratiocinative and Inductive Being: A Connected View of the Principles of Evidence and Methods of Scientific Investigation.* London: Longmans, Green, 1941. (Originally published 1843.)

Nisbett, R. E., and Ross, L. *Human Inference: Strategies and Shortcomings of Social Judgment.* Englewood Cliffs, N.J.: Prentice-Hall, 1980.

Porac, J. F., and Salancik, G. R. "Environmental Interdependence and Causal Reasoning by Academic Department Heads." Unpublished manuscript, University of Illinois, 1982.

Porac, J. F., Salancik, G. R., and Ferris, G. "Employee Valuing and Outcome Interdependence in Organizations." Unpublished manuscript, University of Illinois, 1983.

Salancik, G. R. "A Single-Value Function for Evaluating Organizations with Multiple Constituencies." *Academy of Management Review,* 1984, *9*, 617–625.

Salancik, G. R., and Meindl, J. "Corporate Attributions as Strategic Illusions of Management Control." *Administrative Science Quarterly*, 1984, *29*, 238-254.

Weick, K. E. *The Social Psychology of Organizing.* (2nd ed.) Reading, Mass.: Addison-Wesley, 1979.

# 4

# Organizations as Cognitive Maps

## Charting Ways to Success and Failure

Karl E. Weick
Michel G. Bougon

*Managers basically possess only ideas. Hierarchy, organization, control—these reside primarily in the mind. In fact, management exists only because the manager and managed believe it exists.*

—Joseph McGuire

*VISA is highly structured conceptually, philosophically, and ethically. What we do and why we do it is carefully planned. How we do it is not. We give it just enough procedural structure to make it respectable to those who are enamored of forms, job descriptions, reports, consultants' presentations, statistics, and other such impediments.*

—Dee Hock, chief
executive officer, VISA

Organizations exist largely in the mind, and their existence takes the form of cognitive maps. Thus, what ties an organization together is what ties thoughts together. People who study

102

cognitive maps take those assertions seriously and literally. This chapter shows why.

## Background

To see that what ties an organization together is what ties thoughts together, first, we must consider how we think of organizations in terms of causes and effects, and second, we must examine how we assemble personal cognitive maps from such primitive cause-effect relations.

*Causality as an Epistemological Primitive.* There are only four possible things that can happen among events in an organization. The events can be either similar or different, and they can occur either at the same or at different times. That is it. These four combinations are the primitives of all organizing. This chapter is about the most relevant combination in organization theory: the combination of different events at different times. It is this combination that generates the inferences of causality that are stored in the sets of related causality beliefs we call *cause maps*.

The relationship between the four epistemological primitives and causality can be seen in Figure 1. Cell A, which stands for the same events occurring at the same time, is exemplified by two whistles blowing at the same time; this combination of events is called coincidence or *identity*. Cell B, which represents the same event happening at different times, is labeled *seriality* and would be exemplified by a series of explosions occurring over a period of time. Cell C, which stands for different events occurring at the same time, is characterized as *correlation* and is exemplified by a whistle and an explosion occurring at the same time. Cell D, which exhibits different events occurring at different times, is the situation on which patterns of *causality* are imposed. An example of this combination would be a whistle followed by an explosion. It is conceivable that a person observing these two different events spread over time might conclude that the whistle caused the explosion. It is important to emphasize that linking an earlier event to some later event is a reasonable connection, but it is also arbitrary and speculative (see Hume, [1748] 1955).

Figure 1. Epistemological Primitives.

Time at Which Events Occur

|  | Same | Different |
|---|---|---|
| **Same** | A<br><br>Identity | B<br><br>Seriality |
| **Different** | C<br><br>Correlation | D<br><br>Causality |

Classification
of
Events

*Source:* Copyright © 1981, by M. Bougon.

As Figure 1 indicates, causality is one of only four cognitive archetypes, and it is one of only two archetypes that are rich enough to incorporate the dimension of time. The relevance of causality to organizational issues is evident if we recall the basic way organizations are usually described. Selznick (1957, p. 5) is representative: "The term *organization* thus suggests a certain barrenness, a lean, no-nonsense system of consciously coordinated activities. It refers to an expendable tool, a rational instrument engineered to do a job."

This description emphasizes that the organization is an instrument to do things, a means, a consciously constructed tool. Thus an organization is often valued literally because it embodies causality. Organizations institutionalize means-ends relationships and if-then assertions and transform earlier inputs into very different later outcomes, all of which invite inferences of causality.

*Maps as Epistemological Structures.* In the most general sense, a map "is an aggregate of interrelated information" (O'Keefe and Nadel, 1978, p. 62). Maps help people perceive large-scale environments beyond the range of immediate perception. Since maps focus beyond the range of immediate perception, they deal with phenomena that cannot be observed but rather must be explored. Thus, maps are intimately tied to action. O'Keefe and Nadel use an early position paper by Ittelson (1973) to highlight the close ties between action and maps. " 'Most perception research has been carried out in the context of object perception, rather than environment perception. The distinction between object and environment is crucial, because objects require subjects. . . . In contrast, one cannot be a subject of an environment, one can only be a participant. The very distinction between self and non-self breaks down cold. The environment surrounds, enfolds, engulfs, and no thing and no one can be isolated and identified as standing outside of, and apart from it. . . .' The fact that they surround means that one cannot observe an environment; rather the organism explores it" (pp. 74–75).

Thus, action and mapping have a close relationship. When people build cognitive maps, they start with outcomes, small experiments, and consequences that are produced either by one's own action or by that of someone else. These perceived regularities form the raw materials for cognitive maps.

The key nuance that is preserved when the metaphor of a map is used to describe cognitive structures is the nuance of flexibility. Tolman (1948) is credited with the label *cognitive map*, but what is mentioned less frequently is that Tolman contrasted cognitive maps with something that he called a *strip map*. A strip map develops when a person learns a specific path by rote learning and has a simple stimulus-response memory of how to get from one place to another. A strip map might take the following form: at this point turn left, at the next choice turn right, and then turn right at each of the next six choices. What is distinctive about a strip map is that each choice point calls up the appropriate response, which means that a structural component is unnecessary. All you need to do is learn a sequence of turns; neither do you need to measure distance, nor do you need very precise directions.

This relatively mindless strip map contrasts with a cognitive map, which tells routes, environmental relationships, and alternative ways to get from one position to another. The important point about Tolman's distinction between cognitive maps and strip maps is his feeling that you need to invoke the concept of a cognitive map when there is some evidence of flexible behavior, or when, in other words, we find that people can deal with alternative starting positions and alternative routes to a goal.

*Cognitive Maps as Epistemological Structures.* The concept of maps in organization theory dates back at least to Paul Goodman's attempt (1968) to operationalize Lewin's concept of life-space by applying it to regions unique to organizations (such as the authority region, reward region, salary region, promotion region, organizational problem region, financial region). Goodman's interest was in the extent to which managers differentiated regions that were closer and farther from them personally (salary and promotion regions were seen to be closer to the personality than were financial or authority regions) and whether the degree of differentiation was related to hierarchal level, level of aspiration, job involvement, or cognitive complexity. The issue of variations in differentiation has remained a staple in cognitive approaches, and it remains a relatively neglected property of cause maps.

A cognitive map approach to organizations begins with the recognition that participants edit their own organizational experience into patterns of personal knowledge. A representation of that knowledge is called a *cognitive map.* A cognitive map consists of the concepts and the relations a participant uses to understand organizational situations. When we consider all possible types of relations among concepts, such as contiguity, proximity, continuity, resemblance, and implication, then an exhaustive mapping of these relations can be called a cognitive map. If we limit ourselves to mapping only causality relations, as we do in this chapter, then we talk about a more specific form of cognitive map called a *cause map.* Thus, a cause map is a form of cognitive map that incorporates concepts tied together by causality relations.

Other people have described cognitive maps and cause

maps in roughly similar ways. For example, Eden, Jones, Sims, and Smithin (1981) state that a cognitive map "consists of concepts (idiomatically expressed in the client's own phrasing) linked by arrows representing a causal link between the concepts of the form 'concept A has consequences for or can be explained by concept B' " (p. 40). Hart (1977, pp. 115–116) says: "I will define cognitive maps as sets of causal beliefs or assertions though some scholars use the term to stand for general beliefs about the fundamental characteristics of some aspect of a physical or social environment, whether or not such beliefs are causal. . . . Other scholars are interested in sets of causal assertions as they are used in discussions and arguments among groups of policymakers. Such sets are more correctly called rhetorical maps, because they do not assume that the individuals believe the causal assertions that they make in order to persuade others to go along with a particular policy."

*Cause Maps as Epistemological Structures.* A cause map develops as the mind reflects on experience, constructs concepts in the form of variables, and imposes connections among these variables. When variables are connected, they become meaningful since meaning flows from relationships. Thus, the more equivocality the individual can remove from experience by means of concept-structures, the more the world will make sense to that person, and the more productive that person can be. Structures such as cause maps remove equivocality, both because they place concepts in relation to one another, and because they impose structure on vague situations. Since structures are simpler than the qualities on which they are imposed, they reduce equivocality. These are the basic mechanisms by which a cause map operates, and these mechanisms define the basic properties of a cause map: namely, variables and cause ties.

The concepts contained in cause maps are variables. "A concept variable is something like 'the amount of security in Persia'; something that can take on different values such as 'a great amount of security' or 'a small amount of security.' A cognitive map allows great flexibility in the variables. They may be continuous variables, such as more or less of something; or they may be dichotomous variables, such as the existence or nonexistence of something. But whatever type of concept is represented, it is always regarded as a variable that can take on more than one value" (Axelrod, 1976, p. 59).

Since leaders establish organizations to serve their needs, we expect the language used by the participants in organizations to be rich in variables. We also expect the language and models of analysts of organizations to be rich in those variables. Assume, for example, that an orchestra musician already possesses the higher-level concept "performance." That noun can be elaborated into the variables "quality of performance," "number of performances," "satisfactoriness of performance." Eventually the attributes "quality," "number," and "satisfactoriness" become qualifiers that can be attached to practically any noun to transform it into a variable.

Once people have formed concepts or variables, they begin to tie them together to make sense of them. Concepts can be tied by causality relations based on logic, observed matters of fact, or beliefs when evidence is not available (Hall, 1984, p. 908). In most representations of the causality relations between concepts, the simple notations of plus (+), meaning a direct relationship, minus (-), meaning an inverse relationship, and zero (0), meaning no relationship, are sufficient. These notations are sufficient because decision makers typically do not use a more refined set of gradations than this (Axelrod, 1976, p. 69).

In the cause map procedure called the *Self-Q* technique (Bougon, 1983), a more refined description of the strength of causality ties is used. These Self-Q measures are based on both theoretical considerations (Weick, 1979, p. 227) and empirical findings that indicate experience is *curvilinear*. That is, experience is not just either "+" *or* "-" (as assumed, for example, in the studies of Axelrod and associates) but is "+" *and* "-." This represents the fact that some amount of a variable is good, but too much of the same variable is bad (or vice versa). For example, many studies have demonstrated that as stress increases, task performance improves, yet beyond some optimal level, as stress keeps increasing, performance then degrades.

Even though all experience has this curvilinear quality,

specific experiences sample relatively small portions of the complete curvilinear function. In a single experience, people seldom see the whole range of values as well as the shape of the whole function. What people do experience is relationships that differ, depending on which portion of the curve they operate in. Thus, in the previous example, some of the time more stress leads to more task performance, some of the time more stress leads to less performance, and some of the time (in the vicinity of the optimal level of stress—at the near-flat top of the curve) a change in stress has no effect on performance.

Such partial observations that reveal only portions of the whole curvilinear function are the stuff of which individual reflections on experience are made. For purpose of cause-effect inference, the most accurate way to portray these opposing reflections on the same experience is to say that the experience is *equivocal.* Equivocal does not mean unclear or uncertain; rather, it means that there are two or more clear, distinct meanings for several related variables because the relationships among them differ. Thus, the cause-effect relation between stress and task performance is both more/more (+) *and* more/less (-). A sensitive mapping technique will capture the fact that for a person an experience often means both one thing and its opposite and that what varies is the proportion of time each relation occurs.

*Cause Maps as Collective Structures.* Cause maps are relevant to groups as well as individuals. When people try to make sense of their joint experiences, they must guide each other through three levels of agreement: (1) agreement on which concepts capture and abstract their joint experience (for example, "This is a grievance, but this is humorous"), (2) consensus on relations among these concepts (for example, "Smaller groups lead to higher-quality work"), and (3) similarity of view on how these related concepts affect each party (for example, "I feel ignored in large groups") and on how they themselves can affect the concepts (for example, "In small groups I can make things happen").

Cause maps can be coordinated with relatively little shared understanding (Weick, 1979, p. 91), a characteristic that is important to emphasize given the current emphasis on shared beliefs in organizational culture. Concerted action is possible where there is common relevance of two concepts in two cause maps and a *double interact* (Weick, 1979) to link the maps.

The following example illustrates how two concepts become linked by a double interact: Two actors, A and B, both with quite different cause maps, may become organized when person B wants X and person A has the capacity to fulfill X. To make this example more concrete, assume that A is President Reagan, and he wants person B, Senator Bill Bradley, to vote for his tax program. Concept Y, a vote for the tax program, is an element in both maps but the meaning of that element differs in each map because it is connected to different ideas. Reagan's question is "How do I get Bradley's vote?"

Reagan has to create some object X that Bradley might desire, and then he has to create a desire on Bradley's part for that object. Reagan has to define an X in his own map that he can deliver, and he then has to create a desire for X in Bradley's map. We now have two concepts that are salient to two people, and that is all we need for an initial collective exchange and the possibility for subsequent coordinated action.

In order to coordinate the two maps, three things must happen. First, objects (Xs) for wants need to be identified or created. Second, wants need to be identified or created. And third, wants and objects need to be linked. This process is not easy, since it requires that one person reconstruct someone else's definition of who he or she is. This is difficult to pull off because people often define who they are by what they want ("I want influence"), or by what they have ("I have a Rolls-Royce"), or by what they know ("I know software"), or by what they believe ("I am a Buddhist").

The important point is that the basic condition for starting a collective structure is a situation in which A needs B's Y, and this can occur when B is persuaded to want A's X. What was originally an *interact* (A wanted B's Y, and B's Y could fulfill what A wanted) has become a double interact because for A to get Y, A has to give or create some valued X to B in return.

The core of a double interact is the cause map, since concepts and relationships are what are being negotiated. A double interact forms when we discover that I can be a cause of your X, you can be a cause of my Y, and momentarily we have no better source for these concepts and relationships.

The concepts of interact, double interact, and *assemblage* are illustrated by Hall's (1984, p. 915) description of five separate cause maps for five key departments as the *Saturday Evening Post* (circulation, publisher, editorial, production, and President and Board). The maps constitute a single organization because there are inter-map interacts across the maps. Specific goals in one department become policy variables in other departments. This common relevance of concepts is what ties these departments together into an organization (although their relevance is different in each department).

The important point is that one way to describe collective structure is to identify common elements in diverse cause maps that are linked across maps.

There are two other forms that collective cause maps can take. One form is a *composite cause map,* which is represented in the extensive work done by Eden and his associates (for example, Eden, Jones, and Sims, 1979 and 1983). These consultants-scientists strive to develop a common appreciation of a group situation by first having individuals describe their own idiosyncratic cause maps. Then individuals see both the cause maps constructed by others and a composite map that contains all the concepts and relations found in all the individuals' maps. Using these complex data as a point of departure, people discuss, edit, and reaffirm views in an attempt to build a team map that is both accurate and acceptable. The final team map is developed by a process that resembles the nominal group technique. The resulting composite cause map represents what the group thinks, is likely to perceive, and how it defines itself.

The third form of collective cause map is an *average map* (Bougon, Weick, and Binkhorst, 1977; Ford and Hegarty, 1984; Komocar, 1985, pp. 143–170). To illustrate, in the individual cause maps constructed by the nineteen musicians in the Utrecht Jazz Orchestra, each cell entry was either a –1 (indicating an inverse causality relationship between the column and row variables), a 0 (indicating no causality relationship), or a +1 (indicating a direct relationship). When these entries are added across musicians, the cell entries in the average map could range from -19/19 to +19/19, depending on the number of people who thought a relationship existed and the direction of the relationship. The average map, therefore, is the algebraic mean of the signed links reported by the nineteen participants.

Causality relationships mentioned by a significant number of orchestra members (see p. 610 in Bougon, Weick, and Binkhorst, 1977, for a summary of significant relationships) can then be treated as a consensual view of what the orchestra is. As with any average, no one cause map may coincide exactly with the average map. However, all nineteen musicians share at least two variables in common, so minimal structures are present among all possible pairs. Since these musicians interacted at least four hours every week, they developed common understanding of many variables and similar definitions of new variables that were added to the map.

In summary, collective cause maps can take the form of an assemblage (Hall, 1984), a composite (Eden, Jones, Sims, and Smithin, 1981), or an average (Bougon, Weick, and Binkhorst, 1977). In each case, dependencies between people involve concepts and potential exchanges. The importance of exchange is clearest in the case of an assemblage and least clear in the case of an average map. In an average map, people can share beliefs but not have the mutual dependencies implied by an exchange. However, since most concepts have dependencies built into them (for example, "quality of orchestra performance" involves mutual dependence), average maps usually involve exchange.

## Methods for Gathering Cause Maps

The root of the cause map perspective lies in subjective reality; thus, the closer one gets to the subject, the closer one gets to what he or she thinks and means, and the closer one remains to the language of the subject, the greater the validity of the resulting map. Cognitive maps can be gathered through several different means, but the main ones used so far are

1.  Systematic coding of documents representing the writings or statements of an individual.
2.  Coding of verbatim transcripts of private meetings in which the individual participates.
3.  Eliciting causality beliefs through questionnaires and interviews.

Hart (1977, p. 117) makes the following observations about these three methods. The advantage of documents is that they represent an individual's beliefs and are easy to find. Since they are plentiful, documents allow one to trace changes in beliefs over time. Furthermore, since the individual is usually writing for a general audience, the causality assertions are likely to represent defensible beliefs, although they may not always represent sincere beliefs.

Precisely because of the sincerity problem, many believe that participants are more likely to reveal their beliefs in private decision-making contexts (see, for example, Levi and Tetlock, 1980), which means that verbatim transcripts of private meetings may be more valid sources of cognitive maps than are public documents. However, not only are transcripts rarer but they may also have problems of sincerity. Insincerity also may be a drawback in questionnaires and interviews, although such dissembling can sometimes be assessed by items inserted to detect it. Also, face-to-face interviews may provide crucial nonverbal information that suggests deception.

Insincerity is not the only problem when cause maps are collected. A more stubborn problem is the fact that meaning does not reside in the labels attached to concepts. Instead, meaning lies in the map itself—that is, in the larger pattern among the other labels to which a specific label is linked and between these other labels and the specific label. Only the speaker can know for sure what any concept means, and investigators impute meaning at the risk of misrepresentation.

Researchers should remember that in any cause map "nodes are codes." When participants mention a specific concept (for example, "the home"), the observer cannot know for sure what lies behind that phrase. In order to guard against arrogance, observers need to treat phrases as coded buzzwords that imply a coherent set of meanings in a cause map. Precisely because nodes are codes, it is more defensible to do content-free analyses that examine structures and the placement of concepts than to puzzle over the meanings of the words themselves. Thus, the Utrecht Jazz Orchestra analysis focuses on associations between the placement of concepts in a flow of causality and on other properties, such as controllability, goal stability, and coalitions.

Problems that can occur when observers presume that their own meanings are identical with those a participant would develop are illustrated by a study forecasting energy use. Diffenbach (1982) constructed cause maps to understand which elements were involved in peak-load pricing of electricity, and he developed a composite map on the basis of judgments by three members of a research team (p. 143). Diffenbach's work is exemplary because he makes explicit the reasoning used by his research team to develop the links and concepts they used (see pp. 144–145). Nevertheless, a weakness of the Diffenbach work is that what you really want to know in peak-load pricing is how the electricity users see the situation, since they are the ones who are going to have to choose, for example, between taking a shower at night when the rates are cheap and taking a shower in the morning when they are not. Those are the mundane decisions that will nullify or affirm a peak-load pricing mechanism, yet those are the very data that are unavailable.

In the literature, there are several gradations in the extent to which researchers move closer to the participants and give them greater control over what they insert in their cause maps. For example, Roos and Hall (1980) interviewed and observed people over a three-year period and then drew a cause map for them. That is an improvement over Axelrod (1976) because there is fuller information available than is found in single documents stripped of their context of delivery and intention.

Ford and Hegarty (1984) move one step closer to participants' thoughts and meanings than Roos and Hall. They extracted contingency variables from the research literature, but rather than connect these variables as they thought participants would, they had managers and MBA students connect them. Somewhat troublesome is that these variables are abstract and not anchored in any specific organization, which makes it difficult to tell what referent the subjects had in mind when they, for example, connected size with formalization and division of work. The fact that similar connections were made by MBAs and the managers suggests either common socialization, common ignorance, or equivalent stereotypes. But what we cannot be sure of is precisely what it means when people take labels used by academics and connect them the way academics connect them.

To move even closer, researchers can have participants both create the variables and connect them. This is what happened in the study of the Utrecht Jazz Orchestra. Musicians generated a single list of seventeen variables, which they then causally connected.

There still is the possibility that even though the seventeen UJO variables codify statements made by specific musicians, the labels we have used have more meaning for some musicians than for others. To move even closer to the natural language of participants, Bougon (1983, 1986) developed the self-questioning (Self-Q) technique (see also Baird, 1984a, 1984b). As its name implies, people ask themselves questions about whatever topic is being mapped, and concepts are then extracted from the questions. This format is fruitful because people are not practiced in defending against questions that they ask themselves and over which they have control. Furthermore, since the person is asking questions rather than making assertions, the questions themselves seem harmless.

Once the causality assertions have been collected, they need to be displayed systematically for purposes of analysis.

The general aim of analyses conducted on cause maps is to discover universal structural regularities in these maps. Specific aims include the study of universal relationships between these structural regularities and a person's values, means, goals, emotions, influence, power, expertise, inconsistencies, sense of self, and formation of double interacts leading to the creation of organizations. Another major aim of the analyses is to simplify and clarify individual cause maps to reveal the dominant flow of causality that people impose on their experience.

In the pursuit of these aims, most cause map analyses start with an *adjacency matrix* in which causes are listed at the West side of the matrix and effects are listed at the North side (see Figure 2). Thus the matrix summarizes causality flowing from the concepts listed on the left to the concepts listed on the top.

**Figure 2. The Adjacency Matrix for Summarizing Cause Ties.**

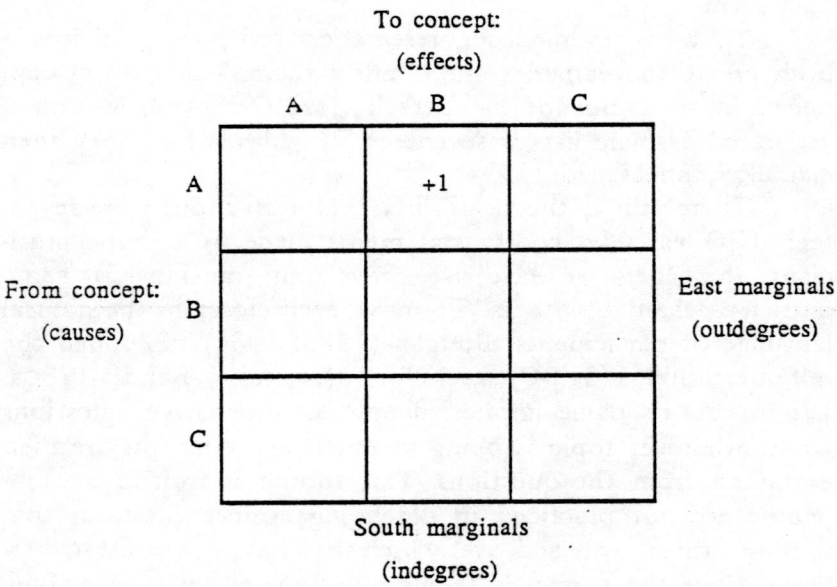

Example:
    IF variable A is "people in the group" and variable B is "I feel ignored"
    AND the person reported the cause-effect relation "The more people in the group, the more I feel ignored"
    THEN entry in cell AB will be +1, indicating a direct (more/more) relation between A and B (from A to B).

In this matrix, if we sum absolute cell values in each North-South column, we learn how many causes terminate in each effect. We write these sums at the South margin of the matrix. These South marginal values are labeled *indegrees* because they summarize the relative density of relationships flowing into a particular variable. Dense flows into a variable correspond to a person's tacit inference of a goal, or end, or outcome (Bougon, Weick, and Binkhorst, 1977; Komocar, 1985).

If we sum absolute cell values in each West-East row, we learn how many effects each cause has created. We write these sums at the East margin of the matrix. These East marginal values are labeled *outdegrees* because they summarize the relative density of relationships flowing out of a particular variable. Theory and data suggest that dense flows out of a variable correspond to a person's tacit inference of a value, or reason, or imperative (Bougon, 1985; Komocar, 1985). More is known about the pattern of South marginals (hence about tacit goals, ends, or outcomes), but the interesting question lies in the degree to which a rank ordering of the East marginals reveals tacit values, reasons, or imperatives imposed on a situation.

The important point about working with marginals in a cause-effect matrix is that they untangle causality relations and reveal order in the information contained in the map. For example, if the flow into a variable is more dense than the flow from that variable, then the North-East portion of the ordered cause matrix will have more or stronger or both more and stronger cell entries than the South-West portion. The ratio of one portion to another tells us both how much structure exists and whether there is a dominant direction in which causality flows. Thus, we are able to specify both a vectorial and a scalar measure of order in a social system.

Cause maps usually contain dense patterns of relations among variables and we need to know which relations are dominant. Each variable in a cause map can have an effect on every other variable, either directly or indirectly through paths involving other variables. Indirect paths can be calculated by using adjacency matrices and then raising the adjacency matrix to successive powers. Squaring an adjacency matrix, for example, will give paths of length 2 (for example, the effect of B on D through C), while raising the matrix to the third power would indicate how many indirect effects there are of B on D through paths that contain three links. Reachability matrices have been used by Axelrod (1976, pp. 350–353), Ford and Hegarty (1984, p. 283), and Bougon, Weick, and Binkhorst (1977), and are the basis on which Bougon (1986) extracts the dominant linkages in a cause map using the Self-Q technique. Two variables that are linked by a large number of strong direct and indirect paths are assumed to be more influential in determining what a person does and sees than are two variables that are linked by fewer weak paths. The more ways one variable can affect another variable, the more robust and dominant that linkage is assumed to be.

### Cause Map Findings

Since much cause map research consists of tool development and atheoretical description, the preceding sections already contain much of what has been found in cause map research.

The two most complete, self-contained organizational analyses of cause maps are Bougon, Weick, and Binkhorst (1977) and Hall (1984). These two works, each devoted to a single organization, provide models for cause map investigations because they are theory-driven, explore collective maps, incorporate both lineal and reciprocal causation, and generate new theory and methodology.

Bougon, Weick, and Binkhorst (1977) develop ways to untangle raw cause data and show how causality flows in an orderly manner that can be highly hierarchal. The study demonstrates that the orderliness of a social structure can be assessed by the structure of causality generated by the members of that structure.

Hall's (1984) longitudinal study of the *Saturday Evening Post* is noteworthy because he shows that in the early stages, the pattern of cause maps led to growth of the firm, but as the pattern among maps changed, these same maps destroyed the firm. Thus, there is clear evidence that maps can have a tangible effect. Hall analyzes cause maps among coalitions, and shows that it is the balance of cause map logics among these coalitions that determines whether the organization survives or disappears. Since all of this is interpreted in the context of strategy and policy, Hall shows the tight fit between cause maps and strategic thinking.

Several specific cause map findings also seem worth pursuing here. We have seen that there are dominant links in any cause map and that they show a distinct pattern, with causality flowing only or almost only from left to right along a causality continuum. Although this finding is content-free, positions along this flow of causation are sensible. Ford and Hegarty (1984, p. 286) found that variables toward the left-hand end of the causality continuum contain context factors, that the middle variables correspond to structure, and that the right-hand end corresponds to performance variables. In the Utrecht Jazz Orchestra, variables at the left were givens (for example, difficulty of number played), variables in the middle were means (for example, time spent rehearsing), and variables at the right were ends (for example, quality of the band's performance). Roos and Hall (1980) describe policy variables as being at the left, intervening variables as being in the middle, and utilities (that is, ultimate pragmatic values) as being at the right-hand end, sorted more finely into utilities for the director and utilities for the sponsoring agency.

Variables at the right that terminate activity sequences have a distinctive character not found in variables at the left that initiate causality sequences. Ends contain significantly fewer logical inconsistencies than do origins, due to a greater abundance of deviation-amplifying loops at the right end of the causality continuum. Thus, ends are more sensible but also more unstable and subject to change because they are nested in positive feedback loops (Bougon, Weick, and Binkhorst, 1977, p. 624).

Not only are different positions along the causality continuum sensible, but different positions also seem to have different degrees of controllability. As we found in the Utrecht Jazz Orchestra, if a variable is controlled by other variables (it has a high indegree value), people tend to say they have control over that variable. Apparently, if a variable is controlled by several other variables, then people feel that they too can control that variable because they too are causal agents. These findings support what we have called the *confluence model*. If there are lots of paths to a variable, then there is a better chance that an individual can affect one of those paths and the variable itself.

Notice, however, that the degree of personal influence is dependent on where the individual tacitly places himself or herself in that flow of causation. If self as a concept is placed at the right, then many variables affect it, and the self has relatively little effect on any other variables. This would correspond to a situation often described as *external locus of control.* If the position of self moves more toward the left-hand end of a causality continuum, then this is more consistent with an interpretation of an internal locus of control, high self-efficacy, or being an origin rather than a pawn.

Cause maps contain the two basic components of cognitive complexity: differentiation and integration. *Integration* is measured by the number of connections among differentiated concepts. *Differentiation,* the number of characteristics or dimensions of a problem that are included, is often fixed by the observer, but when it is not, complexity can be assessed. For example, in Self-Q assessments, degree of differentiation is measured by the number of concept variables in a question relative to the logarithm of the number of words in a question (the logarithm reduces the influence of variations in the length of the questions). Levi and Tetlock (1980) found that cognitive complexity, coded from transcripts using Schroder, Driver, and Streufert's (1967) content rules, correlated significantly (0.57) with complexity in cognitive maps developed to portray the same events. Thus, maps may provide a means to examine requisite variety and the development of complicated thinking (Bartunek, Gordon, and Weathersby, 1983).

One of the more durable findings in studies of cognitive process is that crisis-produced stress leads to low-quality information processing. This finding has received modest support in work on cause maps (for example, Hall, 1984, p. 922), although it is not clear that the proposition has yet been tested adequately. Levi and Tetlock (1980) studied transcripts of conferences in 1941 among Japanese policy makers who were discussing whether to go to war against the United States. It was found that from June 15, 1941, to December 7, 1941, there was a slight tendency for cause maps to become simpler, this effect being most pronounced for the navy chief of staff, Nagano. Levi and Tetlock question whether this is a strong test of the disruptive stress hypothesis since a key aspect of crisis—namely, surprise—was missing, and since the Japanese had relatively high control over their environment and could do unilateral planning rather than face an escalation of mutual antagonism and hostility (spirals of mutual hostility seem to force simplification).

Since there is good evidence that decision makers in crisis consider less information, focus on shorter term consequences, and stereotype more, it seems likely that cause maps would not be shielded from these effects. Specifically, as stress increases, dominant links should exert relatively stronger effects over what is perceived. Concepts that are more complex and more recently learned would be likely to disappear from maps sooner than older, simpler concepts. Cause loops, which are hard enough to understand in times of quiescence, would be likely to seem especially baffling in crisis and to be ignored (see Hall, 1984, for data supporting this deduction). If a crisis lowers perceived control over events, then the more severe the crisis, the more "self" would be shifted toward the right end of the causality continuum. A shift of self toward·the right might even induce the perception that an event is a crisis, since less seems to be under one's personal control. If stress simplifies cognition, variables with extreme indegree and outdegree values (that is, variables at the Ends and Values extremities of the causality continuum) should remain salient, but variables with intermediate values should become merged, indistinguishable, and of relatively little value in sensemaking.

A puzzling finding, especially considering the origin of cause map technique (Maruyama, 1963), is that feedback loops are relatively rare in cause maps. This finding takes on added importance because executives of the *Saturday Evening Post* neglected the one prominent cause loop that existed in their cause maps: namely, having more readers leads to a lower advertising rate per reader, more advertising pages, and more magazine pages, which in turn attracts yet more readers. Neglect of this prominent cause loop eventually led to the demise of their organization (Hall, 1984, pp. 916, 923).

When cognitive maps are coded from documents, it is rare

to find loops (for example, Hart, 1977; Levi and Tetlock, 1980). When Hall simulated the *Saturday Evening Post* on a computer, subjects were unable to detect any of the six feedback loops that were built into the model. Even more important, when the loops were pointed out to them, they could not interpret them (p. 915). This pattern of no significant strong loops was found in the Utrecht Jazz Orchestra data, although numerous weak loops were found.

Axelrod (1976) and Porac (1981) found two-step cause loops when people responded to concepts two at a time, which is the format used in the Utrecht Jazz Orchestra. When people generate their cause maps spontaneously, loops are less likely to be found. Diffenbach's (1982, pp. 140-141) cause map had several loops, but recall that three persons experienced in electrical engineering produced that map. Roos and Hall (1980) found important loops in their study of an extended-care hospital.

Given the potential importance of loops for survival and change (Maruyama, 1963; Ashton, 1976; Masuch, 1985), how are we to interpret the fact that loops seldom appear in cause maps (Axelrod, 1976, pp. 231-239) or appear under unusual conditions? One answer is that loops do not appear because they are not there when people act. Despite the fact that we talk about feedback all the time, there is evidence that people who normally perceive loops ignore them and impose a clear, categorical, lineal structure on their experience when there is uncertainty (Steinbruner, 1974). Hall (1984, p. 919) argues that when there is indeterminacy, executives often pick the simplest and most direct arguments that offer immediate, tangible results, and favor the dominant coalition. These preferences effectively rule out loops. Levi and Tetlock (1980) find that maps tend to be simplified under stress. Since uncertainty produces stress and since organizations operate under uncertainty much of the time, we might expect to find relatively simple, nonrecursive structures in dominant cause maps.

It could also be argued that lineal relationships are sufficient to get things done in a world where there is so much turnover that the effects of an action seldom affect the originator, who has left by the time the consequences become clearer. A lineal view of causality may also be an appropriate perception, especially in the early stages of organizing. When people explore situations, they take several actions, only some of which have consequences. In the early stages of exploration, simple stimulus-response connections are sufficient to portray what is happening.

Dominant loops also may be absent from cause maps either because loops are relatively weak (weak loops can still produce regularity if they cycle often enough) or because it takes parts of several different individual maps to form a dominant loop. The connected variables that form loops in Maruyama's (1963) description of how cities deal with refuse are connected only because several actors acted interdependently. The assemblage of their maps made one dominant loop and that loop is what provided stability for the larger social systems (see also Axelrod, 1976, p. 242).

In summary, cautioned by the reminder that nodes are codes and that inferences need to be triangulated (that is, verified by multiple independent measurements), there are several things we can learn from cause maps. We can look for the degree to which the relationships are structured, the degree to which tacit goals are singular or plural, and what the content of those goals might be. We can also ask whether the tacit values that drive activities are singular or plural, what the content of those values might be, and what the dominant linkages are. It is important to assess the degree to which the self is seen as an origin (is it far to the left?) or a pawn (is it far to the right?) in the flow of causality, the extent of equivocality present in the cause relations, and the degree to which the Values or Ends extremities of the causality continuum contain relatively more or fewer logical inconsistencies. Finally, cause maps can reveal the extent to which loops either stabilize or destabilize that portion of the causality continuum where the loops cluster; for example, in the UJO, destabilizing loops clustered around the indegree pole and therefore tended to destabilize goals. We can also learn what concepts exist that may enable one person to be linked with another person and thus create an organization.

## Implications

Cause mapping is attractive because it lends substance to phenomenology, is an alternative to case studies as a means to analyze social construction of reality (Pfeffer, 1985, p. 385), and is a means to move higher in Boulding's (1956) hierarchy of systems levels. A cause map starts where people actually are in their understanding of issues and preserves the natural language of their understanding. Respect for understanding, however, does not occur at the expense of analysis, since structure is analyzed while content is left in the subject's own words.

Cause maps also represent a blend of the rational and the nonrational (Shweder, 1984). Maps contain inconsistencies, equivocal relations, tacit values, and concepts originating in metaphors, yet they also contain the more rational components of means-ends relations—that is, observed regularities, consensually validated relationships, changes in response to experience, and sensible inconsistencies.

*Implications for Research.* Axelrod's data suggest that people do act rationally within the limits of the map they build, but the map is simplified because loops and inconsistent pathways are ignored. People are both rational (they make correct explanations, predictions, and deductions) and irrational (by ignoring data, they form a map from which it is easy to make deductions). "The picture of a decision maker that emerges from the analysis of cognitive maps is of one who has more beliefs than he can handle, who employs a simplified image of the policy environment that is structurally easy to operate with, and who then acts rationally within the context of his simplified image" (Axelrod, 1976, p. 244).

The research question implied is "under what conditions can people build, maintain, and apply more complex maps so that a wider range of problems is represented appropriately?" As we are better able to assess differentiation and integration in cause maps, and as we are better able to state the conditions under which people can complicate their understanding, the attention bottleneck implied by maps with no loops and inconsistencies will be removed and appropriateness should improve.

Against this background, it becomes crucial to see how the cause maps of experts differ from those of novices. We need to know such things as whether experts differentiate more, integrate more, have less hierarchy and more loops or whether the reverse is the case. We also need to know whether experts change their maps less often or more often, and whether they change only those links that are minor and preserve those links that are strong links or whether the opposite is the case. Do experts consistently place "self" in positions with greater control over causality flows, or do they place "self" at different positions depending on their expertise concerning the issue being addressed? Questions such as these are variations on the theme that structure, rather than competencies in making inferences, predicts when decision makers will make better policy choices.

Aside from the issue of the ratio of rational to nonrational components in a cause map and the relevance of these ratios to appropriate perception, there are several other research implications of what has been reviewed.

The level of analysis appropriate for a cause map is the individual. Thus, psychological processes suggest conditions under which cause maps should be especially influential (Levi and Tetlock, 1980, p. 196; Holsti, 1976). Cause maps should exert influence when the situation is nonroutine and requires something more than standard operating procedures. Maps will have more effect when key actors are relatively free of organizational constraints, when overload necessitates simplifying strategies, when stress impairs the performance of cognitively complex tasks, and when ambiguity is high.

Hall's (1984) examination of changes in cause maps over twenty years at the *Saturday Evening Post* raises the important issue of how maps develop. Documentation of the development of maps is crucial because of primacy effects, the regression under crisis conditions to first-learned concepts, and the likelihood that assimilation is less cognitively effortful than is accommodation (meaning that older meanings dominate and incorporate newer information). Study of the development of cause maps is also important because groups and collectivities form around concepts and because concepts that are shared early should exert disproportionate effects on who is judged to be similar and thus available for future interaction.

A plausible sequence for the development of cause maps is suggested by the dimensions of presumed analyzability of the external environment (high/low) and intensity of search processes within the environment (active/passive) (Daft and Weick, 1984). The presumption of high analyzability occurs when people assume that the environment is measurable, determinant, logical, and that correct interpretations can be discovered. The presumption of low analyzability occurs when people assume that the environment is indeterminant and subjective, and that interpretations are created and imposed. Active search occurs when people move around in the environment and act to see what responds and with what consequences. Active searchers perform trials in order to learn what an error is and are often described as proactive. Passive search occurs when people accept whatever information the environment gives them, and try to discover the pattern in those data. This style is often labeled reactive.

When the dimensions of active and passive search and analyzable and unanalyzable environment are combined, the sequence shown in Figure 3 is suggested. When people face an unknown environment, they act to see what happens (Cell 1). If some action is repeatedly followed by the same effect, this leads to an isolated if-then proposition (for example, "If I talk about money, then more people pay attention to what I say"). A series of separate actions coupled with separate consequences generates pairs of related concepts that are not linked among the pairs.

As the person continues to act and believes he or she knows the environment more fully (Cell 2), pairs of causally connected concepts become linked into chains, and more remote effects are seen because the person now knows what to look for.

As more chains and more data accumulate, the person spends less time acting and more time analyzing connections that spread among more variables (Cell 3). As a result, some effects are now seen to be causal for earlier events that influenced

Figure 3. Development of Cause Maps.

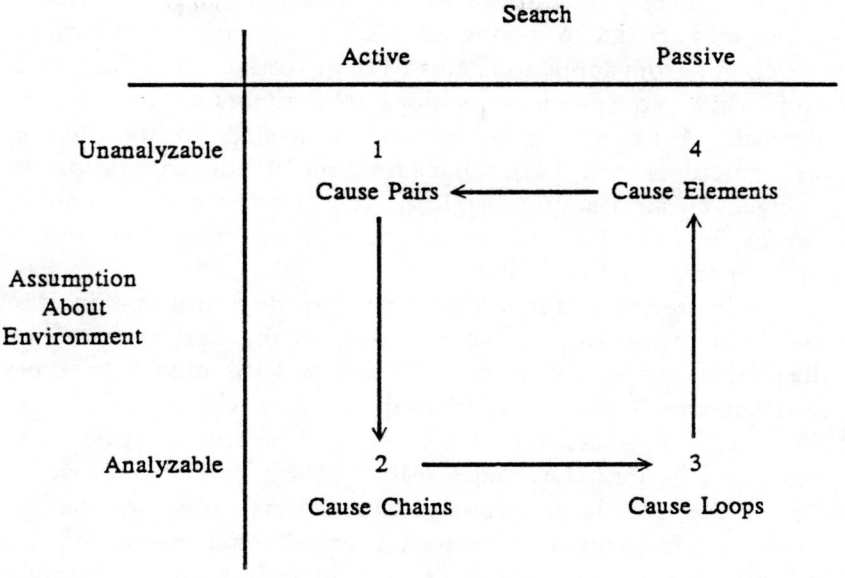

these effects. When loops are added to pairs and chains, the complexity of a cause map increases dramatically and the map may become an armchair cosmology, disconnected and no longer edited by firsthand experience in the world it supposedly represents.

It is this very lack of connection with experience and of updating that now causes the map to disintegrate into arbitrary pairs and chains (Cell 4), none of which correspond to events that can be discovered or created. When a map disintegrates, the person has little choice but to wade back into the world again, act, and see what now happens (Cell 1).

This model suggests several possibilities. Pairs and chains are compatible with action, while loops and elements are not. The maps of active people should have fewer loops than the maps of passive people. If newcomers are socialized by being presented with chains and loops, their sensemaking should be accelerated since chains and loops represent cause maps at a more advanced stage of development. As an organization disintegrates, the maps of its chief actors should move in a reverse direction—namely, from loops to chains to pairs. In this situation, it becomes crucial to distinguish Cell 2 maps from Cell 4 maps. Movement from loops to chains to pairs would signal disintegration, while movement from loops to elements to pairs means, ironically, further development and an attempt to find the simple structures and pairs that are crucial for adaptation to changed circumstances. In short, the life cycle of organizing should be traceable through changes in the maps that reflect and constrain that organizing.

Greater attention has been paid to the South marginals or the Ends region of a cause map than to the East marginals or the Values region of a map. Variables with high outdegrees (East marginals) would be treated as values within the context of the UJO analyses, but this would not be true in other cause map formulations. Levi and Tetlock (1980, p. 201), for example, define a value as a variable that affects utility without affecting other concepts. However, a variable characterized in this way would have low outdegrees, would appear toward the right end of a causality continuum, and would be of questionable meaning since utility is an observer concept, not a participant concept. Since rankings by indegree are not a mirror image of rankings by outdegree, each ranking seems to be tapping something unique. What is being tapped differentially is not yet clear, especially in the case of variables that cluster toward the left end of a causality continuum.

Future research should also spell out the links between cause maps and other organizational concepts. For example, the developmental sequence proposed earlier might parallel the way organizational culture develops (for example, initial agreement on causal pairs followed by agreement on chains and then on loops). Cultural evolution might also follow the stages implicit in the design of Eden, Jones, Sims, and Smithin (1981)—namely, people articulate their own maps, then view other maps, and finally build composite maps.

A cause map is also an ideology (Beyer, 1981) and a basis for a presumption of logic (Weick, 1983). A script (Gioia and Poole, 1984) can be viewed as a strip map—that is, as a frozen deduction from a cause map. Placement of a concept in a map would allow a sharper distinction between causes (at left) and objectives (at right) than has been found in much causal attribution work (Buss, 1978). Hall's (1984) successful prediction of preferred policies from cause maps suggests that policy decisions across time are not a random walk (p. 918). The amount of differentiation and integration in a cause map can be treated as a proxy for requisite variety, which would enable tests of the proposition that it takes variety to destroy variety.

A cause map can represent a motivational structure (House, 1971) if we argue that *expectancies* equal *values, instrumentality* equals *means,* and *valence* equals *goals.* Thus, to put an expectancy theory of motivation in motion, the leader picks means from the middle of an individual's causality continuum and a goal from the right end, shows that high effort will produce a significant change in the means, and that this significant change will cause a desired outcome to occur. Since the leader is working with the employees' own map, rather than with contingencies that are externally imposed and subject to suspicion, linkages should be tighter and motivation higher.

Locus of control is an important variable used by people who study social cognition. Perceptions of control fit neatly into cause maps since the placement of variables toward the right end of a continuum of causality is associated with perceptions of controllability, regardless of the content of the variables. This suggests that future research should explore the effect of placement of variables on perceptions of control, and the effects of controllability on placement. For example, the perception that a variable is a goal might be induced by demonstrating the apparently unrelated idea that the individual is able to control the variable. Conversely, people with an external locus of control might be induced to take more responsibility for a variable if that variable is moved from left to right on the causality continuum and is seen as more controllable.

While there are many more implications for research than we have suggested here, it is important also to discuss implications for practice, since cause maps have several such implications.

*Implications for Practice.* Cause maps are evocative. They lay bare personal cause-effect logic, which in turn forces the individual to confront the reasonableness and validity of tacit cause-effect assumptions. A cause map provides an occasion to think carefully, deeply, and deliberately about an issue.

A decision maker can become a more sophisticated thinker by externalizing and studying a previously implicit map. Particularly attractive is the fact that this externalization does not require dependence on an outside expert and can be done in private.

Axelrod (1976, p. 246) identifies several advantages of "do-it-yourself" mapping. First, the person can be honest in stating beliefs and connections, since no one else will see the map. Second, since the person uses concepts that are personally meaningful, larger maps can be comprehended. Third, the person is not influenced by the preferences and values of an outsider but instead has control over the values that are included. And fourth, "The decision maker will not become overconfident in the methodology . . . since everything is explicit and easy to understand. To the extent that the beliefs are oversimplified so that they can be represented in the format of a cognitive map, the decision maker himself is in a position to evaluate the nature of the oversimplifications, since he made them himself" (p. 246).

When we move from private to public use of cause maps, there is agreement that maps allow groups to diagnose disagreements and manage those disagreements (Pfeffer, 1982, p. 217; Diffenbach, 1982, p. 144). Eden, Jones, Sims, and Smithin (1981), for example, find that a result of negotiations over individual maps among team members is that there is a "careful and gradual change of mutual understanding which is evidenced as each individual map absorbs more concepts from the team maps and, conversely, the team map absorbs more individuality" (p. 43).

Discussions of concepts, relations, and meanings are focused by a cause map graph in ways that are not possible with brainstorming. It is interesting that this focus is accomplished sometimes with less than complete data. Eden, Jones, Sims, and

Smithin (1981) emphasize that they do not assign weights to causality relationships so that people have some latitude for movement during discussion (p. 42). In private, weights are informative, but in public, they may necessitate justification and preclude change. Managers need to develop maps that are easily updateable.

Cause maps have the potential to be used prescriptively and normatively, but this application has yet to be explored. Hart (1977, p. 139) has suggested some standards against which a person's cause map could be judged. First, does the person fail to make distinctions that are commonly made by others? (Hart labels this "conflation of concepts.") Second, do the assertions made agree with those made by people of similar experience and expertise? Third, are the assertions consistent over time? And fourth, do changes in the assertions represent an ability to learn?

Hart summarizes his position about criticizing the cause maps of other people this way: "Perhaps the most important application of cognitive mapping, therefore, would be to provide the user with a list of concepts which he himself distinguished but which others did not, and vice versa. Similarly, one could provide the user with a list of assertions made by others which do not agree with those that he himself would make. The purpose of such an application would be to prevent the sort of talking at cross-purposes that often takes place at political negotiating sessions" (p. 139).

## Conclusion

Maps are guides as well as products. They are guides in the sense that they assimilate uncertain events into an existing structure. Because maps relate an uncertain event to existing concepts, they generate meaning for the event. Maps are also products in the sense that concepts change in order to accommodate new experience.

People often build meaning in novel situations when they impose a structure on those situations and assimilate them. An equivocal situation becomes more sensible when it is assimilated in an existing cause map. Seldom, however, is the fit perfect. Reorganization of concepts often occurs, which means that accommodation is an eventual outcome with cognitive maps. Since cause maps determine what a person will perceive and do in situations, they have a substantial effect on what people call "real."

The important thing to remember about a cause map is that it *is* the organization (Weick, 1979, p. 141). The cause map contains the structure, the process, and the raw materials from which agreements and conflicts are built when people coordinate action.

## References

Ashton, R. H. "Deviation-Amplifying Feedback and Unintended Consequences of Management Accounting Systems." *Accounting, Organizations, and Society,* 1976, *1,* 289–300.

Axelrod, R. (ed.). *Structure of Decision: The Cognitive Maps of Political Elites.* Princeton, N.J.: Princeton University Press, 1976.

Baird, N. "The Use of Cause Maps To Explore an Organizational Question." Unpublished manuscript, Pennsylvania State University, 1984a.

Baird, N. "Procedures for Using the Self-Q Interview for Data Collection." Unpublished manuscript, Pennsylvania State University, 1984b.

Bartunek, J. M., Gordon, J. R., and Weathersby, R. P. "Developing 'Complicated' Understanding in Administrators." *Academy of Management Review,* 1983, *8,* 273–284.

Beyer, J. M. "Ideologies, Values, and Decision Making in Organizations." In P. C. Nystrom and W. H. Starbuck (eds.), *Handbook of Organizational Design.* Vol. 2. New York: Oxford University Press, 1981.

Bougon, M. G. "Uncovering Cognitive Maps: The Self-Q Technique." In G. Morgan (ed.), *Beyond Method: Strategies for Social Research.* Beverly Hills, Calif.: Sage, 1983.

Bougon, M. G. *Uncovering Cognitive Maps: The Self-Q Handbook.* (5th ed.) Privately printed handbook, Pennsylvania State University, 1986.

Bougon, M. G., Gray, B., and Donnellon, A. "Making Sense of Symbols." *Proceedings of the National Academy of Management,* 1985, p. 384.

Bougon, M. G., Weick, K. E., and Binkhorst, D. "Cognition in Organizations: An Analysis of the Utrecht Jazz Orchestra." *Administrative Science Quarterly,* 1977, *22,* 606-639.

Boulding, K. E. "General Systems Theory—The Skeleton of Science." *Management Science,* 1956, *2,* 197-208.

Buss, A. R. "Causes and Reasons in Attribution Theory: A Conceptual Critique." *Journal of Personality and Social Psychology,* 1978, *36,* 1311-1321.

Daft, R. L., and Weick, K. E. "Toward a Model of Organizations as Interpretation Systems." *Academy of Management Review,* 1984, *9,* 284-295.

Diffenbach, J. "Influence Diagrams for Complex Strategic Issues." *Strategic Management Journal,* 1982, *3,* 133-146.

Eden, C., Jones, S., and Sims, D. *Thinking in Organizations.* London: Macmillan, 1979.

Eden, C., Jones, S., and Sims, D. *Messing About in Problems.* Elmsford, N.Y.: Pergamon, 1983.

Eden, C., Jones, S., Sims, D., and Smithin, T. "The Intersubjectivity of Issues and Issues of Intersubjectivity." *Journal of Management Studies,* 1981, *18,* 37-47.

Ford, J. D., and Hegarty, W. H. "Decision Makers' Beliefs About the Causes and Effects of Structure: An Exploratory Study." *Academy of Management Journal,* 1984, *27,* 271-291.

Gioia, D. A., and Poole, P. P. "Scripts in Organizational Behavior." *Academy of Management Review,* 1984, *9,* 449-459.

Goodman, P. S. "The Measurement of an Individual's Organization Map." *Administrative Science Quarterly,* 1968, *13,* 246-265.

Hall, R. I. "The Natural Logic of Management Policy Making: Its Implications for the Survival of an Organization." *Management Science,* 1984, *30,* 905-927.

Hart, J. A. "Cognitive Maps of Three Latin American Policy Makers." *World Politics,* 1977, *30,* 115-140.

Holsti, O. "Foreign Policy Formation Viewed Cognitively." In R. Axelrod (ed.), *Structure of Decision.* Princeton, N.J.: Princeton University Press, 1976.

House, R. J. "A Path Goal Theory of Leader Effectiveness." *Administrative Science Quarterly*, 1971, *16*, 321–338.

Hume, D. *An Inquiry Concerning Human Understanding.* New York: Bobbs-Merrill, 1955. (Originally published 1748.)

Ittelson, W. H. (ed.). *Environmental Cognition.* New York: Seminar Press, 1973.

Komocar, J. M. "Participant Cause Maps of a Work Setting: An Approach to Cognition and Behavior in Organizations." Unpublished doctoral dissertation, University of Illinois at Champaign–Urbana, 1985.

Levi, A., and Tetlock, P. E. "A Cognitive Analysis of Japan's 1941 Decision for War." *Journal of Conflict Resolution*, 1980, *24*, 195–211.

Maruyama, M. "The Second Cybernetics: Deviation-Amplifying Mutual Causal Processes." *American Scientist*, 1963, *51*, 164–179.

Masuch, M. "Vicious Circles in Organizations." *Administrative Science Quarterly*, 1985, *30*, 14–33.

O'Keefe, J., and Nadel, L. *The Hippocampus as a Cognitive Map.* Oxford: Clarendon Press, 1978.

Pfeffer, J. *Organizations and Organization Theory.* Marshfield, Mass.: Pitman, 1982.

Pfeffer, J. "Organizations and Organization Theory." In G. Lindzey and E. Aronson (eds.), *Handbook of Social Psychology.* (3rd ed.) Vol. 1. New York: Random House, 1985.

Porac, J. E. "Causal Loops and Other Intercausal Perceptions in Attributions for Exam Performance." *Journal of Educational Psychology*, 1981, *73*, 587–601.

Roos, L. L., and Hall, R. I. "Influence Diagrams and Organizational Power." *Administrative Science Quarterly*, 1980, *25*, 57–71.

Schroder, H. M., Driver, M., and Streufert, S. *Human Information Processing.* New York: Holt, Rinehart and Winston, 1967.

Selznick, P. *Leadership in Administration.* New York: Harper & Row, 1957.

Shweder, R. A. "Anthropology's Romantic Rebellion Against the Enlightenment, or There's More to Thinking than Reason and Evidence." In R. A. Shweder and R. A. LeVine (eds.), *Culture Theory: Essays on Mind, Self, and Emotion.* Cambridge: Cambridge University Press, 1984.

Steinbruner, J. D. *The Cybernetic Theory of Decision.* Princeton, N.J.: Princeton University Press, 1974.

Tolman, E. C. "Cognitive Maps in Rats and Men." *Psychological Review,* 1948, *55,* 189–208.

Weick, K. E. *The Social Psychology of Organizing.* Reading, Mass.: Addison-Wesley, 1979.

Weick, K. E. "Managerial Thought in the Context of Action." In S. Srivastva and Associates, *The Executive Mind: New Insights on Managerial Thought and Action.* San Francisco: Jossey-Bass, 1983.

# 5

---

# Language and Communication
# in Organizations

## Bridging Cognition and Behavior

### Anne Donnellon

*An overwhelming number of our ordinary, every-
day activities are performed in and through speaking, and most of the rest presuppose linguistic abilities.*

—Coulter (1979, p. 22)

Much the same connection has been said to exist between organization and communication. As long ago as 1938, Barnard
pointed out to us that communication and language are central,
if not critical, factors in the processes of organizing and managing. Other organizational theorists have since sounded the same
refrain, adding that we can learn more about these processes by
studying communication behavior. It has also become well accepted that in order to account for human behavior, we need to
acquire a better understanding of human cognition.

In this chapter, I will integrate these viewpoints into a
concept of organizing as an iterative process of social cognition
and communication. The chapter will review literature that con-
ceptualizes language as a behavioral indicator of cognition, as
social action, and as the context for subsequent behavior. Fur-

thermore, I hope to show that the study of communication behavior is an exceptionally useful vehicle for investigation of the links between cognition and behavior, since communication is indeed the very behavioral code humans have developed in order to display and interpret their cognitions. The central thesis of the chapter is that since much of organizing is an essentially linguistic enterprise, we can profitably investigate the process of organizing by using linguistic data and methods of analysis.

This theoretical perspective on organizational communication implies a different focus of study, as well as a considerably different approach to the data, than most researchers in our field have taken. The focus here is on face-to-face communication behavior in natural organizational settings. The method this chapter proposes is conversational analysis, which derives from several language-related disciplines.

The chapter is organized into seven sections. It begins by presenting a summary of the argument and goes on to define the major terms and concepts used in language description and to provide an overview of some other fields that have examined such data. After discussing the precedents of communication research in the organizational literature, the chapter will suggest a way in which these various perspectives can be integrated and discuss some prospects for research using such an approach. In the conclusion, I will discuss some of the practical implications such a program of study may have.

## The Argument in Brief

The term *social cognition* has come to refer to a body of research that deals with the content and process of our thinking about other people (Taylor and Fiske, 1981). Increasingly, psychologists have recognized that most, if not all, of our cognition is social, by which we mean that it is influenced by other people, starting as early as birth. The developmental argument (Piaget, [1937] 1954; Vygotsky, 1978) is that we comprehend what we experience by comparing our sensory experience with mental schemas developed through interaction with the people around us.

The argument I wish to develop here derives from this psychological perspective: our cognitions develop primarily through our experiences with others and more specifically through communication with those most significant to us (Mead, [1934] 1964). Because of our social nature, we develop codes for the communication of our cognitions and feelings. That is, we have constructed conventionalized rules for the display of our own thoughts and for the interpretation and influence of those of others through our language and communication behavior.

Although such displays are not always intentional, consistent, reliable, clear, or unambiguous, they are nevertheless a key part of our human system for interaction. In order to understand a human activity such as organizing, which involves apparently deliberate, cooperative behavior, we can profitably study the communication through which it occurs. In other words, we can use the means the participants themselves use to make sense of their organizational experience and to take organized action. The sensemaking devices include communication displays and interpretive schemes for comprehending the displays of others.

Before elaborating this argument, I will define some of the terms necessary to the viewpoint that communication behavior can be a useful source of data for understanding organization.

### Definition of Terms

The human system for interaction is essentially a set of communication codes consisting of elements and rules for the behavioral exchange of information. Among the codes commonly used for communication are language, gestures, physical objects such as street signs or architecture, dance, music, and so on. For descriptive purposes, these codes may also be considered to be levels or dimensions of observable communication behavior. Figure 1 is a schematic depiction of these ways of defining communication.

The communication codes this chapter will focus on are language or the linguistic system and the paralinguistic and pro-

Figure 1. Dimensions and Levels of the Human Communication System.

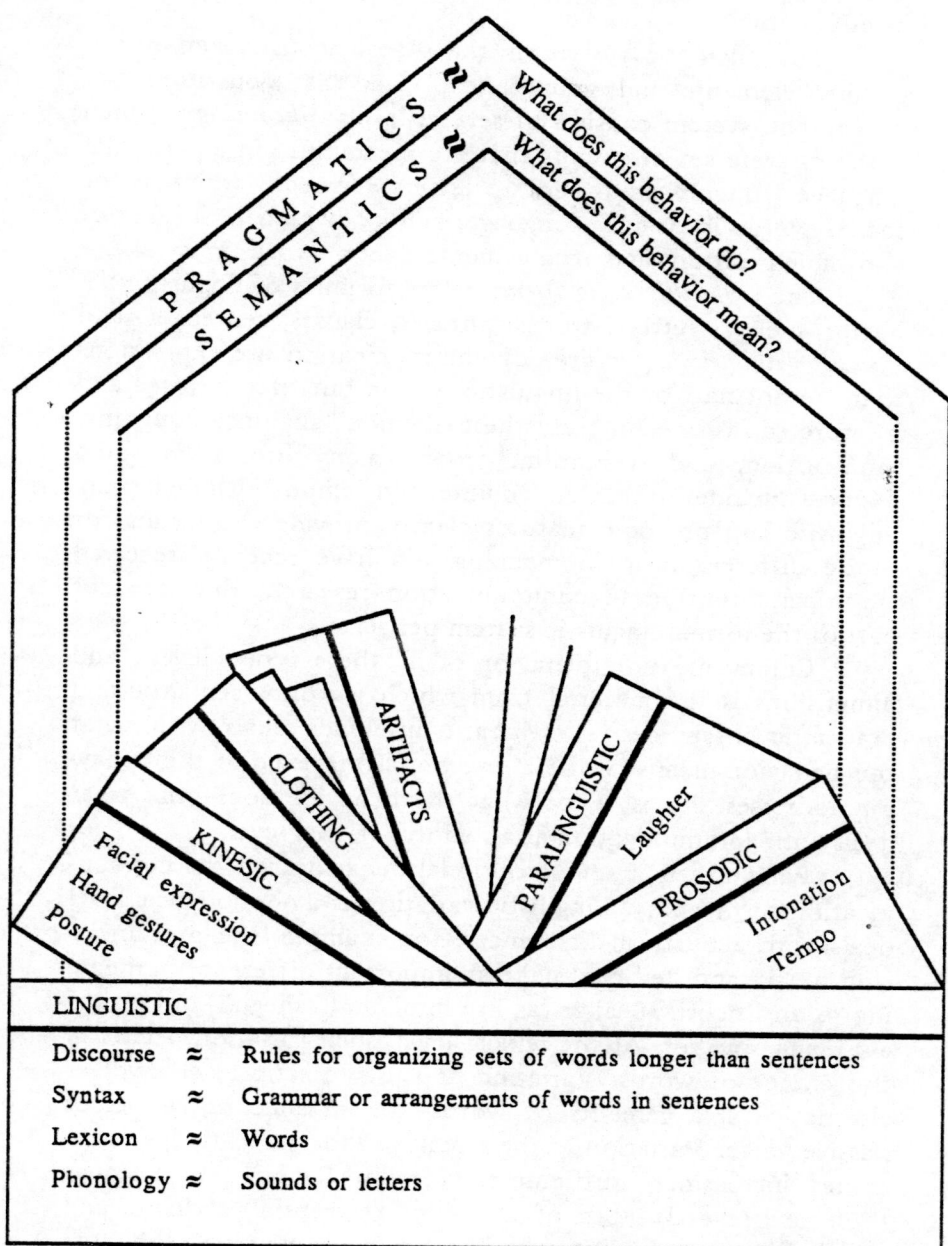

sodic aspects of communication. Each of these terms is defined briefly below.

The *linguistic system* is the set of acoustic and orthographic elements and grammatical rules that constitute language. The system consists of several levels: *phonology,* which is the discrete set of sounds that are meaningful in a particular language (roughly equivalent to letters); *lexicon,* which is the set of words in a given language; *syntax,* which is the set of allowable positions and arrangements a set of words may take.

The term *linguistic forms* refers to units of linguistic behavior such as letters, words, phrases, clauses, sentences, and text. *Paralinguistic features* of communication are expressions that are not part of the linguistic system but that are used and interpreted as meaningful; these include laughing, coughing, interruption, and hesitation, among many others. *Prosodic features* include intonation, volume, and tempo. Although paralinguistic and prosodic features clearly provide the means for subtle differentiation in meaning and have recently received empirical attention in communication research, they are not part of the formal linguistic system per se.

Communication behavior of all these types, levels, and dimensions is the material from which we draw semantic and pragmatic inferences. A *semantic* inference deals with what the behavior means, while a *pragmatic* inference of the behavior addresses the issue of what the behavior does—that is, it deals with communication at a sociofunctional level.

Language is a set of optional behaviors for the communication of meaning. Linguistic variation at a phonological level deals with acoustical differences; for example, the pronunciation of "i" and "e" can make an important difference in meaning to an English speaker (as in "ship" and "sheep") but not to a French speaker. At the lexical level, such variation occurs in the choice of words. Variation at the syntactic level involves alternative arrangements of words—for instance, active versus passive voice. Variation at the semantic and pragmatic levels becomes increasingly difficult to account for, in part because there are several types of meaning: referential, stylistic, and social. For example, active and passive voice may have the same meaning in terms of what they refer to, but from a stylistic perspective, active voice is considered more colloquial and passive more formal or literary. Because this is an issue of active, ongoing controversy in linguistics (Lavandera, 1978), I will not attempt to discuss it further here.

The study of language usage is still in its theoretical and methodological infancy, even in those disciplines that have focused on language. In part this is due to the complexity of communication and to the arbitrary disciplinary lines we have drawn through the phenomenon. In this chapter, I attempt to integrate several perspectives on the use of language into a single approach that investigates the social and organizational functions of communication behavior. I refer to the approach as *conversational analysis* to emphasize that it uses linguistic data and methods to address "nonlinguistic" issues. In other words, conversational analysis is a method to investigate how language is used to accomplish organizational activities like leading and decision making. The complexity of such an undertaking will be seen in the brief descriptions below of language-related disciplines.

### The Study of Communication Behavior in Other Disciplines

This section provides a broad overview of ways in which language has been studied. To organize the discussion, I will use the disciplinary distinctions prevalent among communication researchers. The six perspectives discussed are linguistics, psycholinguistics, sociolinguistics, ethnography of communication, ethnomethodology, and interaction analysis.

*Linguistics.* The central question in the discipline of linguistics has been, What is language? As described above, the linguistic model consists of a discrete set of elements and rules, which are capable of producing all and only the strings of these elements that are considered meaningful and "well formed" (Chomsky, 1957) in the opinion of native speakers of the language under study. The ultimate aim of mainstream linguistics since Chomsky has thus been to account for the knowledge that an idealized speaker must have to form and recognize grammatical sentences. How speakers say what they mean and how utterances are given meaning by listeners are questions that remain outside the purview accepted by most linguists (Dore and McDermott, 1982). The reasons commonly cited for this delimitation are the inadequacy of linguistic models to deal effectively even with the idealized accounts of linguistic behavior and the fact that the meaning of linguistic forms is determinable only by reference to nonlinguistic entities, such as the social context of the utterance.

*Psycholinguistics.* Perhaps a more relevant perspective on the organizational implications of communication behavior is the subfield that merged linguistic with psychological perspectives. This area of study received its impetus and central research issue from Chomsky's (1965) aim of creating a model of the mental structure and processes required to produce linguistic competence at the level of a native speaker. This led to ongoing efforts in psycholinguistics and cognitive psychology to make such cognitive inferences from the experimental study of language acquisition and use (see Palermo, 1978; Weimer and Palermo, 1974).

Psycholinguistic research has discovered numerous important aspects of cognitive processing. For example, as discussed elsewhere in this volume, researchers in this area have demonstrated that people develop, retain in memory, and rely on mental representations of frequent sequences of events (Schank and Abelson, 1977), common situations (Bower, Black, and Turner, 1979; Minsky, 1975), and types of people and things (Cantor and Mischel, 1977; Rosch, 1978; Rosch and Mervis, 1975). All of these insights are based on the operations that research subjects performed using natural language.

Less well-known perhaps is the work that has demonstrated that what people process and recall of natural language is not the exact form of it, but its gist, which they have constructed in the process of comprehending the linguistic data (Bransford and Franks, 1971; Bransford and Johnson, 1972). A related finding of significance to organizational processes is the role of context in determining the meaning of linguistic expressions (Bransford and McCarrell, 1974; Olson, 1970). In general, psycholinguistics has recognized that the way we interpret an utterance is a function not only of the linguistic forms and their ordering (that is, of their syntax) but also of the linguistic text of which they are part and of the social context of the utterance (Anderson and Pichert, 1978; Bransford and McCarrell, 1974; Franks, 1974; Hyde and Jenkins, 1973).

In a study of the linguistic and social influences on the interpretation process, Anderson and Pichert (1978) asked subjects to assume the perspective of a particular type of person as they read a given text (that of a burglar or of a home buyer). They found that the specific details of the text that subjects recalled depended on the perspective taken. Furthermore, when asked to change perspectives during the recall task, the subjects were able to remember additional details of the story. Anderson and Pichert contend that these data support the notion that information unretrievable from one perspective can be recalled if its salience is altered by a shift in perspective.

This study also demonstrates another aspect of cognitive processing supported and elaborated by other studies (Kintsch and van Dijk, 1978; Schank and Abelson, 1977): we process communication hierarchically rather than in the linear sequence in which it is presented to us. That is, we reorganize and structure it according to some basic self-interest, like goals or values. Both the content and process of linguistic comprehension are believed to be influenced by subjects' a priori, top-down sense of what is important (van Dijk, 1980).

How might these psycholinguistic insights contribute to an understanding of organizations? Their usefulness is primarily in what they tell us about how people use linguistic cues to form an understanding of others. It has been said that to construct meaningful linguistic expressions, a speaker must understand hearers, must know what they already know and what they expect and want to hear (Stubbs, 1983). This research suggests that speakers acquire this knowledge by seeking the gist of what others are saying rather than by attending to the actual form, by using the context of the interaction as a guide to interpretation, and by reorganizing the information they hear according to some primary sense of what the whole discourse is "really" about. Using these psycholinguistic insights, we can study the communication behavior in organizations to understand something of what is going on in people's minds (Taylor and Fiske, 1981). For example, the descriptions research subjects provide of organizational events (particularly when contrasted with those of other people and of the researcher) may tell us something about the person's goals, as well as the cognitive strategies directed by these goals (Tetlock, 1985), and about the mental structures developed as maps for such occasions.

Analyses of conversations may tell us what expectations or presuppositions a person has about the state of mind of his listener. We may also be able to ascertain what a person considers to be the critical aspect of a situation by searching for the contingency that organizes a given discussion. For example, Tannen (1977) has suggested that the conjunction "but" and words of negation display a speaker's belief that listeners may be developing inaccurate impressions from the discourse: "I interviewed the job candidate, but I didn't get a good sense of her credentials" indicates that the speaker believes the listener expects an interview to yield such cognitions. Lakoff (1972) argued that adverbs like "technically" and "practically speaking" depict the place that concepts have in fuzzy semantic sets, as when we say, "Technically, she's a secretary," implying that she is only marginally part of that set. By examining such word choices in context, as well as the use of labels and figures of speech, we may discover the mental structures that influence human actions.

In the conclusion of his book on psycholinguistics, Palermo (1978) contends that an adequate theory of semantics must be able to account for context, communication, and metaphor. The essence of his argument is that language exists primarily to serve a communicative function and that the investigation of language requires natural language in context, as well as a recognition of the nonliteral functions of language.

*Sociolinguistics.* Sociolinguists are concerned with developing descriptions of language that include its communicative functions. They describe how language is used and try to account for particular linguistic choices (Lavandera, 1978). Among the most significant findings of this type of research was the demonstration by Labov (1969) that linguistic variation, even at a phonological level, can make a considerable difference in the social or stylistic meaning of an utterance. For example, English speakers recognize "meeting" and "meetin'" to refer to the same event; however, many would consider the former variant more appropriate to some contexts (and people) than the other.

Sociolinguistic researchers argue that many of the "rules" for linguistic choice are as much social as they are linguistic, and that language differentiation both reflects and creates social meaning. Linguistic variation reflects social meaning in that differences in speech have been found to correlate with social variables such as education, economic status, and geographic location. Language differences create social meanings by establishing speech norms, the deviation from which is meaningful.

Empirical studies in sociolinguistics suggest that aspects of organizations can be investigated through an examination of linguistic variation. For example, Gumperz (1977) demonstrated that problems in interethnic relations in the workplace can be related to misunderstandings and misattributions that are based, apparently unconsciously, on the most subtle differences in communication styles. In a series of experiments, Planalp and Tracy (1980) showed that listeners form general competence judgments about people on the basis of their skill in changing topics. In an analysis of a dinner conversation, Tannen (1981) found that regional differences in conversational style defined by rate of interruption, overlapping speech, and pausing lead to unattributable feelings of confusion and irritation by some interactants.

This literature suggests that sociolinguistic analysis of organizational interactions may enable us to identify the interpersonal source of person perceptions and intergroup misunderstanding. For example, if variations in speech tempo were found to correlate with attributions of competence made by professional interviewers but not with those made by line managers, such a finding would have important practical implications for hiring practices.

Perhaps the most important application of sociolinguistic research to organizational study is in the methodological area. The *comprehensive discourse analysis* method introduced by Labov and Fanshel (1977) and Grimshaw (1982) and multilevel approaches to interaction analysis (Dore and McDermott, 1982) not only demonstrate that significant social action is taken through conversation but also provide detailed description of a method for describing and interpreting complex social action.

Theoretically, sociolinguistics has elucidated the connection between social meaning and the communication mechanisms by which it is created and maintained. This insight has led sociologists and anthropologists to view language as "action in context" (Stubbs, 1983, p. 3), which has in turn resulted in the development of approaches that describe context and integrate observations of both communication behavior and context.

*Ethnography of Communication and Ethnomethodology.* Two language-related fields have tried to define the influence that communication behavior has on social and organizational actions. These are the ethnography of communication and ethnomethodology. Using the insights from sociolinguistics as a point of departure, ethnographers of communication have focused on communication as a major component of culture (Hymes, 1962; Bauman and Sherzer, 1974). Making the assumption that the linguistic and the social are mutually determining, they argue that the ability to say how language is used requires description of both the social context and the communication codes used in them (Saville-Troike, 1982; Stubbs, 1983).

In keeping with its anthropological roots, the ethnography of communication entails observation of a particular speech event in its social setting, with the specification of such details as the place, time, roles of participants, function, tone, and purpose of the communication. To test the validity of the observations, researchers compare their insights with those of native participants in the event. This ensures that the social norms of the culture have been accurately described before inferences are made about the meaning of the observed communication.

This research has made several contributions to the

understanding of language usage. Perhaps most importantly, it has identified several functions served by communication beyond the two traditional roles of information transfer and expression of feeling. Hymes (1962) suggested that communication is also used to relieve tension, to relive experience, to crystallize an interpretation of experience, and to organize people. Ethnographers have also identified the contextual features that define communication events culturally and have demonstrated that the fit between communication, context, and action is so critical that even the most subtle changes in communication can alter the meaning and course of action. From an organizational perspective, these insights imply that it might be useful to investigate what communication behaviors characterize different types of organizational events, such as meetings with subordinates versus sessions with peers, and to investigate whether changes in communication can influence changes in cognition or action and thus in the outcome of a given situation.

A similar set of research values is to be found in the studies of the ethnomethodologists (Garfinkel, 1967; Schegloff, 1972; Jefferson, 1972; Sacks, 1972; Sacks, Schegloff, and Jefferson, 1974). Rather than being concerned with the description of the social context of the communication, however, ethnomethodologists use conversational data to understand how the social order of the communication itself is constituted. They study social interaction at the microanalytic level to determine what procedures (or "methodology") members of a community have for creating, participating in, and evaluating social events.

As Coulter (1979) pointed out, the ethnomethodologists contend that what members need to know to participate in orderly social events, such as conversations, is coextensive with native-speaker linguistic intuition. Ethnomethodologists have therefore developed descriptive techniques for determining the rules for conversational action (Sacks, Schegloff, and Jefferson, 1974; Jefferson, 1972, 1978, 1979; Sacks, 1972; Schegloff, 1972). Their techniques include complete transcription and precise timing of interruptions, overlapping speech, pauses, and gazes. The studies have led to the formulation of rules for conversational turn taking, closing, repairs, and joke telling.

Using conversations as data, ethnomethodologists are engaged in the study of sensemaking as a social rather than an individual enterprise. However, as West and Zimmerman (1982, p. 511) point out, the effort is to describe "the reasoning structures" people must have in order to interact in ways that are meaningful to others.

Other communication researchers have extended the descriptive and analytic techniques of the ethnomethodologists to address questions regarding the influence that communication has on the broader social contexts. One such application is the analysis of communication in the professional practices (DiPietro, 1982). Researchers in this area are studying interactions in the courtroom (Nofsinger, 1983), in medical interviews (Tannen and Wallat, 1982; Frankel, 1984), and in clinical therapy (Labov and Fanshel, 1977) to identify the patterns of communication typical in those settings and to discover how language contributes to the accomplishment of professional and organizational ends.

These approaches are very similar to the perspective proposed here for organizational analysis. The data in both instances would be conversations. I propose that such studies will enable us to improve our understanding of the connections between an individual's cognitions, communications, and actions, and will also advance our understanding of organizational action.

*Interaction Analysis.* McDermott and Roth (1978) suggest that interaction analysis provides the theoretical and methodological means to link the order discoverable in face-to-face communication to the higher social, cultural, and organizational systems. They argue that humans create, learn, and sustain the rules for social order through interaction. Stubbs (1983, p. 29) contends that "roles . . . have to be realized and sustained through particular discourse strategies. Roles such as teacher, doctor, pupil, or interviewer cannot be abstracted from the interactional activities which constitute them." Such activities might include the allocation of turns to speak, control of topics for discussion, strategic parrying over conversational resources, and distribution of attention. Each of these interactional activities has been found to have important social effects beyond the immediate conversation. For example, Dore and

McDermott (1982) demonstrate how reading group interaction strategies result in minority children learning less than children of the majority culture. Several studies suggest that specific communication behaviors help sustain the traditional relationship of doctor and patient in our culture (Fisher, 1982; Frankel, 1984; West and Zimmerman, 1982).

In a recent treatise on impression management, Schlenker (1980) suggests that social interaction contributes to the production of self-image as well as to the development of behavioral patterns. His concept of impression management departs notably from Goffman's (1959) in the recognition that self-image also shapes the course of the interaction. Schlenker argues that in interaction, people project (either consciously or unconsciously) self-images in "performances that shape their identities and destinies" (1980, p. 41).

Methodologically, interaction analysis assumes that "a person's behavior is best described in terms of the behavior of those immediately about that person, those with whom the person is doing interactional work in the construction of recognizable social scenes" (McDermott and Roth, 1978, p. 321). Thus, interactional researchers consider behavior as both the subject and criterion for assessing the adequacy of interactional description (Birdwhistell, 1952; Scheflen, 1968; McDermott, Gospodinoff, and Aron, 1978). In their analysis of a classroom interaction, McDermott and others (1978) propose and use four behavioral criteria for identifying and validating units of observed behavior: (1) interactants must behaviorally formulate the interactional order, (2) they must enact this formulation kinesically, (3) they must orient to the order, and (4) they must be observed to hold one another accountable to this order.

Using these criteria, researchers can describe interaction in terms that are demonstrably recognizable to the participants. For example, an utterance may be categorized as a question on the basis of both its internal structure (that is, its distinctive syntax) and on the basis of such behavioral criteria as the shifting postural arrangements of the group from one speaker to the apparent addressee, the repetition of the utterance in the absence of a response, or the subsequent utterance by the addressee.

As this example suggests, interactional approaches to the

study of social behavior are premised on the view that behavior can be defined in terms of the immediate interactional context —that is, in terms of the behavior of all interactants. McDermott and Roth (1978) extend this view, arguing that it is only by reference to the context that we are able to interpret behavior. Thus, all prior behavior becomes the context by which subsequent behavior is generated and interpreted, so that "what I think I am doing is a function of what I think you were doing." For example, the utterance "I'm not finished yet" becomes interpretable as defiance in the context of the supervisor's prior utterance of "I thought I told you to get that truck unloaded." Both statements are critical to a valid interpretation of the supervisor's parting words: "I'm not finished with you yet either."

In this section of the chapter, I have reviewed six approaches to the study of language and communication. I have also attempted to demonstrate how the theory, methods, and findings of each approach may contribute to an understanding of organizational behavior. Before presenting an integration of these perspectives as an approach to organizational analysis, I will briefly review some important precedents of communication research in organizational research.

### Precedents in Organizational Research on Communication

Fortunately, we do not have to begin the observational study of language in organizations without previous experience. Empirical studies are few, and our knowledge is somewhat limited by the fact that much of the previous research is based on laboratory experiments rather than on natural organizational situations. Much of the research also categorized observed communication behavior in fairly abstract units rather than using the multidimensional linguistic categorization. Nevertheless, this previous research provides valuable experience in terms of method development and conceptualization that can be pursued in future field research.

Much of the current interest in face-to-face communication in the organization stems from Mintzberg's (1973) classic investigation into the nature of managerial activities. He found that through brief verbal interactions, managers enact ten distinctive roles; he did not, however, directly observe the communication behavior. In a recent study of the functions of general managers, Kotter (1982) reported that his subjects rely on a few specific communication strategies: asking lots of questions, getting people to identify with them, using finesse, and implying dependency on them.

Recently, a number of observational frameworks for the study of verbal behavior have developed. Jablin (1978) used an a priori categorization scheme to have researchers and participants code videotaped interactions to assess the perceived openness in hierarchical communication and found that it was related to the judgments of the appropriateness of superiors' responses to subordinates' messages. Watson (1982a, 1982b) developed an observational system for identifying the communication behaviors that differentiated leader roles from follower roles. Sims, Manz, and Gioia (Sims and Manz, 1984; Gioia and Sims, forthcoming) have developed and applied an observational scheme for measuring the verbal behavior of both leader and subordinate in performance appraisal interviews. Gioia and Sims have found that verbal behavior is a useful indicator of mutual influence, because after verbal interaction the attributions made by a supervisor of the cause for a subordinate's performance level were often changed.

To capture more of the emergent socially constructed aspects of organizational conversations that are more behaviorally dense, some researchers have begun to use observational methods more consistent with the approaches of the language-related disciplines. Gronn (1983) used interaction analysis and thick description of the ethnographic setting of the conversations of a school administrator and his staff to discover the administrative functions of talk. Donnellon, Gioia, and Sims (1985) determined the sequence of speech acts performed in videotaped interviews in order to discover if these displayed a common cognitive structure for such events. In a discourse analysis of the videotaped interaction of a group, Donnellon, Gray, and Bougon (1985) identified a set of communication mechanisms used in the joint sensemaking and in the implementation of organized action. The conversational behavior of CEOs and top managers as they proceed through their daily routines is currently under study by Donnellon, Sims, and Gioia (forthcoming). This project used the integrated method that will be described in the next section.

## Conversational Analysis: An Integration

The position advanced here is that organizing and managing are accomplished through communication. Language and communication are used in organizations to serve two primary functions: first, to understand what people are thinking and feeling; and second, to create or influence these cognitions and emotions.

Because organizing and managing are manifested primarily as linguistic enterprises, these activities can be analyzed through methods devised for investigating the communication system. However, to study organizational topics such as leadership, decision making, and influence through a communication perspective, we need an approach that integrates the perspectives and methods discussed above. Many researchers in the language-related areas are now expressing a similar need for an integrative approach. In fact, recently some progress has been made toward the integration and application of communication approaches to the practical problems of the everyday world (see DiPietro, 1982; Frankel, 1984; Stubbs, 1983). The discussion that follows owes much to those works.

A classic linguistic analysis of organizational interactions would not in itself be very useful as a means of inferring the meaning of the interaction to participants, because linguistic forms are essentially indeterminate without reference to the context in which they are uttered. The forms are a set of behavioral options we have for generating socially meaningful discourse (Sigman, 1980). The matter of which forms are chosen at any particular time and what meaning they have depends on the primary function the communication is intended to serve (Stubbs, 1983).

The interpretation and prediction of organizational behavior has analogous, if not more serious, limitations. Such behavior is essentially ambiguous and, in fact, indeterminate without knowledge of the context of which it is part. The range of
behavioral options for the display of a concept like leadership,
for example, is so vast that it is virtually impossible to predict
which variant the organizational actor will display or to make a
reasonable inference of the intended meaning unless one makes
reference to the context in which the forms are uttered. For
example, the function of persuasion can be accomplished
through the use of any combination of communication behaviors derived from a very large set. Unless a researcher knows
something about the interactants and the reason for the interaction, he or she is unlikely to be able to predict which behaviors will be observed. However, from an ethnographic description of the interaction, together with a sequential and hierarchical
analysis of the communication itself, we can begin to make inferences about the cognitions of the speakers and eventually to
make predictions about the communication mechanisms like-
liest to be displayed.

The inferential process used in the observational method
described here is similar to that used by the participants themselves as they try to understand what others know, think, or
feel by attending to the details of person, place, timing, and to
the content and manner of the speech of other participants.
However, as researchers we are also attempting to discover the
regularities in such interactions that enable organizational members to achieve some degree of mutual understanding and to implement organized action. This research method thus requires
special techniques for the detection of the "strangeness of an
obstinately familiar world" (Garfinkel, 1967, p. 38).

The first phase of the method entails the selection of particular organizational events for analysis on the basis of some
theoretical interest. For example, a researcher may wish to discover precisely how managers influence the beliefs and positive
affect of employees (Pfeffer, 1981). Therefore, the meeting at
which some innovation is introduced may serve as a fruitful
field for analysis. Generally, both prior and post hoc ethno-

graphic observation and interviewing are required as orientation for the researcher so that he or she can develop an understanding of the principal actors, the nature of the organization's business, its basic terminology, and the central issues of concern to the organizational members.

Once orientation has taken place, it is time to record the selected events on video or audio equipment for subsequent transcription and analysis. An alternative approach consists of continuous recording over a given period of time, with episodes for analysis selected from among this larger set. The selected conversations are then transcribed as completely as possible, including notation of paralinguistic features like coughs, false starts, and laughter as well as prosodic features such as intonation and volume of the voices. This translation of essentially auditory data into written description allows for the "estrangement" of the researcher from data that have at least superficial meaning for him or her because of membership in the same speech community (Garfinkel, 1967). Transcription thus facilitates the detection of the structures in the conversation. This process represents the *etic* (Pike, 1967) or outsider's description of the behavior, which is to be compared subsequently with the participants' to confirm its *emic* status (that is, its subjective meaning).

The functional approach to the conversational analysis (Lavandera, 1978; Dore and McDermott, 1982; Stubbs, 1983) involves the specification of the organizational functions of the communication of interest to the researcher, followed by a multilevel analysis of the interactions to determine how these functions are being served.

As the range of behavioral variants available for the construction of socially meaningful communication is quite considerable, it is rarely possible to predict what the precise categories of findings of such a study would be. However, taking the multilevel approach, the set of possible categories of behaviors that serve organizational functions in such interactions could include variation in pronunciation, intonation, emphasis, syntax, or lexicon. It is also possible that there may be variation in the types and ordering of speech acts, as some researchers have found to be the case in studies of the medical and legal profession (Frankel, 1984; Nofsinger, 1983).

In the example of the influence of a manager on the belief system of the employees, a multilevel analysis of the interaction might begin with the identification of a change in the beliefs of the employee and work backwards to describe the features of the interaction that show the manager trying to influence the thoughts of others. Possible elements of his strategy might be lexical choice, use of conjunctions to suppress a likely but undesired inference, use of phonological variation to convey the manager's own attitude toward the change, and use of passive voice or indirect speech acts to obscure the agent of the change.

To summarize, the integrated methodology described in this chapter entails on-site, ethnographic observation and interviewing, and multilevel, sociolinguistic analysis of tape-recorded conversations.

## Research Implications

Using the method described above, we can conduct conversational analyses of typical organizational events, such as job interviews, training sessions, staff meetings, performance evaluations, and decision making sessions, not to mention day-to-day conversations in the hall. Such analyses may provide novel answers to age-old questions such as, How do people motivate others? What behaviors are used to influence others? How is power expressed? How is it exerted? What is referent power?

The perspective and method proposed in this chapter may also shed light on other, more specific questions, such as the following: Do people use the same communication behaviors in various organizational events or settings, or are they influenced by various contextual contingencies? Is there any correlation between the patterns of communication in certain key activities and organizational success? How do organization members describe the same situations? Do these descriptions display differences in temporal order, in significance, in evaluation? How do differences in speech style correlate with judgments of competence? Do differences in people's ability to "read" or influence others correlate with attributions of competence? Are different types of organizational events characterized by different patterns of communication? Do some managers seem to create opportunities for some subordinates to succeed and others to fail simply by their own speech behavior (for example, by never giving subordinates a chance to ask questions or to feel some personal connection or investment)? How do new organizational members discover the rules for expressing dissatisfaction, loyalty, commitment, or innovative ideas?

## Practical Implications and Applications

Communication plays a central role in perception, learning, adaptation, and influence. In this section, I will discuss the operation of these basic human processes in organizations and suggest ways that organizational activities may benefit from a better understanding of the role of communication.

As any interviewer or supervisor knows, adults come to organizations with their heads full of preconceived notions and expectations. Perhaps this knowledge of human nature accounts for the popularity of the interview as a selection device: it is a communication event in which perception and learning occur on both sides. As the research reviewed earlier suggests, attention to communication displays can provide information on cognitions, emotions, and values. Additional research on interview interactions may show not only how candidates translate their experiences into cognitions and words but also how interviewers use their own norms for linguistic interpretation to arrive at evaluations of candidates' competence and to make hiring decisions.

Discovering how the dual processes of displaying and interpreting cognitions from communication behavior work should lead to the development of improved techniques for selection. Personnel responsible for interviewing and selection may be taught to "read" people better. Programs may be developed for discovering the values and attitudes candidates hold by eliciting the cognitive schemas and scripts they have developed and the expectations they have. The interview process itself may be improved by training personnel to look beyond stylistic differences in communication behavior to see more fundamental differences in candidates. Through studies of interview interactions, we might also observe and learn to correct tendencies for interviewers to create contexts in which only certain types of behavior can be enacted by job candidates.

Once the individual has joined the organization, he or she immediately begins the process of making sense of the new experiences. Cognitive psychologists have demonstrated that sensemaking and learning processes occur through the matching of experience with existing mental structures (Palermo, 1978). It has also been recognized that communication is not only the most common experiential input to the matching process but also the medium through which people develop their cognitive structures (Taylor and Fiske, 1981). These insights have important practical implications for training in organizations. First, they suggest that to be effective, training should start with a framework for organizing material that already exists in the minds of the trainees. Second, these insights suggest that since people continue to learn and modify their cognitions as they communicate with others, training should anticipate and possibly compensate for the early socialization influences that new employees will inevitably experience as they assume their new positions and begin to communicate with their new colleagues. Training might therefore be enhanced if it were conducted on the actual site of the job assignment or if it included a post-assignment module for the assessment of on-site influences on the mental structures that have been developed in training.

As Louis (1980) has pointed out, socialization into a new organization is often characterized by surprise, as the new employee observes and is told "how we do things here." For all the official, usually written, communication about the new organization and its expectation, this period of socialization usually occurs in face-to-face interaction with fellow employees and supervisor. As Jablin (1982, p. 266) suggests, "Sensemaking is essentially communicative in nature."

Selection and training are two substantive aspects of organizational action, and I have attempted to show how they are significantly affected by communication. The argument that has been implicit up to this point is that language and communication are as much a part of the substance of management activity as they are of the symbolic side of that activity (Pfeffer, 1981). In other major organizational activities such as decision making, controlling, and innovation, language plays both substantive and symbolic roles. Each of these activities involves influence, which is ultimately parleyed through communication. In the activities of motivating and controlling employees, communication is the means by which organizational leaders make experience meaningful to others. This may occur through the articulation of performance goals and linkage of employee behavior to a system of rewards; or it may occur through inspirational activity, like creating a company motto such as "We try harder."

In virtually every phase of a joint decision-making effort, communication plays a critical role. Various strategies for communication may be used to influence the way a problem is formulated and the manner in which decision criteria are established, as well as the presentation of alternatives and the crediting or discrediting of individual evaluations. Once decisions are made, the processes of implementing change are based almost entirely on communication.

At a more general level, it is obvious that there are basically three practical reasons for investigating the role of language and communication in organizations. First, such research can help practitioners develop an understanding of how they themselves use language to develop and display their own cognitions. Second, it will enable them to perceive similar uses of language by others. Third, a research program on language usage and strategies for communication will result in a taxonomy of communication mechanisms and strategies that practitioners can use to select optimal courses of communicational action.

## Conclusion

I have argued here that communication and language are used in interactions for two primary purposes: to infer the cognitions of others and to influence them. These two functions are at the heart of most organizational activities. Understanding the way people develop and display their cognitions and emotions is a key to understanding their organizational behavior. This chapter proposes an approach to the study of face-to-face organizational communication that can garner new insight into both the behavior of individuals in organizations and into organizational processes in general.

## References

Anderson, R. C., and Pichert, J. W. "Recall of Previously Unrecallable Information Following a Shift in Perspective." *Journal of Verbal Learning and Verbal Behavior,* 1978, *17* (1), 1-12.

Barnard, C. *Functions of the Executive.* Cambridge, Mass.: Harvard University Press, 1938.

Bauman, R., and Sherzer, J. (eds.). *Explorations in the Ethnography of Speaking.* Cambridge: Cambridge University Press, 1974.

Birdwhistell, R. L. *Introduction to Kinesics.* Washington, D.C.: Foreign Service Institute, 1952.

Bower, G. H., Black, J. B., and Turner, T. J. "Scripts in Memory for Text." *Cognitive Psychology,* 1979, *11,* 177-220.

Bransford, J. D., and Franks, J. J. "The Abstraction of Linguistic Ideas." *Cognitive Psychology,* 1971, *2,* 331-350.

Bransford, J. D., and Johnson, M. K. "Contextual Prerequisites for Understanding: Some Investigations of Comprehension and Recall." *Journal of Verbal Learning and Verbal Behavior,* 1972, *11,* 717-726.

Bransford, J. D., and McCarrell, N. S. "A Sketch of a Cognitive Approach to Comprehension: Some Thoughts About Understanding What It Means to Comprehend." In W. B. Weimer and D. S. Palermo (eds.), *Cognition and the Symbolic Processes.* Vol. 1. Hillsdale, N.J.: Erlbaum, 1974.

Cantor, N., and Mischel, W. "Traits as Prototypes: Effect on Recognition Memory." *Journal of Personality and Social Psychology,* 1977, *35,* 38-48.

Chomsky, N. *Syntactic Structures.* The Hague: Mouton, 1957.

Chomsky, N. *Aspects of a Theory of Grammar.* Cambridge, Mass.: MIT Press, 1965.

Coulter, J. "Beliefs and Practical Understanding." In G. Psathas (ed.), *Everyday Language: Studies in Ethnomethodology.* New York: Irvington, 1979.

DiPietro, R. J. (ed.). *Linguistics and the Professions.* Norwood, N.J.: Ablex, 1982.

Donnellon, A., Gioia, D. A., and Sims, H. P., Jr. "Speech Act Analysis and Script Inference: An Exploration of Communication and Cognition in Organizations." Unpublished manuscript, Division of Organizational Behavior, Pennsylvania State University, 1985.

Donnellon, A., Gray, B., and Bougon, M. G. "Communication, Meaning, and Organized Action." Unpublished manuscript, Division of Organizational Behavior, Pennsylvania State University, 1985.

Donnellon, A., Sims, H. P., Jr., and Gioia, D. A. "Communication at the Top." Working paper, Division of Organizational Behavior, Pennsylvania State University, forthcoming.

Dore, J., and McDermott, R. P. "Linguistic Indeterminacy and Social Context in Utterance Interpretation." *Language,* 1982, *58* (2), 374–398.

Fisher, S. "The Decision-Making Context: How Doctors and Patients Communicate." In R. J. DiPietro (ed.), *Linguistics and the Professions.* Norwood, N.J.: Ablex, 1982.

Frankel, R. M. "From Sentence to Sequence: Understanding the Medical Encounter Through Microinteractional Analysis." *Discourse Processes,* 1984, *7*, 135–170.

Franks, J. J. "Toward Understanding Understanding." In W. B. Weimer and D. S. Palermo (eds.), *Cognition and the Symbolic Processes.* Vol. 1. Hillsdale, N.J.: Erlbaum, 1974.

Garfinkel, H. *Studies in Ethnomethodology.* Englewood Cliffs, N.J.: Prentice-Hall, 1967.

Gioia, D. A., and Sims, H. A. "Cognition-Behavior Connections: Attribution and Verbal Behavior in Leader-Subordinate Interactions." *Organizational Behavior and Human Decision Processes,* forthcoming.

Goffman, E. *The Presentation of Self in Everyday Life.* New York: Doubleday, 1959.

Grimshaw, A. D. "Comprehensive Discourse Analysis: An Instance of Professional Peer Interaction." *Language in Society,* 1982, *11,* 15–47.

Gronn, P. C. "Talk as the Work: The Accomplishment of School Administration." *Administrative Science Quarterly,* 1983, *28* (1), 1–21.

Gumperz, J. J. "The Conversational Analysis of Interethnic Communication." In E. L. Ross (ed.), *Interethnic Communication: Proceedings of the Southern Anthropology Society.* Athens: University of Georgia Press, 1977.

Hyde, T. S., and Jenkins, J. J. "Recall of Words as a Function of Semantic, Graphic, and Syntactic Orienting Tasks." *Journal of Verbal Learning and Verbal Behavior,* 1973, *12,* 471–480.

Hymes, D. "The Ethnography of Speaking." In J. Fishman (ed.), *Readings in the Sociology of Language.* The Hague: Mouton, 1962.

Jablin, F. M. "Message-Response and 'Openness' in Superior-Subordinate Communication." In B. D. Ruben (ed.), *Communication Yearbook 2.* New Brunswick, N.J.: Transaction Books, 1978.

Jablin, F. M. "Organizational Communication: An Assimilation Approach." In M. E. Roloff and C. R. Berger (eds.), *Social Cognition and Communication.* Beverly Hills, Calif.: Sage, 1982.

Jefferson, G. "Side Sequences." In D. Sudnow (ed.), *Studies in Social Interaction.* New York: Free Press, 1972.

Jefferson, G. "Sequential Aspects of Storytelling in Conversation." In J. Schenkein (ed.), *Studies in the Organization of Conversational Interaction.* Orlando, Fla.: Academic Press, 1978.

Jefferson, G. "A Technique for Inviting Laughter and Its Subsequent Acceptance/Declination." In G. Psathas (ed.), *Everyday Language: Studies in Ethnomethodology.* New York: Irvington, 1979.

Kintsch, W., and van Dijk, T. "Towards a Model of Discourse Comprehension and Production." *Psychological Review,* 1978, *85,* 363–394.

Kotter, J. P. *The General Managers.* New York: Free Press, 1982.

Labov, W. "Contraction, Deletion and Inherent Variability of the English Copula." *Language,* 1969, *45,* 715–762.

Labov, W., and Fanshel, D. *Therapeutic Discourse: Psychotherapy as Conversation.* Orlando, Fla.: Academic Press, 1977.

Lakoff, G. "Hedges: A Study in Meaning Criteria and the Logic of Fuzzy Concepts." In *Papers from the Eighth Regional Meeting, Chicago Linguistics Society.* Chicago: Linguistics Department, University of Chicago, 1972.

Lavandera, B. R. "Where Does the Sociolinguistic Variable Stop?" *Language in Society,* 1978, *7* (2), 171–182.

Louis, M. R. "Surprise and Sense-Making: What Newcomers Experience in Entering Unfamiliar Organizational Settings." *Administrative Science Quarterly,* 1980, *25,* 226–248.

McDermott, R. P., Gospodinoff, K., and Aron, J. "Criteria for an Ethnographically Adequate Description of Concerted Activities and Their Contexts." *Semiotica,* 1978, *24* (4), 245–275.

McDermott, R. J., and Roth, D. R. "The Social Organization of Behavior: Interactional Approaches." *Annual Review of Anthropology,* 1978, *7,* 321–345.

Mead, G. H. *Mind, Self, and Society.* Chicago: University of Chicago Press, 1964. (Originally published 1934.)

Minsky, M. A. "Framework for Representing Knowledge." In P. H. Winston (ed.), *The Psychology of Computer Vision.* New York: McGraw-Hill, 1975.

Mintzberg, H. *The Nature of Managerial Work.* New York: Harper & Row, 1973.

Nofsinger, R. E. "Tactical Coherence in Courtroom Conversation." In R. T. Craig and K. Tracy (eds.), *Conversational Coherence.* Beverly Hills, Calif.: Sage, 1983.

Olson, D. R. "Language and Thought: Aspects of a Theory of Semantics." *Psychological Review,* 1970, *77,* 257–273.

Palermo, D. S. *Psychology of Language.* Glenview, Ill.: Scott, Foresman, 1978.

Pfeffer, J. "Management as Symbolic Action: The Creation and Maintenance of Organizational Paradigms." In B. M. Staw and L. L. Cummings (eds.), *Research in Organizational Behavior.* Vol. 3. Greenwich, Conn.: JAI Press, 1981.

Piaget, J. *The Construction of Reality in the Child.* New York: Basic Books, 1954. (Originally published 1937.)

Pike, K. *Language in Relation to a Unified Theory of the Structure of Human Behavior.* The Hague: Mouton, 1967.

Planalp, S., and Tracy, K. "Not to Change the Topic But . . . : A Cognitive Approach to the Management of Conversation." In D. Nimmo (ed.), *Communication Yearbook 4.* New Brunswick, N.J.: Transaction Books, 1980.

Rosch, E. "Principles of Categorization." In E. Rosch and B. B. Lloyd (eds.), *Cognition and Categorization.* Hillsdale, N.J.: Erlbaum, 1978.

Rosch, E., and Mervis, C. B. "Family Resemblances: Studies in the Internal Structure of Categories." *Cognitive Psychology,* 1975, *7,* 573–605.

Sacks, H. "On the Analysability of Stories by Children." In J. J. Gumperz and D. Hymes (eds.), *Directions in Sociolinguistics.* New York: Holt, Rinehart and Winston, 1972.

Sacks, H., Schegloff, E., and Jefferson, G. "A Simplest Systematics for the Organization of Turn-Taking for Conversation." *Language,* 1974, *50,* 696–735.

Saville-Troike, M. *The Ethnography of Communication.* Baltimore, Md.: University Park Press, 1982.

Schank, R. C., and Abelson, R. P. *Scripts, Plans, Goals, and Understanding.* Hillsdale, N.J.: Erlbaum, 1977.

Scheflen, A. E. "Human Communication: Behavioral Programs and Their Integration in Interaction." *Behavioral Science,* 1968, *13,* 44–55.

Schegloff, E. A. "Notes on Conversational Practice: Formulating Place." In D. Sudnow (ed.), *Studies in Social Interaction.* New York: Free Press, 1972.

Schegloff, E. A. "The Relevance of Repair to Syntax-for-Conversation." In T. Givon (ed.), *Syntax and Semantics.* Vol. 12: *Discourse and Syntax.* Orlando, Fla.: Academic Press, 1979.

Schlenker, B. R. *Impression Management: The Self-Concept, Social Identity, and Interpersonal Relations.* Monterey, Calif.: Brooks/Cole, 1980.

Sigman, S. J. "On Communication Rules from a Social Perspective." *Human Communication Research,* 1980, *7,* 37–51.

Sims, H. P., Jr., and Manz, C. "Observing Leader Verbal Behavior: Toward Reciprocal Determinism in Leadership Theory." *Journal of Applied Psychology,* 1984, *69* (2), 222-232.

Stubbs, M. *Discourse Analysis.* Chicago: University of Chicago Press, 1983.

Tannen, D. *Well, What Did You Expect?* Berkeley: Berkeley Linguistic Society, University of California Press, 1977.

Tannen, D. "New York Jewish Conversational Style." *International Journal of the Sociology of Language,* 1981, *30,* 133-149.

Tannen, D., and Wallat, C. "A Sociolinguistic Analysis of Multiple Demånds on the Pediatrician in Doctor/Mother/Child Interaction." In R. DiPietro (ed.), *Linguistics and the Professions.* Norwood, N.J.: Ablex, 1982.

Taylor, S. E., and Fiske, S. T. "Getting Inside the Head: Methodologies for Process Analysis in Attribution and Social Cognition." In J. H. Harvey, W. Ickes, and R. F. Kidd (eds.), *New Directions in Attribution Research.* Vol. 3. Hillsdale, N.J.: Erlbaum, 1981.

Tetlock, P. E. "Accountability: The Neglected Social Context of Judgment and Choice." In L. L. Cummings and B. M. Staw (eds.), *Research in Organizational Behavior.* Greenwich, Conn.: JAI Press, 1985.

van Dijk, T. A. *Macrostructures.* Hillsdale, N.J.: Erlbaum, 1980.

Vygotsky, L. S. *Mind in Society.* Cambridge, Mass.: Harvard University Press, 1978.

Watson, K. H. "A Methodology for the Study of Organizational Behavior at the Interpersonal Level of Analysis." *Academy of Management Review,* 1982a, *7,* 392-402.

Watson, K. H. "An Analysis of Communication Patterns: A Method for Discriminating Leader and Subordinate Roles." *Academy of Management Journal,* 1982b, *25,* 107-120.

Weimer, W. B., and Palermo, D. S. *Cognition and the Symbolic Processes.* Vol. 1. Hillsdale, N.J.: Erlbaum, 1974.

West, C., and Zimmerman, D. H. "Conversational Analysis." In K. R. Scherer and P. Ekman (eds.), *Handbook of Methods in Nonverbal Behavior Research.* Cambridge: Cambridge University Press, 1982.

# 6

# How Cognitive Structures Affect Organizational Design

## Implicit Theories of Organizing

### H. Kirk Downey
### Arthur P. Brief

*Not until the years following World War II and Henry Ford's death [emphasis added] was the Ford administrative pattern reshaped along lines similar to those of General Motors, and only then did the Ford Motor Company become an effective competitor once again.*

—Alfred Chandler

This chapter deals with the broad issue of what role cognition plays in the development of organizational structures. In addition to arguing that cognitions play a central role in the development of organizational structures, this chapter will develop two control ideas. First, we will suggest that cognitive structures of organizational members are, in fact, an essential ingredient in organizational functions. Second, we will attempt to demonstrate that an understanding of the ways in which cognitive structures might exert their influence is critical to practicing managers.

Before discussing the role of cognitions in the design of

organizations and the reactions of organization members to those designs, it may be useful to review the development of the thinking about cognition and organizational design presented in this chapter. In addition, we will place our main arguments in context by discussing our beliefs about the study of purposeful behavior. After discussing our main notions about the role of cognition in organizational structure, we will anticipate problems in this chapter's central ideas, suggest the kind of research required to support and address the issues we have raised, and explore the implications of our ideas for managers of organizations.

## Background

At this point, it is important to digress in order to explain our own interest in cognitive structures and organizations and the background that has led to our current views. This explanation will be most useful to managers and to academics from other disciplines—that is, those who might not be familiar with the literature on which our arguments are based.

While we have had an interest in cognitive approaches to individual behavior for some time, we (and we suspect many others) have not tended to associate these notions with larger organizational issues, such as structure and design. In 1975, Staw forced us to consider cognitions, in the form of attribution processes, in our thinking about organizations. In that work, Staw demonstrated that group members' perceptions of what are usually thought of as concrete events in groups can be influenced by whether group members believe that those events have led to desirable outcomes. In short, Staw demonstrated that group members create visions of reality consistent with their notions of how they think groups operate. In order to do so, the subjects of Staw's study must have had a cognitive schema of how groups function, which they then used to observe and understand the organized setting. By *cognitive schema*, we mean an abstract structure represented in thought which an individual uses to represent real-world phenomena.

Initially, Staw's results had a chilling effect on those of us who had spent time and effort studying organizations by asking organization members to describe elements within their organized settings. How could we believe our own research results? One of the authors of this chapter suspected that Staw's results were an artifact of his research methods and set out to show him to be mistaken. These efforts resulted in a series of methodological studies (for example, Downey, Chacko, and McElroy, 1979) that consistently supported Staw's initial findings. Other researchers, like Denisi and Pritchard (1978), conducted similar tests of Staw's results and reached similar conclusions. Not only were the results reported by Staw essentially correct, the phenomenon was found to be more pervasive than originally suspected. Partly because of this research, it now seems clear that organization members use cognitive schemas to observe and understand the organized settings in which they find themselves.

In parallel, several theorists have argued for some time, in a more general way, for inclusion of cognition in the explanation of organizational phenomena. For example, Mitroff and Kilmann (1976) and Weick (1977, 1979a, 1979b) have long argued that cognitive processes play an important role in organizations. We will return to these theorists later and explain how our approach builds on their earlier work.

All of the above led us, in the early 1980s, to develop a set of ideas regarding specific cognitive mechanisms that could help to explain organizational structures. That work, which is summarized in Brief and Downey (1983), uses a specific type of cognitive structure called *implicit theories* to attempt to explain both how organizations are structured by organizational elites and how organization members respond to those structures. This chapter is an extension of that work.

## Research on Purposeful Behavior

Scientific inquiry in any area begins with sets of preassumptions concerning the phenomena under study and the necessary methods for gaining insight into those phenomena. These preassumptions form what Kuhn (1962) has called "a research paradigm." As others have pointed out, these paradigms are not tested by the research itself. Rather, the paradigms are kept or abandoned based on the overall usefulness of all research that is guided by the paradigms. As such, these preassumptions, or paradigms, are faith statements about what is being studied and how to study it.

In some ways it might be ideal if researchers began every inquiry with an intellectually clean slate and were able to develop approaches and methods free from previous experiences. In fact, however, we all bring our past research experiences with us to any inquiry. Consequently, we many times fail to rethink the basic notions or paradigms that we use. In our own case, it has been helpful to rethink our basic notions about organizations and their structures because it is easy in macro-oriented research to lose sight of the centrality of the human actor.

Two specific notions need emphasis here concerning research involving purposeful behavior in organized settings. These notions concern first, the contrived nature of organizations, and second, the nature of human choice. As for the first notion, following a long tradition of social scientists, we view organizations as social inventions of the human mind. Consequently, organizations are whatever their designers and members think they are. Etzioni (1964) provides a direct statement of this view when he begins his discussion of organizations with the statement that "Organizations are social units (or social groupings) deliberately constructed and reconstructed" (p. 3). This idea of deliberate construction is important in that it places human decision processes in the center of thoughts about organizations and their structures.

As for the nature of human choice, we follow in the tradition of Simon (1976) when he stated that "social choices are choices. . . . We neither need nor want separate theories of social thinking and other thinking" (p. 254). This view of human choice means that the choices that are made by organization members, be they designers or other members responding to design, must conform to our notions about human decision making in general. These basic notions about organizations and human choice need not and should not be distorted by our attempts to study organizations and their design.

In short, our view of organizations and the centrality of human choice in the functions of organizations led us to begin our inquiry with the preassumptions that human actors create organizational structures and do so through processes of choosing that are consistent with more general social choices and decision making. This places us squarely in the position of assuming that the cognitions of an organization's designers strongly influence the decisions that result in organizational structures and that these decisions are purposeful.

It remains for us to explain the manner in which these cognitions lead to organizational structures. The assumption of purposeful behavior alone leads us to a faith adherence to a cognitive orientation for our inquiry. We emphasize the faith nature of this cognitive orientation because we make no attempt here to defend the basic notion that organizations are deliberately created through social choices by human actors. That is an assumption on which our work rests.

### Cognitive Theories of Organizing

In an earlier work (Brief and Downey, 1983), we argued that individuals make choices and respond to their surroundings on the basis of well-developed ideas of how the world in which they find themselves operates. That is, they respond on the basis of their "theories" about their world. Further, we argued that the implicit theory concept can be particularly helpful in understanding how individuals choose to act in organized settings and how others respond to those actions. The implicit theory concept that is used here is borrowed from nonorganizational studies and brings a new perspective to discussions of organizational design. The newness of this perspective stems from the unique characteristics of implicit theories and from its strong inclusion of the human actor in the organizational design process. This emphasis on the human actor is consistent with our earlier insistence that research in organizational design must rest on an assumption of purposeful behavior and thus must include elements of human choice.

Although the use of implicit theories of organizing is

relatively new in organizational studies, the general notion of implicit theories is well entrenched in studies of individual behavior. Prior to introducing the concept of implicit theories, it is important that we restate our position that it is neither necessary nor desirable to invent "new" theories of human choice simply because we are going to focus our attention on a narrow type of choice setting like organizational design. Thus, the idea of borrowing the concept of implicit theories is meaningful in both an analogical and an analytical sense. That is, the concept is useful as an analogy in that it will lead us to consider organizational design differently; and it is useful as an analytical tool in that students of individual behavior have already learned a number of things about implicit theories in other settings.

Early interest in implicit theories centered on attempts to understand individual behavior (for example, Heider, 1958; Jones and Davis, 1965; Kelley, 1967). The term *implicit theory* itself stems from Bruner and Tagiuri (1954). Observing the tendency for individuals to assume causal relationships among attributes of people with whom they interact, Bruner and Tagiuri called the network of these assumed causal relationships "naive, implicit personality theories." They are theories in the sense that they seek to explain, they are naive in that they tend to be simple and noncomplex, and they are implicit in that they are usually unstated and unconsciously held. At about the same time, Cronbach (1955) was using the term *lay theory of personality* to describe a similar observation.

These observations and the observations of other students of individual behavior led to a growing cognitive orientation; in effect, not only do we think, but we also think about how we think. Further, we seem to develop and use rather stable, albeit simple and implicit, schemas to guide these thought processes. By 1973, Schneider was able to synthesize these earlier concepts by defining an implicit personality theory as a set of assumptions that we each have about why people behave as they do.

The most developed applications of implicit theories involve the more narrow interest in attribution processes. Using the implicit theory ideas of Heider (1958) and Jones and Davis (1965), Kelley (1967) states that attribution processes are "processes that operate *as if* the individual were motivated to attain a *cognitive* [emphasis added] mastery of the causal structure of his environment" (p. 193). Further, Kelley emphatically urges that we not think of the attribution process as a mere reflection of the individual's attempt to understand. Rather, he asserts that individuals make attributions about the causes of others' behavior in order to seek control of their world through active intervention. In short, Kelley means that individuals develop cognitive schemas about others in order to understand them and in order to act. While the former of these reasons may be of deep intellectual interest, the latter is of more direct interest to an understanding of organizational structures.

Our discussion here is not restricted only to the more well-developed concepts of attributions. In fact, we will later argue that the tendency for some students to restrict their discussions of implicit theories only to attribution processes can be problematic for our notion of implicit organizing theories. Rather, we are interested in four basic commonalities that can be seen in all discussions of implicit theories. First, implicit theories are *assumptions* about causal factors. In this sense they are inductively derived; if $x$ is so, $y$ must have caused it. Second, individuals are more likely to use implicit theories to understand and to reinforce their understandings than they are to predict behavior. That is, we tend to be more interested in developing and confirming our cognitive schemas than in testing them. The third characteristic of implicit theories flows from the second, and it is that we seldom revise or alter our implicit theories even in the face of contrary evidence. Since we are usually trying to understand what has already happened, we do not give ourselves much of an opportunity to be wrong. Thus, we do not have to change our implicit theories—we simply change our application of them to events. Last, implicit theories are an important input into our actions. This last characteristic essentially restates the fact that our actions are a result of purposeful behavior and that purposeful behavior assumes a cognitive schema to guide action.

### Implicit Organizing Theories

We earlier pointed out that our interest in implicit theories was stimulated for methodological reasons by Staw. Our interest here, however, is much broader. If individuals use implicit theories to guide their behavior vis-à-vis other individuals, it is likely that individuals develop and use similar cognitive schemas to guide their behavior vis-à-vis other features in their environment. What is more, in a modern and complex society organizations represent one of the environment's most important and obtrusive elements. It is therefore reasonable to expect that we develop and use implicit theories about organizations to guide our behavior vis-à-vis organizations. Finally, our earlier agreement with Simon regarding the common elements of human choice leads us to expect that the nature and use of implicit organizing theories should parallel those of other implicit theories, such as implicit personality theories.

The following notions about implicit organizing theories stem from our observations about organizations coupled with what students of individual behavior have told us about implicit theories in general. The type of concepts presented here are not new to observers of organizations and their structures. What is new is the use of specific theories of human choice to predict phenomena at which others have hinted. For example, Weick (1977) has continually prodded scholars to consider the socially constructed nature of our perceptions of organizations. This cognitive orientation toward organizations is an intellectual forerunner of our present constructions. Similarly, Pondy and Mitroff (1979) have talked about organization members' use of "organizing rules." Here we will attempt to extend these earlier thoughts with some of the specifics of organizational design.

Before we proceed, there are a few things we should note about how we will treat organizational structure in this chapter. While we are obviously quite content to see our approach as consistent with those of a socially constructed reality (for example, Berger and Luckman, 1967; McLeod and Chaffee, 1972; Salancik and Pfeffer, 1978; Weick, 1977, 1979a, 1979b), we have chosen to treat organizational structure in a strictly "objective, concrete" way in this discussion. This choice is necessary if we are to use the notion of implicit theories to mediate between the empirical, observable characteristics of organizations and our perceptions of those same characteristics.

Further we have chosen to use the term *organizational structure* in a summative manner; that is, we wish to use the term as a shorthand to refer to a larger collection of variables. This larger collection would include such concepts as formality, complexity, and so on. While actual research aimed at exploring our ideas would require us to treat these structural variables individually, the discussion here does not do so.

## The Role of Implicit Organizing Theories

While it might be intellectually satisfying to posit the notion that individuals use implicit organizing theories in their interactions with organizations, that observation by itself is not particularly useful if not expanded. We will attempt to expand this observation in two important ways. First, we will explore the role that implicit organizing theories play in organized settings. After doing so, we will be in a position to suggest specific research that might incorporate the potential of implicit organizing theories as a concept.

We have identified five important roles that implicit organizing theories play in the way organizations function. Briefly, implicit organizing theories (1) guide organization elites in the design of organizations; (2) help organization members respond to the organization's structural dimensions; (3) contribute to the ability of a single organizational setting to satisfy organization members with dissimilar goal structures; (4) elicit change in organizational structures; and (5) bond organization members to each other and to their organization.

*Design.* The prominent role that implicit organizing theories play in the design of organizations is a direct extension of the basic thrust of this paper. If design decisions constitute purposeful behavior and if individuals use implicit theories in purposeful choices, it follows that those responsible for decisions that result in characteristics of the organizational structure use implicit organizing theories to guide their actions. As was pointed out early in our discussion, the fundamental basis of implicit theories is that their holders seek to use them to create an environment in which they will have some elements of control. Weick (1979a) touched on this notion when he talked about managers enacting the reality of their environments. In our terms, this would involve managers seeking to operationalize relevant implicit organizing theories to the extent that they have control over the organization.

This role that implicit organizing theories play in the design of an organization requires two important clarifications. First, the notion that implicit organizing theories play a role in design assumes that organizational structure characteristics are the result of choices made by organization members (Child, 1972). Second, this notion rejects the idea that organizational structures are the result of some natural evolutionary processes (Aldrich, 1979). This does not mean that the choices that resulted in organizational structure had to have been made by individuals who defined themselves as facing a situation in which organizational design is at stake. Decision makers are likely to draw upon more than one implicit organizing theory when facing a situation involving complex choices.

For example, suppose an executive creates a new sales group in order to provide more intense sales efforts aimed at institutional buyers. This choice is likely to involve the use of many implicit organizing theories. Some of these theories may involve marketing factors and some may involve structural factors. In this case, the implicit organizing theories that involve structure may be less salient compared to the marketing ones while still being influential. If this is so, the executive is likely to have considered the situation as being a marketing one while still using implicit organizing theories that have to do with the overall structure of the organization. At the other extreme, a manager might define the situation as an organizational design choice. If so, we would expect a set of implicit organizing theories regarding design to play a more prominent role in the choice.

In a recent work, Donaldson and Lorsch (1984) have produced strong support for our position put forth here. In a longitudinal, clinical study of the decision making of twelve CEOs of major corporations, they found that the CEOs' "beliefs" about organization processes were an important constraint on their choices in a variety of arenas. Donaldson and Lorsch chose to label these constraints "beliefs" in order to convey a stronger meaning than is normally communicated with such terms as "values." They state that their observations led them to need a term that would mix "convictions about normative matters (such as values and desired goals) with those about decision rules—cause and effect relationships" (p. 199). Donaldson and Lorsch point out, furthermore, that the beliefs that they had observed concerning the appropriateness of organizational arrangements were "a conviction or persuasion that something is true," and they emphasize "that persons (even senior executives) often have a deep emotional attachment to such convictions" (p. 79). In short, Donaldson and Lorsch seem to be describing the importance of implicit organizing theories in the behavior of the executives they studied.

For a longer example of the use of implicit organizing theories in the design of organizations, the reader is referred to an earlier work in which we used the case studies of Henry Ford and Will Durant to illustrate the ability of two organization designers to create two very different organizations in seemingly very similar settings (Brief and Downey, 1983).

*Organization Member Response.* The role of implicit organizing theories in the creation of organizational design is quite easy to assert. The second role of implicit organizing theories—that is, their role in organizational functions—is less obvious but equally important. This second role involves the use of implicit organizing theories by organization members to respond to the structures of organizations in which they find themselves. If an organization's structure were such that it carried a complete behavioral script for each organization member, this role of implicit organizing theories would not be needed. The structures that are created by organization designers as they seek to enact their implicit organizing theories represent only a skeletal guide to behavior for the organization members. Organization members must exercise discretion in the full elaboration of their organizational roles.

Some of the ambiguity in an organization member's role will likely be used by the member to fulfill some of his or her own personal goals or ambitions. It is likely, however, that the

organization member will also "fill in" or refine the role definition by making inferences from structural cues that are ubiquitous in the organizational setting. In order to refine the role, the
organization member must observe the outcome (structure) of
someone else's process (organizational design) and to impute or
infer a cause (design intent). To do so, the organization member
must apply a theory in reverse causal order, which is, of course,
exactly the purpose for which implicit theories are most often
used. In short, the organization member will fill in his or her
prescribed role using his or her personal implicit organizing
theory.

     This interpretation of design intent using implicit organiz-
ing theories means that the degree to which the organizational
structure is successful in eliciting the desired behavior is a function of the implicit organizing theories of both the designer(s)
and the organization members. Failure to recognize this phenomenon leaves most managers repeatedly "amazed" at how
their most carefully thought out reorganizations can seemingly
always be "fouled up" in implementation.

     The ability of organization members to "read" the needs
of the organization has been recognized by previous observers
of organizations. What is added here is an explanation of the
cognitive mechanism by which the organization member accom-
plishes this reading. For example, Jacques (1956) observed the
relationship between an organization member's pay and the
length of time that is required before the organization receives
feedback on the adequacy of the member's performance. The
members for which these times are the longest are paid the
most. Presumably, this is because these organization members
have a larger amount of discretion in their jobs. The greater the
required discretion, the greater the value of the member. *Value*
here can be expected to be a function of the degree to which
the organization can rely on the member to have and to use the
appropriate implicit theories in the enactment of his or her organizational role.

     Thompson has put forth a set of notions that are very
similar to those of Jacques. Thompson (1967) observed that
jobs in an organization tend to be arranged in such a way that

career advancement demands the ability to exercise increasing discretion. Ability to exercise this discretion can also be expected to be related to the organization member's ability to read the organization and to enact the proper role on the basis of that reading. The arrangement of jobs sequentially allows the organization to test the ability of the member to handle increasing amounts of discretion on an incremental basis. This incremental testing is meant to avoid disasters in placement decisions.

In summary, implicit organizing theories elicit behaviors from the members of the organization by allowing those members to infer the intent of the organization's design. This means that implicit organizing theories are the cognitive mechanism at work in the production of member behavior from organizational structure.

*Satisfying Dissimilar Goal Structures.* One of the most often cited discussions of general implicit theories involves the so-called performance-attribution effect. This effect involves the tendency for individuals to use performance as an important cue in their detection of all sorts of characteristics in a situation. For example, it is well documented that we tend to attribute success to ourselves and failure to our environment. For a review of this effect, the reader is referred to a recent work by Gioia and Sims (1985). The performance-attribution effect assumes that individuals use their implicit theories to attribute these characteristics in the setting. For this reason, the presence of the characteristics can be more a result of the members' implicit theories than the actual presence or absence of these characteristics. It is important to recognize, however, that performance is not the only cue (outcome) that individuals might use as a basis for attributions. Nevertheless, the performance-attribution effect is a well-documented phenomenon that, in fact, served as the basis for Staw's work, which we reported to be the original stimulus for our work.

The performance-attribution aspects of implicit organizing theories are also important because they allow us to posit a third role for implicit organizing theories—namely, the ability of organizations to satisfy the dissimilar goal structures of organization members. Let us take a look at how this works.

The basic driving force behind the attribution process is the assumed need to understand one's surroundings. In terms of performance attributions in organizations, individuals can be expected to observe performance outcomes and then attribute characteristics to the organization that are consistent with their implicit organizing theories. This attribution process may or may not be accurate in that individuals may or may not attribute the "correct" characteristics to the organization. For example, if an organization member's implicit organizing theory suggests that successful organizations are usually those that *lack* centralized decision processes, any signs of successful performance by the organization will lead the individual to tend to attribute decentralized characteristics to the organization. Other individuals, either internal or external to the organization, may attribute the exact opposite to the same organization because their implicit organizing theories suggest centralization as a requisite for success.

Note that this observation should not be interpreted to mean that we believe that people see anything they want to see in an organization. It does mean, however, that a large number of the relationships in an organization require individual perception and thus provide great latitude for different interpretations. This role of implicit organizing theories can be particularly important when different individuals value different organizational attributes. This is likely to be the case in organizations that employ individuals with heterogeneous backgrounds and training, which is true, of course, of most modern complex organizations.

Because implicit theories are by definition simple and contain few variables, people are likely to hold more than one implicit organizing theory with regard to a large, complex organization and to apply them when they feel the setting is appropriate. This would allow the individual to attribute very different characteristics to different parts of the organization. Indeed, this would allow individuals to attribute dissimilar, and perhaps even inconsistent, characteristics to the same organization at different times and for different subjects.

*Structural Change.* The fourth role of implicit organizing

theories is to serve as an elicitor of change in organizations. This role, like the third, is based on the performance-attribution process. When performance of an organization is poor, those associated with it will be likely to attribute characteristics to it that are associated with failure. To the extent that the individuals are in a position to change structures or to agitate for change, they are likely to initiate the process of change. Although this seems to be a desirable role for implicit organizing theories, it may prove to be problematic in actual practice. First, the attributions may be incorrect in the sense that the "real" causes of the poor performance might not have anything to do with the organization's structure. Events outside the organization's control (for example, changes in the general economy) or even chance occurrences (for example, luck) may be the actual cause of a specific performance outcome. To the extent that this is true, poor performance can bring on needless, and perhaps harmful, change, while success can breed satisfaction with structures that are not actually contributing to performance.

A second, highly speculative aspect of this role of implicit organizing theories involves the placement of attributions. Implicit theories applied to individual behavior have repeatedly demonstrated a tendency for individuals to attribute the causes of success to themselves and failure to others. While we will return to this question shortly, it remains to be seen if there is an organizational counterpart to this phenomenon. If so, agitation for change because of failure will be weakened and reinforcement because of success will be strengthened. Popular notions about managers would seem to confirm this tendency to attribute success to the organization and failure to the environment. This can be seen in the often repeated stories of managers who refuse to change even in the face of disaster, believing that success is "just around the corner." Likewise, it has been repeatedly demonstrated that achieving change needed for the future in a successful organization can be particularly difficult.

*Organization Bonding.* The final role of implicit oganizing theories is to contribute to social bonding of organization members. It has long been recognized by social scientists that individuals who share a belief system are likely to develop strong social attraction (Terborg, Castore, and DeNino, 1976). As such, they are more willing to associate, interact, share information, and remain together. All of these tendencies have positive outcomes for organizations. Organization members with these strong social bonds could be expected to be more willing to join the organization, work willingly together, communicate openly with each other, and be reluctant to leave the organization. Implicit theories are belief systems. In an organizational setting, an individual's implicit organizing theories should be particularly salient. Shared implicit organizing theories, sometimes called *consensual implicit theories*, can be expected to contribute to increased social bonding among organization members and its resultant positive effects.

The lack of social bonding can, of course, be expected in organizations in which individuals hold highly dissimilar implicit organizing theories. The effects would, by definition, be the opposite of those just described. This might be expected to be the case in an organization that employs a large number of individuals with highly dissimilar backgrounds and training.

Finally, it is important to note that the social bonding discussed here has nothing to do with the "correctness" of the shared implicit theories. In this sense, implicit organizing theories can be shared and can thus become organization myths. As is true of myths in any social system, their functionality is not necessarily related to their correctness. Armies have marched off to disasters believing themselves unbeatable, and organization members have happily worked the organization into bankruptcy waiting for the world to discover their felt superiority.

## Origins of Implicit Organizing Theories

For the most part, we will not discuss here the manner in which individuals come to hold particular implicit organizing theories. The reader is referred to Brief and Downey (1983) for a more complete discussion of this topic. Briefly, we suggest that individuals acquire implicit organizing theories through one of four processes. The first process is simply *sensemaking*. This process refers to the tendency for individuals to attempt to make sense of the world. They develop explanations of important activities around them. A more elaborate explanation of sensemaking is suggested by Weick (1979a), who describes "efferent sensemaking" as the process by which ideas are extended outward, implanted, and then rediscovered as knowledge. A second acquisition process involves what we would normally call *learning*. We learn implicit organizing theories, both directly and vicariously, by observation of covariation between stimuli in our environment. Third, we suggest that many of our implicit organizing theories are culturally provided in the same manner that we acquire other cultural meanings. These means would include games, rituals, literature, and other important transmitters of cultural meaning. Finally, we suggest that some implicit organizing theories seem to be intuitively acquired. In this intuitive process, the individual usually has generalized one implicit organizing theory to a new setting and is unaware of having done so.

## Problems with Implicit Organizing Theories

At this juncture, the preceding treatment of the origins and functions of implicit theories of organizing is best viewed as a set of interrelated propositions that, in large part, await empirical scrutiny. That is, while each of the propositions advanced may appear plausible and the connections between them reasonable, data directly relevant to their verification are scarce. Most empirical work in this area has not attempted to address the issues involved in the broad use of implicit theories in organizations. The initial work that has been done (for example, Gioia and Sims, 1985) has focused on narrow segments (for example, attribution location) of cognitive processes. For example, we are aware of only one test of the broad proposition that "those responsible for decisions which result in organizational structure characteristics use implicit organizing theories to guide their actions" (Walton, Brief, and Austin, 1985). Walton, Brief, and Austin sought to assess, with a laboratory experiment employing graduate business students as subjects, the causal relationship between structure-effectiveness attributions and organizational design decisions. They failed to detect any such relationship. Clearly, the external validity of the Walton, Brief, and Austin study is open to question. But the mere fact that it is the *only* study that has supplied data bearing directly on the proposition emphasizes the tenuous nature of implicit organizing theories.

More generally, one can turn to the literature on the relationships between cognitions and behaviors to examine further the propositions we have advanced about implicit organizing theories as causes of organizational behaviors. In summarizing this literature, Fiske and Taylor (1984) concluded, in part, the following:

1.  Consistency between cognitions and behaviors "will be highest when one examines behaviors that are prototypically related to particular cognitions, but that cognition-behavior consistency will be lowest when one examines behaviors that are less centrally related to the cognitions in question" (p. 371).
2.  "Cognitions that emerge from personal rather than indirect experience, and cognitions that have implications for one's future outcomes, may predict behavior better than cognitions that develop merely from mild curiosity or passing interest" (p. 374).
3.  "If cognition-behavior linkages are salient, cognitions and behaviors may typically cohere, but when situational norms are salient, behavior may be consistent with those norms" (p. 375).
4.  "All individual difference variables can be interpreted as moderators of the cognition-behavior relationship in that they predict what chronic goals people have cross-situationally, what kinds of situations they prefer, and what they do when they get to those situations" (p. 378).

Each of these four conclusions has clear implications for testing the set of propositions we have offered. First of all, organizational behaviors that are prototypical for particular implicit organizing theories should be looked for. Second, those implicit organizing theories should be identified that are most likely to have behavioral consequences. The organizational context should be examined for factors that make particular implicit organizing theories salient. Finally, individual difference variables (for example, the self-monitoring pointed to by Snyder, 1974) and self-consciousness (Fenigstein, Scheir, and Buss, 1975) that may moderate the relationship between implicit organizing theories and organizational behavior should be identified.

Even presuming these suggestions are followed, however, based on Fiske and Taylor's summary it must be assumed that the relationships between implicit organizing theories and organizational behavior will be found to be complex and elusive. Support for this assumption can be found in the work on the relationship between leader attributions about the causes of subordinate behavior and leader behavior. For example, Mitchell (1983), a person intimately involved in this research, concludes to his dismay that results regarding the relationships are mixed and that the predictive power of leader attributions is low. Moreover, Mitchell's conclusions are confirmed in a recent review of the nonorganizational attribution-behavior literature (Kelley and Michela, 1980).

A final and possibly more disturbing word of caution is in order. In the abstract, our idea of implicit organizing theories exhibits a marked similarity to Kelley's (1972) notion of causal schemas. The adequacy of Kelley's notions has not gone unchallenged. For example, Fiedler (1982) notes that "the formalistic notion of schema structures abstracted from meaning and content seems inadequate" (p. 1001); and Shaklee (1983) argues that "research outside of the attribution tradition must be considered in drawing conclusions about naive causal reasoning" (p. 1010). Shaklee, along with Fischhoff (1976), suggests that this other research includes that concerned with information processing. Thus, as a final suggestion for research on the relationships between implicit organizing theories and organizational behavior, we urge readers not to ignore work like Cappella and Folger's (1980) on an information processing explanation

of attitude-behavior inconsistency and like Shaklee and Fischhoff's (1982) on nonstrategies of information search in causal
analysis.

To sum up, there are problems with implicit organizing
theories. Most of these we optimistically see as stemming from
the scarcity of data. We feel that additional data, collected
with the suggestions we have offered, will demonstrate the utility of thinking about implicit organizing theories. But without
these data, further theorizing seems unwarranted.

## Implications for the Management of Organizations

Because there has been so little empirical research on
implicit organizing theories, any speculation about their importance to the management of organizations is highly speculative.
At the same time, a moderate amount of speculation seems to
be both fun and worthwhile at this point—fun for the mental
exercise and worthwhile in the sense that the projected implications will most likely determine whether further research is actually worth the effort. The reader is, of course, encouraged to
join the speculation as to the implications of implicit organizing
theories for the management of organizations. We will offer
some speculations of our own for starters.

The first implication for the management of organizations involves the individuals who contribute heavily to the design process. At present, their use of implicit organizing theories
is likely to be an intuitive, unconscious process. Given the un-
planned manner in which implicit organizing theories are likely
to be acquired by these individuals, design decisions would appear to include a strong element of chance. It might be argued
that success and failure of individual managers will eventually
produce designers with appropriate implicit organizing theories.
This argument assumes, of course, that we (both the organization and the individual) can bear the costs involved until that
"eventually" arrives and that once in the proper place, the individual would not be moved to a position in which his or her implicit organizing theories are inappropriate. In short, it may be
possible to lessen the cost of acquiring appropriate implicit or-

ganizing theories through open examination of them and through experience (acquired, perhaps, through training) aimed at the development of implicit organizing theories with specific characteristics.

The second implication involves the manner in which we treat results in organizational settings. At the present time, it is normal to assume that results which meet expectations are a function of our effort. Consequently, few organizations spend a significant amount of resources or energy retrospectively analyzing the reasons for success. This tendency may be the result of our tendency to attribute success to ourselves. In many cases, this may be more a function of the attribution process than a reflection of reality. If this is so, it might be wise for organizations and organization members to institutionalize something like the military practice of debriefing for specific operations. These debriefings are aimed at identifying both reasons for failure and for success.

The third implication is closely related to the second and has to do with achieving change in the organizational setting. If attributions related to implicit organizing theories work in ways that are similar to implicit theories in general, we will need to pay special attention to the performance-attribution process in our strategies for change. Recent evidence suggests this is the case (for example, Staw, McKechnie, and Puffer, 1983; Salancik and Meindl, 1984). This process would lead us to speculate that organization members, especially organization designers, are likely to attribute the causes of favorable performance to the organization's designs and unfavorable outcomes to elements in the environment. There is, of course, some probability that these attributions will be correct, but they obviously need not be so. In short, strategies for change will need to take special account of this process and find ways to short-circuit it.

Finally, the notions put forth in this chapter, if found to be valid, have implications for the importance of rituals and myths in organizations. (We use the term *ritual* here to refer to such things as group sharing of "war stories," the development of global mission statements, and Christmas parties. We use the term *myth* to refer to the stories, some true, some false, that circulate in any organization. These include the story of the time a young executive—no one can remember his name—defied the boss and lived to tell about it or the story of the new revolutionary product that is always just about to come from R&D.) These rituals and myths are important for two reasons. First, they may represent one of the important ways that organization members acquire their implicit organizing theories and have them reinforced over time. For example, many experienced managers may, from time to time, purposely implant the stories behind myths in informal communications because of their indirect impact. Second, rituals and myths may be important in that they represent an opportunity for organization members to share their individual implicit organizing theories in order to discover their similarities, which, in turn, would be expected to lead to increased social bonding.

## Summary

In this chapter we have attempted to present the framework for an understanding of the potential importance of a specific type of cognitive process in organizational design. We have done so by using what is known about implicit theories and by applying this information to a specialized setting for human choice—namely, organizational structure. We emphasize that our ideas are speculative and that moving beyond speculation with this topic will not be easy. We hope we have demonstrated, however, that the rewards for doing so could be substantial.

## References

Aldrich, H. *Organizations and Environments.* Englewood Cliffs, N.J.: Prentice-Hall, 1979.

Berger, P. L., and Luckman, T. *The Social Construction of Reality.* London: Penguin, 1967.

Brief, A. P., and Downey, H. K. "Cognitive and Organizational Structures: A Conceptual Analysis of Implicit Organizing Theories." *Human Relations,* 1983, *36* (12), 1065–1090.

Bruner, J. S., and Tagiuri, R. "The Perception of People." In G. Lindzey (ed.), *Handbook of Social Psychology.* Vol. 2. Reading, Mass.: Addison-Wesley, 1954.

Cappella, J. N., and Folger, J. P. "An Information-Processing Explanation of Attitude-Behavior Inconsistency." In D. Cushman and R. D. McPhee (eds.), *Message-Attitude-Behavior Relationship: Theory, Methodology, and Applications.* New York: Academic Press, 1980.

Child, J. "Organization Structure, Environment and Performance—The Role of Strategic Choice." *Sociology,* 1972, *6,* 1-22.

Cronbach, L. J. "Processes Affecting Scores on Understanding of Others and Assumed 'Similarity.' " *Psychological Bulletin,* 1955, *52,* 177-193.

Denisi, A. S., and Pritchard, R. D. "Implicit Theories of Performance as Artifacts in Survey Research: A Replication and Extension." *Organization Performance and Human Behavior,* 1978, *21,* 358-366.

Donaldson, G., and Lorsch, J. W. *Decision Making at the Top.* New York: Basic Books, 1984.

Downey, H. K., Chacko, T., and McElroy, J. C. "Attributions of the 'Cause' of Performance: A Constructive, Quasi-Longitudinal Replication of the Staw Study." *Organizational Behavior and Human Performance,* 1979, *24,* 287-299.

Etzioni, A. *Modern Organization.* Englewood Cliffs, N.J.: Prentice-Hall, 1964.

Fenigstein, A., Scheir, M. F., and Buss, A. H. "Public and Private Self-Consciousness." *Journal of Consulting and Clinical Psychology,* 1975, *43,* 522-527.

Fiedler, K. "Causal Schemata: Review and Criticism of Research on a Popular Construct." *Journal of Personality and Social Psychology,* 1982, *42,* 1001-1013.

Fischhoff, B. "Attribution Theory and Judgments Under Uncertainty." In J. Harvey and others (eds.), *New Directions in Attribution Research.* Hillsdale, N.J.: Erlbaum, 1976.

Fiske, S. T., and Taylor, S. E. *Social Cognition.* Reading, Mass.: Addison-Wesley, 1984.

Gioia, D. A., and Sims, H. P., Jr. "Self-Serving Bias and Actor-

Observer Differences in Organizations: An Empirical Analysis." *Journal of Applied Social Psychology,* 1985, *15,* 547–563.

Heider, F. *The Psychology of Interpersonal Relations.* New York: Wiley, 1958.

Jacques, E. *Measurement of Responsibility.* London: Tavistock, 1956.

Jones, E. E., and Davis, K. E. "From Data to Disposition." In L. Berkowitz (ed.), *Advances in Experimental Social Psychology.* Vol. 2. Orlando, Fla.: Academic Press, 1965.

Kelley, H. H. "Attribution Theory in Social Psychology." In D. Levine (ed.), *Nebraska Symposium on Motivation.* Vol. 15. Lincoln: University of Nebraska Press, 1967.

Kelley, H. H. "Causal Schemata and the Attribution Process." In E. Jones and others (eds.), *Attribution: Perceiving the Causes of Behavior.* Morristown, N.J.: General Learning Press, 1972.

Kelley, H. H., and Michela, J. L. "Attribution Theory and Research." *Annual Review of Psychology,* 1980, *31,* 457–501.

Kuhn, T. S. *The Structure of Scientific Revolutions.* Chicago: University of Chicago Press, 1962.

McLeod, J., and Chaffee, S. H. "The Construction of Social Reality." In J. Techleschi (ed.), *The Social Influence Processes.* Hawthorne, N.Y.: Aldine, 1972.

Mitchell, T. R. "Attributions and Actions: A Note of Caution." *Journal of Management,* 1983, *8,* 65–74.

Mitroff, I. I., and Kilmann, R. "On Organizational Stories: An Approach to the Design and Analysis of Organizations Through Myths and Stories." In R. Kilmann, L. Pondy, and D. Slevin (eds.), *The Management of Organization Design: Strategies Implementation.* New York: Elsevier North-Holland, 1976.

Pondy, L. R., and Mitroff, I. I. "Beyond the Open Systems Model of Organization." In B. Staw (ed.), *Research in Organizational Behavior.* Vol. 1. Greenwich, Conn.: JAI Press, 1979.

Salancik, G. R., and Meindl, J. R. "Corporate Attributions as

Strategic Illusions of Management Control." *Administrative Science Quarterly*, 1984, *29*, 238-254.

Salancik, G. R., and Pfeffer, J. "A Social Information Processing Approach to Job Attitudes and Task Design." *Administrative Science Quarterly*, 1978, *23*, 224-253.

Schneider, D. J. "Implicit Personality Theory: A Review." *Psychological Bulletin*, 1973, *79*, 294-309.

Shaklee, H. "Causal Schemata: Description or Explanation of Judgment Process? A Reply to Fiedler." *Journal of Personality and Social Psychology*, 1983, *45*, 1010-1012.

Shaklee, H., and Fischhoff, B. "Strategies of Information Search in Causal Reasoning." *Memory and Cognition*, 1982, *10*, 520-530.

Simon, H. A. "Discussion: Cognition and Social Behavior." In J. S. Carroll and J. W. Payne (eds.), *Cognition and Social Behavior*. Hillsdale, N.J.: Erlbaum, 1976.

Snyder, M. "The Self-Monitoring of Expressive Behavior." *Journal of Personality and Social Psychology*, 1974, *30*, 526-537.

Staw, B. M. "Attributions of the 'Cause' of Performance: A General Alternative of Interpretation of Cross-Sectional Research on Organizations." *Organizational Behavior and Human Performance*, 1975, *13*, 414-432.

Staw, B. M., McKechnie, P. I., and Puffer, S. M. "The Justification of Organizational Performance." *Administrative Science Quarterly*, 1983, *28*, 582-600.

Terborg, J. R., Castore, C., and DeNino, J. A. "A Longitudinal Field Investigation of the Impact of Group Composition on Group Performance and Cohesiveness." *Journal of Personality and Social Psychology*, 1976, *34*, 782-790.

Thompson, J. D. *Organizations in Action.* New York: McGraw-Hill, 1967.

Walton, E. J., Brief, A. P., and Austin, E. J. "Cognitive and Organizational Structures: An Empirical Analysis." *Human Relations*, 1985, *38* (8), 723-738.

Weick, K. E. "Enactment Process in Organizations." In B. Staw and G. Salancik (eds.), *New Directions in Organizational Behavior*. Chicago: St. Clair Press, 1977.

Weick, K. E. *The Social Psychology of Organizing.* Reading, Mass.: Addison-Wesley, 1979a.

Weick, K. E. "Cognitive Processes in Organizations." In B. Staw (ed.), *Research in Organizational Behavior.* Vol. 1. Greenwich, Conn.: JAI Press, 1979b.

# 7

# The Managed Thought

## The Role of Self-Justification and Impression Management in Organizational Settings

Jennifer A. Chatman
Nancy E. Bell
Barry M. Staw

*So you want to know what I think about my job? If I'm satisfied?*

*Well, I've got a couple of answers for you. When I was first offered the job, I was so excited about it that I could hardly wait for the first day of work. Then reality struck. I realized that this place had real problems and that my position in the operation was one of the worst. Still, I didn't give up, I didn't jump ship. I worked hard at this miserable job until I saw its merits. I tell you, someone's got to do the dirty work around here, and if I quit, the whole place might fall apart. I tell my story to all the new recruits each year, and of course they fail to see the merits of my argument, initially at least. But just wait a few years and you'll see how they come around.*

*What was your question again—was it about*
*job satisfaction?*

—Confessions on the
managed thought by a
devoted corporate
citizen

Much of the recent literature on individual and social cognition
has deemphasized the roles of both the person and the social
context. Researchers have been concerned with finding patterns
and limitations of a rather mechanical model of information
processing—that is, they have been concerned with exploring
shortcomings in the input, storage, and recall of information.
This mode of research has at its core the metaphor of man as
"intuitive scientist" (Kelley, 1967), with theory and research
centered on cognitive processes and heuristics that people use to
process information and make attributions.

Like the professional scientist in the laboratory, the intuitive scientist is conceived of as collecting and analyzing information in a dispassionate manner. This perspective, unfortunately, makes little allowance for the influence of emotional
preferences, nor are individual motivations and intentions often
considered as explanations in the formulation and communication of information. Likewise, the social context is given very
little weight in explaining how information is derived, manipulated, and presented in interpersonal settings. These omissions,
we would argue, are serious shortcomings of most information-
processing theories, because there is evidence that thoughts can
be "managed" and that cognitions are subject to motivational
and contextual forces.

This chapter is therefore concerned with two related issues: first, with bringing people back into the study of individual cognition by formulating a more motivational model of
information processing; and second, with emphasizing the role
that the social context plays in providing the content for a
greater understanding of social cognition. We will concentrate
on two cognitive theories that invoke motivational premises and

constraints: self-justification and impression management. We will briefly review the origins of and recent literature on each of these models and then show how they may be used productively in organizational research. Our concern will not be to discredit prevailing cognitive approaches or to debate the role of motivation in social cognition. Instead, we will argue that it is necessary to ground cognitive formulations in their relevant context, taking into account individual and social influences, if we are ever to accurately describe the role of cognition in organizational settings.

## Self-Justification Theory

Self-justification theory is an outgrowth and refinement of Festinger's classic work on cognitive dissonance. *Dissonance,* as defined by Festinger (1957), is a motivational state aroused in individuals when two cognitive elements are inconsistent. Dissonance theory is conceptually very broad since cognitive elements can be interpreted as any knowledge, opinion, or belief about oneself or one's environment, and inconsistency among such elements can be implied by perceptual rather than factual or logical incongruity. The outcome of cognitive inconsistency is predicted to be tension or motivational arousal, at least until "cognitive work" lowers the number or the importance of cognitions that are discrepant. Such cognitive work often produces attitude change. For example, if a person joins an organization to work at a dissatisfying job, the dissonance between his behavior (holding the job) and his attitude (job dissatisfaction) should be reduced by changing either the behavior (quitting the job) or the attitude ("discovering" more positive aspects of the job). Because it is often easier to change attitudes than to change behavior, people may grow to like the jobs they are performing.

There have been three major contexts or paradigms for testing cognitive dissonance. One type, known as the *forced-compliance paradigm,* has examined attitude change as a consequence of induced compliance (Festinger and Carlsmith, 1959; Gerard, 1967). The typical forced-compliance study has asked subjects to write essays contrary to their own attitudes or positions on an issue. Some subjects were asked to comply with this request with little external pressure (for example, paid nothing or $1) while others were paid more generously (for example, $20) for writing such a counterattitudinal essay. Dissonance theory has predicted and found an inverse relationship between payment and attitude change. Subjects who were given a relatively high reward ($20) for writing the essay have shown little change in their attitudes, since the payment presumably provided a sufficient explanation or justification for their counterattitudinal act (Festinger and Carlsmith, 1959; Wicklund and Brehm, 1976). In contrast, when subjects were given only a small reward for writing a counterattitudinal essay ($1), their attitudes changed more significantly in the direction of the essay. Apparently, being paid poorly to perform a counterattitudinal act sets up dissonance that can be reduced by changing one's attitude on the issue.

A second, and closely related, area of work has concerned the consequences of initiation rites (see Aronson and Mills, 1959; Salancik, 1977). The general finding has been that people become more attracted to a group or organization after they perform difficult or unpleasant tasks to attain entry into that group. Their enhanced attitudes apparently result from attempts to align the performance of difficult (and sometimes very distasteful) tasks with their desires to enter the group. For example, cognitive dissonance theory would predict that attraction to an organization would be enhanced by going through initiation rites, since in order to satisfy the need for consistency, organization membership would have to be seen as being worth the effort it takes to attain it.

A third area of empirical work on cognitive dissonance has focused on individuals' tendencies to enhance the perceived value of chosen alternatives (Brehm, 1956; Cooper, 1971). In one of the earliest experiments testing cognitive dissonance theory, Brehm (1956) gave subjects the choice between two appliances. Following their choice, subjects tended to reevaluate the two appliances in such a way as to downgrade the unchosen appliance and enhance their liking of the chosen appliance. The cognitive dissonance interpretation is that after making a difficult choice, people experience tension because cognitions about any negative attributes of the preferred object are dissonant with having chosen it, and cognitions about the positive attributes of the unchosen object are dissonant with not having chosen it. So, in order to reduce dissonance, people emphasize the positive aspects of the chosen object and emphasize the negative aspects of the unchosen object (Festinger, 1964).

*From Dissonance to Self-Justification.* In an early review and interpretation of dissonance theory, Aronson (1968) pointed out that dissonance arousal appeared to occur only when an individual's self-concept was involved. In fact, Aronson argued that the tests of cognitive dissonance may have actually tapped threats to the self-concepts of individuals. For example, when one considers the self-concept as represented by a number of statements like "I am an honest person" and "I am an intelligent person," such beliefs are likely to be threatened in the typical cognitive dissonance experiment. Thus a person's beliefs about the level of his or her competence and performance may determine whether or not dissonance will be aroused. A positive self-concept may therefore be an important boundary condition for the occurrence of dissonance effects, with individuals with a poor self-concept (people who perceive themselves as incompetent or unintelligent) experiencing typical forced-compliance situations as compatible rather than dissonant with their self-concepts.

Staw (1980) has taken Aronson's argument a step further by proposing that most of the dissonance experiments have tapped a need for self-justification rather than a need for cognitive consistency. Individuals, he argued, may seek to justify their own actions, decisions, and attitudes in order to protect their self-concepts as rational decision makers. Thus, while dissonance-predicted effects are presumed to be motivated by a need for cognitive consistency, self-justification effects are assumed to be motivated by threats to one's ego, or valued self-image. Dissonance-reducing behaviors would therefore be expected to occur in situations where an individual's perception of his or her own consistency is challenged, while self-justifying behaviors would be expected to occur in situations where the individual's sense of rationality or competence (or any other important element of the self-concept) is challenged.

It is clear that the concepts of dissonance and self-justification are closely related and that situations that evoke a combination of both types of motives and behaviors are likely to arise. An explanation for this link is that society has tended to associate consistent behavior with rational or utility-maximizing behavior. A difference between the approaches relates to the source of arousal and target of attitude change. Cognitive dissonance theory argues that one's motivation (to change one's beliefs or attitudes) is based on the desire to appear consistent to oneself—that is, to resolve the tension resulting from inconsistent cognitive elements. In contrast, self-justification theory views attitude change as a way to resolve threats to the ego, primarily stemming from adverse events in the person's environment. At the extreme, Staw (1980) has considered self-justification as a motive to demonstrate competence to oneself and/or others in a social setting—to prove to either oneself or others that one is a rational and worthwhile person. If we use this latter definition, self-justification starts to overlap with impression management theory.

## Impression Management Theories

Impression management is not a single coherent theory but a set of common descriptions of behavior based on several shared assumptions. Usually, the term *impression management* refers to an interpersonal motive to impress others or to satisfy external publics. Whereas dissonance and self-justification refer to intrapsychic desires to reduce inconsistency or protect one's ego, impression management refers to the desire to please or impress others. The impression management view generally examines the behavioral strategies that people use to create and maintain desired social images and identities (Tetlock and Manstead, 1985). This approach analyzes people's considerations of their moral responsibilities, their reasons or justifications for behaviors, and their desires and attempts to present positive views of themselves to others.

Forced-compliance situations have been a particularly useful means of articulating the assumptions of impression management theories. In contrast to the approach of dissonance theorists, forced-compliance situations are viewed as evoking a state of interpersonal defensiveness rather than a need for cognitive consistency. This state is triggered by negative affective states, such as embarrassment or shame that subjects feel because of the predicament they have been placed in. Additionally, people are assumed to act in accord with subtle societal norms, such as cooperating with an authoritative figure, in an attempt to maximize the favorability of their image to others. Thus, in forced-compliance situations subjects may not perceive free choice, contrary to what cognitive dissonance researchers assume. Finally, impression management theory assumes that any attitude changes occurring in a forced-compliance situation, or in analogous real-life situations, can represent uninternalized, temporary, and feigned shifts that serve the function of managing an individual's social identity rather than real or fundamental shifts in attitudes and beliefs.

Theorists have differing views about the appropriate restrictions to impression management theories. Tedeschi and Rosenfeld (1981), for example, argue that impression management is an applicable interpretation of behavior only when salient and external audiences are present. In contrast, theorists such as Schlenker (1982) argue that real audiences do not have to be present for a person to feel negative repercussions. This is because the actor may have "internalized," via socialization, particular standards, constructed a self-concept, and become aware of what others require him to be.

Impression management theorists also differ in the topics they cover and the methodologies they use. Tedeschi and Rosenfeld (1981) divide impression management into three types of approaches. The evaluation-apprehension approach (Rosenberg, 1968) looks at the demand characteristics and the potential social desirability biases that may cause subjects to attempt to maintain consistency in experimental situations. The situated-identities approach (see Alexander and Knight, 1971; Tetlock, 1980) argues that people are aware of the social norms of how others judge behaviors in a given situation. Thus, situations constrain the kinds of behaviors that can be emitted, and this restricts the kinds of identities actors can claim. A third approach, which is usually simply referred to as impression management (see Tedeschi, 1981; Schlenker, 1982), argues that individuals do not have an intrinsic need to be consistent as proposed by Festinger. Instead, people have a social concern or an underlying motive to *appear* consistent, honest, intelligent, and so on, to others.

Many experiments that support impression management approaches have used the *bogus pipeline procedure*. This procedure attempts to convince subjects that their responses are being monitored by a device that can determine when they are lying (the device is not actually able to detect lies, hence the term *bogus*). An example is a study by Gaes, Kalle, and Tedeschi (1978). Subjects were induced to write an essay against toothbrushing, which, they were told, would be read to junior high school students. Then half the subjects were given the typical paper-and-pencil attitude questionnaire, while the other half were hooked up to the (bogus) lie detector. Compared with control subjects, those subjects in the paper-and-pencil condition reported significant attitude change in the direction of the counterattitudinal behavior (the typical forced-compliance finding). In contrast, subjects whose attitudes were measured via the bogus device did *not* manifest attitude change. The experimenters concluded that subjects *feigned* attitude change only when they thought that their responses could not be verified or demonstrated to be insincere (presumably because the consequences of being exposed as a liar are worse than appearing inconsistent).

*Comparing Self-Justification Theories with Impression Management Theories.* A salient feature in comparing cognitive dissonance and self-justification with impression management theories is the source of motivation that each hypothesizes. The dissonance and self-justification approaches are intrapsychic theories in which individuals are seen as needing or desiring to view themselves in a particular way (for example, competent, certain, consistent). In contrast, impression management theories argue that the motivation for many behaviors and expressed attitudes is based on the individual's desire to create and maintain external social identities.

In a sense, intrapsychic and impression management explanations are not alternative or competing modes of dealing with the predicament of inconsistency between behaviors and attitudes. Rather, the two responses are designed for different audiences: impression management to placate the external audience, and intrapsychic theories to placate the self. To clarify this point, consider the example mentioned earlier of a person who works in a dissatisfying job and who subsequently changes his attitude about his job by "discovering" more positive aspects of that job. Such an attitude change may serve two purposes: first, it may resolve a threat to the person's inner sense of consistency or efficacy (by allowing the person to avoid asking himself why he is working in a job that he finds dissatisfying); and second, the attitude change can help to manage a desirable impression to others (that he is well adjusted). Taken to an extreme, however, the distinction between internal and external sources of motivation can also become rather arbitrary. For example, impression management theorists could argue that when there is no external audience present, subjects may still be attempting to maintain their images, but to *internalized* audiences. Unfortunately, it is impossible to distinguish internalized audiences from the intrapsychic explanation.

Tetlock and Manstead (1985) identify seven strategies that researchers have used in attempts to distinguish between intrapsychic theories (for example, cognitive dissonance) and impression management theories. The categories are as follows: public versus private, manipulation of audience beliefs, contextual manipulations, sincerity of response manipulations, social identity implications of behavior, personality variables (for example, self-monitoring or self-attention), and physiological arousal. For each of these categories, Tetlock and Manstead describe what each theory would predict, and they discuss the problems each category has in conclusively distinguishing between intrapsychic and impression management explanations. Because it is nearly impossible to construct a strong compara-

tive test of the two approaches, Tetlock and Manstead urge researchers to look for similarities that underlie *both* classes of
theories. An additional motivation for this research strategy is
the possibility that both self-justification and impression management might be *simultaneously* present in a given situation.

One important similarity of self-justification and impression management theories is that they are both motivationally
based. With either of these approaches, information processing
is more than the mechanical input, storage, and retrieval of
data. Both self-justification and impression management approaches bring individuals back into models of cognition, because they emphasize human bias and the adjustment of beliefs
to fit behavior. They also bring the social context back into social cognition, because they help identify interpersonal influences in information processing and the transmission of data.
According to these two models, individuals seek to regulate
cognition by managing their beliefs in a way that conforms to
internal, personal standards (such as honesty or rationality) or
external organizational standards (such as a demand for competence or consistency). A future task of cognitive researchers
is therefore to identify the content, functions, and derivation
of behavioral standards as they affect individual cognitive processes.

## Implications for Theory and Research

Our intent in the second part of this chapter is to propose
some ways in which self-justification and impression management processes may be manifested in organizations. We have
chosen to explore a number of organizationally relevant topics:
job satisfaction, career images, socialization, decision making,
and organizational images. We have chosen topics that cross
levels of analysis: the first topics are concerned mainly with
individuals as the units of analysis, while the latter topics move
into a more macro or organizational unit of analysis. The purpose of the discussion that follows is to illustrate the importance of amending the machine model of social cognition by including two potentially important sources of data biasing:
individual motivation and social context.

*Job Satisfaction.* Survey evidence indicates that most workers report that they are satisfied with their jobs, only about 10 percent reporting dissatisfaction (Freeman, 1978). One reaction to such a small percentage of dissatisfied jobholders would be to take this information at face value and to conclude that people in general simply like their work. If, however, one were somewhat suspicious of this conclusion, one might want to look for underlying mechanisms that could explain conformity in the expression of job attitudes.

A self-justification theorist might argue that being in a dissatisfying job is an ego-threatening situation. Since our society puts a value on being happy and on freedom of choice, it is important for people to feel that they are able to choose situations in which they feel content. The two cognitions "I am unhappy in this job" and "I choose to be in this job" are therefore inconsistent. Similarly, the cognition "I am in this job without the freedom to go to another job" will be inconsistent with the view of oneself as competent and self-determining. Thus, a person who is dissatisfied with his job would be expected to make some adjustment in order to appease his internal need for consistency between his attitudes and his behaviors. This adjustment could take the form of a change in behavior, such as quitting one's job.

But what about those who do not choose turnover as their dissonance-reduction mechanism? Perhaps a portion of those individuals who report that they are satisfied with their jobs may have at one time been less so and may have cognitively reevaluated their jobs in order to resolve the inconsistency between dissatisfaction and staying on the job. Such cognitive reevaluation would be most likely in situations where the person was a member of a work group in which other members of the group had already engaged in a similar reevaluation process. Organizational stories or accounts, which are exchanged and shared by the group, could be a mechanism for the transmission of such information, supporting the reevaluation process.

An impression management view of reported satisfaction might reason as follows: one desired social identity in our society is to appear well adjusted, and consequently people should not report that they willingly stay in unpleasant situations. To do so would convey an impression of nonoptimal social adjustment. For this reason, respondents to job satisfaction questions might overstate their job satisfaction in order to manage a public impression of adjustment—that is, to appear consistent between attitudes and behavior or at least to avoid being perceived as a "complainer." Of course, since job attitudes surveys are usually anonymous, impression management would have to be of the variety that allows for internalized audiences (Schlenker, 1982)—that is, one that is close to well-learned social norms for individual behavior and beliefs.

Although self-justification and impression management can both serve as forces for consistency between job attitudes and behavior, there are important cases where such inconsistency persists. Richard Freeman (1978), for example, describes an interesting case where low reported job satisfaction is associated with low turnover. This seemingly inconsistent state of affairs is found in the case of unionized workers. Unionism tends to reduce turnover, while also *reducing,* or in some data sets holding constant, job satisfaction. In explaining this anomaly, Freeman contends that union members express dissatisfactions through the "voice" mechanism—that is, through the grievance procedure and through formal contract negotiations. Therefore, although at first glance this looks like a case of behavior not matching attitudes, this finding can still be explained in light of self-justification and impression management processes. With recourse to the grievance procedure, to a strike, or to a negotiating position, union members can account for their continued tenure in the job by convincing themselves that they are acting to improve the situation.

An interesting way of researching our speculations about job satisfaction may be the situated-identities approach (see Alexander and Knight, 1971; Tetlock, 1980). This technique could be used to uncover the particular norms that operate in organizations. For example, one organization may be more tolerant and constructive with employees who express job dissatisfaction, while another organization may impose strict sanctions when such dissatisfaction is expressed. This would mean that the first organization, which holds honesty and openness in high esteem, would not foster as much distortion in job attitudes as the second organization, which is more concerned with face-saving and public appearance. Also, an organization that provides positive channels for criticism would more likely possess individuals who are both dissatisfied and, at the same time, closely identified with their jobs. With a means of expressing dissatisfaction, individuals need not justify their very presence or identification with the firm.

*Career and Organizational Images.* A second area of inquiry where thinking in terms of self-justification and impression management can provide useful insights is how individuals manage their career images and what the consequences of such career image management might be. As we know, work plays a role in defining one's image or identity, both to self and to others (Gouldner, 1957; Kahn, 1980). However, one's work identity may be defined both by the particular type of job one does (for example, engineer or secretary) and by the organization (for example, IBM or Boeing) for which one works. We would therefore predict that the means by which a person uses his or her organizational or professional associations to manage his or her career may vary according to the type of job, the organization, and the person's perception of socially relevant or desired images.

It is proposed that when the individual perceives *both* the organization and the job to be prestigious (as might be the case, for example, with a systems engineer who works for IBM), both will be presented to others with equal frequency. If the job is not seen as prestigious but the organization is (for example, a janitor at the Pentagon), it is likely that the individual will present himself to others as working for the organization and refer less to the particular job he performs. Conversely, if the profession is highly prestigious but the organization is not (for example, a Ph.D. college professor who works for a low-status junior college), the individual will be more likely to present herself as belonging to the profession. Finally, if both the job and the organization are perceived by the individual as low on prestige, it is likely that the person will not identify himself in terms of his work; rather, other affiliations will be the important identity categories (for example, a dishwasher who works in an unpopular greasy-spoon restaurant may be more likely to discuss her bowling club membership than her work). For each of these propositions, it is assumed that perceived prestige is a function of the person's own beliefs and values and also of the perceived norms and values of significant others. The perceived norms and values can change according to the particular audience that is important to the actor at a given time.

Besides prestige association, there can be other advantages and disadvantages to the individual for associating his or her image with an organization. The negative side could be demonstrated when an organization is involved in a serious violation either of social norms or of the law. (There is no shortage of examples of such violations: the A. H. Robins Company's problems with the Dalkon Shield, the Union Carbide incident in Bhopal, and the Bank of Boston's alleged mafia affiliations are only a few.) An organization member in such a situation is caught in a "predicament," since he may share some responsibility for the organization's negative actions. Feelings of shared responsibility can arise from an individual's direct involvement with the negative event; or the member can perceive that he is "guilty" or responsible simply because he is associated with the organization, even if he has had nothing to do with the particular event.

The member's reaction to this kind of predicament is difficult to predict. It will be affected by his or her perception that the organization's actions are inconsistent with the member's own beliefs and values about the way the organization should conduct its business, the perceptions the individual has about how *others* perceive the organization's actions, and the degree of responsibility the individual feels with respect to organizational events. The publicity of the event will also be important in the sense that the more times the person is called upon by others, both external and internal to the organization, to explain or justify the event, the more salient will be the need to resolve cognitive inconsistencies or to create favorable impressions. Finally, the equivocality of the evaluation of the event

will be important, since ambiguity both reduces the need to resolve the predicament and allows more flexibility in constructing an appropriate explanation of the event.

The individual who is caught in such a predicament has a
few options:

- Try to deny one's responsibility in the actual event ("That
  wasn't my division").
- Minimize one's association with the organization ("I only
  work here").
- Withdraw functionally from the organization via such be-
  havioral avenues as absenteeism or sabotage.
- Withdraw physically from the organization (quit).
- Try to change the organization while maintaining one's
  loyalty to it.
- Point to the "hidden" positive features of the negative event.
  Such reasoning or justification may take the following form:
  "Bhopal prevented this from happening in other places" or
  "The Bank of Boston incident led to a more honest system
  because other banks admitted to having unrecorded transac-
  tions."

It may be that the strategies an individual uses to deal with
negative organizational events depend on the particular type of
attachment that person exhibited prior to the event. It has been
found that the bases of an individual's attachment to an organization can be described by three orthogonal factors: compliance, identification, and internalization (O'Reilly and Chatman,
1985).

Drawing on Kelman's (1958) typology, compliance occurs
when attitudes and behaviors are adopted in an organization
not because the individual shares the beliefs of the organization but rather to gain specific rewards. Since their association is based on an instrumental exchange with the organization,
individuals whose basis of attachment is compliance will be
more likely to use a strategy of minimizing their association
with the organization, or denying their responsibility for the
actual event.

The second dimension, identification, refers to cases in which the individual accepts the influence of the organization in order to maintain a satisfying relationship; that is, the individual respects the values and accomplishments of the organization without necessarily adopting them personally. A person who identifies with the goals and values of the organization would more likely adopt a strategy of withdrawal (either physically or functionally) from the organization. Because those who identify are placed in a predicament when negative circumstances arise, withdrawal or a reduction in affiliation may provide a "solution" to such predicaments.

Finally, internalization occurs when influence is accepted because the induced behavior is congruent with the individual's own values; thus, the values of the individual and the organization are one and the same. In contrast to the case of identification, individuals who internalize the goals and values of the organization may not have the option of withdrawing from the organization because the values and goals in question are a part of the individuals themselves. Therefore, those who have internalized organizational goals and values would be more likely to rationalize or justify the organization's actions.

*Organizational Socialization.* Self-justification and impression management theories also provide useful insights into the issues surrounding organizational socialization. Socialization is the process by which new recruits learn the value system and behavioral norms of an organization (Schein, 1979). It is also the process by which commitment or identification with the organization is built. Thus, socialization is a process where both the behavior and the attitudes of the recruit are targets of change. A new employee may have to engage in many work behaviors that are potentially quite different from previous work behaviors, and that are public, explicit, and promise little or no immediate reward. In this sense, the socialization process is a real-life analog of the forced-compliance research paradigm discussed earlier.

In the commonly cited case of fraternity initiation rites, it is generally predicted that the pledges will realign their attitudes about the fraternity in order to justify all the effort and costs undergone in the pursuit of membership. Although the rites of initiation for new organization members are usually less extreme than those for fraternity pledges, the socialization experience of new employees may be equally powerful in producing attitude change. New organization members find themselves in the position of having to learn many new and difficult behaviors, and often organizations intensify this socialization experience by giving new members the most unpleasant tasks or by withholding benefits until new members have proven themselves. In order to resolve threats to the ego (such as maintaining a self-concept of competence) or threats to a social need (such as managing a positive public impression), the new organization member's attitudes may change in the direction of greater congruence with organizational values and norms. There is, of course, also the risk that the new recruit will resolve the inconsistency between the realities of the job and his or her self-concept or social needs by exiting the organization.

Perhaps the reason that few people leave an organization as the result of a difficult socialization experience can be found in the job selection process. A whole set of formalities exists in the screening, selection, and hiring processes that potential job candidates must go through. Although these procedures may have some validity, many of them are only marginally predictive of later job performance (Cascio, 1978). Such entrance procedures may, however, serve the function of increasing commitment to the organization, because of the time the job candidate has invested in trying to get the job. In this way, even before entering the organization, self-justification and impression management may be operating to move the potential employee's attitudes into alignment with organizational values.

*Decision-Making Processes and Commitment to a Course of Action.* Socialization processes usually refer to the positive aspects of committing organization members to values or behaviors—but such commitment also has negative potential. Once an individual is committed to specific behaviors, the results can be disastrous if the behaviors are counterproductive for the organization. If such commitment occurs at the top levels of the organization, for example, it could contribute to inflexibility in action and failure to adapt to changing environmental conditions. At the extreme, leaders may even need to be replaced to bring the organization in line with changing products and forces in an industry.

Motivational models of decision making (for example, Janis and Mann, 1977) recognize that decisions take place in a social context or "natural decision environment" (Tetlock, 1985). In this environment, decisions may be imbued with affective considerations, as opposed to the "cool," machinelike model of rational problem solving (Abelson, 1963; Janis and Mann, 1977). "Hot," or affect-laden, cognitions may cause the decision-making process to become one of rationalizing rather than one that is normatively rational. For example, in the course of defending against a threat, rationalizing may lead to a search for exonerating explanations (excuses), a falsely positive reevaluation of negative outcomes or losses (justification), and an attempt to recoup losses by escalating commitment to a failing course of action ("throwing good money after bad").

Self-justification theory has already been used to develop a large literature on the escalation of commitment. A common finding has been that individuals tend to invest further resources in a losing course of action when they have been personally responsible for failure (for example, Staw, 1976). However, as the escalation literature has grown, impression management principles have also started to be considered. For example, decision makers have been found to be more likely to become committed to a course of action when they have needed to protect their external reputations or when social norms have dictated consistency in action (see Brockner and Rubin, 1985, and Staw, 1981, for reviews). There is also evidence that decision makers may manipulate information sent to others as a means of justification or impression management (Caldwell and O'Reilly, 1982). Thus, because of self-justification and impression management, organizations may neither process information appropriately, nor make proper decisions about failing policies and courses of action.

In addition to the literature on the escalation of commitment, there are other ways in which self-justification and impression management affect the decision-making process. Given that there is a high degree of uncertainty surrounding most organizational decision-making processes and that strong norms of accountability exist, decision makers may make those decisions that will be most justifiable later on. Often this may mean that decision makers follow an "acceptability heuristic" (Tetlock, 1985) rather than engaging in a thorough information search and evaluation of the problem at hand. In some cases decision makers may gather too much information, since administrators may be more interested in avoiding external criticism than in avoiding the cost of useless data (Feldman and March, 1981). In both instances, the motivating force behind decision making may be an effort to manage external impressions of rationality rather than the desire for accurate and effective action. The result of such impression management may be a reduction in creativity at the organizational level, since actions that are less than totally defensible will be avoided.

*Organizational Images.* So far, our discussion has been primarily concerned with how individuals use justification and impression management. However, these processes may also apply at the organizational level. As noted by Staw, McKechnie, and Puffer (1983), organizations may put substantial effort into rationalizing action and events to themselves (akin to self-justification) or managing the appearance of rationality with outside constituencies (akin to impression management). Although a number of mechanisms can be used to manage the appearance of rationality, analyses of annual reports (Bettman and Weitz, 1983; Salancik and Meindl, 1984; Staw, McKechnie, and Puffer, 1983) have demonstrated that organizations engage in self-serving biases (taking credit for success and avoiding blame for failures) to justify their behaviors to important constituencies.

Organizations may also evidence justification and impression management processes in their routine operating procedures. Rules, regulations, standardization, and planning may all serve to increase efficiency, yet they also function to legitimate the organization to its various constituencies (Meyer and Rowan, 1977). Such organizational features, rather than being essential for task performance, may be used to convey to constituents (including internal organizational constituencies) that the organization is rational, competent, and systematic. This legitimation reassures constituents, and it allows them to avoid having to question the reasons for their own continued affiliation with and support of the organization.

Finally, it should be noted that the organization may not always want to manage or present the most positive image of itself. For example, when faced with a demand for higher wages, the organization may want to create an impression among workers (particularly unionized workers) that things are not good. To this constituency, management tells a sad story: profits are down and there is no money for raises. In contrast, when the organization is presenting data to stockholders, bankers, and potential customers, the future is bright and resources plentiful. Thus, depending on the constituency involved, information can be biased by organizations in either an optimistic or pessimistic direction. Managing these two such conflicting impressions can, of course, be no easy feat.

## Conclusion

In this chapter we have done two things. First, we reviewed the self-justification and impression management approaches, and we noted how they can enhance our knowledge of social cognition by including motivational and contextual elements. Second, we discussed some of the ways in which self-justification and impression management theories can be applied in organizational settings. It should be apparent that this latter discussion was very speculative, mainly because there has been so little organizational research using these cognitive theories.

In exploring the organizational implications of self-justification and impression management theories, a theme that we hoped to emphasize is the importance of viewing cognitive theories at both the micro and macro levels of analysis. Crossing levels of analysis is, we believe, especially useful for two reasons. First, the psychological theories of self-justification and impression management are simply process theories whose content and predicted consequences depend on the social context in which they are imbedded. Second, there is conceptually an overlap between individual and organizational behavior that is seldom acknowledged. This is because when we look at individual behavior in organizations, we are actually seeing two entities: the individual as himself, and the individual as a representative of his collectivity (which could be the work group or the organization). Thus, the individual not only acts on behalf of the organization in the usual agency sense, but he also acts, more subtly, "as the organization" when he embodies the values, beliefs, and goals of the collectivity. As a result, individual behavior is more "macro" than we usually recognize, and organization behavior is more "micro" than is generally acknowledged.

Much more research needs to be done in order to fully ground the study of cognition in organizations. So far, cognitive research in organizations has been borrowed directly from atomistic rather than contextual models of individual functioning (McGuire, 1984), without the richness of either individual motives or the features of organizations that may serve to cue these motives. It is thus our contention that we need to recapture the "individual" in individual cognition, as well as the "social" in social cognition. These will be no easy tasks, yet they should bring us a more accurate model of organizational life and a better understanding of "the managed thought."

## References

Abelson, R. P. "Computer Simulation of 'Hot Cognitions.' " In S. Tomkins and S. Mesick (eds.), *Computer Simulation of Personality.* New York: Wiley, 1963.

Alexander, C., and Knight, G. "Situated Identities and Social Psychological Experimentation." *Sociometry,* 1971, *34,* 65–82.

Aronson, E. "Dissonance Theory: Progress and Problems." In R. Abelson and others (eds.), *Theories of Cognitive Consistency: A Sourcebook.* Skokie, Ill.: Rand McNally, 1968.

Aronson, E., and Mills, J. "The Effect of Severity of Initiation on Liking for a Group." *Journal of Abnormal and Social Psychology,* 1959, *59,* 177–182.

Bettman, J. R., and Weitz, B. A. "Attributions in the Board Room: Causal Reasoning in Corporate Annual Reports." *Administrative Science Quarterly,* 1983, *28,* 165–183.

Brehm, J. "Post-Decision Changes in the Desirability of Alternatives." *Journal of Abnormal and Social Psychology,* 1956, *52,* 379–382.

Brockner, J., and Rubin, J. Z. *Entrapment in Escalating Conflicts.* New York: Springer-Verlag, 1985.

Caldwell, D. F., and O'Reilly, C. A. "Responses to Failure: The Effects of Choice and Responsibility on Impression Management." *Academy of Management Journal,* 1982, *25,* 121–136.

Cascio, W. *Applied Psychology in Personnel Management.* Reston, Va.: Reston, 1978.

Cooper, J. "Personal Responsibility and Dissonance: The Role of Foreseen Consequences." *Journal of Personality and Social Psychology,* 1971, *8,* 354–363.

Feldman, M. S., and March, J. G. "Information in Organizations as Signal and Symbol." *Administrative Science Quarterly,* 1981, *26,* 171–186.

Festinger, L. *A Theory of Cognitive Dissonance.* New York: Harper & Row, 1957.

Festinger, L. *Conflict, Decision, and Dissonance.* Stanford, Calif.: Stanford University Press, 1964.

Festinger, L., and Carlsmith, J. "Cognitive Consequences of Forced Compliance." *Journal of Abnormal Social Psychology,* 1959, *58,* 203–210.

Freeman, R. B. "Job Satisfaction as an Economic Variable." *American Economic Review,* 1978, *68,* 135–141.

Gaes, G. G., Kalle, R. J., and Tedeschi, J. T. "Impression Management in the Forced Compliance Situation." *Journal of Experimental Social Psychology,* 1978, *14,* 493–510.

Gerard, H. "Compliance, Expectation of Reward, and Opinion Change." *Journal of Personality and Social Psychology,* 1967, *6,* 360–364.

Gouldner, A. W. "Cosmopolitans and Locals: Toward an Analysis of Latent Social Roles—I." *Administrative Science Quarterly,* 1957, *2,* 281–306.

Janis, I. L., and Mann, L. *Decision Making: A Psychological Analysis of Conflict, Choice, and Commitment.* New York: Free Press, 1977.

Kahn, R. *Work and Health.* New York: Wiley-Interscience, 1980.

Kelley, H. H. "Attribution Theory in Social Psychology." In D. Levine (ed.), *Nebraska Symposium on Motivation.* Vol. 15. Lincoln: University of Nebraska Press, 1967.

Kelman, H. C. "Compliance, Identification, and Internalization: Three Processes of Attitude Change." *Journal of Conflict Resolution,* 1958, *2,* 51-60.

McGuire, W. "A Contextualist Theory of Knowledge: Its Implications for Innovation and Reform in Psychological Research." In L. Berkowitz (ed.), *Advances in Experimental Social Psychology.* Vol. 16. Orlando, Fla.: Academic Press, 1984.

Meyer, J. W., and Rowan, B. "Institutionalized Organizations: Formal Structure as Myth and Ceremony." *American Journal of Sociology,* 1977, *83,* 340-363.

O'Reilly, C. A., and Chatman, J. A. "Organizational Commitment and Psychological Attachment: The Effects of Compliance, Identification, and Internalization on Prosocial Behavior." Paper presented at 45th annual meeting of the Academy of Management, San Diego, Aug. 1985.

Rosenberg, M. "Hedonism, Inauthenticity, and Other Goals Toward Expansion of a Consistency Theory." In R. Abelson and others (eds.), *Theories of Cognitive Consistency: A Sourcebook.* Skokie, Ill.: Rand McNally, 1968.

Salancik, G. "Commitment and the Control of Organizational Behavior and Belief." In B. Staw and G. Salancik (eds.), *New Directions in Organizational Behavior.* Chicago: St. Clair Press, 1977.

Salancik, G. R., and Meindl, J. R. "Corporate Attributions as Strategic Illusions of Management Control." *Administrative Science Quarterly,* 1984, *29,* 238-254.

Schein, E. H. "Organizational Socialization and the Profession of Management." In D. A. Kolb, I. M. Rubin, and J. M. McIntyre (eds.), *Organizational Psychology: A Book of Readings.* (3rd ed.) Englewood Cliffs, N.J.: Prentice-Hall, 1979.

Schlenker, B. *Impression Management: The Self-Concept, Social Identity, and Interpersonal Relations.* Monterey, Calif.: Brooks/Cole, 1980.

Schlenker, B. "Translating Actions into Attitudes: An Identity-Analytic Approach to the Explanation of Social Conduct." In L. Berkowitz (ed.), *Advances in Experimental Social Psychology.* Vol. 15. Orlando, Fla.: Academic Press, 1982.

Staw, B. M. "Knee-Deep in the Big Muddy: A Study of Escalating Commitment to a Chosen Course of Action." *Organizational Behavior and Human Performance,* 1976, *16,* 27–44.

Staw, B. M. "Rationality and Justification in Organizational Life." In B. Staw and L. Cummings (eds.), *Research in Organizational Behavior.* Greenwich, Conn.: JAI Press, 1980.

Staw, B. M. "The Escalation of Commitment to a Course of Action." *Academy of Management Review,* 1981, *6,* 577–587.

Staw, B. M., McKechnie, P. I., and Puffer, S. M. "The Justification of Organizational Performance." *Administrative Science Quarterly,* 1983, *28,* 582–600.

Tedeschi, J. *Impression Management Theory and Social Psychological Research.* Orlando, Fla.: Academic Press, 1981.

Tedeschi, J., and Rosenfeld, P. "Impression Management and the Forced Compliance Situation." In J. Tedeschi (ed.), *Impression Management Theory and Social Psychological Research.* Orlando, Fla.: Academic Press, 1981.

Tetlock, P. E. "Explaining Teacher Explanations for Pupil Performance: A Test of the Self-Presentation Position." *Social Psychology Quarterly,* 1980, *43,* 283–290.

Tetlock, P. E. "Accountability: The Neglected Social Context of Judgment and Choice." In B. M. Staw and L. L. Cummings (eds.), *Research in Organizational Behavior.* Vol. 7. Greenwich, Conn.: JAI Press, 1985.

Tetlock, P. E., and Manstead, A. "Impression Management Versus Intrapsychic Explanations in Social Psychology: A Useful Dichotomy?" *Psychological Review,* 1985, *92,* 59–77.

Wicklund, R., and Brehm, J. *Perspectives on Cognitive Dissonance.* Hillsdale, N.J.: Erlbaum, 1976.

# 8

## Affect in Organizations

### How Feelings and Emotions
### Influence Managerial Judgment

Oh Soo Park
Henry P. Sims, Jr.
Stephan J. Motowidlo

*I can sum it up this way: it is both a positive and
negative thing. I feel good about it at times and I
feel bad, nervous, and uncomfortable about doing
it sometimes. . . . You try to approach it in a positive way, although that can be tough because of
time pressures or poor performance or you're having a rough day or week or whatever. I don't know
anyone that really loves doing the appraisal, and
yet it can be a good thing and it can be enjoyable
. . . but it can also be real difficult, uncomfortable,
even an anxious thing for both of us. I have mixed
feelings . . . but it is part of the job that you have
to take seriously and you can't neglect even if you
don't like doing it. It is your responsibility to do it
and that is it. Your feelings change and are influenced by the circumstances surrounding each appraisal you do. I've had some real highs doing it
and some real lows, let me tell you. You just try*

*and do the best you can to make it a positive thing*
*for your people because they deserve it.*

—Longenecker, 1984, pp.
221–222, quoting a
senior executive

In recent years, affect has taken on new importance in cognitive psychology and, at least potentially, in the study of organizational behavior. In addition to asking how individuals process information, related investigations have explored the nature of feelings, moods, and emotions, and how these forms of affect, in turn, influence behavior. Some might question whether affect should be a part of cognitive psychology, since the term cognition implies thought, while conversely affect implies feeling. Nevertheless, because most of the affect investigations have grown from the field of cognitive psychology, research on affect is most often related to cognitive research. Moreover, much of the thrust of affect research explores the interaction and relationships between affect and cognitions.

In this chapter, we will review some of the important contributions emerging from affect research in cognitive psychology and speculate on how this affect research might provide important insights into behavior in organizational situations. In particular, we will explore how affect research might be helpful in providing new understanding about managerial judgment in organizational situations. Later, we will focus on a specific type of organizational event, the performance appraisal, as an application of the ideas developed here.

Affect itself is not new to organizational behavior. Indeed, affect-like variables such as satisfaction (Locke, 1976), valence (Vroom, 1964; Mitchell, 1974), and preference (Cyert and March, 1963) have historically been extremely important parts of theories of organization. Furthermore, some organizational theories have given serious attention to so-called nonrational components in choice processes (March, 1978; March and Olsen, 1976; Weick, 1979). Also, conceptual frameworks utilizing affect have recently been successfully applied to the organizational context. For example, we have seen research on effects of affective variables on task perceptions (Caldwell, O'Reilly, and Staw, 1983), expectation and performance (Park, Sims, and Motowidlo, 1984), job performance (Motowidlo, Packard, and Manning, 1985), judgments of performance effectiveness (Srinivas and Motowidlo, 1985), citizenship or prosocial behavior (Motowidlo, 1984; Bateman and Organ, 1983; Smith, Organ, and Near, 1983; Moore, Underwood, and Rosenhan, 1984), turnover decisions (Motowidlo and Lawton, 1984), and personnel decisions (Jaccoud, 1984; Longenecker, 1984). Nevertheless, we believe the especially recent viewpoints on affect from cognitive psychology provide a relatively new perspective. The challenge for us is to explore whether these theories have potential relevance in thinking about how managers and organizations function.

In this chapter, we will first attempt to define affect in terms of more precise concepts, such as emotion, feeling, and mood. We will explore distinctions of meaning and nuances among the concepts. We will then describe some selected recent theoretical developments that center on affect as an important component of human cognition and behavior. Finally, we will suggest how these concepts and theories might be usefully applied to organizational behavior, with a particular emphasis on managerial judgment and performance appraisal.

### What Is Affect?

The term *affect* is generally considered to be broad and encompassing. It is a generic term for a wide range of feelings and emotions (Arnold, 1960; Fiske and Taylor, 1984) and is frequently used as an overarching concept that encompasses more specific terms like *emotion, mood,* and *feeling.* For the purposes of this chapter, it is convenient to distinguish between two categories of affect: differentiated affect and undifferentiated affect.

Differentiated affect is aroused by a specific target or situation (Arnold, 1960; Ewert, 1970; Clark and Isen, 1982; Roseman, 1980; Fiske, 1981), and describes an individual's emotional reaction toward that target or stimulus (Fiske, 1982; Zajonc, 1980). It is thought to be related to specific cognitive processes such as attribution (Weiner, 1980b, 1982; Brown and Weiner, 1984; Weiner and Graham, 1984), arousal or attention (Schacter and Singer, 1962; Norman, 1975; Mandler, 1975), or schematic processing (Leventhal, 1980; Clark and Isen, 1982; Lang, 1984). Thus, differentiated affect is defined as an emotional response to a specific target, person, or situation.

Undifferentiated affect, or mood, has no specific target (Clark and Isen, 1982; Fiske, 1981). It is pervasive and ongoing, for at least some period of time (Zajonc, 1980; Clark and Isen, 1982; Bower and Cohen, 1982), and permeates all one's experiences (Fiske, 1981). Both types of affect, differentiated and undifferentiated, are discussed in the following section, where we review selected theories of affect derived mainly from the cognitive psychology literature. The theories we review are not necessarily exhaustive; they have been selected with two criteria in mind. First, each of these theories has attained a certain measure of prominence and attention in cognitive psychology. Second, we believe that potentially each of these theories has pragmatic ramifications for the study of organizations.

### Selected Theories of Affect

*Affect and Cognition: Which Precedes Which?* Affect and cognition are understood as separate yet interrelated, interactive, and interdependent systems. One point of view regards affect as a consequence of cognitive processes. Many researchers have suggested that cognition elicits affect or that affect results from the evaluation of a stimulus (Arnold, 1960; Arieti, 1970; Lazarus, Averill, and Opton, 1970). Also, some suggest that emotion (affect) is experienced or elicited through the perception of unique physiological changes (Tomkins, 1970), or through cognitive interpretation of a general arousal state (Mandler, 1975, 1982; Royce and Diamond, 1980; Roseman, 1980). And more recently, Lazarus (1982, 1984) argues that cognition is a necessary precondition for affective arousal. A contrasting viewpoint is that emotion is an antecedent of cognition, and that affective responses can occur without extensive prior cognition (Zajonc, 1980, 1984; Zajonc and Markus, 1982, 1984).

There is no full agreement about whether cognition is a *necessary* precondition for the affect. However, it is generally recognized that under certain conditions, cognitive factors contribute importantly to emotional processes, such as emotional expression, symbolization, and labeling of emotion. Actually, we suspect that parts of this argument stem from semantic differences in the definition of affect and from differences in research perspectives. It is also important to note that Zajonc does not assert that affect *always* precedes cognition. He suggests that affect can be generated without prior cognitive processes "in a certain situation" (1980) and that affect precedes cognition "at times" (1984). Royce and Diamond (1980) also suggest that the argument over the causal precedence of affect and cognition is not a critical issue because the phenomena can be referenced with language such as "cognitive basis of emotion" and "affect-laden cognition."

In the long term, however, the issue of affect/cognition precedence may potentially have important ramifications for the study of organizational behavior. If, for example, affect is fundamental and relatively instantaneous as Zajonc suggests, then managerial judgments may frequently be made almost entirely subconsciously, before any "real" cognition is brought to bear on the issue. This suggests at least a certain degree of *predecision.* That is, the theory suggests the possibility that important decisions are initially (and perhaps therefore predominantly) affect-driven rather than "rational" or cognitively driven. Zajonc's seminal 1980 article describes the amusing incident of Phoebe's decision of whether to accept a position at another university. She says, " 'I get half way through my [decision-making] sheet and say 'Oh hell, it's not coming out right! Have to find a way to get some pluses over on the other side!' " (Zajonc, 1980, p. 155).

The more important question is not which causes the other—affect or cognition—but rather how do affect and cognition interact to influence patterns of behavior in work settings.

Affect and cognition may exist as independent entities, but the processes or activities of each are likely to be interactive with each other. Their relationship might best be understood as a *cognitive basis of affect* and/or an *affective basis of cognition* rather than a one-way deterministic relationship.

*Memory and Mood.* Recent studies have begun to examine effects of mood on memory, thinking, social learning, and social judgment (Bower, 1981, 1983; Bower and Cohen, 1982; Srull, 1983; Gilligan and Bower, 1984; Clark and Isen, 1982; Wright and Mischel, 1982). From a managerial perspective, this suggests that one's immediate affective state—mood—may have an influence on a judgment to be made. Bower and his colleagues suggest that mood is an associative element tagged to other cognitive elements in memory. These affective tags are linked to each other in a rich associative network of concepts, schemas, and events. In this associative network, emotion serves as a memory unit, and activation of this memory unit retrieves events associated with that emotion.

Bower (1981) describes two ways in which undifferentiated affect or mood might influence such cognitive processes as learning, memory, perception, and judgment. The first is the mood-congruity effect: events that convey an emotional tone that matches an individual's current mood are attended to most closely and learned best. For example, people who feel happy tend to pay more attention to and learn more thoroughly information about a happy than an unhappy incident. The second is mood-state-dependent retention: superior retrieval from memory occurs when the mood state at the time of recall matches the mood state experienced during learning. For example, people in a negative mood can recall information that they learned while in a negative mood better than information that they learned while in a positive mood.

Other recent research is similar in perspective to Bower's research but has focused on the influence of affect on problem solving, decision making, judgment, and/or evaluation (Isen, Shalker, Clark, and Karp, 1978; Isen and Shalker, 1982; Isen, Means, Patrick, and Nowicki, 1982; Isen and Means, 1983; Isen, 1984; Isen and Patrick, 1983; Isen and Daubman, 1984; Hill, Lippitt, and Serkowneck, 1979). Most of this research by Isen and her colleagues has dealt with normal ranges of emotional intensity that might be experienced in everyday life rather than extreme or traumatic affective states. In addition, their approach has focused more on the effects of positive affect than on the effects of negative affect. They propose that a positive mood influences evaluation, judgment, and decision making by shaping decision-making strategies and by increasing the likelihood that positively toned material will be retrieved from memory. According to their research, a subject who feels good is more likely to be efficient in decision making through a more effective use of information related to the decision making (Isen, Shalker, Clark, and Karp, 1978; Isen, Means, Patrick, and Nowicki, 1982; Isen and Means, 1983). In general, a person who is feeling good will be better able to create solutions to problems requiring ingenuity (Isen, 1984).

Isen and her colleagues have also explored the influence of affect on risk taking (Isen, Means, Patrick, and Nowicki, 1982; Isen and Patrick, 1983). They suggest that positive affect will increase the risk-taking tendency when risk is low. Under high risk, the influence of affect is not conclusive. They propose that positive affect, through its influence on memory and judgment, leads to more optimistic expectations about possible outcomes. In turn, these more favorable expectations lead to a higher propensity for risk-taking behavior (Isen and Shalker, 1982; Isen, Shalker, Clark, and Karp, 1978).

*Schema-Triggered Affect.* Fiske and her colleagues (Fiske, 1981, 1982; Fiske and Linville, 1980; Abelson, Kinder, Peters, and Fiske, 1982; Fiske, Beattie, and Milberg, 1983; Fiske and Taylor, 1984) describe two modes of affective response in person perception. One is category-based or *schema-triggered affect,* which results when a target person "matches" or fits a category that also has strong affective overtones. (As defined elsewhere in this volume, the term *schema* refers to a cognitive knowledge structure—that is, a mental map or network in which concepts are organized into some systematic pattern.) A category prototype is a particularly vivid representation of a schema. For example, Jaccoud (1984) has clearly demonstrated the widespread existence of the "extroverted salesman" as an example of a person-in-situation type of category prototype. Another is piecemeal-based affect, which results when a target person fails to fit a clear category.

In *piecemeal-based affect,* affective reactions are based directly on the information given, and bits of information accumulate independently with their own valences. This piecemeal-based affect is a slow process that involves attribute-by-attribute judgment (Fiske, Beattie, and Milberg, 1983). In contrast, schema-triggered affect results when a target person matches an affect-laden category; it is a rapid, configural judgment. According to the empirical findings of Fiske and her associates, good matches of a person to schema elicit stronger positive or negative affect than no matches. Fiske, Beattie, and Milberg (1983) support the hypothesis of schematic efficiency (or stereotyping efficiency). In other words, schemas enable more rapid affective responses than are possible without such social categories.

Fiske's concept of schema-triggered affect is similar to other concepts that involve automatic or holistic processing of information about affective experience. Leventhal (1980), for example, suggests that an emotional schema is a memory of the emotional experience itself and that it represents a form of automatic recognition. Clark and Isen (1982) apply the distinction between automatic and controlled processing of information suggested by Posner and Snyder (1975) and propose that a person's experience of a feeling state automatically cues similarily toned materials in memory. Lang (1984) also regards the emotion-information network as a sort of prototype or schema, which is processed as a unit under certain conditions.

Thus, a schema-triggered model of interpersonal affect suggests two interesting propositions. One is that perceptions of persons are represented as instances of categories and that affect is inextricably linked to this categorization. Another is that schema-triggered affect is efficient and quick because affective reactions do not require complex, volitionally controlled processes.

In sum, two models have been developed to explain affective reactions to persons as social entities: a schema-triggered model and a piecemeal model. As Fiske and her colleagues argued, "Neither model is exactly wrong or exactly right. It is not a question of which model fits, but of when each fits" (Fiske, Beattie, and Milberg, 1983, pp. 3-4). When a target person fits an affect-laden category (or schema), schema-triggered affect results from automatic, holistic processing of information; when a target person fails to fit any schema, however, more controlled processes, driven by more volitional dynamics, slip into gear, and piecemeal-based processing of information produces the affective response.

*Attribution and Affect.* A theory of affective consequences of achievement-related attribution has been proposed by Weiner and his colleagues (Weiner, 1980a, 1980b, 1982, 1983; Weiner, Russell, and Lerman, 1978, 1979; Weiner and Graham, 1984; Weiner and Brown, 1984; Brown and Weiner, 1984; Weary, 1982). They suggest that emotion in an achievement-related context is a function of performance outcome and the specific causal ascription for this outcome. Weiner (1980b, 1982) differentiated two kinds of affect: outcome-dependent affect and attribution-dependent affect. Outcome-dependent affect represents broad positive or negative affective reactions (for example, happy or upset) stemming from success or failure, regardless of the causes of these performance outcomes. This outcome-dependent affect is an intensively experienced emotion, and it is independent of causal attribution (though not free from other cognition). In contrast, attribution-dependent affect is related to particular causal attributions, and it is likely to be a sharply differentiated affect like anger, pride, pity, guilt, or surprise. Attribution-dependent affect is thought to be a longer lasting affective state than outcome-dependent affect. It might also be more strongly influenced by cognitive mediation—that is, it might reflect more the results of active thinking about and analysis of information related to performance outcomes—than outcome-dependent affect.

For the attribution-dependent affect, different causal attributions elicit qualitatively distinct affective reactions (Weiner, 1980b, 1982, 1983; Brown and Weiner, 1984; Weiner and Graham, 1984). For example, leaders who attribute subordinates' failure to lack of effort would show more anger toward the subordinates than would leaders who attribute subordinates' fail-

ure to lack of ability. Leaders who attribute the failure of subordinates to external causes, such as bad luck or the difficulty
of the task, tend to show pity or sympathy.

Research in this area has focused primarily on ability and
effort as potential attributional causes and on affective responses like pride, anger, pity, sympathy, and guilt. One overall
theme that seems to emerge from these studies is that attribution to either effort or ability seems to make a bigger difference
in the nature of the subsequent affective response (pride, anger,
and so on) when the performance outcome is failure. When the
performance outcome is success, the effects of attributed cause
on affective response are weaker.

In sum, according to this line of research, the observed
outcome—the success or failure of another person's performance—and the nature of the perceiver's causal attribution
about that outcome both influence the perceiver's affective response, but they do so differently. Outcome-dependent emotions are elicited regardless of the nature of the causal attribution. The causal beliefs about the performance or outcome
influence the observer's affective reactions to the performer,
especially if the performance outcome is failure.

*Summary.* All these conceptual frameworks and empirical studies fall into one of two major categories. One category
involves the notion that affect is automatically triggered by
schema. Concepts such as Zajonc's cognition-affect preference,
Fiske's schema-triggered affect, Leventhal's emotional schema,
Lang's emotional prototype, Clark and Isen's automatic processing of affect, and Weiner's outcome-related affect share this
perspective. The second category involves the notion that affect
results from volitional cognitive processes. Concepts such as
Lazarus's primacy of cognition, Fiske's piecemeal-based affect,
Leventhal's conceptual processing of emotion, Lang's control of
emotion, Clark and Isen's controlled processing of affect, and
Weiner's attribution-induced affects share this perspective.

## Affect and Emotion in Performance Appraisal

The literature we have reviewed highlights the importance
of affect as a major set of variables in understanding and ex-

plaining individual behavior. Yet little is known about how affective variables and cognitive variables interact to shape behavior in organizational settings. Neither is much known about their effects specifically on evaluative, judgmental, and decision-making processes in organizations. Of the many potential behavioral and judgmental issues in organizational behavior that might be analyzed according to effects of the interplay of affect and cognition, we will single out the issue of performance appraisal. One reason that performance appraisal seems an appropriate subject for analysis in these terms is that the performance evaluation literature is currently undergoing a special focus on the psychological processes underlying the transformation of informational cues into evaluations of the effectiveness or goodness of observed job performance. Consequently, we believe an analytic perspective that draws from the literature on affect and cognition in human behavior can help illuminate the processes that govern performance evaluation in organized work settings.

In the following pages, we will show how theories of affect can be applied to performance appraisal in organizational settings. Also, we will explore the relationship between affect and cognition in the performance appraisal process and discuss how this relationship can be applied to the problem of understanding the complex process of managerial judgment in a performance evaluation situation.

*Information Processing in Performance Appraisal.* Before we undertake an affect perspective, it would be useful to briefly review some of the more recent cognition-oriented developments in the performance appraisal literature. For example, Borman (1978) and Cooper (1981) describe relatively rationalistic cognitive components of organizing, storing, and retrieving performance-related information. Landy and Farr (1980) suggest a process model of performance rating that more completely integrates context components, cognitive processes, and administrative rating processes. Other theoretical approaches describe even more complex and comprehensive models of cognitive processes in performance evaluation (Feldman, 1981; Landy and Farr, 1983; Ilgen and Feldman, 1983; Denisi, Cafferty, and Meglino, 1984).

These models view ratees as active seekers and processors

of information (Feldman, 1981; Denisi, Cafferty, and Meglino, 1984) who carry out cognitive tasks such as attention, categorization, storage, recall, and integration of performance information. The models describe how raters process performance-related information to make rating decisions about ratees. They generally characterize performance appraisal as a memory-based judgment (Ilgen and Feldman, 1983) rather than stimulus-based judgment.

Behavioral and other kinds of information about ratees is presumed to be utilized to initially classify the individual into a category when the person seems to match a category prototype (or schema). However, when the person does not fit any available category, controlled processes take over and cognitive factors such as causal attributions come to play a more important role in forming the evaluative judgment (Feldman, 1981; Ilgen and Feldman, 1983; Landy and Farr, 1983). If the person fits a category prototype, information is processed automatically and yields an evaluative judgment according to attributes implied by the category prototype rather than according to actual attributes of the person. If it does not fit any available category, controlled processes go into effect and the rater may deliberately search for additional information until a good fit with a category in memory can be made. Then, once the person has been assigned to a category, the assignation produces the related evaluative judgment. However reached, the judgment itself is stored in memory and influences the next episode of performance evaluation by influencing processes of attention, categorization, storage, recall, and integration of subsequent performance-related information.

*Affect in Performance Evaluation.* The information processing model of performance appraisal described above enhances our understanding of how cognitive processes of raters shape their judgments of performance evaluation, but other factors should also be taken into account. In particular, affective processes that influence and that are in turn influenced by cognitive factors are especially important to consider.

For example, undifferentiated affect, or mood states of raters, may influence the way they process information about ratees. As suggested by Bower and his colleagues (Bower, 1981, 1983; Bower and Cohen, 1982; Gilligan and Bower, 1984), mood biases encoding, memory, recall, and judgment of affectively toned events or material. People are more likely to attend to and recall information that is consistent with their mood. This means that a rater in a positive mood should be more likely to notice and remember good things that a subordinate has done. Thus, raters who feel good are more likely to notice and remember information reflecting effective performance on the part of the ratee and for that reason should rate him or her more favorably. This happens because positive mood acts like a filter that selectively reinforces the salience of information connoting high levels of performance effectiveness. Mood can act in this manner at both the attention and retrieval stages of information processing. Mood can thus be a source of bias. In an unpublished qualitative study, Longenecker (1984) quotes executives who recognize this potential source of bias in themselves and describes some of their self-developed strategies to control it.

We also expect mood to influence cognitive processes in the controlled mode. When searching actively for additional information to enable the performer to fit an available category prototype, raters are likely to bias their search in favor of information consistent with their mood. As a result, raters in positive moods operating in a controlled mode are more likely to find evidence of effective performance; raters in negative moods are more likely to find evidence of ineffective performance.

So far, we have described the manner in which undifferentiated affect, or mood, influences automatic and controlled processing of performance-related information and the favorability of the final performance evaluation. At the same time, we might expect a causal effect in the other direction. That is, performance information should have reciprocal effects on raters' affective states. As Fiske and her colleagues suggest (Fiske, 1981, 1982; Fiske and Linville, 1980; Fiske, Beattie, and Milberg, 1983), if social information leads to a close fit with a category prototype in memory, the affective tone associated with that prototype will be automatically elicited. For example, if the rater observes information about the ratee that closely resembles characteristics of a category such as effective performer, and if that prototype is associated with a positive affective response such as liking—that is, the rater wants effective performance from his or her subordinates and likes subordinates who perform effectively—this liking response will be evoked and attached to the ratee under consideration. Essentially, the rater comes to like the ratee because the ratee fits the prototype of effective performer.

Differentiated affect may also be evoked by factors not directly related to job performance itself (for example, dress, hairstyle, race, gender, courtesy). If the performance information is sufficiently dramatic and if it leads to a sufficiently strong differentiated affective response, the rater's subsequent mood could also be influenced. Furthermore, this affective response (liking for the ratee) will influence subsequent cognitive processes (Zajonc, 1980), and perhaps categorization as well (Isen, 1984; Srull, 1984), in the direction of more favorable evaluations of the ratee's performance. In this way, performance-related information and associated cognitions can influence both differentiated and undifferentiated affective states through automatic modes of information processing. These affective states then act to influence subsequent stages of the process leading ultimately to a judgment about performance effectiveness. The major point is that both undifferentiated and differentiated affect can be a source of unsuspected bias in the final rating.

The rater's affective states, both differentiated and undifferentiated, can also be influenced through controlled modes of information processing. When information does not fit any category prototype in memory, raters will search for additional information so that a category fit can finally be achieved. While searching, they make causal attributions for examples of successful or unsuccessful performance that they observe. As we mentioned earlier, these attributions can elicit differentiated affective responses such as pride, pity, sympathy, or anger. If sufficiently strong, they may also lead to positive or negative moods.

In sum, the judgment process is likely to involve a complex and dynamic interplay between various forms of affective responses and cognitions related to information about the ratees and their job performance. Through both automatic and controlled modes of information processing, performance information and associated cognitions can elicit both differentiated and undifferentiated affective responses, which distort subsequent attention, categorization, and retrieval processes. This explains how factors that lead to good moods in raters and positive regard for ratees operate to inflate the favorability of performance evaluations and how bad moods and negative regard for ratees deflate evaluation favorability. Examining both differentiated and undifferentiated affect within the performance appraisal context also suggests a more fundamental issue—namely, the possible interaction of relationships between the two kinds of affect. Does an initial mood evoke a concurrent differentiated affect toward a target person? Will differentiated affect influence subsequent mood? Since rating favorability can be increased or decreased by these mechanisms, rating accuracy must be affected as well.

## Implications

Recent theoretical and empirical developments in the study of affect and cognition in human behavior can help unravel the complex psychological processes underlying evaluative judgments in organized work settings. There is evidence that two kinds of affective variables, undifferentiated affect or mood and differentiated affect directed toward specific referents, can influence and be influenced by cognitive processes. Moods can be affected by affectively colored information or thoughts. They can also influence the affective tone of information that is attended to, encoded into, or retrieved from memory. Differentiated affective responses such as anger, liking, or pity can also be elicited by affectively colored information and by cognitive processes such as causal attribution. What is more, differentiated affective responses can also influence the affective quality of information attended to or retrieved from memory. In a word, a person's overall mood and specific feelings about another individual (1) can be influenced by information about that individual and (2) can influence the nature of the information that the person notices or recalls about the individual.

These relationships have important implications for managerial judgment, especially judgments and decisions about other individuals. In the context of performance evaluation, they suggest that a manager's moods and feelings about an employee can be influenced by information about that employee, including information about his or her job performance, and can influence judgments about that employee's level of job effectiveness. Most managers ordinarily want their subordinates to perform effectively. If effective subordinate performance is personally desirable to the manager, the manager probably attaches positive affect to that performance (Jaccoud, 1984). The manager is likely to have positive feelings for subordinates who perform especially well and is likely to slip into a good mood upon seeing a subordinate perform especially well.

If this relationship between subordinate effectiveness and managerial affective response holds, it sets the stage for the possibility that a manager's mood and feelings about a particular subordinate will distort his or her judgment about the subordinate's job performance. Managers who are in a good mood or who have positive feelings for subordinates when they observe their performance are apt to be particularly attentive to signs that the subordinate is performing well and is doing a good job. Managers who have these positive moods or feelings while trying to judge a subordinate's effectiveness are apt to recall signs that the subordinate performed well in the past. Thus, these positive moods and feelings cause positive information about the subordinate to be weighted in a judgment of performance effectiveness more heavily than they deserve. As a result, the manager will evaluate the subordinate more favorably than the subordinate deserves. In a similar way, negative moods and feelings lead to evaluations less favorable than subordinates deserve.

While we have chosen to focus on performance appraisal as a pragmatic example, the theoretical notions developed here have potential ramifications for other organizational issues as well. For example, in the reciprocal determinism between leader and subordinate (Sims and Manz, 1984; Sims and Gioia, 1984), leader cognitive process and verbal behavior are more likely to be influenced by affect. In addition, selection decisions are likely to be highly influenced by affect. Even decisions beyond the interpersonal realm, such as strategy issues, are potential applications of these theoretical notions. For example, strategy decisions may be influenced by an executive's differentiated affect toward certain alternatives—"I just *like* being in that business!"

Affect influences on managerial judgments are subtle, insidious, and pervasive. We need to know more about how they operate. We need to understand in more complete detail exactly how affective responses such as these come about and how they influence judgments and decisions in ways that might detract from judgmental accuracy and managerial effectiveness. Better insight into the affective and cognitive processes involved should point the way toward strategies and interventions to help managers avoid the potentially disfunctional effects of affective and emotional states on information processing, judgment, and decision making.

## References

Abelson, R. P., Kinder, D. R., Peters, M. D., and Fiske, S. T. "Affective and Semantic Components in Person Perception." *Journal of Personality and Social Psychology*, 1982, *42*, 619-630.

Arieti, S. "Cognition and Feeling." In M. B. Arnold (ed.), *Feeling and Emotion: The Loyola Symposium*. Orlando, Fla.: Academic Press, 1970.

Arnold, M. B. *Emotion and Personality*. New York: Columbia University Press, 1960.

Bateman, T. S., and Organ, D. W. "Job Satisfaction and the Good Soldier: The Relationship Between Affect and Employee 'Citizenship.'" *Academy of Management Journal*, 1983, *26*, 587-595.

Borman, W. C. "Exploring Upper Limits of Reliability and Validity in Job Performance Ratings." *Journal of Applied Psychology*, 1978, *63*, 135-144.

Bower, G. H. "Mood and Memory." *American Psychologist,* 1981, *36,* 120–148.

Bower, G. H. "Affect and Cognition." Unpublished manuscript, Department of Psychology, Stanford University, 1983.

Bower, G. H., and Cohen, P. R. "Emotional Influences in Memory and Thinking: Data and Theory." In M. S. Clark and S. T. Fiske (eds.), *Affect and Cognition.* Hillsdale, N.J.: Erlbaum, 1982.

Brown, J., and Weiner, B. "Affective Consequences of Ability Versus Effort Ascriptions: Controversies, Resolutions, and Quandaries." *Journal of Educational Psychology,* 1984, *76,* 148–158.

Caldwell, D. F., O'Reilly, C. A., and Staw, B. M. "The Effect of Mood on Task Perception." Unpublished manuscript, School of Business Administration, University of Santa Clara, 1983.

Clark, M. S., and Isen, A. M. "Toward Understanding the Relationship Between Feeling States and Social Behavior." In A. H. Hastorf and A. M. Isen (eds.), *Cognitive Social Psychology.* New York: Elsevier North-Holland, 1982.

Cooper, W. H. "Ubiquitous Halo." *Psychology Bulletin,* 1981, *90* (2), 218–244.

Cyert, R. M., and March, J. G. *A Behavioral Theory of the Firm.* Englewood Cliffs, N.J.: Prentice-Hall, 1963.

Denisi, A. S., Cafferty, T. P., and Meglino, B. M. "A Cognitive View of the Performance Appraisal Process: A Model and Research Proposition." *Organizational Behavior and Human Performance,* 1984, *33,* 360–396.

Ewert, O. "The Attitudinal Character of Emotion." In M. B. Arnold (ed.), *Feeling and Emotion: The Loyola Symposium.* Orlando, Fla.: Academic Press, 1970.

Feldman, J. M. "Beyond Attribution Theory: Cognitive Processes in Performance Appraisal." *Journal of Applied Psychology,* 1981, *66,* 127–148.

Fiske, S. T. "Social Cognition and Affect." In J. Harvey (ed.), *Cognition, Social Behavior, and the Environment.* Hillsdale, N.J.: Erlbaum, 1981.

Fiske, S. T. "Schema-Triggered Affect: Applications to Social Perception." In M. S. Clark and S. T. Fiske (eds.), *Affect and Cognition.* Hillsdale, N.J.: Erlbaum, 1982.

Fiske, S. T., Beattie, A. E., and Milberg, S. S. "Category-Based Affect: Stereotype Versus Piecemeal Process in Impression Formation." Unpublished manuscript, Department of Psychology, Carnegie-Mellon University, 1983.

Fiske, S. T., and Linville, P. W. "What Does the Schema Concept Buy Us?" *Personality and Social Psychology Bulletin,* 1980, *6,* 543-557.

Fiske, S. T., and Taylor, S. E. *Social Cognition.* Reading, Mass.: Addison-Wesley, 1984.

Gilligan, S. G., and Bower, G. H. "Cognitive Consequences of Emotional Arousal." In C. E. Izard, J. Kagan, and R. B. Zajonc (eds.), *Emotions, Cognition, and Behavior.* New York: Cambridge University Press, 1984.

Hill, B., Lippitt, L., and Serkowneck, K. "The Emotional Dimension of the Problem-Solving Process." *Group and Organization Studies,* 1979, *4,* 93-102.

Ilgen, D. R., and Feldman, J. M. "Performance Appraisal: A Process Focus." In L. L. Cummings and B. M. Staw (eds.), *Research in Organizational Behavior.* Vol. 5. Greenwich, Conn.: JAI Press, 1983.

Isen, A. M. "The Influence of Positive Affect on Decision Making and Cognitive Organization." In T. C. Kinnear (ed.), *Advances in Consumer Behavior.* Vol. 11. Ann Arbor, Mich.: Association for Consumer Research, 1984.

Isen, A. M., and Daubman, K. A. "The Influence of Affect on Categorization." *Journal of Personality and Social Psychology,* 1984, *47,* 1206-1217.

Isen, A. M., and Means, B. "The Influence of Positive Affect on Decision-Making Strategy." *Social Cognition,* 1983, *2,* 18-31.

Isen, A. M., Means, B., Patrick, R., and Nowicki, G. P. "Some Factors Influencing Decision-Making Strategy and Risk Taking." In M. S. Clark and S. T. Fiske (eds.), *Affect and Cognition.* Hillsdale, N.J.: Erlbaum, 1982.

Isen, A. M., and Patrick, R. "The Effect of Positive Feelings on Risk Taking: When the Chips Are Down." *Organizational Behavior and Human Performance,* 1983, *31,* 194-202.

Isen, A. M., and Shalker, T. E. "The Influence of Mood State on Evaluation of Positive, Neutral, and Negative Stimuli." *Social Psychology Quarterly,* 1982, *45,* 58-63.

Isen, A. M., Shalker, T. E., Clark, M., and Karp, L. "Affect, Accessibility of Material in Memory, and Behavior: A Cognitive Loop?" *Journal of Personality and Social Psychology*, 1978, *36*, 1-12.

Jaccoud, A. J. "Categorization, Information Processing, and Interpersonal Affect in the Selection, Promotion, and Appraisal of Employees." Unpublished doctoral dissertation, Department of Organizational Behavior, Pennsylvania State University, 1984.

Landy, F. J., and Farr, J. L. "Performance Rating." *Psychological Bulletin*, 1980, *87*, 72-107.

Landy, F. J., and Farr, J. L. *The Measurement of Work Performance: Methods, Theory, and Applications*. Orlando, Fla.: Academic Press, 1983.

Lang, P. L. "Cognition in Emotion: Concept and Action." In C. E. Izard, J. Kagan, and R. B. Zajonc (eds.), *Emotions, Cognition, and Behavior*. New York: Cambridge University Press, 1984.

Lazarus, R. S. "Thoughts on the Relations Between Emotion and Cognition." *American Psychologist*, 1982, *37*, 1019-1024.

Lazarus, R. S. "On the Primacy of Cognition." *American Psychologist*, 1984, *9*, 124-129.

Lazarus, R. S., Averill, J. R., and Opton, E. M., Jr. "Toward a Cognitive Theory of Emotion." In M. B. Arnold (ed.), *Feelings and Emotions: The Loyola Symposium*. Orlando, Fla.: Academic Press, 1970.

Leventhal, H. "Toward a Comprehensive Theory of Emotion." In L. Berkowitz (ed.), *Advances in Experimental Social Psychology*. Vol. 13. Orlando, Fla.: Academic Press, 1980.

Locke, E. A. "The Nature and Cause of Job Satisfaction." In M. Dunnette (ed.), *Handbook of Industrial and Organizational Psychology*. Skokie, Ill.: Rand McNally, 1976.

Longenecker, C. O. "Executive Cognition and Affect in Performance Appraisal: A Qualitative Study." Unpublished doctoral dissertation, Department of Organizational Behavior, Pennsylvania State University, 1984.

Mandler, G. *Mind and Emotion*. New York: Wiley, 1975.

Mandler, G. "The Structure of Value: Accounting for Taste."

In M. S. Clark and S. T. Fiske (eds.), *Affect and Cognition.* Hillsdale, N.J.: Erlbaum, 1982.

March, J. G. "Bounded Rationality, Ambiguity, and the Engineering of Choice." *Bell Journal of Economics,* Autumn 1978, pp. 587-608.

March, J. G., and Olsen, J. P. *Ambiguity and Choice in Organizations.* Bergen, Norway: Universitetsforlaget, 1976.

Mitchell, T. R. "Expectancy Models of Job Satisfaction, Occupational Preference, and Effort: A Theoretical, Methodological, and Empirical Approach." *Psychological Bulletin,* 1974, *81,* 1053-1077.

Moore, B., Underwood, B., and Rosenhan, D. L. "Emotion, Self, and Others." In C. E. Izard, J. Kagan, and R. B. Zajonc (eds.), *Emotions, Cognition, and Behavior.* New York: Cambridge University Press, 1984.

Motowidlo, S. J. "Does Job Satisfaction Lead to Consideration and Personal Sensitivity?" *Academy of Management Journal,* 1984, *27,* 910-915.

Motowidlo, S. J., and Lawton, G. W. "Affective and Cognitive Factors in Soldiers' Reenlistment Decisions." *Journal of Applied Psychology,* 1984, *69,* 157-166.

Motowidlo, S. J., Packard, J. S., and Manning, M. R. "Occupational Stress: Its Causes and Consequences for Job Performance." Unpublished manuscript, Department of Organizational Behavior, Pennsylvania State University, 1985.

Norman, R. "Affective-Cognitive Consistency, Attitudes, Conformity, and Behavior." *Journal of Personality and Social Psychology,* 1975, *32,* 83-91.

Park, O. S., Sims, H. P., Jr., and Motowidlo, S. J. "Mood and Cognition: Variations and Causal Relationships in the Achievement Context." Unpublished manuscript, Department of Organizational Behavior, Pennsylvania State University, 1984.

Roseman, I. "Cognitive Aspect of Emotion and Emotional Behavior." Unpublished manuscript, Department of Psychology, Yale University, 1980.

Royce, J. R., and Diamond, S. R. "A Multifactor-System Dynamics Theory of Emotion: Cognitive-Affective Interaction." *Motivation and Emotion,* 1980, *4,* 263-299.

Schacter, S., and Singer, J. E. "Cognitive, Social, and Physiological Determinants of Emotional State." *Psychological Review*, 1962, *65*, 121–128.

Sims, H. P., Jr., and Gioia, D. A. "Attribution and Verbal Behavior in Organizational Interaction." Unpublished manuscript, Department of Organizational Behavior, Pennsylvania State University, 1984.

Sims, H. P., Jr., and Manz, C. C. "Observing Leader Verbal Behavior: Toward Reciprocal Determinism in Leadership Theory." *Journal of Applied Psychology*, 1984, *69*, 222–232.

Smith, C. A., Organ, D. W., and Near, J. P. "Organizational Citizenship Behavior: Its Nature and Antecedents." *Journal of Applied Psychology*, 1983, *68*, 653–663.

Srinivas, S., and Motowidlo, S. J. "Effects of Stress on Information Processing in Performance Evaluation." Paper presented at meeting of the Academy of Management, San Diego, Aug. 1985.

Srull, T. K. "Affect and Memory: The Impact of Affective Reactions in Advertising on the Representation of Product Information in Memory." In R. P. Bagozzi and M. T. Alice (eds.), *Consumer Research*. Vol. 10. Ann Arbor, Mich.: Association for Consumer Research, 1983.

Srull, T. K. "The Effects of Subjective Affective States on Memory and Judgment." In T. C. Kinnear (ed.), *Consumer Research*. Vol. 11. Ann Arbor, Mich.: Association for Consumer Research, 1984.

Tomkins, S. "Affect as the Primary Motivational System." In M. B. Arnold (ed.), *Feelings and Emotion*. Orlando, Fla.: Academic Press, 1970.

Vroom, V. H. *Work and Motivation*. New York: Wiley, 1964.

Weary, G. "The Role of Cognitive, Affective, and Social Factors in Attributional Biases." In J. H. Harvey (ed.), *Cognition, Social Behavior, and the Environment*. Hillsdale, N.J.: Erlbaum, 1982.

Weick, K. E. *The Social Psychology of Organizing*. (2nd. ed.) Reading, Mass.: Addison-Wesley, 1979.

Weiner, B. "A Cognitive (Attribution)-Emotion-Action Model of Motivated Behavior: An Analysis of Judgments of Help-

Giving." *Journal of Personality and Social Psychology,* 1980a, *39,* 186-200.

Weiner, B. "The Role of Affect in Rational (Attributional) Approaches to Human Motivation." *Educational Researcher,* July/Aug. 1980b, pp. 4-11.

Weiner, B. "The Emotional Consequences of Causal Attributions." In M. S. Clark and S. T. Fiske (eds.), *Affect and Cognition.* Hillsdale, N.J.: Erlbaum, 1982.

Weiner, B. "Some Methodological Pitfalls in Attribution Research." *Journal of Educational Psychology,* 1983, *75,* 530-543.

Weiner, B., and Brown, J. "All's Well That Ends." *Journal of Educational Psychology,* 1984, *76,* 169-171.

Weiner, B., and Graham, S. "An Attributional Approach to Emotional Development." In C. E. Izard, J. Kagan, and R. B. Zajonc (eds.), *Emotions, Cognition, and Behavior.* New York: Cambridge University Press, 1984.

Weiner, B., Russell, D., and Lerman, D. "Affective Consequences of Causal Ascriptions." In J. H. Harvey, W. J. Ickes, and R. F. Kidd (eds.), *New Directions in Attribution Research.* Vol. 2. Hillsdale, N.J.: Erlbaum, 1978.

Weiner, B., Russell, D., and Lerman, D. "The Cognition-Emotion Process in Achievement-Related Contexts." *Journal of Personality and Social Psychology,* 1979, *37,* 1211-1220.

Wright, J., and Mischel, W. "Influence of Affect on Cognitive Social Learning Variables." *Journal of Personality and Social Psychology,* 1982, *43,* 901-914.

Zajonc, R. B. "Feeling and Thinking: Preferences Need No Inferences." *American Psychologist,* 1980, *35,* 151-175.

Zajonc, R. B. "On the Primacy of Affect." *American Psychologist,* 1984, *39,* 117-123.

Zajonc, R. B., and Markus, H. "Affective and Cognitive Factors in Preferences." *Journal of Consumer Research,* 1982, *9,* 123-131.

Zajonc, R. B., and Markus, H. "Affect and Cognition: The Hard Interface." In C. E. Izard, J. Kagan, and R. B. Zajonc (eds.), *Emotions, Cognition, and Behavior.* New York: Cambridge University Press, 1984.

# 9

# The Structure and Process of Understanding

## Implications for Managerial Action

### Daniel J. Isenberg

"Then you don't know positively that he was robbing Wynant?"

"Sure we know. It doesn't click any other way. The chances are Wynant was going away on a trip the 3rd of October, because he did draw five thousand dollars out of the bank in cash, but he didn't close up his shop and give up his apartment. That was done by Macaulay a few days later. Wynant was killed at Macaulay's in Scarsdale ... because on the morning of the 4th, when Macaulay's cook, who slept at home, came to work, Macaulay met her at the door with some kind of trumped-up complaint and two weeks' wages and fired her on the spot, not letting her in the house to find any corpses or blood-stains."

"How did you find that out? Don't skip details."

"Ordinary routine. Naturally after we grabbed him we went to his office and house to see what

*Note:* This chapter is based on research for a forthcoming book tentatively entitled *Managerial Thinking: Toward Strategic Opportunism.*

*we could find out—you know, where-were-you-on-the-night-of-June-6-1934 stuff—and the present cook said she'd only been working for him since the 8th of October, and that led to that. We also found a table with a very faint trace of what we hope is human blood not quite scrubbed out. The scientific boys are making shavings of it now to see if they can soak out any results for us."* [It turned out to be beef blood.]

*"Then you're not sure he—"*

*"Stop saying that. Of course we're sure. That's the only way it clicks. Wynant had found out that Julia and Macaulay were gypping him and also thought, rightly or wrongly, that Julia and Macaulay were cheating on him—and we know he was jealous—so he went up there to confront him with whatever proof he had, and Macaulay, with prison looking him in the face, killed the old man. Now don't say we're not sure. It doesn't make any sense otherwise. Well, there he is with a corpse, one of the harder things to get rid of. Can I stop to take a swallow of whisky?"*

*"Just one," Nora said. "But this is just a theory, isn't it?"*

*"Call it any name you like. It's good enough for me."*

—Dashiell Hammett,
*The Thin Man*

Researchers and theorists alike have argued the practical importance of understanding how managers understand and act on the events, data, interactions, meetings, reports, hearsay, and other stimuli they encounter in their work (for example, Barnard, 1938; Kiesler and Sproull, 1982; Weick, 1979). Over the past three years I have conducted a series of field studies in order to identify some of the central thinking processes utilized by senior managers in business organizations (Isenberg, 1982,

1983, 1984, 1985a, 1985b, 1985c, forthcoming). The methods have included content analyses of senior managers' think-aloud protocols collected while they were at work, analyses of think-aloud protocols of managers and students solving a standard case study, in-depth interviews of senior managers, multidimensional scaling, and on-the-job observation. A total of eighteen senior managers ranging from division general manager (thirteen) to chief executive (three), in ten corporations, have been studied in depth. Additionally, a number of senior managers participated in interviews only.

The phenomenon of managerial inference has repeatedly emerged from this research program as critical to the process by which the senior manager achieves and maintains an understanding of the internal workings and external environment of his organization. Here is a quick summary of some of the findings:

- In a problem-solving task, managers used more reasoning processes than did students.
- Those managers who reasoned more by drawing analogies between their own experience and the problem at hand generated plans for action that were subsequently rated as more effective by expert judges.
- Managers allocated significant amounts of attention and cognitive effort to figuring out some puzzling aspect of their work.
- Forty-nine percent of managers' think-aloud protocols were coded as using inferential reasoning from facts or as speculating about some aspect of their situation.
- Protocol analyses showed how managers developed and tested mental "models" reflecting their emergent understanding of problematic or puzzling situations.

Thus, the research clearly showed that the process of understanding is an important aspect of managerial thinking. It also showed that understanding is closely related to managers' ability to effectively plan action. These observations give us strong impetus to understand managerial understanding—that is, to find out how managers "figure out" what is going on around them. In order to shed light on this question, I will draw on a number of key concepts in the cognitive sciences, including plausible reasoning, knowledge structures, and probabilistic thinking. I will argue that managers develop *plausible,* as opposed to necessarily *accurate,* models of their situations, and that managers develop and efficiently use *knowledge structures* (stereotypes, schemas) that guide how the senior manager recognizes, explains, and plans. Underlying all aspects of the process of understanding is the uncertain or probabilistic nature of managerial information, organizational events, and managerial action.

## Plausible Reasoning and the Process of Knowing

Alan Collins and his associates (Collins, 1978; Collins, Warnock, Aiello, and Miller, 1975; Gentner and Collins, 1981) have developed the concept of plausible reasoning as part of a project to develop a procedural theory of human reasoning that can be implemented on a computer. This concept is particularly appropriate to understanding managerial thinking because it specifies how various kinds of information and reasoning processes increase or decrease the certainty with which inferences are drawn from incomplete information. The element of plausibility is important because it stands in contrast to accurate or logical reasoning. Accurate reasoning is possible only in a world where information is complete and certain, where criteria are unambiguous, and where cause and effect links are known. The conditions that allow accurate reasoning rarely exist in the world of the manager.

Instances of managers engaging in plausible reasoning abound. For example, a division general manager in my study attempted over a period of several weeks to build a coherent and reasonable understanding of the relationship between bookings, inventory management done by customers, the hiring activities of customers, and the business conditions in the geographical area. A second general manager utilized plausible reasoning when thinking through a case of an administrative anomaly—

namely, a group of purchasing executives responding favorably to a memo outlining a new purchasing procedure, which was followed by their complete noncompliance in practice. A third general manager verbalized the following thoughts: "I guess I'm a little surprised that there... weren't some letters that suggested that the idea itself was not a very good one.... I guess the thing that comes quickest to my mind is there's probably something in the corporate culture that says that if you have a problem like this, you don't confront it... you just find a way to gloss over it... pat 'em on the head and keep doing your own thing."

To sum up years of research on plausible reasoning, it is now clear that although people frequently reason, they do not do so in strictly logical terms. For example, in response to the question in 1985, "Have you ever met Ronald Reagan in person?," our immediate answer may be negative. Yet have we ever paused to wonder how we arrived at such a rapid and certain conclusion? It is both impractical and wasteful to survey every experience we have ever had of meeting someone in person and then to ask whether that person was Ronald Reagan. Instead, we reason, "If I had met a president of the United States, I would have remembered the meeting. Ronald Reagan is a president of the United States. I don't remember meeting him; therefore, I did not meet him." Plausible? Yes, because of the reasonable premise that a meeting with a president of the United States would be very salient and therefore easily recallable. Logical? No, because it is founded on a likely or plausible premise, not on an accurate or certain premise.

Plausible reasoning involves going beyond the directly observable or at least consensual information to form ideas or understandings that provide enough certainty (begging the question for now as to how much is "enough"). That is, like Hammett's detective, we develop an understanding of the situation that fits enough of the fairly certain pieces together and has no glaring logical holes in it but may not be entirely correct. There are several ways in which this process departs from a logical-deductive process. First, the reasoning is not necessarily correct, but it fits the facts, albeit imperfectly at times. Second, the reasoning is supported by a rationale, an argument. And third, the reasoning is based on incomplete information.

*Developing Plausible Mental Models.* Senior managers reason plausibly in order to "figure things out," that is, in order to develop and test their mental models of the situations they confront. These uncertain situations range from understanding a difficult conflict between two vice-presidents well enough to reduce it, to second-guessing a group president's agendas during his upcoming visit to the division, to anticipating how competitors will respond to a new service or product.

The process of plausible reasoning is perhaps most clearly observed when it is difficult, when the manager does not easily succeed in putting all of the pieces together into a coherent whole. Just such a process was triggered when a general manager, WS, was negotiating with potential buyers for his own division, including one large Japanese conglomerate that had already sent more than one team of experts to examine the operational facilities. WS was puzzled and worried when he heard that a senior Japanese executive, whom we'll call Mr. Kiko, was reportedly blocking approval of the sale within his own company. The figuring out process involved several distinguishable steps. Let us take a closer look at each of them.

First of all, WS received information that Mr. Kiko was holding up the purchase process and that the potential buyer required more time and study before it could make a decision. Mr. Kiko apparently wondered whether the technology developed by WS's division could be used in the buyer's production processes. WS considered this information useful but potentially unreliable. In the second step, WS inferred that Mr. Kiko did not understand that the technology was in fact appropriate for their production processes.

The third step consisted of WS's recognition of an apparent inconsistency. Someone from the parent company named Mr. Kiko (WS thought) visited the major test site of WS's division, which should have given Mr. Kiko the understanding about the technical capabilities of the production technology. This contradicted the new information that Mr. Kiko was holding up the purchase based on an apparent technical misunderstanding.

WS speculated that one possible explanation was that there were two persons named Mr. Kiko. So WS began to search for some information that would clarify the situation. In the fourth step, WS called an outside lawyer who had extensive experience in dealing with the Japanese and who had been instrumental in the current negotiations. The lawyer said he would try to find out something. Next, WS wondered whether he could locate Mr. Kiko on the organization chart, because another piece of information supplied by the lawyer was that Mr. Kiko was a managing director of the company, and this did not square with WS's understanding that Mr. Kiko—the one who visited the test site—was a department manager. If one Mr. Kiko was the department manager, it did not seem likely to WS that he could be the one holding up the purchase; therefore, perhaps there were two Mr. Kikos.

At this point, WS made explicit four possible explanations.

- There are two persons with the same name. If WS knew how common a name that was in Japan, he might change his belief in this explanation.
- WS does not understand the Japanese organization chart, and a managing director could be a department manager.
- WS heard the wrong name of the person who visited the site.
- Mr. Kiko has been promoted from department manager to managing director.

Next, WS ruled out the latter possibility on the plausible assumption that such a leap would be extremely unusual.

At this point, WS called the lawyer and a senior staff person within his own corporation. After listening to WS's speculations, the lawyer gave WS a fairly elaborate explanation of his own. The crux of the explanation was that a senior managing director and director of corporate planning for the Japanese parent company with a similar-sounding name, whom I shall call Mr. Kuko, was favoring the purchase because an affiliate of a company in which they had a stake had developed a technological process complementary to the one that WS's division had developed. Mr. Kuko would be in favor of the purchase if in fact the parent company would have access to the affiliate's complementary technology. Mr. Kuko received much of his information about WS's technology from Mr. Kiko, who was indeed a department manager and not a managing director. The final step consisted of WS's tentative acceptance of the lawyer's explanation on the basis that it encompassed all the reasonably certain facts and also fit WS's conception about the way organizations worked and the availability of alternative technologies in the marketplace.

One of the outcomes of the process of plausible reasoning is an elaborate rationale that managers provide when they are asked to describe their thoughts while engaged in action. In addition to describing those thoughts, they frequently explain the reasoning behind the acts themselves. For example, one senior executive described to me in detail why he presented a new executive compensation scheme to the company president by penciling in an informal chart rather than making a formal slide presentation. Part of the rationale included the manager's conception of the company as priding itself on having a very informal culture, and since the notion of a formal executive compensation policy was countercultural, he felt that he should make an effort to downplay the rigidity and formality of the scheme.

*Certainty Conditions.* A number of factors acted to increase or decrease WS's certainty at various points in the process of figuring out what was going on with Mr. Kiko. Typically, the certainty by which managers evaluate and interpret events taking place around them is not static; rather, it increases or decreases in response to new information and inferences that they make. Consider the following thought experiment: you are driving to an appointment in an unknown part of a familiar city and are already late. You have no map, but you know the names of some of the major streets. You know that you have to turn left one short block before Washington Street as you travel on Lincoln. You also know that once you go past Washington, it will be hard to get back. You see a major street ahead (you know that Washington is major) and the street goes north and south. You strain your eyes to read the street sign, but all you can make out is a few letters. How many letters, and which letters, would you need in order to become confident enough that the street ahead is Washington Street and thus decide to make your left turn? As you believe you recognize the last letters "on," you recall that Washington Street goes north and south, and Lincoln Street goes east and west.

This example illustrates that certainty is a function of both facts and reasoning processes. Specific conditions (for example, the presence and location of particular letters at the end of the street name, the fact that the street in question is major and runs north and south) combine to increase the driver's confidence until he or she is willing to reach a conclusion, which may then lead to action. Collins (1978) has elaborately described the various types of inference and the conditions that increase certainty for each inference type. One type of inference, for example, is the lack-of-knowledge inference, the one used to infer that we have never met Ronald Reagan—that is, because we have no knowledge of meeting him, we infer that we never did meet him. Some of the conditions that increase the certainty of lack-of-knowledge inferences include:

- The importance of the particular subject (for example, the importance of Ronald Reagan).
- The likelihood that the event occurred (for example, the chance likelihood of meeting a president).
- The degree of importance of the given event (for example, the importance of meeting a president).
- The number of similar events recalled that have a similar property (for example, a memory of meeting Ephraim Katzir just before he became president of Israel).

In other words, the certainty of a lack-of-knowledge inference is increased if the subject is important, if the event is important, if the chance likelihood of a similar event is low, and if we can easily recall similar events.

*Plausible Reasoning and Managerial Action.* The world of management is a world of action, and it is on the effectiveness of this action that the viability of the business enterprise rests.

The major strength of the concept of plausible reasoning is that it suggests that managers need to abandon the search for certainty before taking action. Instead, plausible reasoning suggests that managers should increase the certainty conditions beyond some critical threshold that changes as certainty conditions, riskiness, stakes, and other factors change.

My own observation is that many senior managers have implicitly learned how to do this. For example, one general manager received a phone message from a product expediter in a sister division that purchased products from the general manager's own division. The general manager surmised that the expediter could have been calling for one of two reasons: to say something about either price or delivery time on a specific production run. The surmise was based on previous experience with the particular expediter, knowledge that the run was late, and the general manager's impression that he had never interacted with the expediter around any other issue. Before returning the call, the general manager walked by his marketing manager's office and asked a marketing person why *he* thought the expediter called. He received the answer "Price." The general manager then returned the call. Note that the reasoning process rapidly limited the number of hypotheses for the general manager to test and that although the answer constituted a weak test of his hypothesis, the answer considerably increased the manager's certainty with minimal effort and minimal risk. The increase in certainty was enough for him to go back and return the phone call with an idea already developed for how to discuss price with the expediter. It is this latter point that is the critical one: plausible reasoning helps the manager increase his or her certainty to the point of feasible action.

In general, it is possible to describe an idealized process by which many managers use plausible reasoning in planning and implementing action:

1.  The manager needs to develop a different understanding of a phenomenon, often due to an experience of surprise.
2.  The manager tries to take advantage of the data he or she already has in order to speculate about the new situation.

Each speculation is tested against data and assumptions that already exist, and the search for new data at this point is confined to search in long-term memory.

3.  A very selective external search for information is engaged in, particularly in order to confirm one or more of the speculations, although disconfirmation may also occur. The goal of the search at this point is to achieve a degree of certainty that will allow the manager to proceed to step four at minimal cost and minimal risk.

4.  The manager engages in action in the face of an incomplete but tentative understanding of the situation and uses the feedback of his or her actions to complete the understanding (see Isenberg, 1984, on thinking/acting cycles).

## The Structure of Managerial Knowledge

" 'Speculations,' he says, 'are useless until you have all the facts. But I've noticed often enough that it isn't like that with him, really. He begins speculating right away, if you ask me, and his speculations suggest which factors to hunt for next. . . . I really believe he is guessing all the time, and this is what makes him so good a Detective Inspector' " (Innes, *What Happened at Hazlewood*, 1946).

Plausible reasoning is a typically intentional process of "figuring things out," of making sense of the sometimes chaotic and scattered events in the manager's world. For the manager, one outcome of this process of thinking is a mental model of some portion of the manager's world. Over the past twenty years or so, however, experts on human thinking have realized that such models or knowledge structures are not only the result of cognitive processes but also one of the key determinants of cognition (Neisser, 1976). In other words, managers not only develop their models from the perceived facts but also base their understanding of those facts on prior conceptions, expectations, and lay theories about the world. In fact, without some prior knowledge structure, it may be difficult or impossible to notice the facts in the first place. Thus, the manager's knowledge structures help direct his or her attention to the relevant data. The manager's knowledge structures also take advantage of prior experience by helping him or her make inferences without much information.

Research on human thinking has led to a set of theories about knowledge structures, many of which fall under the general rubric of *schema theory* (Hastie, 1981; Neisser, 1976; Taylor and Crocker, 1981). Although the term *schema* has been used in a variety of ways, there is a common definitional core to all of the uses. First of all, a schema represents a person's conscious or unconscious preconceptions or expectations. For example, when a competitor makes an early announcement of the price of a planned new product, it is a market signal designed to elicit a response from us. Figure 1 shows such a market signaling schema. Second, a schema is limited to a given topic or domain, for example, strategic market signaling. Third, a schema connects general concepts with specific features and instances (for example, connecting the instance of Texas Instruments' early announcement of its new memory with the concept "market signaling"). And finally, a schema derives its cognitive efficiency from its applicability to more than one situation. This is true, for example, of the schemas brought into play in competitive relationships among companies.

What impact do schemas have on the way managers think? Schemas have been shown to serve a number of important cognitive functions (see Taylor and Crocker, 1981), many of which are relevant to managerial thinking. In the first place, schemas help managers make inferences about otherwise ambiguous events. A schema would tell us, for example, that our competitor's announcement of a proposed new product is intended to preempt similar new product introductions by weaker competitors. Second, schemas determine the rapidity of thinking about the given domain. Thus, once my market signaling schema is activated, I tend to make rapid inferences about the specific signaling event that triggered the schema. Third, schemas fill in missing data by supplying *default options*. Thus, when a particular schema is activated, the relevant specific features and instances tend to get used in the absence of further information. For example, if we know nothing else about the

Figure 1. An Example of a Schema.

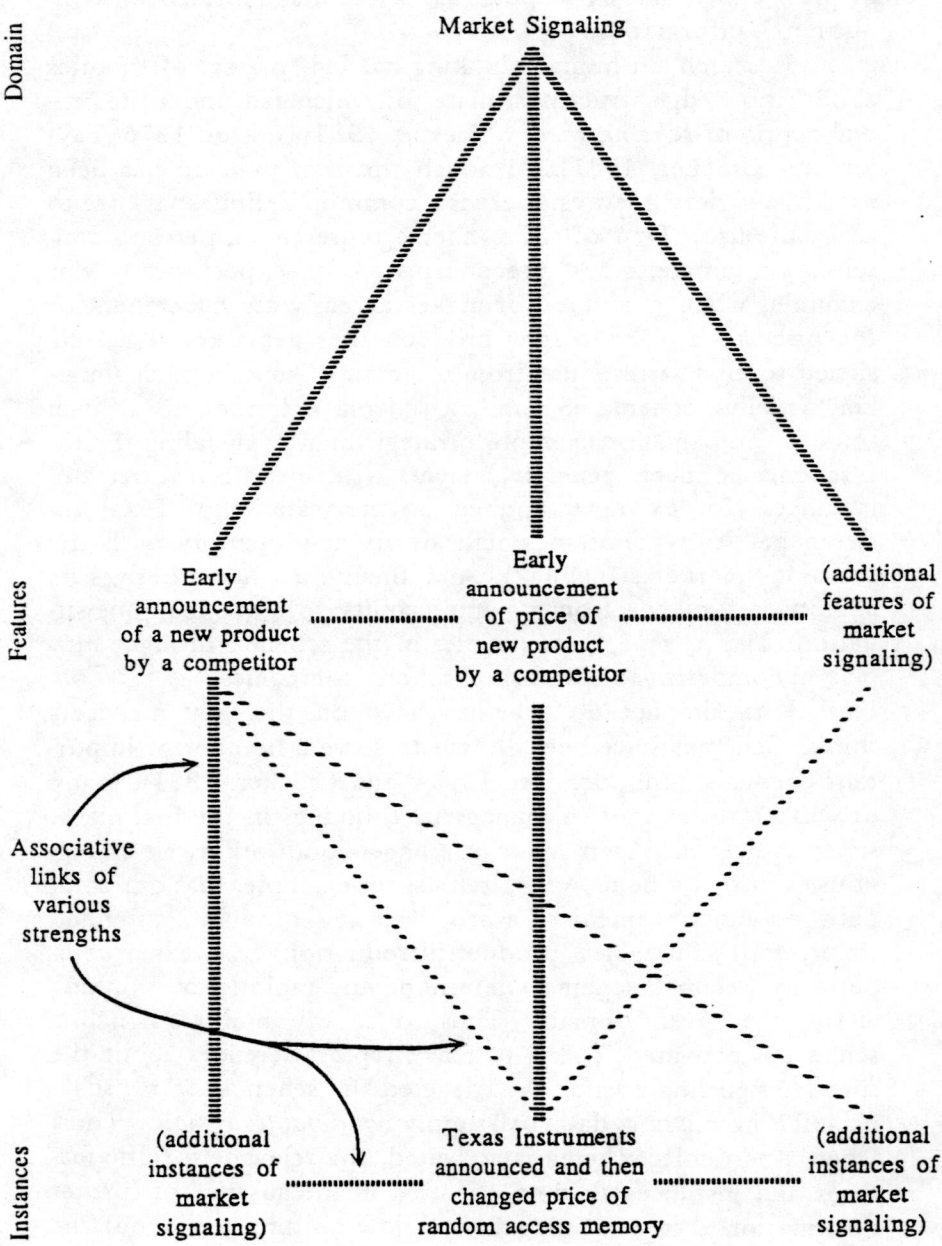

competitor's proposed new product, we fill in that the competitor is preempting when it announces a price as well. It is important to note that this may be an entirely unconscious process. In other words, even though we frequently think that we actually perceived the event or characteristic, in reality the data were supplied by our own preconceptions and expectations. A fourth and related aspect of the use of schemas is that they fill in missing solutions to problems through the recall of past instances. As with the default option function, once a given schema is activated in a particular situation, past responses to the situation are easier to recall and may even pop into mind without conscious effortful search.

A second major set of functions for schemas revolves around the fact that they guide the categorization of events, people, and objects. Schemas include information about *prototypicality* or goodness of fit (Posner and Keele, 1969). Thus, popular schemas about organizations suggest that General Motors and IBM are prototypical business organizations: while IBM is a very "organizationlike" organization, a company like Visa International may be perceived as less "organizationlike." The categorizing function of schemas is closely related to their inferential function. For example, Texas Instruments' advanced price announcement may be a prototypical example of market signaling against which newly encountered instances are matched in order to help us infer whether the ambiguous event we are observing is an example of market signaling.

In addition to guiding categorization, schemas also guide the normative appraisal of events, people, and objects. Thus, in the 1970s the American automotive industry's dire difficulties (when it downsized too late and was caught by increased oil prices and effective foreign competition) were seen, rightly or wrongly, as prototypical of complacent and overconfident management. The fact that the industry was being seen as a type is evidenced by the frequency with which it was used as an example by the business press and business scholars (see, for example, McCaskey, 1982). Arguably the greatest practical strength of *In Search of Excellence* (Peters and Waterman, 1982) has been the fact that it has broadened the number of prototypes of effective organizations that managers can use to evaluate their own organizations.

To sum up, then, perhaps the most important aspect of schemas is that they guide action. Many of the functions of schemas we have just described provide the basis for managerial action: schemas guide the rapid recall of remembered data and solutions, the instantaneous categorization and evaluation of new data, and the default filling in of missing data and solutions via inference. Because schemas operate in this way, they account for many behavioral phenomena, from the tennis star's skillful production of a lob to a manager's ability to conduct very sensitive performance appraisals and analyze detailed financial statements.

Having defined what schemas are and given an overview of how they function, we are ready to look at the ways schema theory integrates a number of the findings from the research program on senior managers discussed at the beginning of this chapter.

*Evaluativeness.* One of my most consistent findings is that managers are critically evaluative of people and events that they encounter. They do not just coolly and calmly assess problems on their own merits but are also involved viscerally in what they do. As highly experienced people operating within a familiar environment on difficult problems, managers have a rich network of schemas to draw upon in interpreting information and events. Acting in a manner that is consistent with research on "schematics" and "aschematics" (see, for example, Markus, 1977), managers polarize their evaluations of situations for which well-developed schemas exist. In effect, one result of managers' experience is that they possess a variety of good and bad prototypes. For example, in a recent survey that I conducted in a large British company, of the businesses that the sixty senior managers "admired," one of the twenty-eight companies mentioned was brought up 25 percent of the time, indicating that that company was a good fit for the prototype of a "good" organization. On the basis of evidence provided by Tesser (1978), one can argue that one function such prototypes play is to assist in the evaluation of newly encountered schema-related objects, events, and people, since the more developed a person's schema in a given domain, the more extremely positive or negative that person's evaluations will be.

*Early Action Ideas.* Schemas cause solutions to be brought to mind more readily as problem situations are categorized and schemas for the particular category of problem are activated. Furthermore, under certain situations schemas cause the person to enact behaviors or solutions "mindlessly" (Langer, 1978), without much conscious thought at all. Ideas about what to do pop into mind when a schema is triggered. This is entirely consistent with the way I have observed managers solving many problems: ideas about what to do are often generated very early in the problem-solving process. Schema theory suggests that this is not a willy-nilly process, but that it is instead determined by the existence of action schemas, which consist of prior conceptions of the general features of solutions as well as specific solution instances. When a schema about involving people in the policy formulation process is activated, for example, personal examples of related situations are called to mind, and with them the examples of what other managers have done in those situations. Rather than wait until all of the data are in, the schema immediately suggests ideas about what actions are feasible. Thus, schemas are one of the bases of what we often refer to as intuition.

*Inference.* As discussed above, one of the central functions of schemas is to assist managers in attributing meaning to otherwise ambiguous events, in making sense of inherently ambiguous phenomena, and in adding unobservable inference to observable data.

*Model Building.* In the context of schema theory, the process managers go through in order to develop models of a problem situation is the process of developing a schema about that situation. Model building is often initiated when the manager is surprised or puzzled by facts that do not fit together. We saw this when WS tried to understand how Mr. Kiko could be against the purchase of WS's division given what else he knew (or thought he knew) about Mr. Kiko. Another example was the general manager who was puzzled about the decline in his bookings, his customers' return of orders, and his customers' accelerated hiring programs. In both cases we could hypothesize that the managers were "aschematic" with respect to their specific problems: they lacked a mental framework for attributing meaning, for categorizing events, for evaluating good and bad, for filling in missing data, or for formulating and taking action. One could extend this analysis to argue that schema development is a critical function for management education and for the subsequent development of skilled managerial performance, and that our systems for developing managers should provide the technology and process for facilitating the development of managerially relevant schemas.

It is of paramount importance that our analysis of managerial schemas sheds light on how managers skillfully perform. The literature on the cognitive basis of expertise (see, for example, Glaser, 1984) shows that the structure of knowledge is one of the key distinguishing characteristics of experts: their knowledge bases are both more extensive and more highly organized, both laterally and hierarchically, than those of nonexperts. In other words, the expert draws upon a vast store of concrete experiences and general rules, all of which are richly interrelated in a dense web of knowledge. Much of this knowledge exists in the form of schemas that as units of knowledge imply one another. This hypothesis is strengthened by the fact that experts and schematics themselves share common characteristics: both are evaluative (Tesser, 1978; Schön, 1983), both generate action ideas rapidly (Simon, 1978; Taylor and Crocker, 1981), both infer heavily (Bouwman, 1982; Taylor and Crocker, 1981), and both engage in mutually reinforcing cycles of thinking and acting (Connolly, 1982; Isenberg, 1984; Neisser, 1976). As Fiske and Kinder (1981) state in their review of the literature on expert understanding of politics, "In any realm, the uninitiated, the novice, and the expert will differ in the complexity and richness of schemata available and in the schema-driven processing strategies employed. . . . The uninitiated do not have appropriate schemata available; novices possess concrete versions of consensual schemata and use them in simpleminded ways; and experts possess abstract schemata that they use in sophisticated ways (pp. 186–187)."

## Summary: Uncertainty and Probabilistic Thinking

" 'When murders are committed by mathematics,' I said, 'you can solve them by mathematics. Most of them aren't, and this one wasn't. I don't want to go against your idea of what's right and wrong, but when I say he probably dissected the body so he could carry it into town in bags I'm only saying what seems most probable. That would be on the 6th of October or later, because it wasn't until then that he laid off the two mechanics Wynant had working in the shop—Prentice and McNaughton—and shut it up. So he buried Wynant under the floor, buried him with a fat man's clothes and a lame man's stick and belt marked D. W. Q., all arranged so they wouldn't get too much of the lime—or whatever he used to eat off the dead man's features and flesh—on them, and he re-cemented the floor over the grave. Between police routine and publicity we've got more than a fair chance of finding out where he bought or otherwise got the clothes and stick and the cement.'

. . . 'I hope so,' she said, not too hopefully' " (Hammett, *The Thin Man,* [1934] 1942).

*Uncertainty.* Perhaps more than most experts, managers work within uncertain environments, knowable and known only in equivocal terms. The manager attributes this uncertainty both to internal conditions—that is, to his own ignorance—and to external factors—that is, to the fact that reality, in the form of future events, is currently unknowable. In general, the existence of uncertainty cuts broad and deep. It is broad because everything—from the physical existence of an object to our perceptions of that object, to scientific experiments—can be characterized as probabilistic. Thus, two psychologists even refer to perception as a bet (Kahneman and Tversky, 1982), and experts in medical decision making consider medical diagnosis and intervention a gamble (Bursztajn, Feinbloom, Hamm, and Brodsky, 1981). Uncertainty cuts deep because many things that our language and culture teach us to take for granted—our ability to speak coherently, our recognition of objects, our sense of self—are in reality probabilistic. This very fact underlies psychologists' fascination with understanding optical illusions, slips of the tongue, and consistent systematic errors in human judgment (Lindsay and Norman, 1977).

Uncertainty is inherent in managers' attempts to understand their worlds, whether through plausible reasoning or through schematic information processing. In applying the theory of plausible reasoning to managerial thinking, we have seen that at the heart of this process are the many mechanisms that managers use to reduce uncertainty. To the extent that various certainty conditions are met, the manager feels that his or her conclusions are plausible. In fact, the essence of plausibility is that uncertainty is reduced by a process of reasoning. Thus, as described earlier in this chapter, one can become more and more confident about inferences made from lack of knowledge as event likelihood increases, as event importance increases, and so on.

Schematic information processing, a less consciously driven process than plausible reasoning, is also a series of bets, although the bets are more implicit ones. In this vein, Langer (1978) has argued that much of social interaction is "mindless": we unthinkingly apply action schemas to situations. The "gambling" nature of this information processing becomes clear when absurd situations arise, such as the commonplace example of someone greeting us by saying, "Fine, thanks," before being asked, "How are you?" At that point it is apparent that we have implicitly "bet" that a person will ask how we are doing when he or she says hello. For managers as well, such gambles are likely to be implicit. For example, one general manager gambled that his vice-president of sales was not telling him about some problem he was working on and further gambled that the vice-president would eventually tell the manager what the problem was. Then, following a conversation with the vice-president of sales, the general manager had this to say:

It was very evident that there was something else on his mind. He just absolutely has got something else he is working on and he is not going to tell me about it till he gets it ready. He operates like that. He does not want to tell me about problems until after he has already worked out a solution to them, but you can always tell when there is one coming. So I'm going to have to figure out how I am going to talk to him sometime today and try to find out what it is. . . . When he did not show [to a luncheon] then I knew there was something going on. That is probably part of it. . . . So the best way to do that is just wait until he gets through with whatever he is doing and he will come in and sit down and he will usually tell me the whole thing.

These gambles about the vice-president informed the manager's strategy of waiting and letting the vice-president take the initiative, but since the unknown problem may have been important for the manager to know about soon, he tried to arrange his activities so that the vice-president would have more opportunities to tell his boss what was on his mind.

*Probabilistic Thinking.* When managers recognize uncertainty and attribute it either to their own ignorance or to objective reality, they engage in probabilistic thinking. Such recognition may be explicit, but just as frequently managers are implicit about the probabilistic nature of their judgments or predictions. The manager just described, for example, showed no explicit awareness that his attribution to his vice-president may have been inaccurate. One result of not explicitly recognizing the probabilistic nature of understanding is that the manager is thus prevented from testing that understanding against reality. Not recognizing that understanding is a gamble, the manager does not place his bets very carefully or may mistakenly treat the bet as a "sure thing." The lack of testability of senior managers' views of themselves and their organizations has been documented in great detail by Argyris (1976), who attributes this characteristic to managers' implicit beliefs or values about how to get things done, particularly while working with other people.

Probabilistic thinking consists of both skills and attitudes.

The skill component is the manager's ability to calibrate his own subjective predictions against actual outcomes. Although such calibration may seem to occur naturally, for example, as the manager receives variance analyses over the years, we would expect accuracy to increase. It has been found, for example, that with extensive feedback over several hundred trials, judges can improve their accuracy at probability assessment substantially (Lichtenstein and Fischhoff, 1980). Much of the calibration results from what might be considered gross adjustments in the early feedback stages. After that, judges do not learn from additional feedback. To my knowledge, however, there is no evidence that in fact managers' predictive accuracy improves with experience, although it is possible that their confidence does (Oskamp, 1965).

The probabilistic thinking managers do also results from an attitude that recognizes the uncertain nature of the managerial environment. This attitude is learned, in part, when the manager makes the transition from a relatively structured functional discipline (such as engineering or accounting) to the more complex and ill-structured general management task. Three of the attitudes that facilitate probabilistic thinking include

- The belief that the manager cannot know all causes of a problem, coupled with the recognition that even if he could, some causes only bring about their associated effects some of the time.
- The belief that managerial action is rule-based gambling. (The term *rule-based* means that the manager does not simply toss a coin but instead uses rules or guidelines as best as possible.)
- The belief that there is no such thing as purely subjective or purely objective knowledge and that there is instead a continuum from subjective to objective (see Bursztajn, Feinbloom, Hamm, and Brodsky, 1981).

I have argued elsewhere (Isenberg, 1984, 1985a) that thinking and acting are not distinct but are rather part of a cycle of activity that enriches both the reflective understanding of past or present and the process of action planning and implementation. One of the implications of probabilistic thinking is that ultimately managers must act despite several kinds of ignorance. The manager must act in at least partial ignorance of the dynamics underlying the current situation to be acted on. Furthermore, like the proverbial manual for riding a bicycle, an action plan can never be entirely spelled out, because there is always another level of operational specificity and also because there are frequent discrepancies between action and intent. What is more, not only must the manager act while partially ignorant of the relationship between his action plan and his subsequent actions, but he must also act in ignorance of the relationship between the actions themselves and their consequences. Even were a manager to have complete understanding of the situation and be able to completely specify his actions, the manager would still be uncertain about whether or not his behaviors would bring about the desired effects.

One implication of my analysis is that the manager launches inquiry into action through informed guesswork. Of course, there is a cost, at least a potential cost, of acting without total understanding—namely, the very real possibility of inaccuracy. However, since the risk is unavoidable, one can at least view the potential cost as an investment and ask how the manager can profit from this investment. If the manager must "sin bravely," to paraphrase Spinoza, at least there should be some benefit or pleasure commensurate with the sin. The most direct benefit is that the results of the action often yield insight and reduce uncertainty when the manager reflects back on the outcomes. Thus, our inquiry into the structure and process of managerial understanding has brought us full circle, from plausible reasoning and schematic information processing, to taking action under uncertainty, to increasingly plausible reasoning when the action is completed. This intimate relationship between managerial understanding and managerial action remains one of the most intriguing areas of inquiry for management scholars to explore further.

## References

Argyris, C. A. *Increasing Leadership Effectiveness.* New York: Wiley, 1976.

Barnard, C. I. *The Functions of the Executive.* Cambridge, Mass.: Harvard University Press, 1938.

Bouwman, M. "The Use of Accounting Information: Expert Versus Novice Behavior." In G. Ungson and D. Braunstein (eds.), *Decision-Making: An Interdisciplinary Inquiry.* Boston: Kent, 1982.

Bursztajn, H., Feinbloom, R., Hamm, R., and Brodsky, A. *Medical Choices, Medical Chances.* New York: Dell, 1981.

Collins, A. "Fragments of a Theory of Human Plausible Reasoning." In D. Waltz (ed.), *Theoretical Issues in Natural Language Processing—2.* Urbana–Champaign: University of Illinois Press, 1978.

Collins, A., Warnock, E., Aiello, N., and Miller, N. "Reasoning from Incomplete Knowledge." In D. Bobrow and A. Collins (eds.), *Representation and Understanding: Studies in Cognitive Science.* Orlando, Fla.: Academic Press, 1975.

Connolly, T. "On Taking Action Seriously: Cognitive Fixation in Behavioral Decision Theory." In G. Ungson and D. Braunstein (eds.), *Decision-Making: An Interdisciplinary Inquiry.* Boston: Kent, 1982.

Fiske, S., and Kinder, D. "Involvement, Expertise, and Schema Use: Evidence from Political Cognition." In N. Cantor and J. Kihlstrom (eds.), *Personality, Cognition, and Social Interaction.* Hillsdale, N.J.: Erlbaum, 1981.

Gentner, D., and Collins, A. "Studies of Inference from Lack of Knowledge." *Memory and Cognition,* 1981, *9,* 434–443.

Glaser, R. "Education and Thinking: The Role of Knowledge." *American Psychologist,* 1984, *39,* 93–104.

Hammett, D. *The Thin Man.* New York: Knopf, 1942. (Originally published 1934.)

Hastie, R. "Schematic Principles in Human Memory." In E. T. Higgins, C. P. Herman, and M. Zanna (eds.), *Social Cognition: The Ontario Symposium.* Vol. 1. Hillsdale, N.J.: Erlbaum, 1981.

Innes, M. *What Happened at Hazlewood.* New York: Penguin, 1946.

Isenberg, D. J. "Managers' Knowledge Structures." Paper presented at meetings of the Academy of Management, New York, Aug. 1982.

Isenberg, D. J. "Drugs and Drama: The Impact of Dramatic Events on Managers' Cognitions." Working paper, Harvard Business School, 1983.

Isenberg, D. J. "How Senior Managers Think." *Harvard Business Review,* 1984, *6,* 80-90.

Isenberg, D. J. "Some Hows and Whats of Managerial Thinking: Implications for Future Army Leaders." In J. Hunt and J. Blair (eds.), *Leadership on the Future Battlefield.* Elmsford, N.Y.: Pergamon Press, 1985a.

Isenberg, D. J. "Thinking and Managing: A Verbal Protocol Analysis of Managerial Problem Solving." Paper presented at meetings of the Academy of Management, San Diego, Aug. 1985b.

Isenberg, D. J. "Research on How Senior Managers Think: Implications for Designing Executive Support Systems." In J. Elam (ed.), *Transactions: The Fifth International Conference on Decision Support Systems.* San Francisco, 1985c.

Isenberg, D. J. "Field Research on Managerial Cognition: Seven Findings, Seven Puzzles." In J. Bishop, J. Lochhead, and D. Perkins (eds.), *Thinking.* Hillsdale, N.J.: Erlbaum, forthcoming.

Kahneman, D., and Tversky, A. "Variants of Uncertainty." *Cognition,* 1982, *11,* 143-157.

Kiesler, S., and Sproull, L. "Managerial Response to Changing Environments: Perspectives on Problem Sensing from Social Cognition." *Administrative Science Quarterly,* 1982, *27,* 548-570.

Langer, E. "Rethinking the Role of Thought in Social Interaction." In J. Harvey, W. Ickes, and R. Kidd (eds.), *New Directions in Attribution Research.* Vol. 2. Hillsdale, N.J.: Erlbaum, 1978.

Lichtenstein, S., and Fischhoff, B. "Training for Calibration." *Organizational Behavior and Human Performance,* 1980, *26,* 149-171.

Lindsay, P., and Norman, D. *Human Information Processing.* Orlando, Fla.: Academic Press, 1977.

McCaskey, M. *The Executive Challenge: Managing Change and Ambiguity.* Marshfield, Mass.: Pitman, 1982.

Markus, H. "Self-Schemata and Processing Information About

the Self." *Journal of Personality and Social Psychology,* 1977, *35,* 63–78.

Neisser, U. *Cognition and Reality.* New York: W. H. Freeman, 1976.

Oskamp, S. "Overconfidence in Case-Study Judgments." *Journal of Consulting Psychology,* 1965, *29,* 261–265.

Peters, T., and Waterman, R. *In Search of Excellence.* New York: Harper & Row, 1982.

Posner, M., and Keele, S. "On the Genesis of Abstract Ideas." *Journal of Experimental Psychology,* 1968, *77,* 353–363.

Schön, D. *The Reflective Practitioner.* New York: Basic Books, 1983.

Simon, H. "On How to Decide What to Do." *Bell Journal of Economics,* 1978, *9,* 494–507.

Taylor, S., and Crocker, J. "Schematic Bases of Social Information Processing." In E. T. Higgins, C. P. Herman, and M. Zanna (eds.), *Social Cognition: The Ontario Symposium.* Vol. 1. Hillsdale, N.J.: Erlbaum, 1981.

Tesser, A. "Self-Generated Attitude Change." In L. Berkowitz (ed.), *Advances in Experimental Social Psychology.* Vol. 11. Orlando, Fla.: Academic Press, 1978.

Weick, K. E. *The Social Psychology of Organizing.* (2nd ed.) Reading, Mass.: Addison-Wesley, 1979.

# 10

## On the Difficulty
## of Learning from Experience

### Jack Feldman

> *What experience and history teach is this—that peo-*
> *ple and governments never have learned anything*
> *from history, or acted on principles deduced from*
> *it.*

—G. W. F. Hegel, 1832

As we examine many individual and organizational practices, Hegel's depressing assertion seems easy to believe. Candidates for high-level positions are often selected on the basis of unvalidated interviews and assessments using projective techniques, despite an almost total lack of validity (Anastasi, 1982; Campbell, Dunnette, Lawler, and Weick, 1970). Bettors and investors lose untold amounts of money on cards, horses, stocks, and commodities using "systems" of one sort or another. In foreign policy, some claim that the United States is committing the same mistakes in Central America as were made in Vietnam. The Soviet Union is said also to be involved in a "Vietnam-like" war in Afghanistan. The common implication is that mistakes tend to be repeated, that people (and organizations of people) do not learn from the results of their own or others' actions.

Is such pessimism warranted? Do people indeed fail to benefit from their experience, or by focusing on failures and

errors do we misrepresent our ability to understand and control
the events shaping our lives? This chapter will examine important psychological processes that influence learning from experience and will outline the conditions that produce errors as well
as those promoting accurate, efficient learning. Finally, suggestions for organizational practice intended to improve the learning process will be made.

## Three Views of Learning from Experience

A concern with errors and biases typifies research on judgment and decision processes. Kahneman, Slovic, and Tversky
(1982) present several papers dealing with systematic errors in
the use of information—for example, improper use of base rates
(Tversky and Kahneman, 1982a), decision and judgment heuristics leading to inaccurate estimation (Tversky and Kahneman,
1982b), improper generalization from sample information
(Tversky and Kahneman, 1982c), incorrect attributional reasoning (Ross and Anderson, 1982), errors in the perception of covariation and control (Chapman and Chapman, 1982; Langer,
1982), hindsight bias (Fischhoff, 1982a), and illusory validity
(Einhorn, 1982). The papers in this single volume summarize
many years of research testifying that human information processing is widely thought to be biased and error-prone. If people
*do* learn from experience, why do such mistakes persist?

A contradictory position also exists. It is obvious that
learning *does* take place, both in daily life and in the course of
deliberate research. The methods by which biases in information processing and decision making themselves were detected
were developed from experience, along with all the rest of human knowledge. Most people and organizations get along very
well on a daily basis, suggesting that "failures to learn" are
unrepresentative exceptions to an efficient and accurate process.

Both positions are somewhat extreme. Our attention is
drawn to spectacular failures, whether personal or international,
making them more accessible and therefore seemingly more frequent than they are (Tversky and Kahneman, 1982d; Taylor,

1982; Taylor and Fiske, 1978). Cognitive theories predict particular kinds of errors in particular settings, inviting tests of those theories focusing on the production of errors. Thus, the research literature is replete with studies of error rather than accuracy. It must be realized, however, that the same underlying processes produce both. To borrow an analogy from Hogarth (1981), the principles of an arrow's flight are the same whether it hits the bull's-eye or misses the target entirely. The most useful questions to ask concern the environmental and individual conditions that promote either errors or accuracy.

It is also important to consider the nature of "accuracy." To say that a task is done incorrectly, one must have some criterion defining "correct" outcomes or processes. For example, "biases" in probability estimation are inferred from discrepancies between people's answers to some questions of likelihood and the output of a normative model such as Bayes's theorem. We say that animals and people exhibit "superstitious" (that is, erroneous) behavior because they behave systematically in response to random reinforcement schedules. People are said to violate the "rationality" of expected utility theory because their stated preferences do not match the calculated utilities of a set of alternatives. We then claim that people do not judge, learn, or decide very well. Hogarth (1981) and Einhorn and Hogarth (1981) point out that this claim is based on the untested, and often untestable, assumption that the criteria themselves actually represent reality. For example, is "superstitious" behavior a special case of a process allowing adaptation to a world in which entirely random reinforcement and punishment are rare? Should people act like expected utility theorists when neither outcome preferences (Fischhoff, Slovic, and Lichtenstein, 1980) nor outcome probabilities may be stable over time? Finally, how far should we generalize the results of studies done without feedback, involving only single judgments, when most of life involves continual interaction with the environment and readjustment of behavior (Hogarth, 1981)? In other words, do the heuristics and biases of judgment and decision research represent reasonable adaptations to the problems of learning from experience?

## Learning Processes and the Environment

*The Role of Cognitive Structures and Strategies in Learning.* Learning can be said to be based on association, either between stimuli (cues) or between stimuli, responses, and outcomes. Interstimulus associations create categories, which are relatively permanent and hierarchically organized cognitive structures (Posner and McLeod, 1982). These can be thought of as being represented by prototypes—that is, by abstract images combining the most frequent and representative features of category members (Rosch, 1977). Psychological categories have some characteristics of "fuzzy sets," in that inclusion is based on the possession of attributes only probabilistically related to membership. Some category members are more "prototypical" than others (just as, for example, a robin is a more "prototypical" bird than an ostrich). Categories develop from experience, representing observed covariation (or instruction); they are an important source of cognitive economy, since a stimulus, once categorized, may be responded to in terms of the category prototype.

Stimulus-response-outcome associations, whether learned from direct experience or instruction, may be generalized into "rules" (Siegler, 1983), which may be organized into "cognitive strategies" (Posner and McLeod, 1982), or "schemas" (see Feldman, forthcoming). Rules are applied to a problem on the basis of the problem's categorical representation—that is, its prototype. Once a problem is classified as "subtraction," for example, one particular rule of an "arithmetic" schema is applied. Similar but more complex processing might apply to a problem of "political subversion" or "falling market share." Expertise implies more complex and differentiated category structures (Rosch, 1977) and correspondingly more complex rules and schemas.

Cognitive structures and strategies differ as a function of experience. Culture, training, and background influence attention to cues and their categorical interpretation. The interpretation of the cues presented by a problem defines its context and the impact of feedback; thus, what one learns is in part a function of what one already knows (Alloy and Tabachnik, 1984; Siegler, 1983). Such a cognitive approach permits a large role for trial-and-error learning, but at the same time recognizes that trials are not randomly generated and that errors may have different effects at different times and for different people. It also permits a substantial role for the environment, since both the accessibility of categories and the salience of cues may be influenced by individual and environmental factors (Feldman, 1981; Ilgen and Feldman, 1983).

Siegler (1983, p. 264) presents five generalizations about cognitive development that may be usefully applied to the question of adult schema and category system learning, allowing for the greater amount and complexity of adult knowledge. These generalizations are as follows:

1. The rule is a useful basic unit for characterizing knowledge.
2. "Premastery" rules are adopted in order of predictive accuracy within the range of environments in which the rule is applied. (That is, partially correct rules are used to the extent that they improve prediction in particular settings.)
3. Reasoning across different concepts is more homogeneous the less knowledge about the concepts possessed by an individual. (That is, the less knowledge, the more likely inappropriate generalizations are to be made.)
4. Learning is determined by the interaction of knowledge and experience. Experiences that contradict existing rules promote the most learning.
5. When contradictions are presented by experience, encoding plays a large role in constructing new rules. (That is, pre-existing and salient category systems influence how events are perceived and relationships inferred.)

Siegler's review supports each of these propositions; they are also consistent with the ideas of social cognition and performance appraisal discussed by Feldman (1981, forthcoming) and Ilgen and Feldman (1983). If the validity of Siegler's arguments is provisionally assumed, learning from experience may be said to occur when an inaccuracy in prediction is made salient, and the resultant feedback is usefully encoded. These conditions are likely to exist when there is already substantial knowledge about the phenomena in question, implying a highly differentiated category system.

*Learning and the Nature of the Environment.* The environment strongly influences the degree to which useful feedback is available. Our experience is necessarily limited to a small proportion of the possible environments; information is obtained irregularly, over time, in a mixture of signal and noise. Outcomes are only probabilistically related to actions, because of a multitude of uncertainties and uncontrollable causal factors in the environment (see Dawes, 1976, pp. 6–7).

One of the most potent environmental factors is the nature of the task itself. Hammond (1980, 1981) has proposed a "cognitive continuum" model that predicts the type of cognitive activity elicited by three general types of tasks. These task types also have implications for the efficiency of learning.

The *analytic task* is represented by tasks such as mathematics problems or mechanical assembly. The determination of sites for convenience stores is a familiar organizational example. The solution process is conscious and can be reliably reported. The problem solver uses relatively few cues, and these cues are previously known, quantitative, and minimally correlated. The nonlinear or nonmonotonic relationship between cues and outcome values requires unequal weighting and configural cue combination processes. Cues are fixed, but different combinatorial strategies may be used, with immediate feedback to the problem solver. Because the tasks used to demonstrate rule learning and modification by experience are analytic, correct rules are learned rapidly when relevant feedback is provided (Siegler, 1983). Most studies demonstrating mistakes in judgment do so by using a situation in which an analytic model applies and then showing that judgments do not correspond to its output.

*Intuitive tasks* represent the opposite end of the continuum, including tasks such as theory generation (for example, the theory of evolution by natural selection) and artistic inspiration. Many "strategic planning" activities require intuition. The process of problem solving is not conscious, and may involve imagery rather than symbolic reasoning. The intuitive task demands that a large number of subjectively scaled, equally weighted and correlated cues be combined; many alternative solutions exist and feedback is equivocal. Because no generally accepted organizing principles exist, a system must first be created and then used to solve a problem. Intuitive tasks are always modeled by weighted-average cue combination processes, but the cues used may vary. The standards for "correctness" of intuitive solutions are subjective, as in the requirement of "elegance" or "beauty" in a scientific theory: "You can't describe it ... if you don't feel it ... you're not susceptible to it. No one can explain it to you" (P. Dirac, quoted in Judson, 1984, p. 43).

Finally, the *quasi-rational task* occupies the midpoint of the cognitive continuum. Simon's (1979) concept of "bounded rationality" describes the thought process elicited by these tasks: for example, attribution problems, similarity judgments, and multi-attribute preference tasks. Heuristics or linear models represent the judgment or decision process. Quasi-rationality combines elements of both intuition and analysis, taking the form of a weighted-average compromise (for example, "Our team will win because we have a good pitching record [analytic] and because our players have the most 'desire' [intuitive]") or of an alternation (for example, "The Subaru may be the cheapest and most dependable car [analytic], but the Buick fits my image of a lawyer [intuitive]"). Quasi-rational tasks are perhaps the most frequently encountered. Processes represented by linear models and heuristics can be adaptive in situations where analytic solutions are absent (Dawes, 1979; Einhorn and Hogarth, 1981; Hogarth, 1981; Hammond, 1980). For example, "adjustment and anchoring" may yield accurate judgments in negotiations with a previously unknown opponent (Hogarth, 1981, p. 207).

From the discussion above, it seems obvious that the task cannot be considered apart from its performer (see Siegler's Rule Four). What to the novice is a hopeless jumble of parts is a straightforward assembly job for the master mechanic; a confusion of numbers and labels to the layperson is a balance sheet to the accountant. While some tasks are inherently analytic (for example, arithmetic problems) and some are fundamentally intuitive (for example, theory development), the expertise of the performer is always a factor in task definition.

The outcomes of one's task activities constitute feedback. Here it is necessary to distinguish two types of feedback: outcome and process (Einhorn and Hogarth, 1981). *Outcome feedback* refers to the consequences of actions; *process feedback* refers to the correctness of reasoning. Process feedback is rare in the natural environment. Typically, outcome information alone is available. It is only when dealing with analytic tasks that outcome feedback may be used efficiently to induce a correct rule, and then only when the range of tasks is sufficient to show the failure of incorrect rules (Lichtenstein, Fischhoff, and Phillips, 1982; Fischhoff, 1982b). Siegler (1983), for instance, showed how an incorrect rule can generate correct answers as long as only a restricted range of problems is encountered (see Rule Two). Dulany's (1961) studies of the role of hypotheses in human operant conditioning showed that partially correct hypotheses can result in substantial reinforcement rates. Dawes (1979) likewise demonstrated that formally incorrect linear models yield substantial predictive accuracy. In short, in the absence of an explicit analytic model, quasi-rational cognition may provide better than chance predictive power, and its use is reinforced by outcome feedback. The drawback is that in cases where an analytic model is either inapplicable or unknown, outcome feedback may be mediated by the environment in such a way as to create an "outcome-irrelevant learning structure" (Einhorn, 1982).

In intuitive task settings, the ambiguity of outcome feedback is pronounced. Here, we are dealing with the conceptualization of a problem, the generation of a theory from experience. The only way to assess the usefulness of a theory is to apply analytic methods, but these cannot be informative unless the intuitive "vision" is stated rigorously. Many theories (for example, the notion of a "need hierarchy") are stated so loosely that any outcome may be interpreted as consistent with them (Locke, 1976). Because these intuitions have the psychological immediacy of perception (Hammond, 1980, 1981), they can be contradicted only via process feedback, and then only if the recipient agrees to the assumptions of the process statement.

*Summary.* It is possible to create situations in which individuals make suboptimal decisions and "learn" illusory relationships, but there is a real question about the representativeness of these settings and tasks. Learning seems to involve the creation of cognitive structures or category systems, in which categories are represented by abstract prototypes; it also involves cognitive strategies or schemas, which include hierarchical organizations of rules or scripts for action. Rules are applied based on a problem's categorization; the results of rule application, in particular the failure of a rule to produce a correct solution, provide the impetus for learning. What is learned, however, depends on the pre-existing cognitive structure. The more differentiated it is, the more readily can experience be encoded and used to induce new rules and structures.

The type of tasks one encounters and the type of feedback received are also important. Analytic tasks, having explicit rules, few cues, and consciously accessible procedures, allow rapid learning via outcome feedback. Intuitive tasks, using multiple cues, imagery, and largely inaccessible processes, require process feedback, which is relatively rare. Quasi-rational tasks, which are the most frequently encountered decision and judgment problems, elicit the use of heuristics and linear decision models that, though often sufficiently accurate for daily life, may be misleading when applied to new problems. Especially where intuitive and quasi-rational tasks are concerned, learning from outcome feedback alone is difficult.

## Learning from Experience: Problems and Their Origins

Having stated the nature of the problem in general terms, it is now useful to consider specific factors influencing the accuracy of learning from experience. The discussion will be organized around the questions posed by Einhorn and Hogarth (1978, 1981): Is there something to be learned? What is learned? When have we learned?

*Is There Something To Be Learned?* In order to realize that learning is necessary, one must notice errors. Given the uncertain connection between actions and outcomes, this is not always easy. For example, how does one know that an organization's reward system is less effective than it might be, given "satisfactory" productivity and turnover levels? Both environmental and psychological barriers exist that may prevent recognition of the need to learn. Einhorn and Hogarth (1978) discuss one such barrier under the label of the "illusion of validity."

People seem to represent frequency rather than probability in memory, perhaps because probability estimation requires attention to *nonoccurrences* of events, which are not as salient as occurrences. Furthermore, action taken on the basis of some hypothesis effectively blocks information on the outcomes of an alternative decision. Finally, people tend not to be sensitive to base-rate information unless it has causal significance (Ross and Anderson, 1982; Tversky and Kahneman, 1982a). Suppose that an action were taken based on an invalid rule—for example, executives were hired on the basis of astrological signs—and that these people were selected from an experienced and capable cohort with a success rate of 65 percent. Most hiring decisions would seem to be correct, because only the frequency of success among those chosen would be known to the decision maker.

The illusion is further strengthened by "Pygmalion" effects. Eden and Shani (1982), for example, found that a randomly introduced positive expectancy had a strong effect on the performance of military recruits. Eden (1984) reviews a number of studies with similar results. The supportive treatment given those selected tends to raise the observed success rate above the base rate (compare Einhorn and Hogarth's "treatment effect"), thus strengthening the illusion. In both social interaction and job interview settings, "self-fulfilling prophecies" produce behavior that confirms initial impressions (Darley and Fazio, 1980; Dipboye, 1982). Not only does the environment present information in a way that is difficult to analyze, but behavior in response to our interpretation of the environment tends to *create* support for our expectations.

Illusory validity is present in other situations as well.

Kahneman and Tversky (1973) note that experienced flight instructors believe that punishment is more effective than positive reinforcement. They have observed that poor performance, leading to criticism, is usually followed by improvement; good performance, leading to praise, is usually followed by a decline. This conclusion reflects ignorance of "regression toward the mean," a statistical concept that is not easy to induce without an abstract analytic schema and carefully recorded observations. In this case, the most salient information is flying performance and some impression of the student's rate of progress. Furthermore, students improve over time regardless of treatment; the effect of positive reinforcement might be seen in a faster rate of progress or higher overall performance, but this cannot be detected without a controlled experiment. Thus, the fact that most students do succeed and the availability of data from immediate experience "confirm" an invalid belief. Without the researcher's methodological schema, outcomes are not assessed or encoded in a manner revealing the true relationship.

There are other factors that prevent one from knowing when learning is necessary. Attentional biases direct attention to expectation-confirming events when disconfirming information is also available. Darley and Gross (1983), for example, unobtrusively induced subjects to categorize a young girl as middle or lower-class and showed that subsequent impressions and memories of her IQ test performance were biased by the categorization. Similar effects have been demonstrated in interview settings by Dipboye, Stramler, and Fontonelle (1984). Such behavior is apparently "thoughtless" or automatic, and is based on the salience of cues relevant to the most accessible category (Feldman, 1981; Ilgen and Feldman, 1983).

When disconfirming events are made salient, an active process of searching for information may begin (Kelley and Michela, 1980; Pyszczynski and Greenberg, 1981). Paradoxically, the processes generated may justify rather than correct the original expectation. Kulik (1983), for example, showed that a person's category-inconsistent behavior may be explained situationally, even in the absence of supporting evidence. Regan, Strauss, and Fazio (1974) and Taylor and Jaggi (1974) found that the positive actions of liked individuals are attributed internally, while negative actions are attributed externally; the opposite pattern exists for disliked people. Gilovich (1983) reported that gambling losses tended to be explained (and discounted) as unrepresentative "flukes." Weber and Crocker (1983) showed that stereotype-inconsistent behavior concentrated within a few members of a stereotyped group led to the differentiation of "subtypes," preserving the original stereotype. Since information about single events (or people) is usually encountered, general beliefs will be slow to change; "exceptions" may be readily dismissed as unrepresentative.

Hindsight bias (Fischhoff, 1982a; Wood, 1978; Hasher, Attig, and Alba, 1981) creates another barrier to realizing the need for learning. People given feedback on the correctness of their information or their predictions tend to remember themselves as favoring the correct answer more than they actually had. That is, mistakes may be explained as temporary aberrations, leaving people's assessments of their knowledge unchanged. Although hindsight bias may be overcome (Hasher, Attig, and Alba, 1981; Wood, 1978), rather strong and uncommon manipulations are necessary.

Yet another factor interfering with recognition of the need to learn is categorical bias in memory. Research reviewed in Feldman (1981) and Ilgen and Feldman (1983) strongly supports the proposition that stimulus persons, categorized either automatically or via a conscious attributional process, are thereafter thought of in terms of the category. Systematic errors in memory occur as a result of this impression; category-consistent behaviors that never occurred are falsely recognized, and category-consistent behaviors are most accurately recalled (Berman, Read, and Kenny, 1983; Johnson and Judd, 1983). Although this seems to disagree with Hastie's (1984) findings, they can be reconciled by postulating a "threshold of inconsistency," such that large or frequent contradictions attract attention and demand controlled processing, but small deviations from expectation do not. Memory is not "schematic," in the sense that only categorical information is stored (Alba and Hasher, 1983). Rather, the prototype serves as a "default option" when the time or motivation for a systematic memory search is lacking. A casual scan of memory is more likely to turn up confirming instances of behavior, thereby reducing the likelihood of useful outcome feedback.

Finally, there are purely social factors that influence the nature and effect of feedback, and thus the awareness of a need to learn. Much of the reinforcement and information obtained in everyday life comes from other people. When intuitions are involved, social reinforcement or "consensual validation" is often the only feedback available. Agreement with opinions that are not objectively verifiable is especially reinforcing and is one major reason that we tend to like those similar to ourselves (Byrne, 1969). In highly cohesive groups, where common values, category systems, and schemas exist, mutual reinforcement may easily lead to "groupthink" (Janis, 1972). This is particularly likely where individuals are selected to be "team players" (as in presidential cabinets and groups of executives) or when the reward system punishes dissent. Even in groups of strangers, conformity pressure may be high; for example, lasting belief change can be produced in ambiguous situations (Allen, 1965). Because social support for dissent is unlikely to be absent in highly cohesive groups, and because people tend to be reluctant to communicate unwelcome news, feedback indicating a need for learning is unlikely (Allen, 1975; Tesser and Rosen, 1975). It might be speculated that the American automobile industry failed to respond effectively to foreign competition because of the isolation of industry executives from the consumer and a social atmosphere that prevented the rapid change in design, production, and marketing schemas demanded by a changing environment. The same might be said of the British motorcycle industry, which no longer exists.

*Summary.* A prerequisite to learning is awareness of errors. Often, however, an incorrect rule or invalid category system does not lead to complete failure. In the absence of information about the results of alternative rules, a suboptimal policy may seem satisfactory; also, actions taken on the basis of that policy may make it seem even more effective. Furthermore, attention and memory seem conservative, in that they are biased in the direction of expected events and existing explanations. Often, only an explicit "methodological schema" can provide enough salient information to counteract tendencies to notice, remember, and create the events we expect, and to explain isolated contradictions as exceptions to a general rule. Norms of social behavior and interpersonal reinforcement promoting conformity also contribute to the perseverance of incorrect schemas.

*What Is to Be Learned?* Realization of the need to learn does not imply that new learning will be error-free. In intuitive and quasi-rational task environments, the events that capture one's attention may be strongly influenced by existing category systems and schemas.

The "illusory correlation" (Chapman, 1967; Chapman and Chapman, 1967, 1969; Hamilton, 1979) is one example. Even experienced, expert observers report associations between events (for example, drawings with eye emphasis and paranoia) matching common semantic associations. Moreover, these tendencies are strong enough to hide real associations existing in the data. Given the tendency of expectations to be self-confirming (as noted earlier), illusory "new learning" can easily persist.

At times the environment may present distorted information. This is seen in stereotype formation, as discussed by Campbell (1967). If interaction with members of some group is restricted to a small range of situations, behaviors demanded by those situations will be the most frequently experienced. Behaviors salient to the perceiver are the most likely to be encoded and remembered; due to a general tendency to perceive causality as inherent in persons (Ross and Anderson, 1982), behaviors will be explained as dispositions of the individual. The tendency to generalize from small samples or single instances of behavior exaggerates the effect (Hamill, Wilson, and Nisbett, 1980; Quattrone and Jones, 1980; Read, 1983). Thus, for example, it is easy to form a stereotype of the Japanese based on behavior observed where formal norms of politeness apply and to thus "explain" the success of Japanese industry based on the compliance and cooperativeness of the work force, while ignoring the complexities of organizational reward systems and investment in new technology.

The environment also influences our learning by making certain stimuli more salient than others. Relatively intense or vivid stimuli draw our attention and lead to stronger causal attributions (Taylor and Fiske, 1978; Taylor and Thompson, 1982). For example, a group member who is in some way unique (for example, in race or sex) is seen as more influential than the same person is when the group contains others of his or her category. Vividness due to purely situational factors (for example, visual or auditory prominence) produces the same effect (Robinson and McArthur, 1982; Ross and Anderson, 1982). Stimulus intensity, which influences salience, has been found important in nonsocial settings with both human and animal subjects (Alloy and Tabachnik, 1984). The environmental salience effect is quite robust in social perception, resisting a number of manipulations (Taylor and others, 1979). Other sources of salience, however, can overcome it (Borgida and Howard-Pitney, 1983).

Very general schemas may influence what is learned. The general rule that the environment may be controlled, for example, guides much of human behavior. Langer (1982) introduced skill-related cues into tasks whose outcomes were determined by chance and found that people responded as if they could control the outcome. For example, they bet more when drawing cards against an awkward opponent than against a "dapper" one. Similar effects are seen in the production of "superstitious behavior" (Alloy and Tabachnik, 1984), in which people "detect" contingencies that do not exist. For example, where one of four keys had to be pressed within a certain interval to obtain reinforcement, subjects developed complex response patterns involving the irrelevant keys.

The role of schemas in the detection of relationships (both true and illusory) is highlighted by research on depression, "learned helplessness," and "learned irrelevance" (Alloy and Tabachnik, 1984; Coyne and Gotlib, 1983). Basically, people see the contingencies they expect, for both themselves and others, when the situation is such as to elicit their generalized schemas of "controllability." Broadly speaking, what is learned depends on the salience or intensity of information in the environment and the kind of relationship one expects (see also Crocker, 1981).

This presents a seeming contradiction. When information is presented in the laboratory, those with no expectations about association are better at detecting covariation. Those with highly-developed schemas—that is, experts—should therefore be *less* accurate at detecting true relationships than novices. Yet expertise also implies greater attention to *exceptions* to schema-based expectations, and therefore greater accuracy in detecting unexpected or changed relationships (Fiske, Kinder, and Larter, 1983). It should be realized that in real life *no* perceptions are schema-free, and thus the novice is more likely to perceive relationships or contingencies in keeping with his or her relevant and salient (but invalid) schema (for example, hiring people because of the shape of their faces, as some Egyptian managers are said to do—see Summers, 1984).

Experts are not free from judgmental biases; Slovic, Fischhoff, and Lichtenstein (1982) report that the differential accessibility of causal information produces judgmental overconfidence in experts similar to that observed in laymen. It may well be that experts' category systems and schematic representations blind them to things that a layman with a "fresh perspective" will notice. It must also be pointed out that the expert logically ought to be more sensitive to environmental feedback. The problem is that in some situations, the cost of the mistakes that provide feedback is very high—design failures in aircraft, for example.

*Summary.* Pre-existing category systems and schemas, in interaction with environmental factors, influence what is learned. Cues associated with accessible category prototypes are habitually more noticeable, as are cues tied to general schemas, such as "controllability of outcomes." Thus, the frequency with which salient cues occur is more likely to be encoded and then used to infer or perceive a relationship. Salience due to environmental factors operates in the same manner and is one way in which invalid category prototypes (for example, stereotypes) are formed and maintained. Experts are as prone to such biases as others, but because their category systems are more differentiated, unexpected events may be more salient, and therefore learning may occur more readily in response to outcome feedback. The conditions under which experts are more or less likely than novices to learn effectively need further investigation.

*When Have We Learned?* In a sense, this topic has already been covered, since deciding when one has learned seems like the mirror image of realizing that learning is needed. We may take as a starting point the idea that when one's predictions reach some hypothetical "satisfactory" level of accuracy, or when a satisfactory level of outcomes is received, learning will be perceived to be sufficient. It follows that the same factors that influence the recognition of the need to learn operate at this phase as well.

One process remains to be discussed, however. Subsequent to the formation of hypotheses, the perceiver might seek to test them. Hypothesis testing that relies on unaided inference may be biased toward confirmation of the newly formed hypothesis, just as perceptions are biased toward information that is compatible with existing beliefs. Since hypothesis-confirming information is generally regarded as more "informative" (Alloy and Tabachnik, 1984; Crocker, 1981), it is not surprising that people have been found to search for it systematically. When choosing questions to ask others, for example, questions likely to confirm hypotheses are preferred (Snyder and Swann, 1978) unless subjects are instructed otherwise (Snyder and White, 1981). A memory-based hypothesis test may likewise be biased toward confirmation (Snyder and Cantor, 1979). The availability or content of memories can be biased by newly formed attitudes (Read and Rosson, 1982; Ross, McFarland, Conway, and Zanna, 1983). Ross and others also show that biased recall may strengthen the attitude. Together, these accessibility and credibility effects help explain why people may be overconfident of newly formed hypotheses (Koriat, Lichtenstein, and Fischhoff, 1982), and why experimentally induced self-perceptions persist in the face of attempts to discredit them (Fleming and Arrowood, 1979; Jennings, Lepper, and Ross, 1981). Some of the perseverance of discredited theories of human behavior (for example, need hierarchies, two-factor theory) may be due to the ease with which "confirming" examples are generated.

Bias is not universal, however. Trope and Bassok (1982)

found that diagnostic evidence was preferred to confirmatory information under conditions making diagnosticity salient. Beyth-Marom and Fischhoff (1983) also found that diagnostic information was used when the hypothesis to be tested was stated in a competitive form. In memory-based judgments, Lingle and Ostrom (1979) found a preferential search for disconfirming (negative or incongruous) evidence, provided incongruity was initially encoded (Lingle, Dukerich, and Ostrom, 1983). Sackett (1982) found no evidence for a confirmation bias in an employment interview setting with experienced subjects, and Brugnoli, Campion, and Basen (1979) found (hypothesis-confirming) racial bias in job sample ratings only when irrelevant tasks and global evaluation forms were used, and when attention was *not* drawn explicitly to behavior. Thus, where an analytic hypothesis-testing schema exists, where an expert's category system directs attention to relevant cues, or where the task is appropriately defined, bias may be reduced or avoided. The fact that bias can be reduced suggests that both training and situational interventions may be useful.

*Summary.* To decide whether one has learned, systematic tests of hypotheses may be performed. One salient schema guiding such tests causes a search for confirming information and can be systematically misleading. More appropriate schemas do exist, however, and can be elicited by instructions, training, or task presentation.

## Suggestions for Practice: How to Improve Learning from Experience

The preceding discussion has focused on the equivocality of outcome feedback, especially in intuitive and quasi-rational task environments, and the biases in learning resulting from reliance on highly overlearned and perhaps incorrect category systems and schemas. The improvements to be suggested focus on increasing the amount and usefulness of feedback within an analytic data gathering process, bringing about changes in the social environment promoting explicit hypothesis testing, and implementing reward systems intended to motivate more effective learning. Since performance at any task is a function of ability and motivation, within environmental constraints, my suggestions will be organized around these categories.

*Environment*

*Suggestion One.* Increase the amount and immediacy of useful feedback. Lichtenstein, Fischhoff, and Phillips (1982) and Fischhoff (1982b) point out that the predictions of weather forecasters and horseracing handicappers are "well calibrated" (the estimated probabilities of events closely match their relative frequencies) due to the availability and rapidity of feedback. Such accuracy requires substantial learning. Of course, there are analytic tasks, allowing unequivocal predictions using a small number of cues, but most situations are more ambiguous. The challenge is to arrange the environment so that the learning task becomes more analytic, and the relevant cues and outcomes become salient and easily codable.

This problem was addressed some time ago by Campbell (1969). One solution involves making specific predictions as to the results of actions or interventions, and setting up a data collection and interpretation system making feedback inevitable. Research becomes a part of every decision or innovation and must be designed to eliminate ambiguities, insofar as that is possible. For example, the decision to implement work redesign should be accompanied by a statement of exactly what benefits are expected and what form they should take. Measurement of relevant variables (for example, dimensions of job satisfaction, absenteeism, and productivity) should accompany the intervention, which itself may be carried out in a quasi-experimental fashion. Tests to eliminate alternative hypotheses (for example, that the higher pay required for enriched jobs accounts for satisfaction increases, or that the higher ability required of those performing the jobs accounts for productivity improvements) should be built in. Although the *basis* for many innovations or decisions may be intuitive or quasi-rational, analytic methods *must* be used to assess their outcomes. Without such specificity, it is all too easy to create an outcome-irrelevant learning structure (Einhorn, 1982).

*Suggestion Two.* Create a social environment that requires

learning. Many of the cues we attend to, and many of the ways our environment is interpreted, reflect a "social reality." Part of the problem is a natural tendency to surround ourselves with people similar to us and also to become like those who mediate information and reinforcements. To counteract the problems resulting from this sameness of world view requires a deliberate restructuring of organizational roles. First, the role of "devil's advocate" ought to be institutionalized. For any major decision, an individual should be assigned to present all the reasons any course of action would be wrong; for any hypothesis, the devil's advocate should be assigned to construct alternatives. These alternatives should then direct part of the data analysis discussed above. Both Fischhoff (1982b) and Lord, Lepper, and Preston (1984) report that the deliberate consideration of alternative possibilities reduces judgmental bias. In combination with formal evaluation procedures, devil's advocacy may substantially improve the rate of learning. Even if a minority opinion does not influence a particular decision, its statement may have substantial effects on future choices (Maass and Clark, 1984).

*Ability*

*Suggestion Three.* Hire or train employees to be experts in both substance and process. Substantive expertise includes both "knowing the business" and formal academic knowledge. Abstractions such as financial theory must be applied in a particular context (for example, in the context of the electronics industry). Furthermore, effective decisions require an understanding of the entire organization and the factors influencing its success, not simply one particular function. The expert schemas and category systems required for the effective use of feedback must refer to the entire organization and its environment. Such knowledge is best produced by a wide range of experience within the organization, in addition to training in some functional specialty.

Job rotation as practiced in Japanese industry is one means of producing an integrated conceptual structure (Hatvany and Pucik, 1983). The fast-track promotion/hiring philosophy should be avoided, because rapid advancement within (or between) organizations cannot produce the kind of substantive expertise that allows sensitivity to the need to learn. By the time the results of the fast-track manager's policies become known, he or she may well have moved on.

Process, or methodological expertise, means more than training in research design. Rather, it means training in the conception of problems and decisions in ways leading to useful feedback. The fact that most people prefer confirming information unless instructed otherwise and the tendency for intelligent, well-trained people not to use analytic thought outside their own areas of expertise (for example, the frequency with which well-paid professionals fall prey to "tax shelter" swindles) make the need for process training evident. The skill required to state hypotheses in testable form, to evaluate evidence for and against those hypotheses, and to propose tentative generalizations to be tested against experience is not a common one. Fischhoff (1982b) reports that "calibration training," with "intense, personalized feedback" (p. 437) was effective in reducing overconfidence in judgment, but exactly what sort of training is required to promote habitual hypothesis statement and testing is unknown. For the moment, it might be useful to make training in the framing of questions and the use of feedback a part of professional curricula and management development seminars as well as a skill to be measured in assessment centers.

*Motivation*

*Suggestion Four.* Don't expect infallibility. The biggest motivational problem in learning from experience can be stated simply: "Everyone wants to learn, but nobody wants to be wrong." Learning from experience requires one to be wrong at least part of the time, but both public and private organizations tend to punish mistakes. Actions are taken based on the presumption that they will be "successful" (Campbell, 1969). Those recommending a given action are rewarded for showing that they were correct, not for accurate evaluation. Sometimes, these contingencies are frozen into organizational policies; for example, some organizations insist that training effects are not measurable (Campbell, Dunnette, Lawler, and Weick, 1970, p. 49). In short, in many organizations the evidence needed to learn from experience may be deliberately ignored (or hidden) because it would be damaging to the individual in charge.

Campbell's (1⁹ ɔ) fifteen-year-old advice is still the best: change the focus from the *solution* to the *seriousness of the problem*. Reward people for the thoughtfulness of their analysis and the extent to which they properly evaluate their diagnoses and proposed solutions. This may seem to fly in the face of political reality, but no one really knows the degree to which an electorate (or a group of stockholders) would respond to a sincere emphasis on experimentation and honest evaluation. Certainly "blood, toil, tears, and sweat" is not a bad promise. In business organizations, "political reality" and ideology ought to be secondary to long-term organizational and societal well-being.

One workable system requires reward for desirable outcomes, determined by the structure and technology of the organization (Lawler, 1981), and an additional reward for information gathering and evaluation. Penalties should be imposed not for being wrong but for refusing to learn. Another benefit of job rotation and promotion from within is that it provides opportunities for mistakes and corrective feedback in relatively low-cost circumstances and a more accurate assessment of each individual's willingness and ability to learn. It follows that disagreement can be a source of new hypotheses to be tested and may indicate that long accepted practices need changing. Such creative conflict cannot occur unless people are selected and rewarded on the basis of real, measured ability and contributions, and not on the basis of irrelevant personal characteristics. These sentiments are not simply academic niceties, but reflect the observation of successful managers (see, for example, Townsend, 1971, pp. 21, 35, 56, and 57–65).

The strategy outlined here does not mean that an organization must be paralyzed by interminable study of each and every action. Rather, action and evaluation should be linked, so that whether a decision is made quickly or not, its consequences may be evaluated, the basis for the decision considered, and the *next* decision made better. That is, after all, what learning is about.

# References

Alba, J. W., and Hasher, L. "Is Memory Schematic?" *Psychological Bulletin,* 1983, *93,* 203-231.

Allen, V. L. "Situational Factors in Conformity." In L. Berkowitz (ed.), *Advances in Experimental Social Psychology.* Vol. 2. Orlando, Fla.: Academic Press, 1965.

Allen, V. L. "Social Support for Nonconformity." In L. Berkowitz (ed.), *Advances in Experimental Social Psychology.* Vol. 8. Orlando, Fla.: Academic Press, 1975.

Alloy, L. B., and Tabachnik, N. "Assessment of Covariation by Humans and Animals: The Joint Influence of Prior Expectations and Current Situational Information." *Psychological Review,* 1984, *91,* 112-149.

Anastasi, A. *Psychological Testing.* (5th ed.) New York: Macmillan, 1982.

Berman, J. S., Read, S. J., and Kenny, D. A. "Processing Inconsistent Social Information." *Journal of Personality and Social Psychology,* 1983. *45,* 1211-1224.

Beyth-Marom, R., and Fischhoff, B. "Diagnosticity and Pseudodiagnosticity." *Journal of Personality and Social Psychology,* 1983, *45,* 1185-1195.

Borgida, E., and Howard-Pitney, B. "Personal Involvement and the Robustness of Perceptual Salience Effects." *Journal of Personality and Social Psychology,* 1983, *45,* 560-570.

Brugnoli, G. A., Campion, J. E., and Basen, J. "Racial Bias in the Use of Work Samples for Personnel Selection." *Journal of Applied Psychology,* 1979, *64,* 119-123.

Byrne, D. "Attitudes and Attraction." In L. Berkowitz (ed.), *Advances in Experimental Social Psychology.* Vol. 4. Orlando, Fla.: Academic Press, 1969.

Campbell, D. T. "Stereotypes and Perception of Group Differences." *American Psychologist,* 1967, *22,* 812-829.

Campbell, D. T. "Reforms as Experiments." *American Psychologist,* 1969, *24,* 409-428.

Campbell, J. P., Dunnette, M. D., Lawler, E. E., III, and Weick, K. E. *Managerial Behavior, Performance, and Effectiveness.* New York: McGraw-Hill, 1970.

Chapman, L. J. "Illusory Correlation in Verbal Report." *Jour-*

*nal of Verbal Learning and Verbal Behavior,* 1967, *6,* 151–155.

Chapman, L. J., and Chapman, J. P. "Genesis of Popular but Erroneous Psychodiagnostic Observations." *Journal of Abnormal Psychology,* 1967, *73,* 193-204.

Chapman, L. J., and Chapman, J. P. "Illusory Correlation as an Obstacle to the Use of Valid Psychodiagnostic Signs." *Journal of Abnormal Psychology,* 1969, *74,* 271-280.

Chapman, L. J., and Chapman, J. P. "Test Results Are What You Think They Are." In D. Kahneman, P. Slovic, and A. Tversky (eds.), *Judgment Under Uncertainty: Heuristics and Biases.* Cambridge: Cambridge University Press, 1982.

Coyne, J. C., and Gotlib, I. H. "The Role of Cognition in Depression: A Critical Appraisal." *Psychological Bulletin,* 1983, *94,* 472-505.

Crocker, J. "Judgment of Covariation by Social Perceivers." *Psychological Bulletin,* 1981, *90,* 272-292.

Darley, J. M., and Fazio, R. H. "Expectancy Confirmation Processes Arising in the Social Interaction Sequence." *American Psychologist,* 1980, *35,* 867-881.

Darley, J. M., and Gross, P. H. "A Hypothesis-Confirming Bias in Labelling Effects." *Journal of Personality and Social Psychology,* 1983, *44,* 20-33.

Dawes, R. M. "Shallow Psychology." In J. Carroll and J. Payne (eds.), *Cognition and Social Behavior.* Hillsdale, N.J.: Erlbaum, 1976.

Dawes, R. M. "The Robust Beauty of Improper Linear Models in Decision Making." *American Psychologist,* 1979, *34,* 571-582.

Dipboye, R. L. "Self-Fulfilling Prophecies in the Selection-Recruitment Interview." *Academy of Management Review,* 1982, *7,* 579-586.

Dipboye, R. L., Stramler, C. S., and Fontonelle, G. A. "The Effects of the Application on Recall of Information from the Interview." *Academy of Management Journal,* 1984, *27,* 561-575.

Dulany, D. E. "Hypotheses and Habits in Verbal Operant Conditioning." *Journal of Abnormal and Social Psychology,* 1961, *63,* 251-263.

Eden, D. "Self-Fulfilling Prophecy as a Management Tool: Harnessing Pygmalion." *Academy of Management Review,* 1984, *9,* 64–73.

Eden, D., and Shani, A. B. "Pygmalion Goes to Boot Camp: Expectancy, Leadership, and Trainee Performance." *Journal of Applied Psychology,* 1982, *67,* 194–199.

Einhorn, H. J. "Learning from Experience and Suboptimal Rules in Decision Making." In D. Kahneman, P. Slovic, and A. Tversky (eds.), *Judgment Under Uncertainty: Heuristics and Biases.* Cambridge: Cambridge University Press, 1982.

Einhorn, H. J., and Hogarth, R. M. "Confidence in Judgment: Persistence of the Illusion of Validity." *Psychological Review,* 1978, *85,* 395–416.

Einhorn, H. J., and Hogarth, R. M. "Behavioral Decision Theory: Processes of Judgment and Choice." *Annual Review of Psychology,* 1981, *23,* 53–88.

Feldman, J. M. "Beyond Attribution Theory: Cognitive Processes in Performance Appraisal." *Journal of Applied Psychology,* 1981, *66,* 127–148.

Feldman, J. M. "Instrumentation and Training for Performance Appraisal: A Perceptual-Cognitive Viewpoint." In K. Rowland and G. Ferris (eds.), *Research in Personnel and Human Resource Management.* Vol. 4. Greenwich, Conn.: JAI Press, forthcoming.

Fischhoff, B. "For Those Condemned to Study the Past: Heuristics and Biases in Hindsight." In D. Kahneman, P. Slovic, and A. Tversky (eds.), *Judgment Under Uncertainty: Heuristics and Biases.* Cambridge: Cambridge University Press, 1982a.

Fischhoff, B. "Debiasing." In D. Kahneman, P. Slovic, and A. Tversky (eds.), *Judgment Under Uncertainty: Heuristics and Biases.* Cambridge: Cambridge University Press, 1982b.

Fischhoff, B., Slovic, P., and Lichtenstein, S. "Knowing What You Want: Measuring Labile Values." In T. Wallsten (ed.), *Cognitive Processes in Choice and Decision Behavior.* Hillsdale, N.J.: Erlbaum, 1980.

Fiske, S. T., Kinder, D. R., and Larter, W. M. "The Novice and the Expert: Knowledge-Based Strategies in Political Cognition." *Journal of Experimental Social Psychology,* 1983, *19,* 381–400.

Fleming, J., and Arrowood, A. J. "Information Processing and the Perseverance of Discredited Self-Perceptions." *Personality and Social Psychology Bulletin*, 1979, *5*, 201–205.

Gilovich, T. "Biased Evaluation and Persistence in Gambling." *Journal of Personality and Social Psychology*, 1983, *44*, 1110–1126.

Hamill, R., Wilson, T. D., and Nisbett, R. E. "Insensitivity to Sample Bias: Generalizing from Atypical Cases." *Journal of Personality and Social Psychology*, 1980, *39*, 578–589.

Hamilton, D. L. "A Cognitive-Attributional Analysis of Stereotyping." In L. Berkowitz (ed.), *Advances in Experimental Social Psychology*. Vol. 12. Orlando, Fla.: Academic Press, 1979.

Hammond, K. R. "The Integration of Research in Judgment and Decision Theory." Report no. 226, Center for Research on Judgment and Policy, University of Colorado, 1980.

Hammond, K. R. "Principles of Organization in Intuitive and Analytical Cognition." Report no. 231, Center for Research on Judgment and Policy, University of Colorado, 1981.

Hasher, L., Attig, M. S., and Alba, J. W. "I Knew It All Along: Or, Did I?" *Journal of Verbal Learning and Verbal Behavior*, 1981, *20*, 86–96.

Hastie, R. "Causes and Effects of Causal Attribution." *Journal of Personality and Social Psychology*, 1984, *46*, 44–56.

Hatvany, N., and Pucik, V. "Japanese Management Practices and Productivity." In K. Pearlman, F. Schmidt, and W. C. Hamner (eds.), *Contemporary Problems in Personnel*. (3rd ed.) New York: Wiley, 1983.

Hogarth, R. M. "Beyond Discrete Biases: Functional and Dysfunctional Aspects of Judgmental Heuristics." *Psychological Bulletin*, 1981, *90*, 197–217.

Ilgen, D. R., and Feldman, J. M. "Performance Appraisal: A Process Focus." In L. Cummings and B. Staw (eds.), *Research in Organizational Behavior*. Vol. 5. Greenwich, Conn.: JAI Press, 1983.

Janis, I. L. *Victims of Groupthink*. Boston: Houghton Mifflin, 1972.

Jennings, D. L., Lepper, N. R., and Ross, L. "Persistence of Impressions of Personal Persuasiveness: Perseverance of Errone-ous Self-Assessments Outside the Debriefing Paradigm." *Personality and Social Psychology Bulletin*, 1981, 7, 257-263.

Johnson, J. T., and Judd, C. M. "Overlooking the Incongruent: Categorization Biases in the Identification of Political Statements." *Journal of Personality and Social Psychology*, 1983, 45, 978-996.

Judson, H. F. "Century of the Sciences." *Science 84*, Nov. 1984, pp. 41-43.

Kahneman, D., Slovic, P., and Tversky, A. (eds.). *Judgment Under Uncertainty: Heuristics and Biases*. Cambridge: Cambridge University Press, 1982.

Kelley, H. H., and Michela, J. L. "Attribution Theory and Research." *Annual Review of Psychology*, 1980, 31, 457-501.

Koriat, A., Lichtenstein, S., and Fischhoff, B. "Reasons for Confidence." *Journal of Experimental Psychology: Human Learning and Memory*, 1982, 6, 107-118.

Kulik, J. A. "Confirmatory Attribution and the Perpetuation of Social Beliefs." *Journal of Personality and Social Psychology*, 1983, 44, 1171-1181.

Langer, E. J. "The Illusion of Control." In D. Kahneman, P. Slovic, and A. Tversky (eds.), *Judgment Under Uncertainty: Heuristics and Biases*. Cambridge: Cambridge University Press, 1982.

Lawler, E. E., III. *Pay and Organization Development*. Reading, Mass.: Addison-Wesley, 1981.

Lichtenstein, S., Fischhoff, B., and Phillips, L. D. "Calibration of Probabilities: The State of the Art to 1980." In D. Kahneman, P. Slovic, and A. Tversky (eds.), *Judgment Under Uncertainty: Heuristics and Biases*. Cambridge: Cambridge University Press, 1982.

Lingle, J. H., Dukerich, J. M., and Ostrom, T. M. "Accessing Information in Memory-Based Impression Judgments: Incongruity *vs.* Negativity." *Journal of Personality and Social Psychology*, 1983, 44, 262-272.

Lingle, J. H., and Ostrom, T. M. "Retrieval Selectivity in Memory-Based Impression Judgments." *Journal of Personality and Social Psychology*, 1979, 37, 180-194.

Locke, E. A. "The Nature and Causes of Job Satisfaction." In M. Dunnette (ed.), *Handbook of Industrial and Organization Psychology.* Skokie, Ill.: Rand McNally, 1976.

Lord, C. G., Lepper, M. R., and Preston, E. "Considering the Opposite: A Corrective Strategy for Social Judgment." *Journal of Personality and Social Psychology,* 1984, *47,* 1231–1243.

Maass, A., and Clark, R. D., III. "Hidden Impact of Minorities: Fifteen Years of Minority Influence Research." *Psychological Bulletin,* 1984, *95,* 428–450.

Posner, M. I., and McLeod, P. "Information Processing Models— In Search of Elementary Operations." *Annual Review of Psychology,* 1982, *33,* 477–514.

Pyszczynski, T. A., and Greenberg, J. "The Role of Disconfirmed Expectancies in the Instigation of Attributional Processing." *Journal of Personality and Social Psychology,* 1981, *40,* 31–38.

Read, S. "Once Is Enough: Causal Reasoning from a Single Instance." *Journal of Personality and Social Psychology,* 1983, *45,* 323–334.

Read, S. J., and Rosson, M. B. "Rewriting History: The Biasing Effects of Attitudes on Memory." *Social Cognition,* 1982, *1,* 240–255.

Regan, D. T., Strauss, E., and Fazio, R. "Liking and the Attribution Process." *Journal of Experimental Social Psychology,* 1974, *10,* 385–397.

Robinson, J., and McArthur, L. Z. "Impact of Salient Vocal Qualities on Causal Attribution for a Speaker's Behavior." *Journal of Personality and Social Psychology,* 1982, *43,* 236–247.

Rosch, E. "Human Categorization." In N. Warren (ed.), *Studies in Cross-Cultural Psychology.* Vol. 1. Orlando, Fla.: Academic Press, 1977.

Ross, L., and Anderson, C. A. "Shortcomings in the Attribution Process: On the Origins and Maintenance of Erroneous Social Assessments." In D. Kahneman, P. Slovic, and A. Tversky (eds.), *Judgment Under Uncertainty: Heuristics and Biases.* Cambridge: Cambridge University Press, 1982.

Ross, M., McFarland, C., Conway, M., and Zanna, M. P. "Reciprocal Relation Between Attitudes and Behavior Recall: Committing People to Newly Formed Attitudes." *Journal of Personality and Social Psychology,* 1983, *45,* 257-267.

Sackett, P. R. "The Interviewer as Hypothesis Testee: The Effects of Impressions of an Applicant on Interviewer Questioning Strategy." *Personnel Psychology,* 1982, *35,* 789-804.

Siegler, R. S. "Five Generalizations About Cognitive Development." *American Psychologist,* 1983, *38,* 263-277.

Simon, H. A. "Rational Decision Making in Business Organizations." *American Economic Review,* 1979, *69,* 493-515.

Slovic, P., Fischhoff, B., and Lichtenstein, S. "Facts *vs.* Fears: Understanding Perceived Risk." In D. Kahneman, P. Slovic, and A. Tversky (eds.), *Judgment Under Uncertainty: Heuristics and Biases.* Cambridge: Cambridge University Press, 1982.

Snyder, M., and Cantor, N. "Testing Hypotheses About Other People: The Use of Historical Knowledge." *Journal of Experimental Social Psychology,* 1979, *15,* 330-342.

Snyder, M., and Swann, W. B., Jr. "Hypothesis-Testing Processes in Social Interaction." *Journal of Personality and Social Psychology,* 1978, *36,* 1202-1212.

Snyder, M., and White, P. "Testing Hypotheses About Other People: Strategies of Verification and Falsification." *Personality and Social Psychology Bulletin,* 1981, *7,* 39-43.

Summers, L. S. "When in Cairo . . ." *Industrial-Organizational Psychologist,* 1984, *22* (1), 26-30.

Taylor, D. M., and Jaggi, V. "Ethnocentrism and Causal Attribution in a South Indian Context." *Journal of Cross-Cultural Psychology,* 1974, *5,* 162-171.

Taylor, S. E. "The Availability Bias in Social Perception and Interaction." In D. Kahneman, P. Slovic, and A. Tversky (eds.), *Judgment Under Uncertainty: Heuristics and Biases.* Cambridge: Cambridge University Press, 1982.

Taylor, S. E., and Fiske, S. T. "Salience, Attention, and Attribution: Top of the Head Phenomena." In L. Berkowitz (ed.), *Advances in Experimental Social Psychology.* Vol. 11. Orlando, Fla.: Academic Press, 1978.

Taylor, S. E., and Thompson, S. "Stalking the Elusive 'Vividness' Effect." *Psychological Review,* 1982, *89,* 155-181.

Taylor, S. E., and others. "The Generalizability of Salience Effects." *Journal of Personality and Social Psychology,* 1979, *37,* 357–368.

Tesser, A., and Rosen, S. "The Reluctance to Transmit Bad News." In L. Berkowitz (ed.), *Advances in Experimental Social Psychology.* Vol. 8. Orlando, Fla.: Academic Press, 1975.

Townsend, R. *Up the Organization.* New York: Fawcett, 1971.

Trope, Y., and Bassok, M. "Confirmatory and Diagnosing Strategies in Social Information Gathering." *Journal of Personality and Social Psychology,* 1982, *43,* 22–34.

Tversky, A., and Kahneman, D. "Evidential Impact on Base Rates." In D. Kahneman, P. Slovic, and A. Tversky (eds.), *Judgment Under Uncertainty: Heuristics and Biases.* Cambridge: Cambridge University Press, 1982a.

Tversky, A., and Kahneman, D. "Judgment Under Uncertainty: Heuristics and Biases." In D. Kahneman, P. Slovic, and A. Tversky (eds.), *Judgment Under Uncertainty: Heuristics and Biases.* Cambridge: Cambridge University Press, 1982b.

Tversky, A., and Kahneman, D. "Belief in the Law of Small Numbers." In D. Kahneman, P. Slovic, and A. Tversky (eds.), *Judgment Under Uncertainty: Heuristics and Biases.* Cambridge: Cambridge University Press, 1982c.

Tversky, A., and Kahneman, D. "Availability: A Heuristic for Judging Frequency and Probability." In D. Kahneman, P. Slovic, and A. Tversky (eds.), *Judgment Under Uncertainty: Heuristics and Biases.* Cambridge: Cambridge University Press, 1982d.

Weber, R., and Crocker, J. "Cognitive Processes and the Revision of Stereotypic Beliefs." *Journal of Personality and Social Psychology,* 1983, *45,* 961–975.

Wood, G. "The Knew-It-All-Along Effect." *Journal of Experimental Psychology: Human Perception and Performance,* 1978, *4,* 345–353.

# 11

# Image Theory
# and Organizational
# Decision Making

Terence R. Mitchell
Kenneth J. Rediker
Lee Roy Beach

*The study of institutions is in some ways compara-*
*ble to the clinical study of personality. . . . In both*
*personality and institutions, "self-preservation"*
*means more than bare organic or material survival.*
*Self-preservation has to do with the maintenance*
*of basic identity, with the integrity of a personal or*
*institutional "self."*

—Selznick (1957, pp.
141-142).

Our purpose is to present the central ideas of a new theory of decision making, called *image theory* (Beach and Mitchell, 1985), and to extend some of these ideas to the subject of organizational decisions. We will begin by discussing the considerations that gave rise to image theory, its background, its descriptive rather than prescriptive nature, and how it differs from both the "normative" and the "heuristics and biases" views. After briefly outlining the theory, we will extend it from

individual decisions to organizational decisions by drawing theoretical parallels between the two and by elaborating on these
parallels in terms of organizational culture.

## Background

Image theory is proposed as a descriptive theory rather
than a normative, prescriptive theory. Its formulation was motivated by the failure of formal, prescriptive models from economics, statistics, and the like to adequately account for the
ways in which people actually make most decisions.

Prescriptive models all presume that decision makers
make thorough evaluations of the potential consequences of
available actions and select that action for which the consequences appear, on balance, to have the greatest expected utility. Although this view of the decision-making process sounds
quite reasonable and simple, in fact it involves some very strin-
gent assumptions. Such a model makes strong assumptions, for
example, about the nature of the evaluations in terms of preference strengths or preference orderings, as well as assumptions
about the metrics and mathematics of whatever doubt the decision maker may have about whether the consequences actually
will or will not occur if the action in question is selected and
executed. Prescriptive models also make strong assumptions
about the conditions that permit the evaluations to be summarized for alternative actions, to be compared among those alternative actions, to be added to or subtracted from, and the like.
Finally, a prescriptive model makes strong assumptions about
the cognitive and physical capabilities of the decision maker—
how much can be attended to at a time, how precise the evaluations can or must be, and so on. Indeed, most of the research
has focused on the tenability of these assumptions. Unfortunately, the results are very mixed and surprisingly little can be
said with certainty about the conditions under which these assumptions are satisfied sufficiently to permit the appropriate
application of the relevant prescriptive model.

In contrast, image theory is not prescriptive and does not
assume that people necessarily use analytic evaluation proce-

dures or attempt to maximize payoffs when making decisions. On the contrary, image theory assumes that most decisions are based upon very simple rules that require a minimum of analytic thought, but, as we shall see, these rules are not the heuristics and biases that have received so much attention in the recent decision literature (Kahneman, Slovic, and Tversky, 1982).

Attempts to use formal theoretical models of decisions to describe organizational decision making have met with much the same results that they have for individual decision making. On a very general level, these models appear to provide an attractive way of thinking about how the decisions are made. But a close look quickly shows this to be an illusion (for example, Bower, 1970; Cyert and March, 1963; Lindblom, 1959; Mintzberg, Raisinghani, and Theoret, 1976; Quinn, 1980). In both individual and organizational settings, the problem is the same: decision making is much richer and more subtle than the formal models would suggest, while at the same time it is less thoroughly thought through and less premeditated than the formal models demand (March and Olsen, 1979).

In the next section, image theory will be described briefly with special attention to concepts that will later be extended to organizations viewed as cultures rather than as mere collectives of individual participants. It is our opinion that the cultural view of organizations has the advantage of permitting examination of the organization as a unique entity. This advantage is similar to that enjoyed by the philosopher Karl Popper (1972), who conceived of knowledge as first, separate from the physical world that serves as its subject matter, and second, separate from the minds of the people who contribute to it. This conception permitted Popper to explore the structure of knowledge as a phenomenon in and of itself, a conceptual step that proved to be of great value in the advancement of epistemology. In the same way, being able to think of an organization as an entity, as a unit with unique characteristics over and above the characteristics of the individuals it comprises, may permit us to see the parallels between individual decision making and organizational decision making, and, we hope, to learn more about both in the course of doing so.

Image theory is an attempt to describe how people actually make the major decisions that affect their lives. It is *not* an attempt to document the qualitative or quantitative difference between what people do and the prescriptions of formal, normative decision theory and its ancillary models. We realize that there is merit in examining the descriptive adequacy of normative prescriptions. However, we think that the recent single-minded emphasis upon departures of actual decision behavior from such prescriptions has led to a distorted and unduly negative picture of human decision making (Christensen-Szalanski and Beach, 1984). This picture's central themes are chaos and irrationality; yet few of us, even (one assumes) the researchers who present that picture, regard our own decision making as so wholly inadequate. True, we all rue decisions that have not worked out, but few of us would, as a result, be willing to turn all of our future decisions over to some normatively programmed external agent.

Briefly, image theory views decision makers as having images of themselves, their pasts, their presents, and their futures. One image features principles or prescriptions for how one ought to behave (with all the affect that word implies) and for what is important and valuable to pursue. Another image features the goals that follow from these principles. A third image features the ways in which one may pursue the goals that make up the second image. Our principal thesis is that these images, including their structures, how they come to be and how they are changed, and their interrelationships, form the bases for decision making. For the most part, decision makers look at the paths that are open to them in terms of how well each fits with these images, and they adopt those paths that are congruent with the images and reject those that are incongruent.

In contrast to the prevailing negativistic view, the image theory is of fairly orderly decision processes that are a good deal richer than one would expect on the basis of formal decision theory or on the basis of the heuristics and biases literature. A critic might argue that if image theory is an accurate characterization of human decision processes, then insofar as this theory departs from decision theory, it incorporates the suboptimality and irrationality of these processes. However, such a criticism assumes that the models that make up decision theory are the best and only ways in which to make decisions, an assumption that itself has many critics (see Beach, Christensen-Szalanski, and Barnes, 1986, for a review, and Hogarth, 1981). Be that as it may, the fact is that people's decisions frequently serve them well; in the main we tend to survive and often we even prosper. Insofar as human decision making adequately serves its purpose, it is difficult to believe that it is impossibly chaotic and irrational. The goal of image theory is to represent precisely those aspects of decision making that are orderly, and furthermore to demonstrate that what may appear to be irrational from a normative viewpoint may, from a descriptive viewpoint, be quite the opposite.

Image theory is a natural outgrowth of earlier work (Beach and Mitchell, 1978) that proposed a theory of how decision makers select specific decision strategies for use with specific kinds of decisions. In this theory it was suggested that people use three broad categories of decision strategies called *aided-analytic, unaided-analytic,* and *nonanalytic strategies.* Aided-analytic strategies require the use of a decision tool or aid—for example, pencil, paper, and a formula, decision analysis, or some other formal, analytic paradigm upon which to base the decision. Unaided-analytic strategies also involve the use of some form of analytic paradigm, but the paradigm may not be normatively defensible and it is executed without the help of tools—for example, trying to maximize subjective expected utility, or balancing costs and benefits of an action by doing the entire analysis in one's head. Nonanalytic strategies simply involve the use of rules of thumb, reliance upon advice, use of habits, and so on.

Subsequent research (for example, Christensen-Szalanski, 1978, 1980; McAllister, Mitchell, and Beach, 1979; Smith, Mitchell, and Beach, 1982; Waller and Mitchell, 1984) examined how use of these different kinds of strategies is related to the primary constructs of the theory, such as the complexity of the task, the irreversibility of the decision, the degree to which the decision maker is accountable for the decision outcome, the effects of time constraints on strategy selection, and so on. The results of the research have been very supportive of the theory, but two disquieting themes have emerged. First, most people make most decisions (even very important ones) using nonanalytic strategies, which from the viewpoint of decision theory looks irrational but which, upon close inspection, is not in the least chaotic and appears to be reasonably successful. Second, the theory as it was originally formulated in 1978 did not go far enough in capturing the diversity and subtlety either of the nonanalytic strategies or of the unaided analytic strategies that people use when they are really trying hard to be careful, thoughtful decision makers. Image theory is the consequent attempt to extend the 1978 theory in order to better describe the impressive diversity of human decision making.

The motivation for formulating image theory derives from the Beach and Mitchell (1978) theory and the research that it generated, but it also has its roots in what has come to be called *control theory*. In psychology, the most notable example of control theory, at least until recently, was Miller, Galanter, and Pribram's *Plans and the Structure of Behavior* (1960). More recently, control theory has been revived and expanded by Powers (1978) and Carver and Scheier (1982). Throughout, the theme is that behavior is a complex process that is guided by goals and feedback about how well the organism is progressing toward those goals. Those who have read Miller, Galanter, and Pribram (1960) may remember the TOTE system (test, operate, test, exit) as its main contribution. However, great attention was also given, first of all, to images, which are private representations of the actor's self and his or her world. Images, moreover, were seen as guiding plans, which control behavior. Computer programs served as the metaphor for plans, and the general idea was that the actor executed a plan in order to realize an image—that is, in order to make reality conform to some favored state of affairs (in short, a goal). In image theory we have adopted the notion of images from Miller, Galanter, and Pribram's 1960 work (see also Boulding, 1956) and adapted it specifically to decision making.

In addition to our own work and to control theory, image

theory has roots in work on personal development (for example, Neugarten, 1977; Levinson and others, 1978), on career development (for example, Mihal, Sorce, and Comte, 1984; Rhodes and Doering, 1983), and on philosophy (for example, MacIntyre, 1981). All of this work has expanded the idea of images as guiding concepts in behavior. Images are thought of both as one's recollection and reconstruction of one's past (where one has been), and as one's dreams and aspirations for the future (where one hopes one is going). Most important, images constitute one's view of oneself, what one stands for, what one wants to be, and what one wants and likes to do. As the philosopher Alasdair MacIntyre states, "There is no present which is not informed by some image of some future and an image of the future which always presents itself in the form of a *telos*—of a variety of ends or goals—toward which we are either moving or failing to move in the present" (1981, p. 200). Image theory is an attempt to represent the role of such images and such goals and to discuss how such "moving or failing to move" is assessed in human decision making.

Finally, in addition to the three areas described thus far, image theory has roots in recent research on post-decisional commitment. One line of such research comes from organizational behavior (Janis, 1972; Northcraft and Wolf, 1984; Staw and Ross, 1978), and another comes from social psychology (Brockner and Rubin, 1985). The respective terms that are used are *commitment* and *entrapment*, and they both describe cases in which decision makers stick with a course of action (and invest more time, effort, or money) even though doing so is failing to achieve desired goals. That is, these researchers describe the tendency for decision makers (both individuals and organizations) to stay with the status quo beyond the point at which some neutral observer (particularly one operating on normative principles) would advise a change in course. According to image theory, decision makers stick with the status quo because of its centrality to their images and their great resistance to changing these images. Thus, image theory broadens the commitment and entrapment concepts by regarding them as special cases of a more general tendency to stick with the status quo, whether that status quo is a failing course of action or a successful one. The implication of this tendency for decision making is of general importance, and it constitutes a major part of image theory.

In summary, we are convinced that most decisions are made in a more gestalt, "fittingness" way than in the utility maximization way traditionally espoused by theorists who study decision making. We believe that decision makers have images of their pasts, presents, and futures, and that some of these images contain goals, including both those that already have been reached and those that have yet to be attained. Indeed, it is the continuity of past and future goals that lends continuity to one's view of one's life. These images are central and important, and the goals provide both motivation and justification for action. Moreover, it is difficult for decision makers to make great changes in their images, with the result that they tend to favor "business as usual," the status quo. All of these ideas serve as the foundation for the following more formal presentation of image theory. What follows is necessarily brief. A detailed description of image theory is presented in Beach and Mitchell (1985).

## Image Theory

We begin with the assumption that decision makers possess four informational representations, called *images,* that are the bases of decision making. The construction and coordination of these four images constitutes the decision process.

First is the *self-image,* which is composed of *principles* that reflect the way one sees oneself and the precepts that guide one's life. These principles dictate the *goals* (events and states) to which the decision maker aspires, and they serve as the backdrop against which new goal-candidates (prospective goals) are compared and evaluated. Additionally, the self-image embodies the standards against which *actions,* which are considered as ways to achieve those goals, are evaluated, so that actions too are congruent with the goals and the principles from which the goals derive.

Second, the *trajectory image* consists of one's view about

where, *ideally*, one is going. It is the blueprint, however vague, for how one thinks the present should be and how and when future events and states (goals) should be achieved. It includes the ends one thinks it appropriate to pursue in light of the self-image and the landmarks one anticipates along one's idealized course. In short, the trajectory image provides the chronological ordering of one's goals.

Third, the *projected image* consists of the chronological ordering of the events and states that one anticipates will occur if the flow of current activities, the *status quo*, is not changed. It is called the projected image because it describes one's view of the anticipated future. One can anticipate, with some degree of certainty, what will happen if one maintains one's course, and one can anticipate what might happen if one changed that course. Clearly, a key comparison is that between the trajectory image and the projected image, because it is this comparison which provides "fittingness" information about whether one is likely to achieve one's goals if one continues doing what one is doing.

Fourth and last, the *action image* consists of *plans* of action for reaching goals and for reconciling troublesome incongruities among the first three images. When the projected image (the anticipated events and states) differs sufficiently from the trajectory image (how things ideally should unfold), the decision maker is motivated (initially, at least) to modify the action image and to implement the modified plan by executing specific *tactics*, which are concrete behaviors that are intended to produce congruence between the trajectory and projected images, or, in other words, the behaviors that will allow one to attain the goals on the trajectory image.

Construction and coordination of these images, in turn, involve two types of decisions: first, *adoption decisions*, which are about adoption or rejection of new or potential principles, goals, strategies, or tactics as components of their respective images; and second, *progress decisions*, which are about whether the incongruity between the trajectory and projected images is sufficient to indicate lack of progress toward goals and to motivate an adoption decision that will remedy things.

While adoption and progress decisions are the two major types of decisions, they can each appear in two contexts, which are called *optional change* and *nonoptional change* decisions. An optional change decision is one in which the status quo is viable as one of the alternatives to be considered. When one contemplates changing jobs, having a child, diversifying one's investment portfolio, taking up exercise or some other health maintenance program, launching a new product, or building a new production plant, the status quo is one of the alternatives, and the new alternative(s) is (are) compared to it.

Most decisions made by individuals and organizations are optional change decisions. On the other hand, there are occasions that occur either because of developmental circumstances (one graduates, one's children leave home, demand for a product or service decreases, technology changes) or environmental circumstances (one gets fired, one becomes ill, new regulations are imposed, a strong competitor enters the market) in which the status quo ceases to be an option: it is no longer one of the alternatives that one can decide to select. These nonoptional change decisions occur less frequently than optional change decisions, but they compel one to consider new courses of action because the old ones cease to be viable.

Be they optional or nonoptional, adoption and progress decisions are made using either of two evaluative criteria. The first criterion is *congruence,* which includes (1) the degree of "fit" between a particular candidate for adoption and the existing principles, goals, plans, or tactics that already constitute the images, and (2) the degree of "fit" between the trajectory and projected images. Congruence is measured in terms of *lateral attractiveness.* The second evaluative criterion is *contingent benefit,* which is the degree to which a candidate for adoption appears to offer positive consequences over and above congruence alone. Contingent benefit is measured in terms of *marginal attractiveness.*

To make decisions, congruence and contingent benefit estimates are subjected to either of two decision rules. The first decision rule is *sufficiency,* which means that lateral or marginal attractiveness exceeds some variable threshold that is contingent on the characteristics of both the decision maker and the circumstances in which the decision is made. The second decision rule is *maximization,* which means that among competing candidates, all of which have sufficient lateral attractiveness, the candidate with the greatest combined lateral and marginal attractiveness (overall attractiveness) is selected for adoption as a component of the image in question.

There is one more concept, *doubt,* that plays an important role in all of this. Predicting one's future, either ideally or as a consequence of what one is doing, involves doubt about the accuracy of the predictions. Moreover, using marginal attractiveness (as opposed to lateral attractiveness) for evaluating candidates for adoption also involves doubt, as does the use of the maximization rule. Doubt arises from many sources: for example, from incongruence, estimates of one's ability, complexity of plans, the time frame involved in goal attainment, personal versus environmental control, and physical and situational barriers. Doubt discounts the attractiveness of an alternative much as probabilities discount utilities in traditional decision theory. However, image theory makes no a priori assumptions about the logical (mathematical) or metric properties of doubt.

The preceding concepts, together with collateral concepts that are not crucial here, combine to form two general strategies for decision making—that is, strategies that are available to the decision maker to use depending upon the circumstances. The first strategy is nonanalytic and involves the least demanding alternatives presented above. Most such decisions are of the adoption type and occur in optional change contexts: Does one want to change from the status quo to some decidedly different course of action or to pursuing some decidedly different goal? The evaluative criterion for the nonanalytic approach tends to be congruence with existing principles, goals, plans, and tactics (lateral attractiveness), and the sufficiency rule most often is employed. Such a strategy often makes decisions look like nondecisions because the status quo tends to win out. Research clearly shows that there is a strong bias to remain with the status quo unless the alternative is excessively attractive or very pressing (for example, Beach, Hope, Townes, and Campbell, 1982).

The second approach is analytic and involves the more

demanding alternatives presented above. These decisions tend to be about whether to change one's course of action because it is failing to produce progress toward one's goal (progress decisions) or about adoption of new constituents for the images when the status quo is no longer an option (nonoptional change decisions). The criterion for the analytic approach tends to be the benefits that one expects from the change that one will make (marginal attractiveness), and a maximization rule most often is employed.

## Image Theory and Organizational Decision Making

Image theory's four images are seen as the basic elements for individual decision making. We propose that they play a similar role in organizational decision making (for the script theory counterparts, see Gioia and Poole, 1984).

First, the *organizational self-image* consists of the members' key shared beliefs, values, and so on, about the organization. This image is descriptive of the organization as organization and is not a simple aggregation of members' values and beliefs. It is what gives rise to the organization as a distinctive collective that transcends its merely technical functions (Selznick, 1957). Only at the founding of the organization, or during a very threatening crisis to the organization's survival, is the organizational self-image closely associated with specific individuals, and then the association is usually with the most powerful members of the organization (Kimberly, 1979; Pascale and Athos, 1981).

While clues about the organizational self-image may be obtained from charters, constitutions, and mission statements, such formal documents do not fully convey the image. Informal aspects of the image also are important. Moreover, while the imperative (expressive) implications of both the formal and informal parts of the organizational self-image are crucial, its strictures against certain beliefs, values, and consequent behaviors also are important (Peters and Waterman, 1982).

Second, the *organizational trajectory image* extends the organizational self-image into the future as an agenda of desirable states and events. That is, the organizational trajectory image represents the projection of what the organization hopes to become and what it wants to achieve; it contains the landmarks that characterize the organization's ideal future (for example, being number one, entering international markets). Although the organizational trajectory image is often articulated only in the minds of top managers, its basic constituents (key goals) and their relative importance must be diffused throughout the organization in order to influence decision behavior at all levels of the organization.

Third, the *organizational projected image* summarizes, at any specific time, the organization's projection of its operating environment and the implications (in terms of the principles and goals of the self-image and trajectory image) of continuing with currently implemented plans (the status quo). The organizational projected image is a synthesis of the products of the various formal and informal information-processing networks present in most organizations. The key role played by the organizational projected image is as a "reality test" by which progress toward realization of the organizational trajectory image is monitored. For many organizations, the organizational projected image is, in large part, quantitative in nature, because this image is based on "hard" data that are easily quantified for extrapolation. Nevertheless, difficult judgments also are required to assess the implications of "softer" data and to evaluate the causes of apparent gaps between the organization's trajectory and projected images.

Finally, the *organizational action image* consists of the plans and tactics that are the guides for subunit and individual behavior. The intended organizational action image is manifested in documents such as strategic plans and operating budgets, but it is most accurately reflected by actual decisions, behaviors, and resource allocations (Mintzberg, 1978). In other words, there is an important distinction between the organizational action image as intended and the organizational action image as implemented. This distinction is reflected in the commonly encountered difficulty of determining whether a performance gap is due to a poorly conceived action image or to a badly implemented action image. The judgment that the action image was poorly conceived directs attention to the self- and trajectory images. If poor performance is attributed to the implementation process, adjustments are restricted to the action image.

As was the case for individuals, the decisions of organizations are of two types: first, adoption decisions, which involve addition (or rejection) of new constituents for the organization's self-, trajectory, or action images; and second, progress decisions, which result from a comparison of the congruence of the organization's trajectory and projected images. If the congruence is low (that is, there is a large performance gap), the decision makers will first be motivated to reexamine the action image. If the action image appears to be instrumental for goal attainment, then the reasonableness of the goals on the trajectory image might be questioned. In rare instances, if the latter yields no remedy, there may be attempts to change the organizational self-image (for example, through divestment of a major portion of an organization's traditional business or the wholesale replacement of top managers).

Organizations, like individuals, encounter two decisions contexts: optional change and nonoptional change. Optional change decisions are those in which remaining with the status quo is an alternative; for nonoptional decisions, the status quo is not a viable possibility. This is a particularly important distinction, since for most organizations the status quo is highly visible. This visibility derives from the numerous forms in which the status quo is manifested: physical plant and production technologies, the distribution of specialized skills among employees, and the attendant employment patterns and status hierarchies.

Thus, nonoptional change decisions are less common in organizations. Such decisions usually occur only under the pressures of severe and unanticipated changes in the environment (Chandler, 1962; Selznick, 1957), which are generally reflected in large performance gaps. By and large, it is only during such crises that managers are willing to induce the internal stress that results from major changes in the status quo. During such episodes, it is likely that particular people will receive heightened attention; for example, incumbents may be ousted so that newcomers can become forces for the establishment of new plans, of a new status quo, and of a new self-image that resolves the crises.

In image theory, lateral attractiveness (congruence, fittingness) is the most common criterion by which candidate principles, goals, plans, and tactics are evaluated. This criterion is also the most common one used in organizational decisions, reflecting the primacy of the status quo. In evaluating an alternative, the organizational decision makers most frequently ask, in effect, "Does this option (candidate) fit well with what we are already doing and with where we want to go?" Note that the emphasis is on fittingness rather than on precise estimates of the costs and benefits (marginal attractiveness) that are most commonly cited as the bases of decisions, and rather than on "satisficing" (Simon, 1957), which is merely adequacy of benefits on key outcomes.

As was true of individuals, organizations use two decision rules: sufficiency and maximization. Sufficiency probably is the key decision rule for most organizational decisions for several reasons. First, alternatives in a particular decision are likely to be screened rapidly and continuously against the status quo— that is, against expected performance levels, established policies, acceptable risk levels, and so on (Mintzberg, Raisinghani, and Theoret, 1976; Witte, 1972). This screening is best done using the relatively simple fittingness evaluation, which minimizes search and calculation effort. It takes considerable time and money to assemble a fully developed set of competing alternatives for which marginal attractiveness (costs and benefits) can be calculated and to which the maximization rule can be applied.

Second, this screening process occurs serially across time as well as hierarchically. Multiple decision alternatives proposed in various units at lower levels in the organization must be screened as they pass through successive levels until one well-developed (or rather well-justified) alternative is proposed for authorization and funding by executive decision makers (Bower, 1970). In short, most potentially multi-alternative decisions become, as they percolate upward, two-alternative decisions, in which one alternative is the status quo. Decisions involving the status quo usually are based upon lateral attractiveness using the sufficiency rule.

Third, and finally, most decision alternatives are, in fact, "designed" to fit with the perceived beliefs and values of the higher-level decision makers (Cyert and March, 1963). The latter are ordinarily responsible for the organization's being on the road it is on (that is, for the status quo). As a result, those subordinates and others who propose candidate goals and actions for adoption give careful attention to making these candidates (at least appear to) fit with the images held by those who hold the final resource allocation power (in Cyert and March's terms, the "dominant coalition"). For these and similar reasons, there are few organizational decisions for which it is necessary to apply the maximization decision rule to multiple candidates, and, as a result, few occasions for application of the analytic decision mode, in spite of what is claimed both by textbooks and by organizational decision makers.

To round out this extension of image theory to organizations, consider the role of doubt in organizational decision making. Doubt arises here for reasons similar to those that give rise to it for individuals (for example, complexity of the decision problem, length of the time horizon, biases of information sources, environmental instability). In organizational settings, however, doubt also arises because of the greater number of individuals and groups involved in both the decision itself and in the implementation processes. In addition, doubt may be generated by the degree of conflict attendant upon a given decision, although this may be substantially offset by the routine application of the screening processes described above. These screening processes act both to minimize the competition among proposals by the time they reach the upper levels of the organization and to eliminate radical proposals or proposals for dramatic change.

## Images in Strong-Culture Organizations

Let us turn now to a more thorough elaboration of two aspects of image theory that have important implications for organizational decision making. These are the organizational self-image as a manifestation of an organizational culture, and the powerful role of the status quo in the (optional change) decisions of organizations.

In the previous section, we drew parallels between individual and organizational decisions within the context of image theory. Although this is all relatively straightforward, we suspect that the parallels hold best for decisions made by what we will call *strong-culture organizations.* Understanding what is meant by this term requires explanation of the idea of organizational culture in general.

Traditionally, culture is an anthropological construct for understanding social behaviors in societies. Recently, however, culture has been increasingly used as a metaphor for the patterns of values, beliefs, and behaviors in organizations; hence its appropriateness to the applications of image theory to organizations. The *Administrative Science Quarterly* (1983), for example, devoted an entire issue to this viewpoint in its many variations. In addition, popular works on organizations also have exploited the metaphor (for example, Deal and Kennedy, 1982; Peters and Waterman, 1982; Ouchi, 1981). In most work using this perspective, the theoretical goal has been to offer an explanation of how large, complex organizations direct and integrate the efforts of diverse individuals and subgroups. In addition, the culture metaphor characterizes organizations as wholes, not as simple aggregates of members.

For our purposes, organizational cultures can be characterized by (1) the existence of an articulated network of beliefs and values (for example, constant innovation, "the customer comes first," best-quality products), (2) shared knowledge of particular symbolic exemplars (such as founder stories, heroes, success and failure stories) that communicate core beliefs and values as well as their behavioral implications, and (3) social processes (such as leadership acts, employee selection and promotion standards, special languages) that serve to maintain the integrity of the group and to give an in-group quality to the organization's culture. An organization in which these and related characteristics are well developed can be regarded as a *strong-culture organization.*

Decisions in a strong-culture organization are significantly influenced by the content of the organization's self-image as well as by its trajectory image. The elements of these two images are potent guidelines for decision behavior throughout the organization. In particular, the widely accepted validity of the organization's self-image, and the landmarks on the trajectory image, provide the philosophical justification for expressive rather than merely reactive or instrumental organizational choices.

Let us clarify this with an example. An organization's belief that, say, "the customer is always right" forms the legitimate basis for certain internally consistent patterns of behavior, such as a personal response to all customer complaints and money-back guarantees. It may be the case that many organizations espouse such beliefs, but observation may reveal that espousal does not carry over to actual behavior, making one question whether the espoused belief is actually part of the organization's self-image, or if the belief is in fact part of the image, whether that image has been adequately communicated to the appropriate levels of the organization.

Such a question would not arise with a strong-culture organization, since its self- and trajectory images are well articulated and widely understood. Consequently, in such an organization, the influence of images is pervasive, in that organization members accept the validity of the images and express this acceptance in behaviors that are congruent with them. To assume such a role for these images suggests important research questions about their genesis and development and about how they are communicated to and accepted by the members of the organization. By the same token, attempts to build strong-culture organizations must examine these same issues and make concrete attempts to accomplish what they imply.

We turn now to some of the things that must be known in order to evaluate the appropriateness and feasibility of creating a strong-culture organization. Knowledge of the historical circumstances present at an organization's founding, of characteristics of founders and other early leaders, and of certain of their key decisions is often necessary to understand "how we got here from there"—that is, to understand the genesis of the organization's self- and trajectory images. Additionally, knowledge about crisis periods, in which organizational survival was threatened, also illuminates the current structure of the organization's self- and trajectory images (Chandler, 1962; Kimberly, 1979; Pascale and Athos, 1981; Pettigrew, 1983; Selznick, 1957). Parallel to the idea that the behaviors of individuals express principles that they have adopted for their self-images early in their lives, analogous "founding principles" shape and define an organization's subsequent self- and trajectory images.

Creation of a strong-culture organization requires more than just historical knowledge, however. In addition, it is necessary to know how the organization's images can be communicated to the members of the organization. This is accomplished by visible and repetitive leadership acts which express the self-image; by careful selection and training of new members; by pay and incentive systems; by the development of specialized languages, slogans, and the like that are based upon the images; by significant ceremonies (such as those that honor founders) that give public recognition and awards for desired behavior. These processes occur in all organizations. In strong-culture organizations, however, they are consciously attended to and are designed to be mutually consistent expressions of the self- and trajectory images (the organization's principles and goals).

Turning to the role of the status quo in decision making, we previously stated that the status quo is highly visible for most organizations. In terms of image theory, this means that most organizational decisions are optional change decisions (see also Chapter Seven in March and Simon, 1958). In a strong-culture organization, these decisions, and their "optional change" nature, will be quite clear. In contrast to traditional views of decision making, this implies that in strong-culture organizations, fittingness and continuity are highly prized and more willingly acknowledged to be the bases of decision making than in organizations that are not as culturally well defined. Indeed, strong-culture organizations, with their crisp self- and trajectory images, are less likely to revise these images than they are to assume that incongruity between the trajectory and projected image must be dealt with by revisions in the action image

--that is, by changes in strategies and tactics. In short, such organizations, rightly or wrongly, tend not to question their goals or their principles; instead, they focus upon formulating the appropriate actions to achieve their goals and to satisfy their principles.

The combination of well-developed and well-communicated organizational self- and trajectory images, the existence of a potent status quo, the predominance of the fittingness criterion, and the focus upon action revision rather than on revisions of goals or principles—all this means that doubt plays only a small role in the decisions of strong-culture organizations. As long as the images are well articulated, acknowledgment of doubt about principles and goals only invites conflict, which could lead to a reduction in the credibility of the self- and trajectory images. Consequently, managers are unlikely to invite, encourage, or communicate doubt about the organizational self- and trajectory images nor explicitly to include such doubt in their decision processes. While there are distinct advantages for decision making in strong-culture organizations, there is also the possibility that appropriate expressions of doubt about principles and goals may be discouraged. The result is that certain key decisions will fail to properly reflect the demands of the circumstances in which they are made.

This risk emerges during "predictable stresses" in the life of organizations (Greiner, 1972) as well as during crises brought on by fundamental shifts in the economic and social environment. In reality, these forces for change often merge and pose survival questions for organizational decision making.

## Concluding Remarks

The purpose of this chapter has been to explore some implications of image theory for organizational decision making. We have suggested that the concept of organizational culture can be helpful in this endeavor. Both image theory and the organizational culture metaphor give prominence to strongly held principles as guides to human and organizational behavior. Strong-culture organizations exemplify conditions in which image theory may profitably be used both to understand organizational decision making and to help those who wish to develop such organizations. It is likely that most organizations will, in fact, house three or four subcultures, each of which possesses a self- and a trajectory image, with attendant implications for decision making. This situation, however, does not reduce the role of organizationwide images. Indeed, in these circumstances the need is even greater for integrating images that bind potentially conflicting subunits into a more unified whole.

Decision making models that highlight the prospective calculation of costs and payoffs and uncertainty, that emphasize discrete and simultaneous evaluation of multiple competing alternatives, that treat the status quo as merely one alternative among others, and that prescribe the universal application of variations of the maximization rule may indeed capture some of what is called decision making, but the description that emerges is pale and incomplete. It fails to acknowledge the role of historical context, of principles in goal adoption, of goal seeking as the essence of decision making, of the opportunism of most individual and organizational decisions, of the degree to which decisions are based on the congruence of alternatives with what already is being done, as well as the fundamental (and perhaps not unreasonable) aversion most individuals and organizations have to abandonment of the status quo.

## References

*Administrative Science Quarterly,* Graduate School of Business and Public Administration, Cornell University, 1983, *28* (3), entire issue.

Beach, L. R., Christensen-Szalanski, J. J. J., and Barnes, V. "On the Quality of Human Judgment: Bad News or Bad Press?" In *Judgmental Forecasting.* London: Wiley, 1986.

Beach, L. R., Hope, A., Townes, B. D., and Campbell, F. L. "The Expectation Threshold Model of Reproductive Decision Making." *Population and Environment,* 1982, *5,* 95–108.

Beach, L. R., and Mitchell, T. R. "A Contingency Model for the Selection of Decision Strategies." *Academy of Management Review,* 1978, *3,* 439–449.

Beach, L. R., and Mitchell, T. R. "Image Theory: Principles,

Goals, and Plans in Decision Making." Unpublished manuscript, University of Washington, 1985.

Boulding, K. E. *The Image.* Ann Arbor: University of Michigan Press, 1956.

Bower, J. *Managing the Resource Allocation Process.* Cambridge, Mass.: Division of Research, Graduate School of Business Administration, Harvard University, 1970.

Brockner, J., and Rubin, J. Z. *Entrapment in Escalating Conflicts: A Social Psychological Analysis.* New York: Springer-Verlag, 1985.

Carver, C. S., and Scheier, M. F. "Control Theory: A Useful Conceptual Framework for Personality-Social, Clinical, and Health Psychology." *Psychological Bulletin,* 1982, *92,* 111-135.

Chandler, A. D., Jr. *Strategy and Structure: Chapters in the History of the Industrial Enterprise.* Cambridge, Mass.: MIT Press, 1962.

Christensen-Szalanski, J. J. J. "Problem Solving Strategies: A Selection Mechanism, Some Implications, and Some Data." *Organizational Behavior and Human Performance,* 1978, *22,* 307-323.

Christensen-Szalanski, J. J. J. "A Further Examination of the Selection of Problem-Solving Strategies: The Effects of Deadlines and Analytic Aptitudes." *Organizational Behavior and Human Performance,* 1980, *25,* 107-122.

Christensen-Szalanski, J. J. J., and Beach, L. R. "The Citation Bias: Fad and Fashion in the Judgment and Decision Literature." *American Psychologist,* 1984, *39,* 75-78.

Cyert, R. M., and March, J. G. *A Behavioral Theory of the Firm.* Englewood Cliffs, N.J.: Prentice-Hall, 1963.

Deal, T. E., and Kennedy, A. A. *Corporate Cultures.* Reading, Mass.: Addison-Wesley, 1982.

Gioia, D. A., and Poole, P. P. "Scripts in Organizational Behavior." *Academy of Management Review,* 1984, *9,* 449-459.

Greiner, L. E. "Evolution and Revolution as Organizations Grow." *Harvard Business Review,* July/Aug. 1972, pp. 37-46.

Hogarth, R. M. "Beyond Discrete Biases: Functional and Dysfunctional Aspects of Judgmental Heuristics." *Psychological Bulletin*, 1981, *90*, 197–217.

Janis, I. L. *Victims of Groupthink*. Boston: Houghton Mifflin, 1972.

Kahneman, D., Slovic, P., and Tversky, A. *Judgment Under Uncertainty: Heuristics and Biases*. New York: Cambridge University Press, 1982.

Kimberly, J. R. "Issues in the Creation of Organizations." *Academy of Management Journal*, 1979, *22*, 437–457.

Levinson, D. J., and others. *The Seasons of a Man's Life*. New York: Knopf, 1978.

Lindblom, C. "The Science of Muddling Through." *Public Administration Quarterly*, Spring 1959, pp. 79–88.

McAllister, D. W., Mitchell, T. R., and Beach, L. R. "The Contingency Model for the Selection of Decision Strategies: An Empirical Test of the Effects of Significance, Accountability, and Reversibility." *Organizational Behavior and Human Performance*, 1979, *24*, 228–244.

MacIntyre, A. *After Virtue*. Notre Dame, Ind.: University of Notre Dame Press, 1981.

March, J. G., and Olsen, J. P. *Ambiguity and Choice in Organizations*. Bergen, Norway: Universitetsforlaget, 1979.

March, J. G., and Simon, H. A. *Organizations*. New York: Wiley, 1958.

Mihal, W. L., Sorce, P. A., and Comte, T. E. "A Process Model of Individual Career Decision Making." *Academy of Management Review*, 1984, *9*, 95–103.

Miller, G. A., Galanter, E., and Pribram, K. H. *Plans and the Structure of Behavior*. New York: Holt, Rinehart and Winston, 1960.

Mintzberg, H. "Patterns in Strategy Formation." *Management Science*, 1978, *24*, 934–949.

Mintzberg, H., Raisinghani, D., and Theoret, A. "The Structure of 'Unstructured' Decision Processes." *Administrative Science Quarterly*, 1976, *21*, 246–275.

Neugarten, B. L. "Personality and Aging." In J. E. Birren and K. W. Schaie (eds.), *Handbook of the Psychology of Aging*. New York: Van Nostrand Reinhold, 1977.

Northcraft, G. B., and Wolf, G. "Dollars, Sense and Sunk Costs: A Life Cycle Model of Research Allocation Decisions." *Academy of Management Review*, 1984, *9*, 225–234.

Ouchi, W. W. *Theory Z*. Reading, Mass.: Addison-Wesley, 1981.

Pascale, R. T., and Athos, A. G. *The Art of Japanese Management*. New York: Warner Books, 1981.

Peters, T. J., and Waterman, R. H. *In Search of Excellence*. New York: Harper & Row, 1982.

Pettigrew, A. "On Studying Organizational Cultures." In J. Van Maanen (ed.), *Qualitative Methodology*. Beverly Hills, Calif.: Sage, 1983.

Popper, K. *Objective Knowledge*. London: Oxford University Press, 1972.

Powers, W. T. "Quantitative Analysis of Purposive Systems: Some Spadework at the Foundations of Scientific Psychology." *Psychological Review*, 1978, *85*, 417–435.

Quinn, J. B. *Strategies for Change: Logical Incrementalism*. New York: Irwin, 1980.

Rhodes, S. R., and Doering, M. "An Integrated Model of Career Motivation." *Academy of Management Review*, 1983, *8*, 631–639.

Selznick, P. *Leadership in Administration: A Sociological Interpretation*. New York: Harper & Row, 1957.

Simon, H. A. *Models of Man: Social and Rational*. New York: Wiley, 1957.

Smith, J. F., Mitchell, T. R., and Beach, L. R. "A Cost-Benefit Mechanism for Selecting Problem-Solving Strategies: Some Extensions and Empirical Tests." *Organizational Behavior and Human Performance*, 1982, *29*, 370–396.

Staw, B. M., and Ross, J. "Commitment to a Policy Decision: A Multitheoretical Perspective." *Administrative Science Quarterly*, 1978, *23*, 40–64.

Waller, W. S., and Mitchell, T. R. "The Effects of Context on the Selection of Decision Strategies for the Cost Variance Investigation Problem." *Organizational Behavior and Human Performance*, 1984, *33*, 397–413.

Witte, E. "Field Research on Complex Decision Processes—The Phase Theorem." *International Journal of Management and Organization*, 1972, *2*, 555–571.

# 12

## Strategic Plan Failures

### The Organization
### as Its Own Worst Enemy

Michael Finney
Ian I. Mitroff

*Three years ago, the group in the Head Shed*
*—that black hole we call the Corporate Office—*
*spent tens of thousands of dollars, countless man-*
*hours, and ate futures reports instead of Wheaties*
*for breakfast so that we would have a five-year*
*strategic plan. The plan was bright, shiny almost.*
*Like burnished armor that was going to protect us*
*into the next decade. It was future-oriented, well*
*conceived, logical.*

*Our work group held a wake for the plan*
*this morning. Actually doused my copy with cham-*
*pagne and put it through the shredder. The toasts*
*were eloquent and, at times, painfully comic. The*
*Head Shed tried. Damn, they tried.*

*Where did the knockout blow come from?*
*Well, no one person or group delivered it. Some-*
*thing danced lightly around the plan delivering in-*
*visible jabs and punches. We call it "The Force."*
*Luke Skywalker doesn't have anything on this or-*
*ganization. Darth Vader wouldn't have a chance*
*against our Force. It seemed like the sum total of*
*the organization's* intentions *climbed into the ring*

*with the plan and the result was a TKO in favor of*
*The Force.*

—Middle manager,
"National Hightech
Company"

Things do go wrong with the best-laid plans. Robert Burns was
not joking when he said long ago that they often go astray.
Anyone who has been involved with the development and implementation of an organizational strategic plan will support the
truth of Burns's poetic statement. The question addressed here
is, do social cognitive processes embedded in the organization's
activities help them go astray?

Most of the writing about strategic planning today focuses
on "how to" or "things to consider." The focus is also usually
on factors external to the organization that pose threats to organizational livelihood. Barriers to livelihood are found in the
great "Out There." Out there are markets, scarce resources, fi-
nancing; out there rests uncertainty. Alan Patz (1981) succinctly reduces the traditional definition of "strategy" to attempts to reduce uncertainty in the environment.

Knowing "how to" is important and necessary. Knowing
what to consider is also critical. But are all threats to continued
organizational livelihood Out There? What about "In Here?" Do
all internal organizational processes facilitate strategy implementation? Are all of management's actions in wholehearted
support of their organization's espoused strategy? While the environment and its uncertainty pose considerable threat to an
organization's espoused strategy, it may be that internal barriers
pose more immediate and critical threats to a strategic plan's
success.

While this is not a novel idea (Patz, 1981; Stonich, 1982),
the science of organizational behavior has lacked a method for
detecting and understanding such barriers. The lack of a methodology for exploring the barriers can be explained in part by
the observation that the barriers are often deeply embedded in
an organization's social cognitive processes. These cognitive pro-

cesses, which will be more specifically defined later in this chapter, are difficult to unearth and not "countable" using the usual quantitative methods. A modification of the stakeholder analysis and assumptions surfacing (SAAS) process (Mason and Mitroff, 1981) is now available (Finney, 1984) as a method for organizational self-reflection (OSR). OSR allows the reflecting of espoused strategy against enacted strategy. In effect, the OSR method allows the detection of internal cognitive barriers to strategic plan implementation.

Chris Argyris (1964) long ago remarked on the discrepancy between what an organization says it is doing and what it does. The OSR method brings to light discrepancies between the two and presents an organization's management with information which will help them design action that will address cognitive barriers to strategic implementation. The Head Shed referred to in the opening vignette need not go against The Force unarmed. Before we review the OSR method along with examples of process results, let us take a look at the rationale for the process.

## Organizational Cognitive Processes

Organizations today are thought of and studied as cultures (Smircich, 1983; Martin and Siehl, 1983; Schein, 1985; and Pettigrew, 1979). Cultures are systems of enduring, socially agreed-on meanings that guide behavior (Berger and Luckman, 1981). Since cognitive processes determine meaning (Glass, Holyoak, and Santa, 1979; Neisser, 1976), it follows that organizations will exhibit behavior that is guided by socially agreed-on meanings, which are in turn sanctioned as legitimate by the social cognitive processes of those individuals and groups working in the organization.

The power of an organization's culture rests in its ability to control the behavior of individuals and groups. Cultures do not emerge overnight—they have a history. If the cognitive processes guiding behavior were successful in the past, they will be repeated in the present and assumed to be successful in the future (O'Toole, 1982). As will be seen later, the cognitive processes guiding organizational culture and behavior are not easily determined. They lie embedded within the thoughts and actions of those working in the organization. The rationale behind the meaning of the cognitive processes may be lost in history and communicated by employees as "It's just the way we do things around here."

The cognitive processes of interest here—those playing a critical role in the success or failure of strategic efforts—are cognitive schemas and cognitive scripts. Cognitive schemas are interrelated knowledge structures (categories, prototypes, implicit theories, and so on) that people use to organize and make sense of social and organizational information (Neisser, 1976; Taylor and Crocker, 1981; Gioia and Manz, 1985). Schemas provide cognitive frameworks for understanding social information (that is, for ascribing meaning) and suggest implications for behavior. The schemas people use are associated with related scripts for action (Abelson, 1981). Gioia and Poole (1984) describe cognitive scripts as schematic knowledge structures, held in memory, that specify behavior or event sequences appropriate for specific situations. Martin (1982) refers to scripts as situations where an individual or group acts out a scene in which the lines (behavior) and climax (results) are fairly stable and predictable. The script is enacted when the appropriate cues are available to actors in any organizational setting.

The focus in this chapter will be on schemas as organization-specific, interrelated knowledge structures and on scripts as specialized schemas prescribing dynamic behavior sequences within an organization. Of particular importance here, and to those designing and enacting strategy, are consensual cognitive schemas and scripts.

By *consensual*, we mean that there is a reasonable amount of implicit agreement among organization members as to the appropriate meaning of information or events. This leads to consensual cognitive scripts prescribing behavior and action (which are also implicitly agreed to as appropriate by organizational members). Organizational culture may be viewed as a phenomenon emerging from networks of related and integrated consensual cognitive schemas and scripts (Smircich, 1983).

Simply having a description in hand of an organization's

culture is of little value to members of organizational management responsible for designing and enacting strategy. Once
understanding and action schemas become embedded in an organization's culture, they can take on an unconscious nature. It
is the unconscious nature of some schemas that makes it difficult for organizational decision makers to perceive the inconsistencies between their espoused and enacted strategies. Without
an understanding of the integrated conscious and unconscious
consensual cognitive schemas and scripts giving rise to the culture, management will be seriously handicapped in coming to
grips with the "Why?" behind the failure, success, or potential
success of a strategy.

It follows from the preceding discussion that organization
members may be thought of as actors on a stage responding
consciously and unconsciously to cues that orient their performance according to socially agreed-on cause-and-effect relationships. This sounds simplistic and seems to imply homogenized behavior by the managerial actors in an organization; that
is, it seems to imply that all actors will respond to the same cues
in the same way in similar circumstances. Yet this view of the
workings of organizational culture does in fact allow for the individual differences in behavior—for the personal styles—that
are clearly observable in everyday organizational life. An example from a real organizational situation may help to explain why
this is so.

Organizational cues and respective outcomes (and the
meanings attached to both) remain fairly stable over time. Individual responses to the cues may vary, but the outcomes are expected to be homogenized. Manager Jane, working for Marketing, Inc., has come to know that precise, statistically supported
business plans are expected by her boss, Ann. The plan is to be
presented in a rigid form designed years before. Jane's personal
style dictates that when the boss asks for a plan for a proposed
marketing project, she is to work hard and alone, in spite of the
assistance her subordinates might provide. If Jane does it alone,
she feels, she can better control the quality and precision of the
plan. She always delivers a plan in the expected form and of the
expected quality.

Manager Bill, who reports to the same boss in Marketing,

Inc., delivers the same high-quality, statistically precise business plans upon demand. His style dictates that he delegate the responsibility to his subordinates and then integrate their several products into the requested plan. Same cue, same results, but different schemas and scripts.

Boss Ann shared a meaning (which she shares with other bosses in Marketing, Inc., through a consensual schema) for "business plans" complete with orienting cues, schema, and script with Jane and Bill. Jane and Bill responded to the meaning they had also come to share, incorporating their personal schemas and scripts, and produced the expected product. The result is schemas and scripts superimposed on schemas and scripts—that is, meaning and action superimposed on meaning and action. This complex and interactive set of meanings directs the enactment of behavior by the individual, the group, and ultimately the organization.

In the real organizational situation briefly described here, Jane and Bill did their work never suspecting that Boss Ann and other Marketing, Inc., bosses made their decisions based first on the form of the plan, and second on its substance. Ann had come to know over time that the statistical precision and structure of a presented business plan was required for top management approval. Almost anything would be accepted if it was couched in the right statistical terminology and format. Content that could not be fitted to the format was disregarded. The consensual schema presented was "Statistical precision and structure lead to approval; content is disconnected with approval." Bringing the meaning behind the schema and script to light helped the organization develop new strategies that allowed the incorporation of information previously disregarded because it was difficult to fit into the statistical models used in the company's business plans.

## The Organizational Self-Reflection Method

Social cognition is frequently invisible to those under its influence. The often unconscious nature of the barriers that oppose espoused strategic intent and that are thrown up by consensual schemas and scripts is difficult to reveal. It is much easier for a management group to attribute strategic failure to external influences than to recognize and give substance to the complex internal "force." We suggest that there is now a process that can identify, describe, and facilitate the understanding of consensual cognitive schemas. The process also presents the consequences of the managerial actions that are prescribed by consensual scripts.

The OSR method is briefly outlined here, along with excerpts from an actual case as an example of its use. The method's greatest value is its ability to present an organization with a description of its present enacted strategy (the one in use). This enacted strategy can then be reflected upon the organization's espoused strategy. It can also be reflected upon proposed strategy to unearth schemas and scripts that might act as barriers to the proposed strategy. The OSR is at its most informative, in effect, if its results are reflected against both the espoused and the proposed.

One important point to keep in mind is that all organizations have strategies, whether or not they are labeled as "strategic plans." "The way things are done around here" is itself a strategy. Yet what the organization is presently doing strategically is not always an accurate reflection of what it says it is doing. What organizational management proposes to do (that is, the changes apparent in a designed strategic plan) is not always facilitated by embedded cognitive schemas guiding its present strategy.

Displaying the inconsistencies between the present strategy, the espoused strategy, and the proposed strategy entails surfacing the meaning of embedded strategy in the present. It involves giving shape and substance to the "Force" referred to in the opening vignette. The Force can be defined as the power of consensual cognitive schemas. Once the substance of the Force—its meaning—is known, it can be changed or reinforced when necessary.

*The Process*

The OSR method presented here is a five-stage process. Excerpts from the product of each stage are presented as exhibits. The origin of these exhibits is disguised; they are drawn from work done with the organization depicted in the opening vignette. The organization will be referred to as "National Hightech," a pseudonym for a real organization. National Hightech is a sophisticated data-processing subsidiary of a large bank holding company. Its customers are the member banks of the holding company.

The OSR is a variation of the stakeholder analysis and assumption surfacing (SAAS) process (Mason and Mitroff, 1981; Mitroff and Emshof, 1979). SAAS has its roots in Hegelian dialectics (Churchman, 1971). The intention of the process, as originally designed, was to achieve a single, synthesized strategic plan composed of the efforts of two or more groups having known dialectical differences on future strategic directions. Dialectics is, of course, the method of logic based on the principle that an idea or event (thesis) generates its opposite (antithesis) leading to a reconciliation, through discourse, of opposites (synthesis).

The OSR's intentions are to reveal unconscious or barely recognized dialectics not only between but also within groups. The within-group dialectic is the difference between espoused strategy and enacted strategy or between enacted strategy and proposed strategy. The process allows the surfacing and examination of the cognitive schemas and scripts associated with the organization's present enacted strategy.

*Stage One.* The initial steps of the process involve generating a clear statement of an organization's espoused strategy. The sources of information for this statement are located in printed material about the organization. Mission statements, annual reports, magazine articles, employee handbooks, policy and procedure manuals, performance appraisal guidelines, and employee newsletters present information relating to strategic plans. All these and many other sources are available for generating the espoused-strategy statement (see Exhibit 1). The content of these documents can be analyzed for themes such as teamwork and importance of employee satisfaction and for environmental sensitivity, values, problem-solving orientation, community relations and responsibility, and security of market

**Exhibit 1. Excerpts from National Hightech's Espoused Strategy.**

---

It is vital that we continue to provide high-quality, cost-effective services to our customers. We work in cooperative partnership with them in determining their future needs. Their satisfaction is our number one goal.

Our success is due to the quality of our staffs in the various functional departments. We maintain a high level of quality in our employees. Maintaining in-house competency in all areas is critical to customer service.

Our efforts reflect our belief that people are our most important resource. Good internal and external communications are essential to our continued success.

Our emphasis on the matrix management style underscores our confidence in the competence of management employees.

---

position. The themes and other issues can be focused more specifically as a result of how the organization presents its problems during the initiation of the OSR. For example, it may indicate, as Marketing, Inc., did in the example earlier in this chapter, that its business plans for new market development are failing and it does not know why. Themes relating to new market development efforts received special attention.

A note of caution is necessary here. Regardless of the organization's present problem, many different meanings associated with many factors have to be investigated. A strategy is usually composed of many substrategies. The design of business plans in Marketing, Inc., was related to the organization's reward system, its beliefs about verifiable knowledge, and its assumptions about competing successfully. Changes in the construction of business plans necessitated changes in these other processes also. Any organization choosing to use the method must be willing to have many, if not all, of its cognitive-based assumptions tested. The process is virtually useless if the systems implications of integrated schemas and scripts are ignored.

*Stage Two.* Usually, a group of senior managers responsible for directing strategy is formed into an *internal search group* (ISG). The ISG has the responsibility of assisting the consulting facilitator in ferreting out the meaning behind assumptions associated with critical stakeholder groups. The ISG at National Hightech was composed of senior executive vice-presidents officed at Hightech's corporate headquarters. All the remaining exhibits (Exhibits 2, 3, and 4) are excerpts from their group work.

In stage two, the ISG is asked to generate a list of organizational stakeholders. *Stakeholders* are defined as those individuals, groups, or organizations having a vested interest in the success or failure of the organization (Miles, 1980; Ackoff, 1974). A list of all possible stakeholders, without concern for importance, is written on a flip chart. From this general list, participants are requested to choose the ten most important, again without regard for priority. Once they agree on ten as important, they are asked to prioritize the list with "1" representing most important and "10" least important. This narrowing down and prioritizing does not dismiss as unimportant stakeholder groups that do not make it to the top-ten. It serves to reduce the list to a manageable size for the purposes of this stage of the OSR method. Other stakeholder groups are processed during later meetings. Exhibit 2 shows the top four stakeholders from National's prioritized list.

**Exhibit 2. Top Four Stakeholders from National Hightech's Prioritized Stakeholder List.**

1. Customers
2. Senior management (of National Hightech)
3. Holding company
4. Middle managers (of National Hightech)

*Stage Three.* The ISG then proceeds on an assumption-surfacing process. Mason and Mitroff (1981, p. 43) state that an organization "may be conceived of as the embodiment of a series of transactions among all of its constituent purposeful entities, that is, its stakeholders. Thus, a strategy may be thought of as a set of assumptions about the current and future behavior of an organization's stakeholders."

*Assumptions* are defined as those factors taken as "givens," "for granted," or "assumed" about a stakeholder by participants. Assumptions reflect the understanding of and meaning associated with stakeholders. The assumptions serve as the data from which the cognitive schemas will be interpreted.

They are asked to verbalize the assumption or assumption sets they have for each stakeholder. Often the ISG will begin by giving descriptive statements about the stakeholder. These should be listed on the flip chart also. Assumption statements differ from descriptive statements in that they usually indicate a consequence. Exhibits 3a, 3b, 3c, and 3d all show excerpts from assumption statements generated by the ISG at National Hightech. Once the ISG exhausts the assumptions about a particular stakeholder, the facilitator asks them to attach behaviors and feelings to the statements. What behaviors follow from the

**Exhibit 3a. Excerpts from Assumptions About Customers.**

- Customers have a short-term focus. (This creates *conflict* with our long-term focus.)
- Customers are driven by local markets. (We have to react passively to individual demands that prevent global solutions: *frustration.*)
- Customers waste resources and prevent economies of scale. (This suboptimizes product integration; our costs go up, which we have to charge back to them, which causes them to criticize us: *frustration.*)
- Customers are obstacles to be overcome in pursuit of our mission/purpose. (We use a defensive strategy with them, have to presell and negotiate our ideas, which wastes a lot of time and energy, so that we use hidden agendas to get our work done.)
- Customers question our ability and legitimacy. (We overcommit, defend our flanks, and become *defensive* in attempting to meet their demands.)

**Exhibit 3b. Excerpts from Assumptions About Senior Management.**

- We all have "loner" attitudes.
- Each of us understands his role and accountabilities.
- We experience conflicts because of personal style differences.
- As a group, we feel a lack of power and control.
- We are dependent on middle management.
- We don't communicate well within our group.
- We don't make full use of each other's abilities.
- We all have the attitude of "fight your own fires, I've got mine."
- We are competitive men.

*Note:* Each item is a mixture of descriptive and assumption statements. Behaviors are omitted because they are communicated in the content of the statements. The ISG here is composed of National Hightech's senior management. Thus, the assumptions and descriptions in this exhibit are self-descriptions.

**Exhibit 3c. Excerpts from Assumptions About Holding Company.**

- They share our purposes and frustration (cooperation follows, understanding at a gut level, turn to them when we need support, frequent communication).
- They are dependent on us (we respond to their needs, display pride and occasional arrogance).
- A distribution of resources by the holding company would better utilize our abilities (negotiation for more power, preselling of ideas).

**Exhibit 3d. Excerpts from Assumptions About Middle Managers.**

- They are in need of development (we don't promote, lack of trust, we show little confidence in them, have training department design new development procedures).
- They are essential to communication and implementation of mission/purpose internally and externally (we have a lot of meetings, high level of communication efforts, waste additional time because of misinterpretation; as far as external communication—with customers—we are doing nothing).
- They are a more scarce resource than other employees (we tolerate incompetence, we default to "known quantities," try to grow our own).
- They are technically competent.
- They are "managerially" incompetent—they lack communication, social, and leadership skills necessary for the job (lack of trust, go around them to supervisors and front line).
- Their competence is a reflection of our competence—internally and externally (we become restrictive and directive).

assumption? What feelings or emotions are associated with the statement? This information is used to surface the scripts associated with the schemas generated in the first step of stage three. Examples of the behaviors are requested for clarification purposes.

The facilitator then asks ISG members to examine what they have said about the stakeholder under consideration and to encapsulate an assumption that best captures their beliefs about the stakeholder. That statement is also written on the flip chart. Each of the ten stakeholders receives the same treatment.

*Stage Four.* The product of stage three is contrasted against the product of stage one. The ISG members are asked to *describe* inconsistencies and consistencies apparent in the contrasting exercise. In stage four, it is important to have participants describe only what can be inferred or is obvious when the two data sets (products) are side by side; prescriptive corrective or reinforcing action is an integral part of stage five. Participants are asked to make a three-column chart (see Exhibit 4) with the following headings in the order presented: Espoused Behavior/Belief; Assumption Facilitators; Assumption Barriers. The Espoused Behavior/Belief column contains bulleted items representing value statements and themes from the product of stage one. Column two contains bullets relating to assumptions about stakeholders—that is, cognitive schemas and scripts that facilitate the espoused strategy. Column three contains assumptions about stakeholders that act as barriers to the espoused strategy. The product of stage four is thus an "Insight Chart." This Insight Chart provides the necessary meaning to begin to give form and substance to an organization's "Force"—that is, to the consensual schemas and scripts empowering and facilitating behavior.

*Stage Five.* This stage of the OSR method involves the creation of action plans that usually require the redesign of meaning—that is, the development of new cognitive schemas and scripts. Reward systems are redesigned so that they support new meanings and reinforce strategies that facilitate traditional meanings. Management development programs are redesigned to stress and enhance the new meanings. The magnitude and complexity of the work done in stage five is difficult to communicate in detail here. Suffice it to say that this stage is the most difficult task to complete. The product of stage five is an inclusive organizational strategic plan concentrating on internal and external stakeholders.

## National Hightech Self-Reflected

National Hightech requested help when its attempt to introduce a new strategy failed. The new strategy was the introduction of matrix management at a core subsidiary location. Although, as the exhibits show, many interesting insights came from using the method, the failure of the matrix strategy will be the focus here. It was, in fact, matrix management that fell to defeat in combat with National Hightech's Force.

When we investigated the problem at National Hightech,

Exhibit 4. Excerpts from National Hightech's Insight Chart.

| Espoused Strategy | Facilitating Assumptions | Barrier Assumptions |
|---|---|---|
| • Cooperative partnership to provide quality service to customers, first and foremost. | • None generated. | • *Customers* are obstacles to be overcome in pursuit of our mission/purpose (which is to serve the strategy of the holding company first). |
| • We maintain a high-quality staff that is competent. | • *Senior Management* knows and understands their roles and accountabilities.<br>• *Middle Managers* are technically competent. | • *Customers* question our ability and legitimacy.<br>• *Middle managers* are "managerially" incompetent.<br>• *Middle managers* are scarce resources—we tolerate incompetence. |
| • Good internal and external communications are essential. | • *Holding Company* shares our purpose and function.<br>• *Middle Managers* are essential to internal and external communications. | • *Senior Management*—loner attitude.<br>• *Senior Managers*—style conflicts.<br>• *Senior Management* doesn't communicate well within the group.<br>• *Senior Management* doesn't make full use of each other's abilities.<br>• *Senior Management*—"Fight your own fires, I've got mine."<br>• *Middle Managers*—we do nothing to improve their external communication with customers.<br>• *Middle managers* are "managerially" incompetent. |
| • Our emphasis on the matrix management style underscores our confidence in management employees. | • None generated. | • *Senior Management*—"Fight your own fires, I've got mine."<br>• *Middle Managers* are managerially incompetent. |

we used modified OSR methodology with each of the functional units at the location in question. Middle managers were responsible for managing the functional units. The results of the investigation most relevant to this discussion were that a consensual schema labeled "information hoarding" typified the relationships between the functional units at the location. Communication across functional boundaries was very low. Communication within units was good. Middle managers and those they supervised in each unit viewed other units as threats to their unit's operational stability. Rapid growth and constant fire-fighting contributed to an environment where managers protected their unit's boundaries from each other's fires. New projects that required integration across boundaries were sprung on other functional units full-blown ("1,000-mile drop-kicks," as one employee reported). This was not an ideal climate for matrix management.

Matrix management requires certain organizational characteristics. Open, frequent communication is essential. Managerial competence must be high. Top management's confidence in that competence is necessary. Matrix management as espoused by National Hightech required teamwork by middle managers across functional units. It required senior management's trust in the abilities of middle managers. It required that senior management "let go" and not be directive or restrictive, especially in decision making. These schemas and scripts were not present at Hightech.

The results from the senior management group work further clarified the meaning behind the consensual schemas guiding the work of middle managers. The middle managers at the location reported to the senior managers who generated the data presented in the previous exhibits. Senior managers did not function as an integrated team. Within the group, there was implicit agreement that they would concentrate on accomplishing their individual responsibilities. If they had a problem that required help from other senior managers, they rarely requested it. They were concerned that they would be viewed by their peers and the CEO as weak and ineffective if they could not handle problems on their own. They fought their own fires.

How were these meanings originated? Many factors over the organization's history contributed, but one factor was significantly contributing to maintenance of the schemas and scripts in the present. The CEO believed in, advocated, and acted on his beliefs that *individual accountability* was the root and source of nourishment for organizational success. His schemas and scripts held senior managers strictly accountable for their successes and failures. A failure would mean public reprimands in staff meetings. No rewards existed to reinforce team-matrixed efforts at the senior level of management.

Given the odds outlined here, it is no surprise that Hightech's strategy fell to the Force and the shredder. Cognitive processes embedded within cognitive processes within still other processes defeated the strategy.

## Implications for Management

Social cognitive processes at varying levels of complexity (organizational, function unit, group, and individual) play a critical role in the success or failure of an organization's strategic plan. They exist as sometimes visible and more frequently invisible facilitators or barriers. An organization concentrating on the external environment as the major source of threat and uncertainty does so at great risk. Its internal environment may create and unwittingly nourish a more formidable foe. An organization can be its own worst enemy.

The OSR method presented here can help the members of an organization to explore the consensual cognitive schemas and scripts operating in the organization. It can provide valuable information for the design or correction of an organization's strategy. Having an accurate self-reflection allows a better informed design for future strategy. Existing barriers can be surfaced and associated meanings changed so that the chances for success with strategies planned in the future are greater.

The cognitive dissonance created by the Insight Chart used in stage four can be startling. But dissonance without action is useless, and action does not always follow dissonance. Action must be designed, if called for, and the implications of any action must also be searched out in the organizational system. Changes in a reward system, for example, that are intended to increase teamwork across an organization's functional departments, may lead managers to punish individual initiative or inadvertently reward groupthink. Redesign can create new cognitive schemas with unintended meanings and consequences. Exploring and planning for the unintended meanings of proposed actions are necessary parts of the self-reflection process.

Frequently, it is to the organization's advantage to have multiple groups representing different hierarchies participate in the OSR method. What the CEO says at the top rarely means the same thing on the front line; the OSR method can be used to uncover the "why" of this chronic organizational problem. Differences in meaning are easily detected in an Insight Chart of slightly different construction. In this instance, the assumptions of each group are listed in a matrix with stakeholders on the left and hierarchy groups across the top. The priority listing of stakeholders by the different groups provides a particularly rich source of information. They are rarely ever the same from one group to the next.

The process has also been used to contrast the social cognitive schemas and scripts between a board of directors and the executive staff of one organization. The results of the OSR between such significant groups led to the uncovering of several stress and conflict factors that were seriously impeding the implementation of a well-conceived, five-year strategic plan.

Like any method, the process described here has its limitations. It is a time-consuming effort not entered into casually. Organizations using it have had to allocate considerable resources of various kinds. The method is well suited to organizations in crisis that have a mandate for self-examination. It is also well suited to organizations that take planning seriously and want to focus inward as well as outward as they design strategy.

The method's side effects can also be stressful. Having organizational—and often individual—reality shaken is difficult to endure. People become wedded to their beliefs and actions, regardless of their functionality. When the OSR method is used, organizational dysfunctionality and those maintaining it come into clear focus. There have been instances in which organizational members wanted to "kill the messenger" because of the content of the message—that old Greek pastime is still alive and well.

In summary, an old Chinese proverb expresses very succinctly the message in this chapter for organizations and those who guide them: "If we do not change our direction, we will end up where we are headed."

## References

Abelson, R. P. "Psychological Status of the Script Concept." *American Psychologist,* 1981, *7,* 715-729.

Ackoff, R. L. *Concept of Corporate Planning.* New York: Wiley, 1974.

Argyris, C. *Integrating the Individual and the Organization.* New York: Wiley, 1964.

Berger, P. L., and Luckman, T. *The Social Construction of Reality.* New York: Irvington, 1981.

Churchman, C. W. *The Design of Inquiring Systems: Basic Concepts of Systems and Organization.* New York: Basic Books, 1971.

Finney, M. L. "The Organizational Self-Reflection Method." Working paper, Department of Management and Organization, University of Southern California, 1984.

Gioia, D. A., and Manz, C. "Linking Cognition and Behavior: A Script-Processing Interpretation of Vicarious Learning." *Academy of Management Review,* 1985, *10,* 527-539.

Gioia, D. A., and Poole, P. P. "Scripts in Organizational Behavior." *Academy of Management Review,* 1984, *9,* 449-459.

Glass, A. L., Holyoak, K. J., and Santa, J. L. *Cognition.* Reading, Mass.: Addison-Wesley, 1979.

Martin, J. A. "Stories and Scripts in Organizational Settings." In H. Hastorf and A. M. Isen (eds.), *Cognitive Social Psychology.* New York: Elsevier North-Holland, 1982.

Martin, J. A., and Siehl, C. "Organizational Culture and Counterculture: An Uneasy Symbiosis." *Organizational Dynamics,* Autumn 1983, pp. 52-64.

Mason, R. O., and Mitroff, I. I. *Challenging Strategic Planning Assumptions.* New York: Wiley, 1981.

Miles, R. H. *Macro Organizational Behavior.* Santa Monica, Calif.: Goodyear, 1980.

Mitroff, I. I., and Emsholf, J. R. "On Strategic Assumption-Making: A Dialectical Approach to Policy and Planning." *Academy of Management Review,* 1979, *4,* 1-12.

Neisser, U. *Cognition and Reality.* New York: W. H. Freeman, 1976.

O'Toole, J. "Declining Innovation: The Failure of Success." Center for Futures Research, Graduate School of Business Administration, University of Southern California, 1982.

Patz, A. L. *Strategic Decision Analysis.* Boston: Little, Brown, 1981.

Pettigrew, A. M. "On Studying Organizational Culture." *Administrative Science Quarterly,* 1979, *4,* 570-581.

Schein, E. H. *Organizational Culture and Leadership.* San Francisco: Jossey-Bass, 1985.

Smircich, L. "Concepts of Culture and Organizational Analysis." *Administrative Science Quarterly,* 1983, *3,* 339-358.

Stonich, P. J. (ed.). *Implementing Strategy: Making Strategy Happen.* Cambridge, Mass.: Ballinger, 1982.

Taylor, S. E., and Crocker, J. "Schematic Bases of Social Information Processing." In E. T. Higgins, C. P. Herman, and M. P. Zanna (eds.), *Social Cognition.* Vol. 1. Hillsdale, N.J.: Erlbaum, 1981.

# Conclusion:
# The State of the Art
# in Organizational
# Social Cognition

## A Personal View

### Dennis A. Gioia

*Thinking is easy, acting difficult, and to put one's thoughts into action, the most difficult thing in the world.*

—Goethe

Goethe's observation applies on several levels to the attempts to grapple with the complexities and nuances of organizational cognition and action. It is a clear statement of one of the fundamental problems facing executives. There are few more telling times in the organizational experience than when one must formulate a plan and implement it. The effectiveness of one's organization, as well as the fate of one's own career, often hinges on the mastery of the ability to turn thought into act. That translation of cognition into action is in a significant sense the essence of management.

On another level, Goethe's statement applies as well to

those of us who study organizations. At times we have to put our thoughts into action (that is, into print) and say what we think we know about cognition, action, and the management of organizations. One of those times is now and is represented by this book and specifically by this chapter. This volume is a collective statement of the state of the art of our thinking about thought and action in organizations, and this chapter is an attempt to synthesize our current knowledge into some coherent patterns.

In one sense, it is pretentious to try to write a chapter that purports to assess the state of the art in any facet of organizational study. In another sense, it is likely to be both informative and instructive to try to step back in order to discern the patterns in our thinking as they relate to our chosen topic of study (even if the process might be somewhat colored by one writer's interpretive schemes). I confess to some ambivalence about this task. Sometimes I think that the state of our art and science is quite advanced and that we have come a fair distance in our knowledge about cognition and action within the social context of organizations and about the nature of organizations in general. At other times I believe that the state of our art and science is almost hopelessly primitive and that we are making progress at a painfully slow pace—perhaps too slow to keep up with the development and burgeoning importance of organizations in modern life.

A little of the same ambivalence befalls me when I read and reread the contributions to this book. On the one hand, I cannot help being struck by the number of times that the authors have bemoaned the dearth of research on the topics they are discussing and by the frank admissions about what we do not know, all of which leads to a disquieting feeling that there is either far too much to study or that our current abilities simply do not allow comprehensive descriptions of significant organizational phenomena. On the other hand, I have to marvel at the innovative conceptions, research overviews, and rich descriptions of cognitive process that attest to some rather well-developed knowledge about organizations. These chapters demonstrate that some serious thought has indeed been given to organizational thinking and that some advanced and useful knowledge has been created. I also note a possible paradox in the number of times that the authors have been forthright about being speculative, which can be taken either as evidence of ignorance and nescience or as evidence of wisdom and pre-science. Having seen these works evolve from drafts into final chapters, my best attempt at a dispassionate assessment still sees these contributions as characterized by scholarship, insight, and erudition. Although ignorance surfaces, it does so in its most laudable form: the honest concession that there is much that we do not yet know and therefore should learn.

Actually, truth be known, I feel quite heartened by the state of our knowledge. If we take a historical view and allow for the fact that we have been engaged in formal theorizing and empirical investigation for a comparatively short time, then we cannot help but conclude that we know much more than even in the recent past about the nature of organizations, how they work, how they can be managed, and perhaps even how they should be managed. Within that same historical view, we can also note cyclical tendencies in the emphasis of one view or another (behaviorism, humanism, Darwinism, and so on), and we can either lament that our current efforts amount to reinventing the wheel or to old wine in a new bottle, or come to the resigned conclusion that "there is nothing new under the sun." That kind of statement, however, displays a superficial sort of perusal of the evolution of organizational thought. On each reiteration, we have managed to perform a useful embellishment or transformation that contributes to both our understanding and our practice. Furthermore, if one looks at the dominant views that have held sway at different times in the past, one discovers, curiously, that they are all simultaneously with us now. The message that can be inferred is that all are useful in some way and all are needed to formulate a complete picture of one of our highest-level systems, our own organizations (Pondy and Mitroff, 1979).

So, if we take the contributions to this book as a kind of surrogate measure for the current state of our art, where then do we stand? What are the themes that emerge most frequently and most forcefully from these twelve portrayals of an action-oriented cognitive life in organizations? In fact, there are quite a number of them; I have identified thirteen overarching "meta-themes" that are shared among many of the chapters. In my way of seeing, these metathemes fall into two main clusters. The first cluster derives from the essentially implicit assumptions that seem to underlie many of the works here. The second cluster subsumes the notions that are explicitly and convergently discussed, often in different ways, by multiple chapters and authors. I would like to devote most of this concluding chapter to a discussion of the seven metathemes that comprise the "implicit" cluster and the six that make up the "explicit" cluster.

## The Implicit Metathemes

*Management as Art/Management as Science.* There is a rather subtle but prevalent metatheme that arises from considering the nature of modern management: namely, the essence of the experience involves both art and science. It is a scientific endeavor in that it requires logical, analytical, rational thinking of the kind usually applied to organizing, coordinating, controlling, planning, deciding, and so on. It is also scientific in that the findings of a "science of management" generated from empirical research are incorporated more and more into its practice. On the other hand, effective management also retains an ample measure of the artistic. Processes that are best described as intuitive, insightful, perceptive, nonrational, and wholistic are increasingly recognized as characteristic of the compleat executive.

In the past, there have been tendencies to dismiss the artistic aspects of management as sophistry. Alternatively, there have also been thinly veiled attempts to demonstrate that what has been labeled as "the art of management" is simply an as-yet-unknown process waiting for science to unmask it and reveal it as another logical process in disguise. On the basis of the chapters in this book, attempts to forge management purely into a science seem misdirected. In a similar vein, there seems to be some inclination, especially on the part of popular writers, to treat the art in management as fundamentally a mystical process, little understood and virtually inaccessible. Although organizations are certainly settings that have their own brands of mythology and mystification, that sort of stance about the art of the process is also misguided.

Both the art and the science of management are necessary topics for investigation. The two facets might require different approaches and produce different understandings, but both require study. We should therefore supplement our current orientation toward the scientific study of management and also focus on ways to understand intuition, processes involved in creative problem solving, and transformative modes of seeing organizational issues. If that effort results in a science-of-art or an art-of-science, all the better; it would imply a useful common meeting ground.

*A Gestalt View of the Organizational Actor.* Another, closely related metatheme paints a portrait of executives, managers, and other organization members that is more global than previous portrayals. Despite the fundamental concern of this book with cognition and despite the obvious case for the pervasiveness of cognitive influence in organizational life depicted here, the cognitive view alone is not represented as a panacea. A strict dependence on the social cognitive perspective, or any other single perspective, is not enough to present a rounded view of organizations as social phenomena. Cognition, however, is quintessentially characteristic of people organizing, and it thus represents a good central foundation from which to explore the many interconnections with other views that can contribute to a wholistic picture.

In addition to the cognitive perspective, first, and perhaps most obviously, a focus on *action* is required before any hope of a holistic view is possible. Action is intimately related to cognition, a point made in our introduction and by almost all the authors. Secondly, the portrait is undeniably incomplete without a focus on *context* and *environmental factors* because cognition and action are never free of contextual/environmental features; the organizational setting makes this fact very clear. Finally, a focus on *affect* is required. As Fiske and Taylor (1984) have so colorfully noted, trying to study social processes without considering the emotional elements is akin to thinking about the Sahara as one might think about a beach without the ocean. A comprehensive picture cannot emerge without entertaining all the important factors. Thus, at the least, we can note that cognition, action, context, and affect are necessary to fashion any ostensibly wholistic view of the social aspects of organizations, and even that statement is made with full recognition of its incompleteness.

*A Bridging Eclecticism.* A further characteristic that relates to the holistic view of the organization member is our own holistic view of the process of thinking about organizations. It is surely apparent that social cognition is not a tabula rasa process. It is performed predominantly by means of assimilating and accommodating new information and new knowledge into existing structures of understanding. Our thinking about organizations takes place in a similar fashion, not by reinventing insight at every turn, but by integrating knowledge and viewpoints from many eclectic sources. And those sources applied to the issues and problems in these pages cover the widest possible spectrum in our attempts to define, describe, and understand organizations. They range from organizational study's obvious connections to the social sciences, like psychology and sociology, to the much less obvious connections with disciplines like linguistics, philology, and philosophy. Viewed as a whole, the contributions to this volume constitute a strong attempt to synthesize what we know about social life into what we know about organizations. As a consequence the collection of contributions here has implicitly laid a foundation for an "organizational science," where fundamental processes relate distinctively to organizational processes.

*The Path to the Goal: A Concern with Process.* In many philosophical traditions there is a dictum that life should be lived less as a process of achieving goals than as a process of understanding how achievement is accomplished. In many ways it is the journey that matters as much as the destination. In this light, a fourth implicit metatheme is the primary focus throughout the book on cognitive *process*—that is, on *how* something is cognitively accomplished as much as *what* is accomplished.

I hasten to add that I recognize that organizations are

settings where action is held to predominate, and that there is an undeniable need for executives to trade in the currency of results, outcomes, and consequences, and so on. But this volume is a tribute to the belief that any possible improvement in the effectiveness of outcomes stems from knowing how to most effectively reach a cognitive conclusion, and then how to put it into action. Focused action is better facilitated by knowing how executives think about action.

This observation about the dominance of a focus on process also reiterates a theme sounded early on—namely, that one of the purposes of this book is to heighten the concern of management study with *understanding* the nature of the process of managing instead of overconcentrating on techniques of prediction and control. From the point of view of the practicing manager, understanding organizational cognition can do either of two potentially beneficial things: it can allow a more effective (and perhaps more humanistic) mode of prediction and control in the future, or it might pave the way for a reduced need for prediction and control. The latter condition would pertain if, for instance, a concern with organizational cognition reveals ways to facilitate a higher degree of self-management (Manz and Sims, 1980) or ways to apply holographic approaches to the design of organizations (Morgan and Ramirez, 1983).

*Redefining the Nature of Cognition.* Another thematic pattern that emerges throughout is an implicit redefinition of what is meant by the term *cognitive process.* As used in these chapters, it is apparent that the domain of activity that is taken as cognitive has been broadened in comparison to traditional conceptualizations. Put simply, cognition is no longer taken only to mean deliberate "thinking"; it also means "having thought," and then having thought, putting that thought into some coherent, meaningful mental structure. Specifically, the implication of this redefinition is that cognition encompasses more than the layperson's view entailing rational, logical, ongoing, and especially *conscious* processing. It also means the inclusion of nonrational, schematic, and, in particular, *unconscious* processing. Indeed, an implied case is frequently presented that perhaps most cognitive work is done in the latter mode.

Organizational life is a complicated endeavor. If people had to consciously reprocess cues anew at every presentation, they would remain hopelessly mired, because the most mundane activities would require far too much cognitive capacity. They simply do not do that. Instead, people tend to save mental energy for problematic or creative situations; therefore, only in the case of novel information or social situations does "thinking" seem to prevail. Yet the influence of "having thought" is ubiquitous. It attends virtually every other situation.

Given the structured nature of organizations and the repetitiveness of many of the actions that take place in them, this dependence on prior thought need not appear surprising. The recognition of the similarity of current experience to prior experience is all that is necessary to presume predictability. Thereafter, one's previous assumptions and reasonings will usually suffice, thus precluding the necessity for cognitive effort and allowing the cognitive miser in us all to operate (Taylor, 1981). Of course, this studied inattention to much of what is happening around us suggests some potential for a hapless organizational existence, with a multitude of mistakes and inaccurate perceptions. In the face of that possibility, how well do we do at this business of managing the cognitive enterprise?

*Success Despite Failure: Organization Members as Master Cue Processors.* Much has been made of the numerous fallibilities and foibles of the human information processor (see Ross, 1977; Tversky and Kahneman, 1974). Attention is fallible; perception is fallible; memory is fallible, and so on. If we focused only on all these shortcomings, we would quickly conclude that we are all hopeless cases, damned to an organizational life that progresses from one cognitive mess to another. Most of us recognize that this characterization somehow does not square with our own experience.

If instead we recognize how competent we all are at the processes of sensemaking and decision making, we might recognize that we are really master cue processors. *Despite* our shortcomings as logical information processors (or maybe *because* of the cognitive shortcuts that derive from our cognitive miserliness and pattern processing), we seem to get along amazingly well in our organizational worlds. If we actually took all the steps necessary to stamp out our tendencies toward bias (a pipe dream at best anyway), we really would be hopeless cases. The effort to learn techniques to improve rational processing is only a partial solution, and one that if carried too far would subvert the more subtle gestalt processes that allow our best managers to see patterns and meanings in events and actions in spite of possible inaccuracies in logical information processing. That is why I note that people in organizations have success despite their failures in logical information processing, and why they can be comfortably labeled as master cue processors, notwithstanding the paradox that label implies. There is more going on than mere syllogistic reasoning when cognitive conclusions must be reached. This observation is perhaps yet more support for the notion that organizational experience, especially the management experience, is a melding of both art and science.

   *The Role of Paradox, Dilemma, Ambiguity, and Equivocality.* A final tacit metatheme is the recognition of the tenuous nature of organizational reality, which is fraught with uncertainty, ill-structuredness, and even contradiction. Decision makers, whether they be middle-level employees or strategic-level executives, must deal with a phenomenology that must have sense imposed on it. Effectiveness implies that people in organizations must become proficient handlers of paradox. There need not necessarily be a "right" answer to a consequential issue. A decision maker must entertain the paradox that two contradictory alternatives might both provide a solution to a problematic situation. They cannot presume, as can a manager of physical phenomenology, that an analytical approach to problems will lead to the most effective solution. Indeed, stepping away from analytic approaches is the essence of creative problem solving.

   Similarly, dilemmas should be seen as characteristic of organizational reality—that is, not something to be avoided but something to be recognized and dealt with. Although we now have strong acknowledgment of the essential nature of organizations as entities characterized by ambiguity and equivocality (see Weick, 1979), we have been slow to argue convincingly that tolerance for ambiguity is the key to competent modern management. Executives now must master the art of dealing with paradox, dilemma, ambiguity, and equivocality, and they must recognize that resolution of paradox and the reduction of equivocality often entail the imposition of subjective standards. For that reason, making sense of a cognitively messy organizational reality is often a matter of deciding what is a good decision, even in the face of having no objective standards for so deciding.

These are the metathemes that I have discerned to be implicit in the preceding chapters. They stem from multiple readings, reviewings, revisions, and ultimately a wholistic effort to grasp the collection of chapters as many related but different attempts to study the phenomena of organization, organizing, and organizational behavior. This cluster of metathemes is, of course, the product of my own sensemaking, as any try at discerning implicit themes must be. I would now like to turn attention to the metathemes that were treated more explicitly by our contributors in order to reveal the elements of social cognition in organizations that are consensual among scholars of organizations.

### The Explicit Metathemes

*Cognitive Structuring.* It is probably appropriate to begin with the metatheme most often mentioned by the contributors to the book. More attention was devoted to the notion of cognitive structuring than to any other concept. Admittedly, cognitive structuring has many guises and labels, but all imply the ordering and interrelationship of knowledge for the purpose of comprehension and action (Gioia and Manz, 1985). A quick review of the chapters in this volume reveals explorations of the spectrum of knowledge structures, including schemas, scripts, cognitive maps, distilled ideologies (a kind of causal schema), categories and their prototypes, and implicit theories and image theories, among others. Obviously, our contributors converge in the belief that the understanding of organizational cognition is centrally concerned with the study of such structures.

In a sense, this focus connotes the shift within the last decade away from the study of "thinking processes" and toward more global "cognitive processes."

There are good reasons for all the attention now devoted to knowledge structures. Many of those reasons have to do with the usefulness of such structures for efficient information processing and sensemaking. Table 1 summarizes the advantages of cognitive structuring touched upon by several of the writers in this book (see Lord and Foti, Chapter One, and Isenberg, Chapter Nine, this volume; also Gioia and Poole, 1984; Taylor and Crocker, 1981).

### Table 1. Benefits of Cognitive Structuring.

1. Facilitates cognitive economy.
2. Imposes structure on organizational experience.
3. Allows interpretation of ambiguous situations.
4. Speeds information processing and problem solving.
5. Supplies missing information with "default options."
6. Furnishes a basis for evaluating people and events.
7. Enables prediction of future events and outcomes.
8. Provides a basis for action.

Of course, the old adage that "There is no such thing as a free lunch" also applies. When cognitive structures provide such wonderful benefits, they must necessarily sacrifice something and exact their costs as well. The deceptive simplicity and elegance of knowledge structuring come with inherent disadvantages, which are summarized in Table 2.

### Table 2. Costs of Cognitive Structuring.

1. Encourages stereotypic thinking.
2. Subverts controlled information processing.
3. Fills data gaps with typical, not veridical, information.
4. Ignores discrepant (and possibly important) information.
5. Biases information processing toward existing schemas.
6. Discourages disconfirmation of present schemas, therefore
7. Resists revision of current cognitive structures.
8. Inhibits creative problem solving.

*Connections Between Cognition and Action.* Studying cognition in a vacuum would not seem to be a very worthwhile pursuit. A somewhat harsh, yet somewhat justified, allegation has been leveled at cognitive study in the past, however, because the focus of the study seems to have been "cognition for cognition's sake." No such provincialism is evident in these chapters. Fully three-fourths of the contributions dealt explicitly with the linkages between thought and action. One probably should expect nothing less in a collection devoted to *organizational* cognition, where action is the most salient concern, especially of those responsible for managing.

Action and cognition are virtually inseparable, as is apparent in the consideration of which of the two has precedence. For Weick (1979; Weick and Bougon, Chapter Four, this volume), action has primacy. How can one know what one thinks unless one sees what one does? Hence, cognition is seen as following from action. It is a profound and compelling argument for the origination of thought. For other writers, cognition is usefully viewed as the antecedent to action. For still others, the question of precedence is not of great concern; what is of concern is the recognition that there is a strong connection that simply cannot be ignored. Probably the most useful avenue is to consider cognition and action as reciprocal processes occurring cyclically over time (see Isenberg, Chapter Nine, this volume; Pondy, 1983; Weick, 1983). Separating the two is an artificial means of trying to understand them and suggests an illusory division where none exists.

Of course, the cognition/action relationship is nothing if not complex. In this volume, both Downey and Brief (Chapter Six) and Finney and Mitroff (Chapter Twelve) have emphasized the problems in understanding, for instance, how specific actions follow from particular cognitive processes. That discussion is beyond the scope of this chapter, however. Our strongest conclusion is simply that one can neither understand nor alter organizational cognition or action without due consideration of the influence of the other.

*Consensuality and Concerted Action.* Another explicit metatheme that was dwelt upon in many chapters was the notion of concerted action. Naturally, this generic theme is common to many discussions about the nature of organizations and is indeed a defining characteristic of being organized. More interesting, however, were the explorations of the concept of consensuality as a necessity for achieving concerted action. They have ranged from the subject of the strikingly minimal requirements for executing interlocked behaviors (discussed by Weick and Bougon in Chapter Four), to the use of language as a vehicle for arriving at shared meaning (Donnellon, Chapter Five), to the process of symbolization for conveying intended meaning (Gioia, Chapter Two), and finally to the recognition of the use of the implicit theories of organizational elites in fashioning a consensual concept that could lead to concerted action (Downey and Brief, Chapter Six).

These four chapters also shared in common a notion that organizational reality is a socially constructed one, forged out of a consensus of vision and action that exists largely or completely in the minds of the organization's members. That shared assumption implied that consensuality and concerted action were often tenuous fabrications enacted for a common purpose, but subject to dissolution if the definition of reality shifted. Other chapters (notably Chapter Eleven, by Mitchell, Rediker, and Beach, and Chapter Twelve, by Finney and Mitroff) dealt with the notions of shared values and beliefs, coordination, and concerted action without the presumption of a socially constructed reality.

*Affect in Cognition.* For two reasons, it might seem unusual that affect would be identified as an explicit theme in this book. First, affect is usually treated as something qualitatively different and separate from cognition; and second, affect typically receives only superficial consideration when cast within the organizational setting. Other processes are usually deemed more important. Yet the role of emotion and/or the impact upon emotion were frequently noted in the context of these discussions about cognition. The most in-depth treatment was rendered by Park, Sims, and Motowidlo in a chapter (Chapter Eight) devoted exclusively to the consideration of affective processes and phenomena. However, emotional processes also received note in Lord and Foti's exposition on schemas (Chapter One), Donnellon's treatment of communication (Chapter Five), Chatman, Bell, and Staw's discussion of self-justification and impression management (Chapter Seven), and Mitchell, Rediker, and Beach's presentation of image theory (Chapter Eleven).

The not so subtle message here is that affect is often a substantial influence in cognitive processing. People are not dispassionate information processors and sensemakers. Perhaps the most descriptive term capturing the influence of emotion in cognition was offered by Abelson (1963) when he labeled affect-laden cognition as "hot cognition." Affective processes are extremely powerful, acting as they do to color impressions and govern decisions and also serving as a vehicle for meaning construction. Thinking and feeling both play potent parts in organizations. Head versus heart dilemmas do not evaporate simply because the setting happens to be organizational. The issue of affect in organizing seems to be one of the most provocative and interesting areas for future conceptualization and research.

*The Role of Assumption.* Recently it has been in vogue to exhort academicians to specify the assumptions underlying their research and theorizing. Many people have recognized that conclusions, in all their myriad forms, are assumption-dependent. In this book, the authors have often taken special pains to note the assumptions on which their arguments, inferences, and conclusions are based. In one sense, that policy could work to make the arguments less convincing, because if the reader disagrees with the assumptions, he or she could then dismiss the conclusions. However, the opposite seems to be the case here: if anything, positions can be seen as more consistent and tenable when the underpinnings are explicitly known. What is more, in this way an alternative view can be entertained and considered for its possible worth without sacrificing one's own favored position.

In another vein, the role of assumption surfaces in relation to our attempts to comprehend decision making and action taking by managers. To understand managerial processes in use, the presuppositions employed in deciding and acting must be understood, a point made in various ways by Feldman (Chapter Ten),

by Isenberg (Chapter Nine), and by Mitchell, Rediker, and
Beach (Chapter Eleven). Ferreting out those assumptions is not
often easy, but it is clearly necessary. Even descriptive approaches to management study remain obscure without accounting for assumptions in use.

Finally, the role of assumption is noted in some depth
by Finney and Mitroff (Chapter Twelve), who tackle the difficult problem of designing a means for surfacing the assumptions
driving organizational action. It is perhaps instructive that the
chapter most devoted to the specification of pragmatic technique should concern itself almost exclusively with a process for
revealing and managing an organization's underlying assumptions.

*Organizational Cognition as a Multilevel Phenomenon.*
Our final consensual metatheme is the observation by many authors that contrary to tradition, cognition in organizations
should not be construed only as a phenomenon occurring at the
level of the individual. This type of commentary was made, in
one form or another, in most of the chapters. It was a theme of
central concern to the chapters by Chatman, Bell, and Staw
(Chapter Seven) and by Mitchell, Rediker, and Beach (Chapter
Eleven) and was also given prominence by Weick and Bougon
(Chapter Four) and by Salancik and Porac, who in Chapter
Three nicely captured the theme of multiple levels of analysis in
the forest versus trees metaphor.

Indeed, there is another pivotal inference that derives
from the widespread concern with the multilevel issue—namely,
the presumed division of organizational phenomena into micro-
and macro-level is most likely just another artifact of our pen-
chant for segmenting wholistic processes for our own convenience in trying to understand them. Unfortunately, that
tendency leads us to see division where unity actually prevails.
Perhaps we should do away with the labels *micro* and *macro*
for various topics of importance to organizations. Maybe the
consensual emergence of an explicit theme concerned with the
multilevel issue in a book about organizational cognition also
suggests that the study of cognitive process is an ideal focusing
point for studying processes that are pan-organizational.

Having attempted to identify the metathemes that emerged either implicitly or explicitly across different views of organizational cognition, I now turn a selective lens deriving from some of these themes on an issue of overriding importance: the instigation of organizational change and adaptation.

## Cognition and Change

Woven throughout these chapters is an abiding fascination with organizational change. Perhaps the attention devoted to the issue is a commentary on our times. Certainly Toffler's (1970) speculations have come to pass. Technological change is occurring at a rate that makes it difficult for mental and behavioral change to keep pace. Given that organizations are probably better characterized as social institutions than technological institutions, the rate of such change now presents yet another paradox. In effect, technological change is necessary for organizational survival, but the very existence of that change has created a different threat to survival: the possible inability of an organization to cope with its own innovation.

Cognition is strongly implicated in organizational change. Adaptation to change can be seen, first and foremost, as a cognitive challenge. How we think about change very much governs how we respond to it. Thus, keeping pace with change implies cognitive adaptation. Developing that adaptive capacity suggests the need for a more complete understanding of the nature of organizational cognition (an expressed purpose of this book). Many of the volumewide themes identified bear directly on the issue of managing effective change in modern organizations.

At the risk of emphasizing the obvious, we must first note that change is a *process*. The same orientation that argues for a more intense focus on the study of the "how" that underlies decision making, for instance, also augers for a deeper understanding of the processes involved in adaptation to change. One of those processes undoubtedly is cognitive structuring. People seem to structure knowledge about virtually everything, including action. In one sense, cognitive structures impede the accomplishment of change because the knowledge that is presently structured is, so to speak, one step behind the current state of affairs. Because such structures are resistant to alteration or change, they can preclude ready adaptability. Schemas help maintain the status quo, thus lending stability to experience, even where stability might be disfunctional.

Nonetheless, because of the widespread influence of schemas, it is obvious that the construction of workable schemas is crucial to organizational development. Much has been made of the need to snap people out of their usual automatic (that is, schema-driven) modes of information processing and into a controlled mode so they can learn new procedures. True enough, but perhaps we should also be looking at another side of the issue and asking whether a more fruitful activity might not be the intentional *cultivation* of schema development, an approach aimed at broadening the repertoire of schemas used to handle new organizational requirements.

What is really needed is schemas for change—schemas that internalize the folk wisdom that one of the few certainties in life is the certainty of change. Schemas are structures of expectation, and people can learn to expect change. We should recognize and capitalize on the capacity of people for cognitive change as well as on their ability to manage their own responses to change through self-reflection. Cronbach's (1955) observation that people not only think but think about how they think can usefully be applied to the change process. Effective response to required organizational change will not be accomplished unless the cognitive basis for responding to change is understood.

Another useful way to view adaptation to change is as a process of making sense of new experience. Sensemaking can entail many of the fundamental processes described by our contributors, including symbolization, causal reasoning, cognitive mapping, implicit theorizing, self-justification, emotional response, and a whole host of other processes. The sensemaking perspective implies consideration of the social construction processes that people use to cope with change. The changing reality with which people must often deal stems from the way they make sense of internal and external events. Therefore, the impetus for change depends on the way meaning is attributed to events. A consensual redefinition of a situation can then engender concerted action to deal with it.

The sensemaking view also offers another perspective on the multilevel theme identified earlier. Sensemaking is often construed as an individual process, but when consensuality is obtained across members, the process becomes an organizational one. For that reason, a comprehensive view of organizational change requires that it be viewed as multidimensional. Change is a process that crosses all levels of organizational analysis.

A final requirement for effective organizational change is organizational creativity. Creativity means looking at usual problems in unusual ways. The process of change is now a perpetual organizational process. Change, therefore, requires widespread redefinition as an opportunity instead of a problem. Coping with the opportunities provided by change implies coping with the paradoxes, dilemmas, ambiguities, and uncertainties inherent in change. As noted earlier, those processes require a broader view of management as simultaneously art and science. They also suggest a more holistic view of the processes of organizing and reorganizing to cope with change.

## Conclusion

In the introduction to this volume, we characterized organizational study as essentially still in its infancy. Despite the advances represented by recent research and by the contributions to this book, that portrayal continues to be a fair one. We know much more than we did only a decade ago, but there is yet much to know. And it is knowledge, even wisdom, that best defines our roles as scholars and managers of organizations. Indeed, it might be to our best advantage to see ourselves as still young in trying to develop our field. That view presents us with a future of high potential, one that allows us to use our burgeoning understanding to engage in our own brand of organizational change.

One of the reasons that social science, and especially organizational science, continues to be characterized as youthful is that the comparison is usually drawn with the physical sciences, using the standards of physical science study. Given the nature of the physical world and the methods required to understand it, an advanced state of paradigm development has been possible. By comparison, the state of organizational science appears underdeveloped, with no "laws" and few unchallenged theories. Thus, assessed by the particular standards of physical science, organizational science is seen as immature, and it may always be labeled that way, given the ambiguous, uncertain, paradoxical nature of our subject of study, if only conventional standards are applied.

Perhaps we have spent too much time and effort trying to emulate the hard sciences, especially in our ontological assumptions and epistemological approaches. Management is not very much like physics, yet we have been tempted to adopt standards of rigor that would try to forge management into a kind of physics. The nature of the social world is not necessarily parallel to that of the physical world. If that is the case, then patterning our work on those traditions and standards will not lead us to where we need to be.

The conduct of inquiry within the organizational sciences has even proceeded according to the customs of the physical sciences. Research has been skewed rather strongly toward positivist approaches. As useful as those approaches are, the overwhelming dominance of their methods of knowing have tended to limit our ability to explore the daunting complexity of organized people. We should not confine ourselves mainly to hypothesis-testing methodologies and deductive approaches.

Strict adherence to those approaches has inhibited our study of some subtle but significant organizational phenomena and has led to a tacit discounting of, for instance, the role of creativity, intuition, and insight, because we do not have "hard" evidence about the nature of such processes. This sort of narrow focus violates a maxim that now deserves more consideration, to wit: absence of evidence is not necessarily evidence of absence.

We should employ a wider domain of inquiring methods, including phenomenological, interpretive, ethnographic, humanist, and structuralist approaches to learning about organizations.

Expanding our assumption, theory, and research repertoires will also allow us to recognize that in the social and organizational sciences, we are involved not only in the discovery of knowledge but also in the creation of knowledge.

Our hope for developing into a mature science of organizations depends on our ability to recognize that such a science is potentially different from what has gone before and been labeled as *science*. Science is simply knowledge. I learned that in the eighth grade. What I now know, however, is that there are many different kinds of knowledge, all valid in some way. Therefore, a science of organizations, although it will always be eclectic to some degree, can be fashioned into a free-standing discipline of study. Moreover, the development of the discipline is likely to depend on progress in that direction.

### References

Abelson, R. P. "Computer Simulation of 'Hot Cognitions.' " In S. Tomkins and S. Mesick (eds.), *Computer Simulation of Personality*. New York: Wiley, 1963.

Cronbach, L. J. "Processes Affecting Scores on Understanding of Others and Assumed 'Similarity.' " *Psychological Bulletin,* 1955, *52,* 177-193.

Fiske, S. T., and Taylor, S. E. "Affect." In *Social Cognition.* Reading, Mass.: Addison-Wesley, 1984.

Gioia, D. A., and Manz, C. C. "Linking Cognition and Behavior: A Script-Processing Interpretation of Vicarious Learning." *Academy of Management Review,* 1985, *10,* 527-539.

Gioia, D. A., and Poole, P. P. "Scripts in Organizational Behavior." *Academy of Management Review,* 1984, *9,* 449-459.

Manz, C. C., and Sims, H. P., Jr. "Self-Management as a Substitute for Leadership: A Social Learning Theory Perspective." *Academy of Management Review,* 1980, *5,* 361-367.

Morgan, G., and Ramirez, R. "Action-Learning: A Holographic Metaphor for Guiding Social Change." *Human Relations,* 1983, *37,* 1-28.

Pondy, L. R. "Union of Rationality and Intuition in Management Action." In S. Srivastva and Associates, *The Executive*

*Mind: New Insights on Managerial Thought and Action.* San Francisco: Jossey-Bass, 1983.

Pondy, L. R., and Mitroff, I. I. "Beyond Open Systems Models of Organization." In B. Staw (ed.), *Research in Organizational Behavior.* Vol. 1. Greenwich, Conn.: JAI Press, 1979.

Ross, L. "The Intuitive Psychologist and His Shortcomings: Distortions in the Attribution Process." In L. Berkowitz (ed.), *Advances in Experimental Social Psychology.* Vol. 10. Orlando, Fla.: Academic Press, 1977.

Taylor, S. E. "The Interface of Cognitive and Social Psychology." In J. H. Harvey (ed.), *Cognition, Social Behavior, and the Environment.* Hillsdale, N.J.: Erlbaum, 1981.

Taylor, S. E., and Crocker, J. "Schematic Bases of Social Information Processing." In E. T. Higgins, C. P. Herman, and M. P. Zanna (eds.), *Social Cognition.* Vol. 1. Hillsdale, N.J.: Erlbaum, 1981.

Toffler, A. *Future Shock.* New York: Bantam Books, 1970.

Tversky, A., and Kahneman, D. "Judgment Under Uncertainty: Heuristics and Biases." *Science,* 1974, *185,* 1124-1131.

Weick, K. E. *The Social Psychology of Organizing.* (2nd ed.) Reading, Mass.: Addison-Wesley, 1979.

Weick, K. E. "Managerial Thought in the Context of Action." In S. Srivastva and Associates, *The Executive Mind: New Insights on Managerial Thought and Action.* San Francisco: Jossey-Bass, 1983.

# Name Index

# Subject Index

## A

Ability, and learning from experience, 282-283

Acceptability heuristic, and decision making, 209

Action: cognition connected with, 5-6, 347; concerted, and consensuality, 3, 347-348; focus on, 340; and maps, 105; and meaning creation, 51, 54-55; and plausible reasoning, 246-248; and scripts, 57-59; and sense-making, 61-62; as symbols, 52-53

Action image, and decision making, 301, 305-306, 311-312

Adjacency matrix, in cause maps, 116-118

Adoption decisions, in image theory, 301-302, 303, 306

Affect: analysis of, 215-237; and attribution, 223-224; background on, 216-217; and cognition, 218-220; and cognitive factors, 226-229; concepts of, 217-218; differentiated, 217-218, 228, 229; focus on, 340-341; implications of, 229-231; and memory, 220-221; outcome-dependent, 223; and performance appraisal, 224-229, 230; piecemeal-based, 222; schema-triggered, 221-222; summary on, 224; theme of, 348-349; theories of, 218-224; undifferentiated, 217-218, 220, 226-227, 229

Aided-analytic strategy, in decision making, 297, 303-304

Analytic tasks, in cognition, 268, 270

Assemblage, and cause maps, 111

Assumptions: in implicit theories, 171; role of, 349-350

Attractiveness, lateral and marginal, in image theory, 302, 303, 304, 307

Attribution: and affect, 223-224; and implicit theories, 170-171, 177-179, 185

Automatic information processing, and schemas, 21, 56

## B

Bank of Boston, and career image, 204

Behavior: and cognition, bridged, 136-164, 182; purposeful, research on, 167-169

Biases, and learning from experience, 273-275

Boeing, and career image, 203

Bogus pipeline procedure, and impression management, 198

Bonding, and implicit theories, 179-180